Date Due

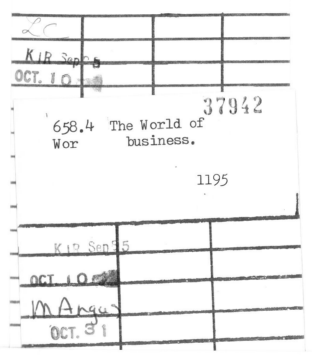

THE WORLD OF BUSINESS
A Canadian Profile

THE WORLD OF BUSINESS

A Canadian Profile

Terry G. Murphy
Head, Business Department
Queen Elizabeth C. & V. I.
Kingston, Ontario

Bob Williams
Business Education Co-ordinator
The Halton Board of Education
Burlington, Ontario

Roy McMillan
Business Education Director
Acton High School
Acton, Ontario

Rob Kelley
Business Education Department
Glendale Secondary School
Hamilton, Ontario

Wiley Publishers of Canada Limited
Toronto

Wiley Publishers of Canada Limited
22 Worcester Rd.
Rexdale, Ontario
M9W 1L1

Business Education Advisor: Terry G. Murphy

Editor: Sylvia Hill
Design and Illustrations: Tibor Kovalik
Cover photo: Birgitte Nielsen

Canadian Cataloguing in Publication Data
Main entry under title:
The World of business
Includes index.
ISBN 0-471-99794-3
1. Business.   2. Business enterprises — Canada.
I. Murphy, Terry G., 1940-
HF5351.W67   658.4   C78-001386-7

Printed and bound in Canada

10 9 8 7 6 5 4 3 2 1

CONTENTS

Preface

This book is an attempt to provide you, the reader, with an introduction to the many aspects of the world of Canadian business and to expose you to many of the courses available in Canadian secondary schools. It is the authors' hope that such an exposure will foster in you a keen interest in your choice of many of these business courses for study in greater depth during your high school career. Because the world of business is an important force around us and because a large number of high school students obtain permanent employment directly after graduation from high school, it is important that you have an understanding of the many facets of business and the manner in which you may be affected by them. All of us–business and individuals are essential to one another for our existence.

To write a book about the world of business requires the co-operation, support, and assistance of many people, businesses, and government organizations. We would like to express our sincere thanks to them all and acknowledge their contributions publicly.

For several years, the overall concept expressed in this text has been a strongly held viewpoint of the authors. This has been supported, reinforced, and proved successful in the classroom by Bob Harkness, Co-ordinator of Business Education for the Hamilton Board of Education, along with the many Hamilton business teachers who contributed their time and talents to the new course outline on which this text is patterned; and to Mary Connolly,

a business teacher at Oakville-Trafalgar High School in Oakville. Their courses are living proof that this concept works and that such courses are essential in the preparation of students for their future role in Canadian society and business.

Our thanks is also extended to Hamilton teachers Jane Lowry and Graham McCallum for their assistance in the organization of the marketing material; to Murray Barnes, a marketing specialist, for reviewing the marketing chapters; to Mary Salamon, a business teacher in Burlington, for her contribution to the shorthand section; to Paul Rehak and Mrs. Dorothy Amirault for their detailed analysis and recommendations for the computer section; to Peter and Ronnie Gerrard for their suggestions for illustrations in the computer section; and to secretary Goldie Herechuck for typing one-quarter of the manuscript.

The business community played a major role in assisting in the production of this book, and this is a very logical collaboration between business and education. The Burlington and Guelph Chambers of Commerce through their Education Committees provided input and the formation of ideas on content to be included in the text. The following people and their business organizations provided suggestions as to content and illustrative materials and we are extremely grateful for their contribution. They are: D.W. Adolph, Assistant Secretary, Bank of Canada; John H. Cranford, Director of Communications, the Insurance Bureau of Canada; Janet E. Dove, Public Relations Assistant, the National

Harbours Board in Vancouver, British Columbia; R.J. Galloway, Director of Corporate Services, Campbell Soup Company Ltd.; R.J. Grimes, Vice-President and Director of Finance, Kraft Limited; Mrs. Dianne Leury, Manager of Retail Marketing and Advertising, Bank of British Columbia; D.R.B. McArthur, Chairman of the Metric Commission Canada; Michèle Ménard, Chief of Public Relations for the Royal Canadian Mint; William E. Pauli, Corporate Relations Manager of Ford Motor Co. of Canada; T.G. Rimmer, Operations Manager of the Better Business Bureau of Canada; Roberta Resnick, Public Relations Manager, Libby McNeill and Libby of Canada Limited; Angela Robertson, Marketing Assistant, Dominion Dairies Limited; B.J. Pipes, Manager of Government and Consumer Relations; Proctor & Gamble Company of Canada; Ms. Jill Stocker, Director of Educational Division and Mrs. Wendy Barnes, Public Relations Officer, Canadian Life Insurance Association; John Szold, Director of Operations Development, Loblaws Limited; Juliana Thompson, Public Relations Officer, the Toronto Stock Exchange; Mrs. Rae Turley, Community Relations Officer, The Royal Bank of Canada; and Mr. R. Walker, Director of Industry Relations, Allstate Insurance Company of Canada.

The suggestions and comments made by these business people and their co-operation should not be construed as an endorsement of the book, although it is in their best interests, as well as ours, to have the final version as correct and as accurate as possible. For the amount of time and numerous telephone calls spent on their related portions of the manuscript, we are sincerely grateful.

Consumer organizations and government personnel also reacted to their respective sections, and we wish to thank especially Carolyn Trudeau, Public Relations Advisor, Consumer and Corporate Affairs Canada; Mr. Marlyn O'Connor, Public Relations Officer for Agriculture Canada; the Consumers' Association of Canada; and the Canadian Standards Association.

Two newspapers, in particular, have been used as sources of photographs and articles. Our thanks are extended to Mr. Alex Beer, Managing Editor of the *Hamilton Spectator,* and to Rita Acton for their assistance in researching photographs and other materials, and to *The Whig-Standard,* Kingston and its reporters and photographers. Special thanks is extended to David H. Ahl, publisher of Creative Computing Press, New Jersey, for permission to reprint several cartoons.

As a result of this collective effort on the part of business and education, we hope that *The World of Business* will open new horizons and opportunities for you and that the study of this text will be the beginning of a series of business studies for you throughout your lifetime.

Terry G. Murphy
Bob Williams
Roy McMillan
Rob Kelley
August 1978

1
Business and You

UNIT A
YOU AND THE WORLD OF BUSINESS

You are in the centre of the business world. It is an exciting place to explore. Business has a great influence on our lives-much greater than you have imagined. Let us examine some of the many ways business affects us.

Business Produces Goods and Services

What has business done for you today? The bed and mattress you slept on were manufactured by businesses. Your house or apartment was built through the co-operation of hundreds of businesses. Some provided raw materials like lumber, nails, and shingles; others provided skilled **services** to build and equip the dwelling. Still other types of businesses help to maintain the dwelling and its contents. Television repair, plumbing, painting, and home repair businesses are common in Canada. Your breakfast was produced by several different farming businesses. These **goods** were delivered by transportation companies, and sold to your family by stores-another type of business. Goods are items of value that have been produced; we can touch them. Services also have value in that we are willing to pay for them, but they do not result in a product we can touch.

Take a walk through a local supermarket. You will see several thousand different goods-fresh and frozen meats and vegetables, perhaps a hundred different dairy products, shelves filled with many different canned goods-"everything from soup to nuts", as the saying goes. You will also see many different packaged goods, crackers, cookies, spaghetti, cereal. Most supermarkets also sell a variety of household articles, pots and pans, toothpaste and soap, and a large number of soaps and cleaning materials. Each of these goods has been provided by businesses-hundreds of them.

Flip through the pages of a department store catalogue. Again you will see thousands of different products: stereos and radios, small and large appliances, hundreds of different clothing items, jewellery and watches, sporting equipment and automotive supplies. The list is almost endless. Many large stores also provide several services; free delivery, mail order, and charge accounts are common examples of services, provided to make shopping more convenient for shoppers.

You have used hundreds of goods and services already today. Think of some of them: your cloth-ing, hairbrush and comb; the lights and appliances and furniture where you live; the food you eat; the bus or car you rode in; your school supplies; your radio and record player. The list is long and each is produced by businesses.

We Have Needs and Wants

Each of us differs in many ways. Our hair colour, facial features, height and mass all serve to make us physically different from one another. We also differ in our needs and wants. Some of us enjoy certain things more than others. Mary likes roast beef, but John prefers chicken. Bill loves to play tennis, and Carol is an excellent golfer.

We all share the need for food, shelter, and clothing. These are called basic **needs**. We need them to survive. Some families call a car or a television set a basic need, because they cannot imagine life without them. The average Canadian household has two radios and one television set. Most have telephone and electrical services. These things are not necessary for our survival, but we have come to take them for granted, and we therefore call them needs.

After our needs have been satisfied, we all have many things we would like to have. These **wants** vary from person to person. Peter wants a bicycle and Anne would like a stereo. Sue would like to go to the baseball game, but Bob wants to see a new movie. Our wants are endless, because we can never satisfy them all. Even if you could make a list of everything you would like to have and were able to obtain everything on the list, you would soon find many other wants to take their place.

Each of us uses many goods and services to satisfy our different needs and wants. For this reason we are called **consumers**. Canada has approximately twenty-three million consumers and there are thousands of different goods and services available to us. Most of these goods and services are provided by businesses.

Business Is Dynamic

In prehistoric times there were no businesses. The cave family had the same basic needs we have today; namely food, clothing, and shelter. The cave family spent all of its time trying to satisfy these needs, and they were happy if they could. Cave

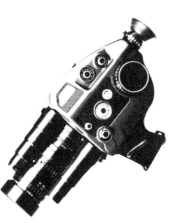

families lived relatively independently of other families, producing all their own goods and services.

As civilization developed, families found that they could satisfy more wants and needs by working together and specializing to produce the goods and services that they were best able to produce. Some people were good hunters, others were skilled at making clothes, and still others were best suited for farming.

Specialization

In Canada today, we are highly specialized. We produce only a few of the goods and services required to satisfy our personal needs and wants. We rely on other people working in businesses to produce the majority of the goods and services we consume. A large steel producing firm employs thousands of people in hundreds of different occupations. The Steel Company of Canada Ltd. employs skilled and unskilled production workers–millwrights, electricians, steam fitters, plumbers, and floor cleaners. Accountants, clerks, secretaries, and computer operators work in offices with managers, buyers, and sales personnel. **Specialization** in our businesses has made it possible to produce many more goods and services than could have been produced if individuals had to provide for their own needs and wants.

In early times, when groups of families began to cooperate with one another, sometimes one group would produce more goods than they needed. This made it possible to trade with another group for a good or service that they had left over. This trading was called **bartering**. Bartering developed into the first businesses. Goods and services were produced to be consumed by others.

Centuries later, money was invented to help people to trade their goods and services. Today in Canada, twenty-three million people use money to help them to trade goods and services. There are several hundred billion such transactions made each year. Each time you buy something at a store you have made a transaction with a business. We have progressed a long way from the time when a little excess grain was traded for a little surplus meat.

There are thousands of businesses operating in Canada. You are familiar with many of them. Think about the last time you visited a shopping mall or the business section of a large town or city. You saw small and large businesses–some employing one person, some employing thousands–producing a few products or services or many. Food, clothing, hardware, jewellery, musical instruments, appliances, carpeting, photography, and furniture stores are but a few of the businesses common in Canadian communities. The Canadian Federation of Independent Business, an association of small businesses, lists over 46 000 members across Canada.

We Are Interdependent

As we have seen, early families were independent. They alone provided for their own needs, and did not rely on others. Today, our society is **interdependent**. To satisfy our wants and needs, we buy the goods and services produced by thousands of different businesses. Businesses are also highly interdependent. The airplane manufacturer buys the goods and services of many other businesses to produce an aircraft.

Imagine the weekly shopping list of a large manufacturing company. Raw materials, parts, machinery, transportation, lubricants, office equipment,

13

paper and pencils, laundry, and window cleaning are only a few of the thousands of goods and services required by large businesses. And the bill for a week's operations often amounts to several million dollars!

Small businesses also rely on many others for successful operation. The neighbourhood variety store relies on many suppliers of the different products to stock the shelves. The local bakery buys flour, sugar, and other ingredients from several businesses, and advertises in newspapers run by still other businesses. For such a system to run smoothly, we must co-operate with one another.

We Need One Another

We rely on businesses to produce many of the goods and services that supply our needs and wants. Most of us earn money to purchase these goods and services by working in a business helping to produce things other people buy. In this way we both contribute to the production and benefit from it.

Business cannot exist without people–we buy its products and we provide our skills to help it produce. In turn, we need businesses to provide us with the goods and services we cannot provide ourselves. All of us are affected by business every day of our lives. What better reason do we need for learning as much as we can about the world of business?

MAYBE THE GOOD OLD DAYS WEREN'T SO GREAT

On days when life gets complicated and confused, it may seem desirable to return to the past, when life was wonderful. But was it?

The average worker of fifty years ago toiled for twelve hours a day, six days a week, and earned very little compared with the average pay cheque Canadians receive today. Children started work before they reached their teens, and people lived on an average to the ripe old age of 50. And not too long ago one child in three didn't live to see a fifth birthday.

Living without modern conveniences was a real treat–freezing temperatures on long winter nights because of inadequate heating. No electricity or running water. Books were very expensive–luxury items. Only the very rich went to school; so they were the only ones who could read. Most families struggled to put food on the table and a roof over their heads. Waking hours were spent "surviving"–no time for television, movies, or entertainment even if they had been invented.

Say what you want, in many ways Canadians today are much better off than they were in the past. Look forward, not backward.

Digest of Business News
April 1978

14

UNIT B

BUSINESS NEEDS YOU

Businesses are people. People start businesses, manage them, and work in them. Without people, businesses would have no need to produce anything. Without people, nothing could be produced.

What Should Be Produced?

A business cannot survive unless it produces goods and services people need and want. Successful businesses are those that know what people want and produce it. Those businesses not producing things people want and need do not stay in business very long.

In Canada, consumers can choose from among thousands of different products. The choices of which things you will buy with your income combined with the choices of all other Canadians determine what goods and services will be produced, and in what quantities. These choices also determine which businesses will be successful. If all Canadians decided that they no longer wanted or needed automobiles, they would not be produced by businesses. Over the years, many products have become obsolete. This means that they have been replaced by newer, more advanced products. Two examples of obsolete products are steam-engine locomotives and stage coaches. Some services have also become obsolete. Fifty years ago, every little town had a blacksmith. Many gas stations today

THOSE JOBS ARE CHANGING

Modern business is becoming more complicated. Products are becoming more sophisticated and their production involves more automated equipment. Today's society takes computers and the accompanying technology for granted, but what is this doing to our job market?

No doubt about it, fewer and fewer unskilled workers are being hired. As machines continue to take over the dull, repetitive tasks previously performed by workers, those workers without skills find it harder and harder to obtain work. But there is a demand for skilled workers—machinists, technicians, and machine operators. Trained people are required to instal, operate, and service the fancy machines of the future that all of a sudden are with us today.

"In just twenty short years we've seen a radical change in our whole industry", said a representative of a large appliance and electronic equipment manufacturer. "Jobs that used to take many men and women days to complete are being done by a computer controlled machine in less than an hour. We still have many employees, but they are doing different things, and they require more training and education."

Digest of Business News
May 1978

15

are self-service; soon all or most may no longer provide the services of pumping gas, checking "under the hood", checking the tire pressure, and washing the windshield of the family car.

An old saying goes: "Build a better mousetrap and the world will beat a path to your door." Businesses are always looking for new and better products to sell to consumers. Successful businesses change as the wants and needs of consumers change. Many products that are available today were not even invented thirty-five years ago. Colour televisions, electronic calculators, and touch-tone telephones are examples.

The types of goods and services we want and are willing to pay for is called our **demand** for those products. Our demand for a particular product depends on several factors. Our needs and wants are different, and we therefore have different demands. Our incomes will determine what types of goods and services we can afford.

It is not enough to merely want a particular product, we must also have the money to pay for it. All of us have many more wants than we have money to pay for. If a person earns $10 000 per year, he or she can purchase only one half as much as someone who earns $20 000 per year. As a result we must make choices. When we do decide to buy a particular product and pay for it, we have expressed our demand for it.

If businesses can provide the types of goods and services we demand at the prices we are willing to pay, they will **supply** them. The supply of goods and services is affected by the costs of producing them, and to some extent by the demand people have for them. If colour television sets could be supplied at $1.00 each, many of us would want to own several. But if ball point pens cost $100 each, most of us would be content with pencils. In general, businesses will produce as many products as people are willing to buy. High prices tend to decrease the demand for a particular product. Low prices tend to increase demand. When hand-held calculators were first introduced they were priced at over $200 each. Few were sold. Now that calculators can be purchased for under $10, most households own at least one.

Businesses must supply goods and services to meet people's demands, and must also earn some **profit** to survive. Few businesses would operate if they could not earn a reasonable profit.

You Are a Producer

Most Canadians are employed by businesses at some time in their lives. Many of you will spend your entire working life employed by one or more businesses. To earn your salary or wages, you will be expected to produce something of value. Production of modern goods and services often requires the cooperation of many people.

A number of skilled people are needed to produce a modern automobile. Engineers and designers, planners and managers, painters, machinists, drill operators, accountants, and office workers are just a few of the hundreds of different people employed by the Ford Motor Company of Canada Ltd. Each person contributes in some way to the completion of the final product. All of them must work together if the business is to be successful.

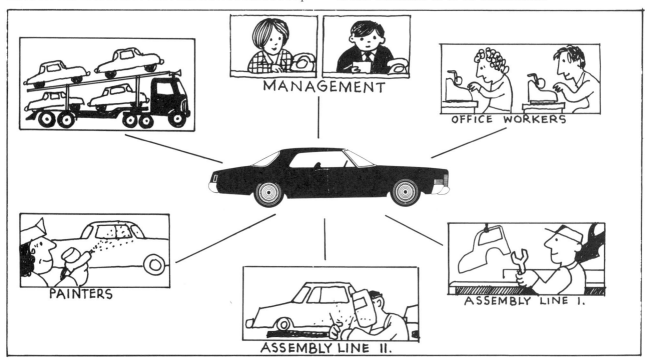

Some of you when you enter the working world will be directly involved in the **production** of goods and services necessary in a modern business. Examples of jobs in production are machine operators, welders, technicians, farmers, and forestry workers. Many of you will be involved in **marketing** jobs. All of the activities involved in getting goods and services from the producer to the consumer are part of marketing. These include many jobs in stores, advertising, transportation, and sales. Still others will work in the area of business **communications.** Modern businesses need many trained office workers–secretaries, stenographers, and clerical workers. In addition, one of the fastest growing job markets is for people trained in computer related skills. Computers assist businesses in many ways. One of the most important is in the financial side of business called **accounting.** Keeping track of all the money coming in and out of a business is a complicated matter, and accounting departments in businesses work to keep accurate financial records. Banks, because they provide a financial service to all businesses, need the skill of many trained accountants.

Businesses need us. As consumers, we purchase the goods and services produced by them. They also need our help to produce these products. What will be your contribution to the business world?

There's nothing wrong with profits

How much profit does the average Canadian business earn on the money it has invested in buildings, equipment, and inventories? A recent poll of Canadians showed that the majority feel that businesses earn more than 35%. That's news to the businesses! Actual profits last year averaged less than 5%. Although many Canadians apparently feel that businesses are "ripping me off", they do not seem to understand the importance of business profits to the health of the economy. For without business profits, Canadians would be worse off.

An individual who invests money in Canada Savings Bonds or a bank savings account earns a greater return on the investment than many businesses earn. And just as individuals have a right to earn interest on savings, so a business has a right to earn a reasonable profit on its investments. The investment made by a business to finance its buildings, equipment, and inventories represents the savings of the individuals who own the business. If businesses cannot earn a reasonable profit, the owners are better off investing their money in savings bonds or bank accounts.

Without the chance of making a profit, people would not invest in a business. Without businesses, we would have no jobs. Without jobs, who would be better off?

Digest of Business News
June 1978

UNIT C
YOU NEED BUSINESS

Few Canadians consume many goods and services they have produced themselves. Some people grow some of their own food, others sew some of their own clothes. In all, average Canadians produce less than five per cent of the goods and services they consume in a year. We rely on businesses for the other things that we use. To be able to buy our clothes and cars, our movies and haircuts, we must produce something of value that will earn us an income.

Most of you will earn this income by working in several different business jobs during your lifetime. You may have several different **careers** during forty or more years as a worker. The average Canadian changes jobs approximately four times in a lifetime. Some experts predict that in the future it will be common for people to change jobs and careers seven or more times during their working lives.

Preparing Yourself for a Career

Should you choose a career because you like it, or should you select a career because it will make you rich? Which is more important–job satisfaction or money? The choice is not easy. There are thousands of possible careers. Many are in business, others are in government services. Different skills and knowledge are needed for different jobs. You can benefit from thinking about possible careers now.

Deciding on a Career

Up to now other people have made most of your life decisions for you. Your career choice, however, should be your own. This book provides you with information and activities designed to help you to make up your mind. The choice you make will affect the rest of your life. Such an important decision deserves much time and thought.

The first step in making a career decision is to know yourself. What are your likes and dislikes? What do you do well? Do you like working with people or alone? Do you enjoy working with tools or with facts and figures? Do you spend most of your time indoors or outdoors? There are some preference tests available to help you to analyse your **aptitudes.** Your teacher or guidance counsellor may provide these for you. Other such devices are avail-

able through the Canada Employment Centre office in your area.

Everyone has different aptitudes and interests. People who choose a career that matches their talents are likely to have job satisfaction and success. Your aptitudes and interests probably differ from those of most of your classmates. There are many career choices available. The previous section introduced you to several jobs in businesses. The second step in making a career decision is to find and to explore jobs that seem to match your interests. To do this you should look at jobs available now, and at those that will likely be available when you graduate, and at jobs available in the future. Several factors will affect the **job market** in the future.

Automation of production processes has eliminated some jobs that existed before advancing **technology** produced the modern machinery used in many businesses. Automation has also created many new types of jobs and careers. Jobs in environmental control, energy conservation, nuclear science, and electronic technology will likely increase in number and importance.

In recent years, Canadians have been using more and more of their incomes to purchase services instead of goods. This trend is expected to continue. The **service industry** needs many employees to work in hundreds of different jobs in hotels, recreational facilities, and repair shops of all kinds.

Some jobs and careers are available in non-business fields such as the governments, education, and medicine. Although business may not directly pay the wages for persons in these fields, a knowledge of business and business procedures is very helpful to people working in them.

Sources of Career Information

How do you find detailed information on jobs and careers of interest to you? There are many sources of information. An obvious source of reliable career information is an interview with people already in these occupations. The guidance department of your school will probably have several sources of information on various careers, and counsellors will be pleased to show them to you, or direct you to other resources. The Federal Department of Employment and Immigration has a computer based

information service on careers called **Choices**. In Ontario, the Ministry of Education offers a similar service called the **Student Guidance Information Service (S.G.I.S.)**. Libraries and resource centres have considerable information on many different careers, including such information as the *Dictionary of Occupational Titles*. Your librarian will be happy to direct you to appropriate resources.

Another source of career information is associations. Groups of people with similar occupations often form an association that sets standards for members and engages in various educational programs. Local offices of labour unions are excellent sources of career information. Most local unions are members of national organizations. Almost all national headquarters operate an educational branch that will provide you with information on careers represented by the union.

To make a wise career decision, it is necessary to have accurate information. Your teacher and other teachers from the Business Education Department in your school will be happy to direct you to appropriate resources.

Choices: Career Decisions

Choices. Our lives are full of them. Some can be made on the spur of the moment. Others, like choosing our careers, take much longer and require very careful thought.

Our choice of life-work colours every facet of our lives. So it is one of the most important we will ever make. Yet most people have only a superficial knowledge of the variety that exists in the working world, and far too many people make the wrong choice! Many make no real choice at all! These people often drift aimlessly from one unsatisfying job to another. Others find and stick with jobs they don't really like simply because they don't know what they would prefer, or how they could get into something better.

Most of us feel that we know ourselves reasonably well. But we have great difficulty in relating this self-awareness to the wide range of career opportunities that may be available for us. To do it really properly we would need a massive library of information on every conceivable type of work, and an effective way of getting information about only occupations that would truly satisfy us. In this way we might very well find out about many occupations that we had never previously considered.

The Department of Employment and Immigration is developing a new system to assist people in making career decisions. It's called, appropriately enough, CHOICES. Choices will help people explore their career alternatives through direct conversation with a computer.

Source: Department of Employment and Immigration Reprinted by permission

Code	Career Name
C5561	Special-Endorsement Clerk
C5674	Statistical Clerk
C5843	Supervisor, Bookkeepers and Accounts Clerks
C5844	Supervisor, Cashiers
C5859	Supervisor, Insurance, Bank Clerks, etc.
C5876	Supervisor, Statistical Clerks
C6017	Teller
C6107	Timekeeper
C6143	Tonnage Compilation Clerk

Minor Group 414
Office Machines and Electronic Data-Processing Equipment Operators

This minor group includes occupations primarily concerned with operating office machines and electronic data-processing equipment.

Code	Career Name
C0039	Adding Machine Operator
C0041	Address Plate Inserter
C0040	Address-Labelling Machine Tender
C0042	Addressing Machine Operator
C0334	Audit Machine Operator
C0517	Billing Machine Operator
C0565	Blueprinting Machine Operator
C0597	Bookkeeping Machine Operator
C0735	Bursting Machine Tender
C0782	Calculating Machine Operator
C0865	Card-Tape Converter Operator
C1206	Coin Machine Tender
C1264	Computer Operator
C1267	Computer Peripheral Equipment Operator
C1481	Cryptographic Machine Operator
C1501	Currency Sorter
C1827	Duplicating Machine Operator
C1957	Embossing Machine Operator
C1996	Envelope-Sealing-and-Imprinting Machine Tender
C2025	Excise-Stamp Cancelling Machine Tender
C2932	High-Speed Printer Operator
C3088	Inserting Machine Tender
C3215	Integrator Operator
C3276	Key Punch Operator
C3601	Magnetic Ink Character Recognition Clerk
C3848	Microfilm Mounter
C3849	Microfilm Records Searcher
C3874	Mimeograph Operator
C4363	Photocomposing-Machine Perforator Operator
C4365	Photocopying Machine Tender
C4679	Proof Machine Operator
C4877	Remote Computer Terminal Operator
C5551	Sorting Machine Tender
C5712	Stencil Cutter Tender
C5855	Supervisor, Electronic Data Processing Equipment Operators

Code	Career Name
C5867	Supervisor, Office Machine Operators
C5915	Tabulating Machine Operator
C6300	Typesetter/Perforator Operator
C6387	Verifier Operator

Minor Group 415
Material Recording, Scheduling, and Distributing Occupations

This minor group includes occupations concerned with examining orders for goods and services; with receiving, storing, scheduling, issuing, shipping, requisitioning, and accounting for material in store or in use. Activities include assigning locations and space to items; verifying quantity, identity, condition, and value; binning, picking, stacking, and counting; preparing or committing stocks for shipment; taking inventory of stock; replenishing depleted items; filling orders; and issuing tools, equipment, or material to workers.

Code	Career Name
C0109	Aircraft Records Clerk
C0306	Assignment Clerk
C0389	Baggage Agent
C0835	Car Supplier
C0872	Cargo Location Clerk
C1011	Checker, Invoice and Order
C1092	Claim Clerk, Lost or Damaged Goods
C1117	Clerk, Cable Transfer
C1330	Control Clerk, Advertising
C1331	Control Clerk, Data Processing
C1757	Dress Checker
C2006	Estimator, Fabric
C2007	Estimator, Jewellery
C2038	Expediter, Purchasing
C2041	Export Booking Clerk
C2936	Highway Scale Operator
C3032	Import Freight Clerk
C3064	Industrial-Order Completion Clerk
C3224	Inventory Clerk
C3252	Job Order Clerk, Manufacturing
C3289	Kitchen Stock Clerk
C3308	Laboratory Clerk
C3497	Linen Room Attendant
C3599	Magazine Keeper
C3606	Mail Order Filler
C3953	Major Vehicle Repair Co-ordinator
C3729	Material Co-ordinator
C3730	Material Estimator, Construction
C4127	Order Clerk, Printing Plates
C4167	Overhaul Planner
C4262	Parts Lister
C4604	Prescription Clerk, Optical
C4625	Price Marker
C4657	Production C
C4658	Pr
C4664	

YOU HAVE INDICATED AN INTEREST IN
                    SECRETARY

        SECRETARY   (CLERICAL)
        SECRETARIAL STENOGRAPHER,
        SCHEDULES APPOINTMENTS, GIVES
        INFORMATION TO CALLERS, TAKES DICTATION
        AND RELIEVES EMPLOYER OF CLERICAL WORK
        AND MINOR ADMINISTRATIVE AND BUSINESS
        DETAILS, PERFORMING ANY OF THE FOLLOWING
        DUTIES:
        READS AND ROUTES INCOMING MAIL. LOCATES
        AND ATTACHES APPROPRIATE FILE TO
        CORRESPONDENCE TO BE ANSWERED BY
        EMPLOYER. TAKES DICTATION IN SHORTHAND
        OR ON STENOTYPE MACHINE, AND
        TRANSCRIBES ON TYPEWRITER FROM NOTES OR
        VOICE RECORDINGS. COMPOSES AND TYPES
        CORRESPONDENCE. FILES CORRESPONDENCE
        AND OTHER RECORDS. ANSWERS TELEPHONE
        AND GIVES INFORMATION TO CALLER, OR
        ROUTES CALL TO APPROPRIATE OFFICIAL, AND
        PLACES OUTGOING CALLS. SCHEDULES
        APPOINTMENTS FOR EMPLOYER AND REMINDS
        HIM WHEN THEY ARE DUE. GREETS VISITORS,
        ASCERTAINS NATURE OF BUSINESS AND
        CONDUCTS VISITORS TO EMPLOYER OR TO
        APPROPRIATE PERSON. COMPILES AND ⌐
        STATIS⌐⌐⌐ ⌐⌐PORTS⌐⌐
        OF

        FOR RELATED CAREERS CONSULT THE MASTER
        LIST UNDER THE MINOR GROUP-------------- 411

    THESE TRAININGS SUPPORT SECRETARY

        EDUCATIONAL SECRETARY TRAINING
        TRAINING FOR SECRETARIAL WORK IN THE
        FIELD OF EDUCATION IS OFFERED AS A SPEC-
        IALIZED, USUALLY ONE-YEAR PROGRAM, AT A
        COMMUNITY COLLEGE LEVEL FOR THOSE THAT
        HAVE THEIR SECONDARY SCHOOL GRADUATION
        DIPLOMA TOGETHER WITH BASIC SECRETARIAL
        QUALIFICATIONS (SHORT HAND, TYPING,
        OFFICE PROCEDURES AND COMMUNICATIONS).

S.G.I.S. HELPS STUDENTS FIND CAREERS

Ontario high school students are now using a million-dollar computer system to find out about jobs and careers that interest them. Known as the Student Guidance Information Service, it is available in all high schools in the province. It is designed to make career planning easier for students, especially those who aren't clear about what they want to do. S.G.I.S. gives students access to descriptions of every type of job in Canada from Administrator to Zoologist. Can you imagine what a "peanut-butter maker" does for a living? The system also tells students where they can get training for the job and entrance requirements that must be met for post-secondary education in the field.

Students indicate on a computer card the jobs in which they are interested. Their requests are sent by courier to the ministry's computer. Within a week the information requested is returned to the student.

The program reduces significantly the amount of time it would take for a student to search through other references, and it makes the information readily available in a form that is easy to understand.

Source: Student Guidance
Information Service
Reprinted by permission

Student Job Office Stays Open

For the first time in its eight-year history the Canada Manpower Centre [Canada Employment Centre] will keep its doors open all winter long.

The centre has been selected as the site for a pilot project–the only one of its kind in Canada–trying to drum up part-time jobs for high school and university students.

"Most of the jobs we're looking for are in the service areas–restaurants, theatres, and the retail business" says Karin Fischer, one of two full-time employees.

"We're also trying to plan ahead for the Christmas rush–any work students could do on the evenings or weekends."

Officially, operations got under way October 1.

Already, Karin and co-staffer Bill Everest can draw from a file of 15 000 students who registered, last spring, for summer jobs.

Sorting through the more recent applications, Bill stresses that only the dependable, responsible students, the ones who will make the best possible referral, will be selected for any given job.

He takes into consideration experience, initiative, and past performance, weeding out the two per cent or so who fail to live up to the centre's reputation.

"We only give two or three chances–and if they don't work out, we cancel their card."

For the householder, willing students will rake the lawn, clean out the garage, move furniture, put up storm windows, and finish those long since forgotten chores at the minimum wage.

For the businessman, they will speed daily operations, and catch up on back orders or short staffing.

So far, it's still in the experimental stage.

"But we make so many contacts during the summer, what do you do in September? Drop them? What about the employers? Their needs don't stop when the kids go back to school," Karin explained.

"A lot of them don't have enough money to keep them going. This gives them that little bit extra.

"And we'll never run dry of students. No matter how many jobs we get we'll have plenty of people to fill them.

"Today, it's a job finding a job."

The Spectator, Hamilton,
October 20, 1976
Reprinted by permission

Educational Requirements

When collecting information on various careers, be sure to discover what the educational requirements are. Most jobs in business require some specialized training, and you can likely select some courses in your secondary school program to help you to achieve these requirements. Many secondary schools offer courses in marketing, business communications and office procedures, accounting, data processing, and other related areas such as law and economics.

The third step in making a career choice, is to prepare a plan. At the end of this course, it is hoped that you will have enough information to develop a plan for yourself. The book examines all of the major areas of business activity, and you are encouraged to discover as much as you can about each, and to explore several jobs in detail.

In day-to-day living, you are a part of the world of business. You use the goods and services produced by business, and face problems in managing your own business affairs. This course can help you to learn how to make better career decisions, and how to solve the problems most consumers face in dealing with businesses.

Innumerable occupations are practised daily under the large roof encompassing Eaton's Centre in downtown Toronto.

REVIEWING
YOUR BUSINESS VOCABULARY

Write the number of each definition.
Write the word that matches the definition number.

UNIT A

barter, business, consumer, good, interdependent, need, service, specialization, want

1. An item such as shoes, a car, a television produced by businesses.
2. An item we require to survive.
3. People producing what they are best suited to produce.
4. Someone who uses goods and services.
5. The term used when businesses and people rely on and need one another.
6. A system in which goods and services are traded for other goods and services.
7. An item we buy, such as a haircut, dry cleaning, television repair.
8. Something we would like to have, but which is not necessary for our survival.
9. An organization that produces goods or services.

UNIT B

accounting, communications, demand, marketing, obsolete, production, profit, supply

1. A process involving senders, receivers, and information.
2. The actual making of goods and services.
3. The activity required to get goods and services from producer to consumer.
4. The quantity of a particular product that people want and are willing to pay for.
5. The financial reward for running a successful business.
6. Products no longer produced because they have been replaced by newer ones.
7. The amount of a particular good or service that a business produces.
8. The job of recording, analyzing and reporting the financial transactions of a business.

UNIT C

aptitude, automation, career, job market, service industry, technology

1. Businesses that sell services.
2. Application of scientific discoveries to produce goods and services.
3. The number and types of jobs available.
4. An ability to do something well.
5. The use of machines to produce goods and services.
6. A choice of lifework.

REVIEW QUESTIONS

UNIT A

1. Explain why you are in the centre of the business world.
2. What is the difference between a good and a service? Give three examples of each.
3. What is the difference between a need and a want? Give three examples of each.
4. Explain two basic ways in which you depend on businesses.
5. What are two major reasons why businesses need you?
6. Explain how businesses are interdependent.

UNIT B

1. How many times does the average worker in Canada change jobs or careers in a lifetime?
2. Why is a career decision an important one for you?
3. What steps should you take to make a career choice?
4. Describe how automation has affected the job market.
5. Is a knowledge of business important to people in non-business jobs? Explain.
6. What are five general sources of career information?

UNIT C

1. What are the two main reasons businesses need consumers?
2. What is the main difference between a successful and an unsuccessful business?
3. Who determines what goods and services will be produced in Canada? Explain.
4. What is meant by production?
5. What is the function of marketing in a business?

APPLYING YOUR KNOWLEDGE

UNIT A

1. Which of the following is a good, and which is a service? Soccer ball; electricity; hair dryer; stove; stereo; eggs; haircut; bus ride; dry cleaning; insurance.
2. List five goods available today that were not available fifteen years ago.
3. Are business firms and governments consumers of goods and services? Explain.
4. Would your needs and wants change if you moved to a sunny, warm island in the Caribbean? Explain your answer in a one-page report.

UNIT B

1. Name two products or services not mentioned in the text that have become obsolete. Why are they obsolete?
2. Everyone who works in a retail store is engaged in a marketing business. Name five kinds of workers such a company needs.
3. Name other courses in your school that explore specific areas of business.

UNIT C

1. Prepare a list of questions that you would like to have answered before selecting a career for yourself.
2. Do you think that a fire prevention officer and an accountant would have the same reasons for job satisfaction? Explain.
3. Supply three sources not mentioned in this unit that provide career information.
4. Name three examples of automation in businesses in your area.
5. Name three occupations you think will become more important in the future. Give reasons for your selections.
6. List five things you hope to learn from this course. Begin each with the words "How to..."

PROJECTS
AND PROBLEMS

UNIT A

1. Examine the Yellow Pages or White Directory for your area. Find the names of ten businesses which you know. For each, name an important good or service which it produces.
2. Name six businesses or types of businesses which depend on the following for their successful operation: a bank; a paper manufacturer; a steel producer; an insurance company.
3. Why is it not possible to satisfy all the needs and wants of everyone? Write a short essay which answers this question.
4. Is education a basic need for Canadians? Prepare a one-page report giving several reasons for your answer.

UNIT B

1. Which was the best selling Canadian-made car in Canada last year? Give several reasons why you think this car was more successful than others.
2. Select a medium or large business in your community. Using the headings *Production, Marketing, Communications, Accounting,* draw up a four-column chart listing three or more types of jobs in each category.
3. Assume that someone has given you $500 to spend in any way you choose. List at least five different possible ways of using this money. State the reasons for your use in a one-page report.
4. Modern businesses need many people who do not contribute directly to the production of goods or services, yet each of these persons is necessary for the successful operation of the firm. In a paragraph for each person, explain what would happen if:
a. Furniture companies had no people in marketing jobs;
b. Book publishers had no office personnel;
c. Banks had no accountants.

UNIT C

1. Draw up a two-column table. In the left column write ten things which you like to do. Include hobbies, interests, and other activities. In the right column list ten things you do not like to do. Provide appropriate headings for the table. What does this information tell you about the types of jobs for which you might be suited?
2. Select one area of business which you are interested in. For this area find at least three other educational institutions which offer courses to train you for jobs in that area. Name the institutions, their locations, a brief description of the courses and the requirements to enrol.
3. Study the *Help Wanted* section of your local newspaper. Answer the following questions:
a. How many different types of jobs are being advertised?
b. How many of the jobs require more education than you have now?
c. Select three jobs you think you might like. Cut out these advertisements and bring them to class.
d. Why does each of these jobs appeal to you?
e. What are the educational requirements of each?
f. Why do you think that you are suited for this type of work?
g. What job satisfaction is available in each of these jobs?
4. The following technical developments are predicted in the next fifty years: control of the weather; automated libraries; nuclear powered fuel-cell automobiles. Select one prediction and in a one-page essay describe how you and the business world will be affected.

CLASS PROJECTS

1. As a class develop a list of specific questions you will use in an interview with people in various jobs. The idea is to find out as much about each job as possible. You may want to include such questions as:
   a. What types of things do you do on your job?
   b. How long have you worked at this job?
   c. Why did you choose your job?
   d. What is the minimum educational level for your job?
   e. What special skills does your job require?
   f. What things do you like about your job?
   g. What things do you not like about your job?
   h. What part of your job gives you the greatest satisfaction?
   i. Is there travel involved in your work?
   j. Does your job have opportunities for promotion?
   k. What other jobs have you held?
   l. What type of a time schedule do you have?
   m. Do you work primarily with other people?

2. Divide the class into groups of two or three students. Each group is to select a business in the local community in which they are interested.

   The class is to agree on a set of questions to be answered for each of the businesses. Consider some of the following:
   a. How long has the business been operating in the community?
   b. What are the major products or services produced by the business?
   c. Who are the major customers of the business?
   d. How many people does the business employ?
   e. What are the types of jobs available in the business?
   f. What have been the major changes in the business in the last twenty years?
   g. What are the predicted changes for the business?
   h. Which major businesses sell goods and services to this company?
   i. Does this company provide other businesses with goods and services?

   After agreeing on a list of questions, each group is to visit their business and interview someone who can answer these questions. Each group can then prepare a report and present it to the class.

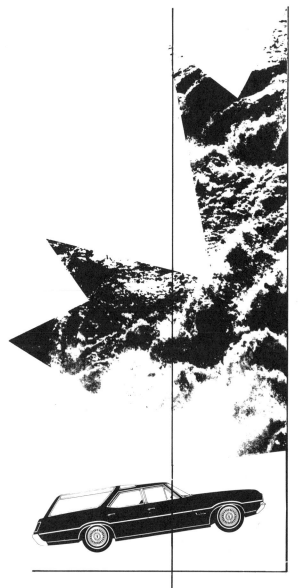

2 Business and the Canadian Economy

UNIT A

OUR "MODIFIED" FREE ENTERPRISE SYSTEM

Canada's economy operates under many government rules and regulations. And all levels of government produce goods and services needed by consumers. Our economy is not a completely free one because of government involvement and is therefore termed a "modified free enterprise system". In a completely **free enterprise** system everyone, businesses and consumers, act independently. Businesses produce what they want to produce and consumers buy what they want.

Our economic system in Canada encourages variety in both goods and services. A visit to a shoe store allows you to see shoes of many styles, colours, qualities, and prices. As a shopper, you buy the shoes of your choice and wear them home. Generally, we find that the goods and services we select have good quality and fair prices. These conditions help both consumers and businesses and there are certain basic rules in free enterprise that make it work this way.

Private Property

The first basic rule of **free enterprise** is that **private property** is encouraged. This simply means that individuals and businesses may own things. You can own clothes, bicycles, a T.V. set, and sports equipment. Adults can own a car, house, furniture, or a cottage. In these cases, the products give satisfaction to their owners–the consumers. The items consumers possess are called consumer goods. Some individuals and businesses may own other types of goods. An individual can own a corner grocery store, and apartment building, a nursery, a barber shop, or a beauty salon. The owner may buy equipment and use the equipment and building to earn a living. Owners also rent buildings to others. They can sell it, give it away, or leave it to their heirs. In all these cases, an owner's rights are protected by law and the law also requires an owner to operate according to certain laws to protect the general public.

Businesses can also own property. Some large businesses own millions of dollars' worth of factories and equipment. They own cars, trucks, ocean liners, planes, and railroads. They own land, race tracks, forests, mines, and fishing rights. Some companies even own other companies whose goods are used to produce other goods–these articles are called **producer goods**.

Profit

The second basic rule of free enterprise is that **profit** is both allowed and encouraged. Profit is the income left over after an owner pays costs and expenses. Profit is the incentive–the reason–for owning and using property, and producing goods. If producers efficiently manage factories, equipment, and workers, etc., they will be able to cover their costs and expenses and have some profit left.

The profit earned belongs to the owner. It is the owner's reward for taking a risk, for there is no guarantee of profit. Profit results from hard work and making the right decisions. After the owner pays part of the profit as taxes, he or she can use the rest any way he or she sees fit. The owner may increase the size of the business, invest in another business, or use it in a personal way. Profit is the incentive for starting a business. It encourages individuals to produce new products, new services, and to keep their costs of production as low as possible. The profit they earn is the reward for their risk and efforts.

In some cases, wrong business decisions are made, costs can become very high, or the business can not sell its products, and the owner may not have enough savings to continue operating. The result is bankruptcy or "going out of business".

Competition

The third basic rule of free enterprise is that **competition** is encouraged. Competition occurs when two or more businesses try to sell the same type of product to the same customer. One business may have a higher quality product. Another may have a lower price. Generally, higher prices and better quality go together but not always. While price and quality are the main items of competition, businesses compete in many other ways. Some businesses offer free services such as delivery, installation, and check-ups. Some offer credit on the spot. Others offer a greater variety in style and colour on consumer goods.

Competition requires businesses to advertise to inform customers of the products that are available and it is a great benefit to consumers. It encourages businesses to produce a variety of products. Customers are able to shop for the quality and price they want and the businesses who satisfy the most customers will be the ones who stay in business: successful businesses are those chosen by the consumer. This is the basis of the slogan "The Consumer Is King" in a free enterprise system.

Benefits of Free Enterprise

Free enterprise gives many benefits to producers and consumers.

Freedom

Business owners and consumers are free to make many decisions. Businesses can produce any product any way they wish as long as they act legally. Owners can produce hot dogs or bicycles. They can also decide whether to hire many workers and fewer machines or to use many machines and hire fewer workers. Their decisions are based on costs and prices.

Consumers also have freedoms. They are free to choose Brand A or Brand X. They are free to select any colour or any model of any product available. Consumers can buy as many products or services as they can afford and as long as jobs are available they are free to work where they want.

Efficient Use of Resources

The manufacture of products requires the use of labour, money, and natural resources. Businesses try to use workers, factories, equipment, and materials as efficiently as possible. This keeps costs down and leaves more money for profit. The desire for profit, therefore, encourages the most **efficient use of resources.**

New Products

Businesses are always attempting to increase their profits. One way to do this is to make new products. Many of these products are fads, such as hula hoops; others such as colour televisions or hi-fi equipment are long lasting. But in either case, the new products satisfy our work and leisure time.

Quality and Price

Consumers want products to work well and last a long time. They also want to pay as little as pos-

sible. Therefore, consumers shop for the best quality product at the lowest possible price suitable to them. Business owners know that they must provide quality products at low prices if they want to stay in business.

Disadvantages of Free Enterprise

Free enterprise also has some disadvantages. Generally these disadvantages apply to consumers.

Waste of Some Resources

Some individuals and businesses accumulate great wealth. These people use their money to buy trivial things at great cost and use of labour. At the same time, other individuals, not so fortunate, cannot earn enough to buy a healthy diet for their families.

Lack of Consumer Knowledge

A free enterprise economy creates so many new products that it is almost impossible for consumers to obtain all the information they need to make good buying decisions. Because of this some products of poor quality are produced and purchased. Consumers soon find that these products are useless and that they have wasted their money.

Unhealthy Products

Free enterprise encourages a great variety of products that are dangerous to health. Even when the products have health warnings printed on the sales packages, they continue to be produced and purchased. The reason such products continue to be sold is the option granted to all of us–that of freedom of choice.

UNIT B

FORMS OF BUSINESS ORGANIZATION

As you drive along any street in a small town or a major city of Canada, you will see a variety of businesses. One of these may be a small barber shop, another a local branch of a nation-wide department-store chain. There will be large businesses and small businesses: some manufacture goods, others provide services. Some have many employees, some few, but in each business case, the reasons for its existence is the same. A business's first purpose is to provide a good or service to its customers. Its second purpose is to provide a profit for the owner or owners.

In order to produce goods or services, a business needs certain items. These items are of four main types and are called **factors of production.** The four factors of production are natural resources, labour, capital, and management.

Natural Resources

Natural resources include land, water, trees, and minerals—iron, nickel, and coal. Oil, natural gas, and uranium are also natural resources and are very important sources of energy for our factories, offices, cars, and homes. A country with an abundance of natural resources can usually produce a variety and quantity of goods and services. Canada is very fortunate in having a great supply of natural resources and our standard of living, which is one of the highest in the world, is in large part dependent on our natural resources.

Labour

Labour includes all physical and mental work needed to produce goods or services. Most work is a combination of mental and physical effort though many jobs do require more of one than the other. Assembly line workers, stock clerks, and many construction workers perform mainly physical work. Designers, lawyers, accountants, department managers, and senior secretaries perform mainly mental work. A high level of production depends on a well trained and efficient labour force.

Capital

Capital includes not only the money invested in a business but also the manufactured goods—machines and other equipment—used to produce other goods. To produce large volumes of consumer goods, a nation needs large quantities of capital goods. Individual businesses use part of their profit to buy capital goods.

Management

Management generally includes the owners and the executive—key personnel—of a business. Management is responsible for making decisions involving production. Management decides what to produce, what materials to buy, and how many employees to hire. They also decide how to use profit, which can be used to buy more capital goods, to increase the wages of the employees, or to give a higher reward to the owners. Management may decide to use its profits in varying amounts for all three purposes.

Business Organizations

Businesses vary in size from small-only one worker, to very large-thousands of workers. The size of a business depends on different factors. The main factors are the product or service produced or the market serviced, the amount of capital needed, and the production processes required. In turn, the size of the business is the main factor that determines the form of a business organization.

Sole Proprietorship–One Owner

A business with only one owner is called a **sole proprietorship.** This form of business is most common in barber shops, beauty salons, neighbourhood stores, small farms, and small factories. The owner performs many different functions in the business. If the business is a restaurant, the owner may purchase the materials to make the snacks and meals, cook and serve the meals, clean the tables, wash the dishes, act as cashier and accountant, and clean the floors. He or she may own the land and building as well as all the equipment needed to carry on business. The money used to buy the capital usually comes from savings and from loans. The result is that the owner supplies his or her own capital, labour, and management. In return, he or she receives all the profits in good times or suffers the losses in bad times. He or she takes the risks accepting these conditions in hopes of good profits.

Advantages of Sole Proprietorship

The owner makes all the decisions regarding what to sell, who to hire, what equipment to buy, and how long to stay open. As a result, the owner is responsible for all decisions. Sole proprietors receive great satisfaction from seeing their own ideas develop into success–and they are their own bosses.

Any profits made by the business belong to the sole proprietor. The owner may use the profits to expand the business, hire more employees, or buy goods and services for his or her family. This encourages the owner to work harder, cut costs, and try any ideas that will benefit the business.

Since the sole proprietorship is usually small, the owner knows all the employees and customers on a personal basis. This situation usually encourages friendly relations and co-operative work habits. The result is often a more efficient and profitable business which is a benefit to customers, employees, and owner alike.

Disadvantages of Sole Proprietorship

The sole proprietor must carry out many duties in the business. The owner may lack the ability to purchase the right supplies, hire and supervise the right people, adequately serve customers, or control the finances. A weakness in any one of these areas can cause the failure of the business.

33

Any losses caused by the business are the owner's. This is a risk the owner takes. This loss may mean that the business does not have enough money to pay all its business debts. Creditors can claim the personal belongings of the owner, such as the house, car, and savings, to cover the business losses. This condition of sole proprietorship is called **unlimited liability**.

The sole proprietor finances the business from savings and whatever can be borrowed. The money accumulating from these two sources is usually small, which makes it very difficult to expand, replace old equipment, or cover emergencies. Situations like this can keep the business small and/or inefficient, and can actually cause failure.

The business activity in a sole proprietorship depends greatly on the owner. A long illness or death may cause the business to fail or be sold. If a buyer cannot be found, the owner's relations may get a poor price for the business.

The Partnership-Two or More Owners

A business with two or more owners is called a **partnership**. Partnerships are found in the same types of business as sole proprietorships. Partnerships are often formed because sole proprietors want to share the work and increase their **capital**. The owners usually continue to own the land and buildings, take an active part in the labour, and contribute most of the capital. When individuals decide to form a partnership, they draw up an agreement called the articles of co-partnership. This signed agreement contains the name and location of the business, the nature of the business, the names of the owners, the duties and responsibilities of the owners, the amount of capital each contributes to the business, and the portion of profits that each will receive.

Advantages of Partnerships

Two or more people now share making the decisions. Therefore better decisions should be made on the basis that "two heads are better than one". One of the partners may be an excellent salesperson and the other may have special buying skills: both these skills are very important in business. With each person concentrating more on his or her best skills, the business should be more efficient and make more profit.

Each partner brings savings. It is also easier to borrow money if there are more partners in the business. If the number of partners is large, the management is usually more efficient, and the credit rating of the business is better.

Disadvantages of Partnerships

Although a partnership can raise more capital than a proprietorship, it is still limited to the funds of a few people. This limited amount of capital restricts the size and type of business suitable for a partnership.

If the partnership fails, each partner can be held personally liable for the outstanding debts of the business. If these debts are large, and one partner has little personal wealth, the other partner or partners can face financial ruin.

In many businesses, conditions change with time. These changes may be in items for sale, profits, extra work, and new duties. If all partners cannot agree on the decisions involving these new conditions, disagreements occur. As a result, efficiency can decrease, profits can fall, and the business can fail.

The Corporation-Many Owners

Another form of business is the **corporation or limited company.** Examples of this form of business are Simpsons, Stelco, Ford of Canada, Bell Canada, and Dominion Stores. These companies require many millions of dollars to buy land, buildings, equipment, and inventory. Therefore, to raise the needed money, many people or owners are necessary.

When a group of business people wish to establish a corporation, they normally contact a lawyer with a knowledge of corporation law. The lawyer helps the group draw up a document, which contains the following:

The name of the corporation

The purposes of the corporation

The amounts of any type of capital that will be raised by the corporation

The location of the corporation

The names of the members of the group setting up the corporation.

This document, when approved by the appropriate government officer, becomes the company's charter.

The corporation's ownership is divided into many small parts, each part called a share or a stock. These shares are sold to individuals and the corporation uses the money to buy its land, buildings, equipment, and inventory. The individual owners are called shareholders. The shareholders meet at least once a year to elect a board of directors, receive the company's financial statements, ask questions regarding the business, and make recommendations to the board of directors. At this meeting, a shareholder receives one vote for each share owned. One share equals one vote, 2000 shares

Because ownership is divided into many small parts, many individuals can become owners. The total investment by these owners means the corporation has a huge amount of capital.

Corporations usually have a large number of employees. These employees have a variety of skills in research, accounting, manufacturing, sales, purchasing, and other business functions. Their skills usually result in a more efficient operation and a more profitable business.

The major advantage of a corporation is that it has limited liability, which means that the owners' liability for the debts of the corporation are limited to the owners' investment. Should the corporation fail, the shareholder loses only the amount invested in shares–no personal property can be claimed by debtors.

Because shares of a corporation can be sold from one individual to another the owners, directors, and executive, of the business change but the business continues to operate. And the business will not cease on the death of one owner. Therefore a corporation business can continue to expand indefinitely. A good example of this is the Hudson's Bay Company established in the seventeenth century and still operating.

Disadvantages of Corporations

The owners of the corporation do not have personal contact with customers or employees. Sometimes this is considered a disadvantage for the customers and employees do not receive the personal attention they might get in a smaller business. And, of course, shareholders who own only a few shares do not take a very active part in managing the business.

In Canada, corporations pay taxes on their profits and shareholders pay income taxes on any dividends they receive causing, in effect, a form of double taxation. There are some tax exemptions in certain cases, but generally speaking, corporation profits are taxed at least twice.

The Co-operative–Customers as Owners

The co-operative is similar to a corporation in many ways. It can be a very large business requiring much capital and many owners. The co-operative requires a government charter to conduct its business. Its ownership is divided into many small parts called shares. The individuals who buy shares are usually the people who use the business and they are called members. For example, many

equals 2000 votes. If a shareholder cannot attend the annual meeting, the shareholder can pass the voting privilege on to someone else, usually a member of the board of directors. This privilege is called a proxy.

The directors set the policies of the company, determine the particular products or services to be produced, and decide how the profits will be used. The directors also appoint the executive of the company to manage the daily operations of the business. This executive is composed of the president, vice-president, secretary, and treasurer. Some companies will have other officers as well. The board of directors is responsible to the shareholders.

The profits of the corporation belong to the shareholders. Usually, some of the profit is used to expand the business by buying more land, buildings, and other assets. In normal years, some of the profit is returned to the shareholders. This payment is called a dividend. The amount of the dividend per share is determined by dividing the amount of profit to be paid out by the number of shares held by shareholders. If a company paid out $250 000 of profit and there were 125 000 shares, each share would receive a share dividend of $2. The owner of one share would receive $2, the owner of 2000 shares would receive $4000.

farmers are members of a grain sales or feed-supply co-operative. Many students at universities own and use co-operative bookstores. Individuals who deposit and borrow money through a credit union become members of that credit union. These members elect a board of directors who in turn appoint an executive to manage the business. However, there is a difference in the voting power of the members of a co-operative compared with a shareholder of a corporation. A member of a co-operative is limited to *one* vote regardless of the number of shares held. This ensures that no one member can control the co-operative.

A second major difference between corporations and co-operatives is in the dividend section. The profit of a co-operative is distributed on the basis of how much the member *uses* the co-operative. A member who buys $2000 worth of goods from a co-operative will receive a dividend twice as large as a member who purchased $1000 worth. This return is called a **patronage refund**. Other conditions under which a co-operative operates are similar to those of a corporation.

FUNCTIONS OF BUSINESS

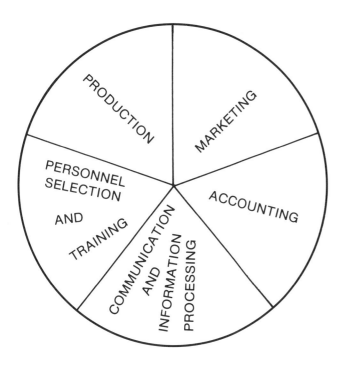

UNIT C

NATURE AND FUNCTIONS OF BUSINESS

As consumers, we depend on business for many of the goods and services we need to survive. These items are called essential goods and services and they include water, housing, and clothing. Business also produces our luxury goods, meaning sports cars, colour television, skate-boards, banana splits, and rock concerts. We also depend on business to provide us with jobs. The money we receive from work is used to buy our essential and luxury goods and services.

Business, naturally, depends on consumers. The money spent by consumers on goods and services is the income of businesses, and businesses depend on consumers for labour. Businesses and consumers are, therefore, dependent on one another.

Modern business is a very complex operation. When we shop for a skate-board or a magazine, we usually think only of the end product, the product that sits on the shelf waiting for us to buy and use it. We seldom think that parts of these products were once raw materials growing in forests or buried underground. And we seldom think of all the operations that occurred to raw materials to change them into the products we buy. Business performs many activities to make these changes.

Nature of Business

Businesses in Canada producing similar products or services are called an **industry**. For example, the auto industry contains all businesses that produce automobiles and parts. The financial industry contains Canada's banks, trust companies, credit unions, and finance companies. The mining industry contains, among others, companies that mine iron ore, nickel ore, uranium ore, and gold ore. These industries are usually separated into three categories depending on the stage of development of the products. These categories are called primary, secondary, and tertiary.

Primary industries, those in the first stage of development of products, take raw materials from land or water. Examples of these industries are mining, fishing, agriculture, forestry, and oil and gas. Many jobs in a primary industry are outdoors. As many primary industries require a large investment in research, equipment, and machinery, the risks against making a profit are often very high.

Secondary industries manufacture raw materials into finished products: gold ore is refined and made into jewellery; iron ore is processed into ingots, steel sheets, and then car bodies or frying pans; crude oil is refined into oil and gasoline, and also processed into synthetic fabrics; wheat is milled into flour and then baked into bread, cakes, or cookies; fish products of many kinds are processed into spreads, sticks, and delicacies; forestry products are used for a variety of building products, furniture, and paper products.

Tertiary industries provide services to consumers, governments, and other businesses. The service industries are becoming more important because they are employing more workers and are taking a larger share of the nation's spending. Some examples of these industries involve transportation of both people and products, television and radio programs, sports, repair services, restaurants, hotels, motels, and financial and credit institutions.

Functions of Business

Because it is impossible to describe the functions of all businesses, this section deals mainly with the secondary or manufacturing businesses. These businesses are responsible for supplying goods purchased by consumers, governments, and other businesses. The functions common to most manufacturing businesses are **production**, **marketing**, **accounting**, **communication**, and **personnel**.

Production

This business function has many parts and one of them is **purchasing**. The purchasing department is responsible for buying the raw materials and supplies necessary for the business. The raw materials may include metal, rubber, wood, and paint for the making of pencils. A bakery needs flour, sugar, fruit, and special decorations. A business producing a more complex product such as an automobile or house has to purchase hundreds of different raw materials. These businesses must also purchase supplies such as paper, pens, typewriter ribbons, tools, and major equipment. A farmer often acts as a purchasing agent in acquiring machinery, livestock, feed, fertilizer, and other supplies.

Businesses that produce only services also need to purchase supplies. Examples of such businesses are barber shops, lawn service businesses, schools, bus lines, and hospitals. No business can operate without supplies.

Retail businesses such as grocery, clothing, furniture, and gift stores depend on a purchasing department. They must have the proper amount of goods on hand at the right time; a shortage results in loss of possible sales, a surplus means money is tied up that could be used in some other way to make a profit.

Processing is another part of production. Processing is the changing of raw materials into finished products. Often more than one business is involved in the chain. Some businesses make only parts while another business assembles the parts into the finished product. Processing methods

FOUR FACTORS OF PRODUCTION

MANAGEMENT

RAW MATERIALS LABOUR CAPITAL

37

depend on the final product. Bread and cakes use a baking process; steel requires a smelting process; most plastic products need a melting and molding process; wooden products normally require sawing, planing, and nailing as part of construction, and many food products require a cooking process.

Another function of production is grading. We usually think of the grading of products when to refer to food products such as eggs, meat, and vegetables. In these cases, the grading indicates size or quality. Higher graded products usually are more expensive. But many other products are also graded. For example, gasoline is often sold in two different grades, regular and premium. Some clothing products with slight defects are classed as "seconds". Some appliance dealers sell their slightly damaged products in a "scratch-and-dent" sale. A wise consumer can often realize good savings on these products and not lose any quality of operation.

Most manufacturing businesses have a quality control department. This department is similar to a grading department except there are only two categories–accept or reject. Very specific standards are set and the products or parts must meet these standards. For example, some steel bars must meet certain strength standards. Any bars not meeting the standards will be scrapped and reprocessed. Car parts not meeting proper standards must be replaced. Certain toys that do not meet safety standards cannot be sold. These standards or grading features protect consumers from defective or unsafe products. They also protect producers from earning a bad reputation, which would decrease sales and profits.

Marketing

Marketing is the process of distributing the goods and services from the producers to the consumers. Many activities are involved in marketing goods and services. A major part of marketing is packaging. Packaging of certain goods is necessary to protect them from damage and from the environment. Packaging also makes it more convenient to move certain products. Imagine carrying home two dozen eggs from the store without a package.

The second part of marketing is storage. Some products often have special seasons for sales. For example, toys have peak sales during November and December; bathing suits have peak sales in spring and summer; and hockey equipment is sold mainly during the winter. Producers wish to spread production evenly over the year, which means that the finished products need to be stored during the slack sales period.

Advertising is the third part of marketing. Advertising is used by producers to inform consumers about goods and services available. The most common forms of advertising are television, radio, newspaper, and magazine.

The fourth part of marketing is transportation. Businesses use many different ways of moving goods to the consumers. Some examples are truck, railroad, plane, ship, and pipeline.

The fifth part of marketing involves research. Research is the process of searching for new materials, new products, or new ways of operating or manufacturing. Research in the plastics industry has resulted in new products that are both strong and light. Medical research has resulted in cures for many killer diseases. Research in technology has resulted in new processes in manufacturing and building. Businesses use research to develop new products, better quality products, and products at lower costs. This helps business make more sales and profits. Consumers benefit from having more products from which to choose, better quality products, and often at lower prices than similar products sold earlier.

Accounting

How often have you heard the statement that money doesn't grow on trees? The statement applies equally to businesses as it does to individuals and families. Businesses face financial decisions every day. To make the right decisions, they must have accurate and up-to-date information. Therefore, businesses usually hire qualified people to handle their financial records. Larger businesses set up their own finance or accounting departments.

The accounting department is responsible for keeping accurate and up-to-date financial records. These records include the purchase of land, factories, and equipment. They also include a record of money spent to buy materials and supplies for production. In many cases these items are purchased on credit, which requires keeping records of future payments. Payroll or salary records are very important, not only for the employees but for the income tax payable to government. The accounting department keeps accurate records on expenses such as heat, water, supplies, materials, and labour. Management uses these records to make decisions on production to keep costs down.

Another important figure recorded by the accounting department is sales–the income of the business. The business starts with this figure, pays all its costs for materials and expenses such as labour, heat, lights, etc., and hopes it has some money left over. The left-over part is its profit. A business needs a profit in order to continue operations.

The accounting department also prepares a

budget for the business. A budget is an estimate of the sales, expenses, and profits for the next one, two, and sometimes even five years. This financial plan allows the business to make plans for future production.

Communications

Communication is the sending and receiving of information. Businesses must communicate constantly. The sales department must contact the customers on a regular basis. The purchasing department must contact the suppliers. The accounting department must receive information from all departments in the business so that it can pay bills on time and prepare the financial statements. The managers and owners must make many decisions. For example they must estimate future sales, plan production schedules, hire the right number of workers, and order the proper amount of materials. To make the right decisions, the information must be accurate, and be received on time. Therefore, a good communication system in a business is necessary to help that business earn a profit.

Businesses use many methods of communication. The most common methods used to contact other businesses are the post office and the telephone. Other methods are telegraph, computer terminals, and private courier systems. Within a business, communication is conducted mainly by letter, memo, telephone, and personal contact in meetings. The future use of electronic equipment using computers and satellites will make communications in business both more efficient and more exciting.

Personnel Selection and Training

The success of a business greatly depends on its employees. If employees like their jobs, receive reasonable wages and salaries, and find the place a pleasant place to work, they are usually efficient workers. That means that the employees work hard and produce more than if they were not happy. The extra products mean more sales for the business and more income for the employees.

The personnel department is responsible for the overall performance of employees. One of the tasks of employees in the personnel department is accepting applications from potential employees. Then the applicants must be interviewed. The personnel department must decide who will be selected for the positions. The lucky applicants must be trained for particular jobs. Training programs are the responsibility of the personnel department.

There are many other duties in this department. Records of all employees are kept here to help select employees for promotions or transfers. The man-

ager is responsible for settling employee problems with the owners of the business. He or she is also responsible for negotiating a wage contract between the employees and the employers, which can be a very difficult and lengthy task. In general, the personnel department is responsible for maintaining good relations between employer and employees.

Costs and Profits

We have read that businesses must earn a profit to survive. This profit is necessary to reward the owners for their risk. We have also read that profit is the income left after the owner pays costs and expenses. For example, if a bicycle sells for $100, and the costs and expenses amount to $75, the profit on the bicycle is $25; these costs and expenses are the results of the functions of business. The larger the costs and expenses, the smaller the profits will be; the smaller the costs and expenses, the larger the profits will be. Business, therefore, will try to keep costs and expenses as low as possible. They try to perform their functions as efficiently as possible.

How Production is Measured

Each year the federal government attempts to discover how well the Canadian economy is doing. This is done by adding together the dollar value of all the goods and services produced in Canada during the year. This total is referred to as the gross national product, or GNP for short. By comparing this total to totals from previous years, the government can determine whether or not any advancement has been made in the wealth of the economy.

Dollar values are the only way by which production can be measured. How else do you add together different items such as steel, candy bars, hair cuts, movies, and train rides?

Digest of Business News
Autumn 1978

REVIEWING
YOUR BUSINESS VOCABULARY

Write the number of each definition.
Write the word that matches the definition.

UNIT A

competition, efficient use of resources,
free enterprise, private property, profit

1. The term used for ownership by individuals and businesses.
2. Keeping costs down, thus having more money for profit.
3. A system in which businesses are allowed to produce any goods and services they wish.
4. The term used for income remaining after payment of costs and expenses.
5. A situation that occurs when two or more businesses try to sell the same type of product to the same customers.

UNIT B

capital, co-operative, corporation, factors of
production, labour, management, natural
resources, partnership, sole proprietorship

1. The term used for the owners and executive of a business.
2. A business with one owner.
3. The term used for all physical and mental work.
4. A business with many hundreds or thousands of owners.
5. Our land, water, trees, and minerals.
6. The money and manufactured goods required to produce other goods.
7. The term that covers all natural resources, labour, capital, and management.
8. A business where the customers are owners.
9. A business with two or more owners.

UNIT C

industry, primary industry, secondary
industry, tertiary industry, purchasing,
processing, marketing, accounting,
communication, personnel

1. The department responsible for buying raw materials and supplies.
2. The general term converting raw materials to finished products.
3. The specific industry that changes raw materials into finished products.
4. The sending and receiving of information.
5. The specific industry that provides services to consumers, governments, and other businesses.
6. The process of distributing goods and services.
7. The specific term for the taking of raw materials from land or water.
8. The department responsible for the overall performance of the employees.
9. The department responsible for keeping accurate and up-to-date financial records.
10. The term for businesses producing similar products or services.

REVIEW QUESTIONS

UNIT A

1. Why is our system called a modified free enterprise system?
2. Explain the basic rules of free enterprise.
3. What does the concept of private property allow individuals to do with their possessions?
4. How does private property affect a business owner?
5. What can owners do with their profits?
6. What factors can cause a business to declare bankruptcy?
7. How does competition help consumers?
8. Explain the economic freedoms for business owners and for consumers.
9. How does profit encourage the efficient use of resources?
10. State two benefits and two disadvantages of free enterprise.

UNIT B

1. What four items does a business need to produce goods and services?
2. List five examples of natural resources.
3. List three jobs that require mainly physical work and three jobs that require mainly mental work.
4. List five examples of capital goods.
5. Why does a nation need a large quantity of capital goods?
6. What are the responsibilities of management?
7. Name three businesses that use the proprietorship form of business organization.
8. Explain the advantages and the disadvantages of sole proprietorship.
9. What is included in the "articles of co-partnership".
10. Explain the advantages and the disadvantages of a partnership.
11. Why does a corporation require many owners?
12. What is included in a corporation charter?
13. How does a shareholder help control a corporation?

14. What are the responsibilities of the board of directors?
15. Explain the advantages and disadvantages of the corporation.

UNIT C

1. How do secondary industries differ from primary industries?
2. Why are service industries becoming more important?
3. Name four functions common to most manufacturing businesses.
4. Why must the purchasing department have the proper amount of goods or materials available?
5. Why do many businesses have a research department?
6. How can a research department in a business help consumers?
7. Why are packaging and storage so important to marketing?
8. What records are kept by the accounting department?
9. What is a budget and why is one prepared?
10. What are the most common methods of business communications?
11. What tasks are carried out by the personnel department?

APPLYING YOUR KNOWLEDGE

UNIT A

1. List ten items of private property owned by you or your family.
2. Select a business in your neighbourhood. List ten items of private property owned by the business.
3. Explain how each of the following could spend the profits they make from their business: a farmer; a fisherman; a housebuilder; a service-station operator; a grocery-store owner; a restaurant owner.
4. Approximately 2500 businesses each year declare bankruptcy. Explain how this situation affects owners, workers, consumers, and government.
5. Select two similar businesses in your area. Explain how they compete with each other.
6. Explain how business competition helps you personally.
7. What economic freedoms do you have as a consumer?
8. List five products you will have to buy some day but which you don't know much about now. Where will you obtain the information you need to make a wise purchasing decision?

UNIT B

1. List four natural resources found in your area.
2. Name five capital goods in your school.
3. Select a particular business that you would like to operate as sole proprietor. What advantages and disadvantages would you face as owner?
4. Explain the differences between a corporation dividend and a co-operative patronage refund.
5. What is meant by the phrase "a variety of businesses"?

UNIT C

1. Name three major industries in your area and three businesses in each one.
2. Select a business in your area. List as many businesses as you can that supply goods or services to that business.
3. Oil is used to produce many different products used by consumers and businesses. List four different products made from oil that are used by (a) consumers, and (b) businesses.
4. List as many materials as you can that are used in the production of a car or a house.
5. Select six different products requiring special storage facilities. Explain why each product requires this individual storage.
6. Why is quality control and grading important in businesses that use peaches.
7. The accounting department of a business deals with consumers on a regular basis. List the financial information from businesses received by your family.

PROJECTS
AND PROBLEMS

UNIT A

1. Meredith has been working as a volunteer in the school cafeteria for the last three years. She hopes to set up her own restaurant within five years. List ten expenses Meredith would have in owning her own restaurant.
2. Select a major business in your area. List six producer goods needed by this business.
3. List four products you buy regularly. For each product, list at least two different producers of that product. Put a check mark beside the business you think produces the best quality product. Explain your reasons.
4. Bring to class three different advertisements that individually emphasize price, quality, and service.
5. Profit is the incentive for starting a business. What business would you be interested in starting that would provide you with a reasonable profit? Explain why you selected this business.

UNIT B

1. Kramer and Pollock are partners in a clothing store. Kramer receives two-thirds of the profit and Pollock receives one-third. Why is this agreement satisfactory to both partners?
2. Explain why barber shops are usually organized as proprietorships rather than corporations.
3. Explain how the limited liability condition of a corporation protects the shareholders.
4. Which would you rather own–ten shares in a corporation or ten shares in a co-operative. Why?
5. Name the oldest business in your community. Explain why you think it has been in business so long.
6. Select a business in your community. Write a short essay on the business that includes: the natural resources it uses; the different types of labour it uses; the goods it uses; the names and positions of its management team.

7. Tom and Sally Walker each have over ten years' experience in working for others in hairstyling shops. They have $20 000 to invest in their own hairstyling business.

a. What form of business organization should they use? Why?
b. What capital goods will they need to purchase?
c. What skills must they have to develop a successful business?
d. What related business activities might they consider to help their hairstyling business?

UNIT C

1. Most of the fresh strawberries that Canadians eat in January are grown in California. List the production and marketing functions necessary for Canadians to have fresh strawberries in January.
2. Barbara loves the deep apple pie that her mother makes. Explain the stages or parts of production necessary to take the apples from the tree and eventually put them in the form of a piece of pie on Barbara's plate.
3. Accounting is sometimes called the language of business. Explain this statement.
4. Describe briefly the types of telephone services available to businesses. Use the telephone directory or reference books in the resource centre for assistance.

3 Marketing in Canada ¿?

UNIT A

PRINCIPLES AND FUNCTIONS

Marketing is a fascinating part of the business world. Without it, many products would never reach the people who want to buy them. What does marketing refer to? You will recall in the earlier two chapters that the producer is the person or enterprise that makes a product (or provides a service). Once the product is made, however, it must reach the consumer for a sale to be made. Marketing is the process of getting the goods from producers to consumers.

Marketing Products

Have you ever been to a "farmer's market"? It's a colourful place where several local farmers bring their fruit, vegetables, eggs, and cheese to sell to people who like fresh produce. The word **market** can mean two things. It can refer to a group of people with similar needs and wants for a product. For example, the people who come to a farmer's market represent a group looking for similar products. **Market** can also refer to the place where buyers and sellers meet. A market can be almost anywhere. If a salesperson comes to your house to sell you a vacuum cleaner, your doorstep becomes the marketplace. In both cases, the farmer and the vacuum cleaner manufacturer are attempting to market, or sell their product directly to the consumer. To **market a product** means to offer it for sale.

This method of marketing is sufficient for a small business operation, but for producers that make thousands of products every day; some way must be found to reach as many people as possible. Most consumer goods in Canada are bought from stores that are not involved in the production of the goods they sell. People who operate stores of this kind are referred to as **middlemen**. There are two kinds of middlemen, one is a retailer, the other a wholesaler.

The Retailer

Imagine yourself in a local shopping mall with a large number of stores. You could probably name several different types of stores found in the shopping centre. Each store owner is a retailer. A **retailer** is a seller who deals directly with the customer. If you made a list of the stores, it might include a grocery store, a jeans shop, a large department store, and a record shop. Businesses that provide services such as hair stylists, banks, movie theatres and dry cleaners are also retailers. Retail businesses are the most common type of business enterprises in Canada and the main method of marketing consumer goods and services. Retailers provide several places through which producers can market their products in large quantities. Of course, in the case of a farmer selling directly to a customer, there is only one seller and one buyer for the product. But within the retail store method of marketing, there are actually two sellers–the producer and the store; and two buyers–the store and you, the customer. This method of selling is referred to as **two-step marketing**.

The Wholesaler

It is possible for a retailer to purchase goods directly from the producer. A corner grocery store may arrange to get fresh fruit and vegetables from local farmers, for example, and several large producers build their own retail stores in order to sell their products. Most tire manufacturers in Canada, such as Firestone and Goodyear, sell their products through their own retail outlets, usually with the same company name. Generally, however, retailers prefer to buy their merchandise from wholesalers.

A **wholesaler** is a merchant who buys goods in large quantities from several producers, and resells them in smaller lots to retailers. A food wholesaler might purchase truckloads of farm products from many vegetable and fruit growers all over the province, then in town, resell them to grocery stores. With this method of marketing, there are three buyers and sellers. The producer sells to the wholesaler. The wholesaler sells to the retailer and the retailer then sells the products directly to the consumer. This is called **three-step marketing**.

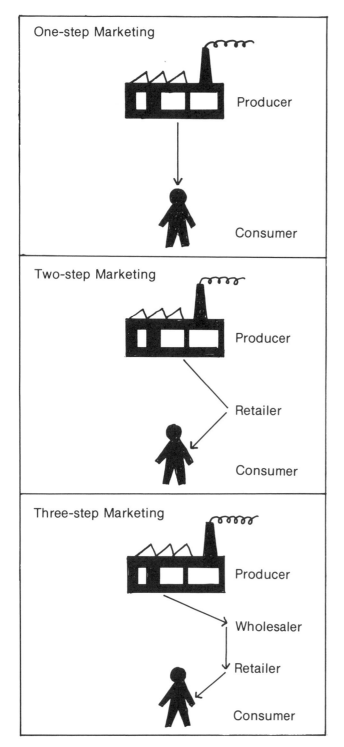

One-step Marketing

Producer

Consumer

Two-step Marketing

Producer

Retailer

Consumer

Three-step Marketing

Producer

Wholesaler

Retailer

Consumer

The Importance of the Middleman

Canada is a vast, resourceful country. It is rich in mineral and oil deposits, agricultural land, timber acreage, and well-stocked fishing waters. Businesses have succeeded in bringing the resources together along with materials imported from other countries in order to produce Canadian goods and services. Marketing these products is a problem because of the distance between markets. **Middlemen,** such as wholesalers, are needed to solve this problem.

Wholesalers provide a way of transporting, storing, and distributing products to the retailers all across Canada. In this way, even a small variety store is able to obtain a large selection of different products with little effort and low cost. The next time you are in a small variety store, read some of the labels to see where the products came from. Without wholesalers, acting as middlemen, most of the shelves would be empty; without retailers, acting as middlemen, you would have to travel to each factory in person to get the products you needed.

Functions of Marketing

The process of marketing usually involves several activities. Suppose, for example, that an electronics firm has just produced a new pocket calculator. Before sales can begin, the packaging department will need to design an attractive, protective box to ensure that the calculator reaches each customer undamaged. The advertising department will need to plan a suitable advertising strategy to introduce the product. Then the sales department can contact wholesalers or retailers that are willing to purchase large quantities of the new calculator.

Sometimes the producer, the wholesaler, and the retailer perform the same marketing activities. Each seller is concerned with storing the product safely and conveniently until a sale is made. To achieve this, the manufacturer and the wholesaler may have their own warehouses. The smaller retailer may simply keep the surplus products in the basement or in a special storage room. Similarly, the producer or middleman may each be involved in other activities, such as transportation and advertising.

The activities of getting the product from the original producer to the point of final sale are known as the **functions of marketing**. Each function increases the cost of the item. As a consumer, you must decide whether or not it is worth paying an extra amount for the value added by each of the marketing activities.

Package Design

Have you ever noticed how many items are sold already packaged in a bottle, can, carton, or wrapper? A well-designed package performs several tasks: it protects the contents; it makes the product easier to carry or to use; it helps to promote the product. The cardboard jacket for a record album, for instance, protects the record from dust and scratches. The square format of the package makes the product more convenient to handle and display. Also, the imaginative, colourful cover created by skilled designers and photographers attract customers and promotes the sale of the record.

Storage

Many products require special storage facilities to maintain their original quality. Perishable products such as meat, vegetables, and dairy products need refrigeration to keep from spoiling. Cereals, paper products, and cake mixes may be damaged if they are not stored in a dry area. Glass products are often packaged with special storage and handling labels such as "fragile" or "handle with care".

Canada has distinctive seasons with reasonably predictable weather conditions. As a result, retailers have to clear and restock shelves to supply the changing needs of their customers. Summer swim suits and short sleeve shirts are replaced by warmer winter clothing. In parts of British Columbia, raincoats and umbrellas mark the winter season. Since moving and storing merchandise is costly and time-consuming, retailers often have seasonal clearance sales. Wise consumers find this an excellent opportunity to get products at reduced prices.

Transportation

Long trainloads of prairie wheat rumble towards a Saskatchewan flour mill. Crude oil surges along pipelines to an Alberta refinery. At the Vancouver docks, a front-end loader lifts several containers of paper on to a cargo ship. A convoy of trucks with packaged, frozen fish leaves a Maritime processing plant and heads towards Toronto. Scenes like these illustrate the many methods of moving products to their final destination. The choice of transport depends upon the nature of the product, the distance, and the cost.

Transportation is an industry in itself. Special railway cars are designed to carry a wide range of products from wheat, automobiles, frozen food, chemicals, petroleum, to steel. The "piggyback" concept allows a tractor trailer with the merchandise still inside it to ride on top of a railway flatcar until it reaches its destination. The use of standardized shipping containers the size of a truck trailer has similar advantages. The storage area can be lifted off the truck trailer and placed on to a railway flatcar, a cargo ship, or put into the hold of a cargo plane. "Containerization" has become highly popular because it eliminates several stages of loading and unloading usually involved with the shipping of merchandise.

Advertising and Promotion

Most producers are confronted with a competitive marketplace. This means that several other companies are selling similar products. In Canada, for example, General Motors, Ford, Chrysler, American Motors, Toyota, Datsun, Volkswagen and a few other companies all compete to sell you the type of car that they manufacture. Car companies rely on advertising to compete for a share of the market.

A variety of media is available to the seller, such as television, magazines, radio, newspapers, direct mail, and billboards. Quite often a company will use a mixture of these methods. Retailers have several other ways of gaining a customer's attention in addition to media advertising. Sales promotion techniques are commonly used and consumers may benefit directly from this form of advertising. When retailers compete with one another, they may reduce their prices, have a sale, give away free samples or bonus coupons, run a contest, even sell something in the store for less than they paid for it. The last item mentioned, referred to as a loss leader, is often used by grocery stores. Sales promotion techniques can be costly to the retailers, especially if they do not attract the extra customers that they had planned for.

Research

The marketing function that receives the least publicity is probably research. Yet most major companies in Canada devote part of their budget towards this function. Product Research is an important step towards the marketing of a new or improved product. A petroleum company, for example, may spend years in chemical laboratories investigating new ways to use their oil. Besides using petroleum for gasoline, engine oil, and diesel fuel, scientists have found ways to use petroleum in fabrics, plastics, drugs, and cosmetics. Much of the clothing you possess has been developed from synthetic fibre refined from petroleum.

A second kind of research involves the investigation of what consumers like to buy. This is called market research. One way of discovering consumer preferences is to interview people in shopping malls, or over the phone, or with questionnaires that you can mail back to the company. A few years ago a company that made cleaning products used a door-to-door survey to find out what new products housewives would like to see. When the survey was analysed, the company immediately began producing the product housewives asked for most–an "easy-off" oven spray. Several months later their competitors found out what a good idea that company had discovered with their market research survey.

Methods of Selling

Marketing a product (offering it for sale) also includes the way in which the seller plans to present the item to the customer. Not all products are sold in the same way. The self-serve method has become popular in grocery stores, department stores, drug stores, and gasoline stations. This method has the advantage of lowering the cost of selling items because fewer salespeople are employed. Personal sales, which includes sales staff, is still needed to sell certain kinds of products. For example, many jewellers, candy shops, clothing and shoe departments have sales clerks to assist you. Clothing and jewellery may require alterations. In the shoe department, clerks are needed to find the right size shoe from the collection they keep in a storage room. Clerks are needed at candy counters to package and cost the candy you have chosen. Personal sales is also needed in order to arrange for delivery, arrange for financing, or explain the warranty and correct way to operate a product.

Mail order selling is another method of reaching the customer. You may have noticed small mail order catalogues in your home, which display items such as wallets, purses, record albums, plants, seeds, and household articles. Many mail order houses specialize in a particular type of product. Record clubs, for example, sell only items related to music to their customers. These might include records, cassettes, eight-track tapes, record cleaners, and tape and record holders.

There are several items to be considered when producers are thinking of marketing their products. These items, known as the functions of marketing, include methods of selling, package design, advertising and sales promotion, research, transportation, and storage. Often some of these functions are performed repeatedly on the same product because different sellers are involved. The seller might be a producer selling to a wholesaler who in turn sells to the retailer who in turn sells to you. If all three sellers are included in the marketing of a product, this method would be referred to as three-step marketing.

UNIT B

ADVERTISING, SALES PROMOTION, AND SELLING

Advertising plays an important role in the business world. All types of companies–manufacturers, retailers, and wholesalers–use advertising to keep consumers aware of products and services that are available. The company that pays for the advertisements is called the **sponsor**. You may recall hearing the familiar cliché "And now a word from our sponsor. . ." during your favourite television program.

Companies often use a mixture of advertising media to reach their potential customers. Commercials on television or radio may be used in combination with outdoor billboards and the local newspaper. Since newspapers are usually thrown out within a few days, local retail stores prefer to use this method of advertising a short-term sale. Magazine advertisements, although more expensive than those in the newspaper, are also frequently used. Studies have shown that each issue of some magazines is passed along to as many as eight or nine readers. This fact is important for some manufacturers who wish their product to be viewed several times.

Some companies prefer to contact their customers individually. In order to do this, people are selected from a mailing list of potential buyers. Each person selected is then sent a personal letter, circular, folder, price list, brochure, or catalogue. The "direct mail" technique is popular because of the personal effect it has on the customer.

If you travelled to school on the bus or subway this morning, you may have noticed several advertisements above the windows. These display cards, which are usually twenty-eight by seventy-two centimetres, are used by a variety of companies. The outside of the bus is frequently decorated with posters as well.

The many choices of advertising techniques available to the producer can make decisions difficult. Some businesses hire **advertising agencies** to design their advertisements and recommend the best mixture of advertising methods for their product. Large business firms may have their own advertising department staffed with an art director, copywriters, photographers, and editors.

Types of Advertising

Advertisers are aware of factors that influence people's buying habits. They use this knowledge to design ads that will convince you that their client's product is preferable to a competitor's. One type of advertisement commonly used is called a **testimonial**. In this type of ad, famous movie stars, television stars, or professional athletes are shown using the product. Comedian-actor Bill Cosby has endorsed Jello Pudding and Ford cars; actress Farrah Fawcett-Majors has endorsed a hair conditioner; actor Robert Vaughn has shown the usefulness of Pond's cold cream and football quarterback Joe Nameth has endorsed boots and aftershave lotion. The intention of the advertiser is to leave the viewer with the impression that the product must be good if these famous people use it.

Emotional advertising is another frequently used method. Advertisers appeal to our emotions such as pride, fear, insecurity, or the desire to be liked. "Will he kiss you again? Be certain with. . ." is an ad that provides a solution to an insecurity that the advertiser could have created in the first place. A coffee ad, that suggests caffeine is bad for you is an example of a fear created by the power of suggestion. Automobile manufacturers may appeal to your pride of ownership, while clothing manufacturers may use pressures of conformity to induce you to buy their latest products. Clearly, emotional advertising can have a powerful influence on our buying habits.

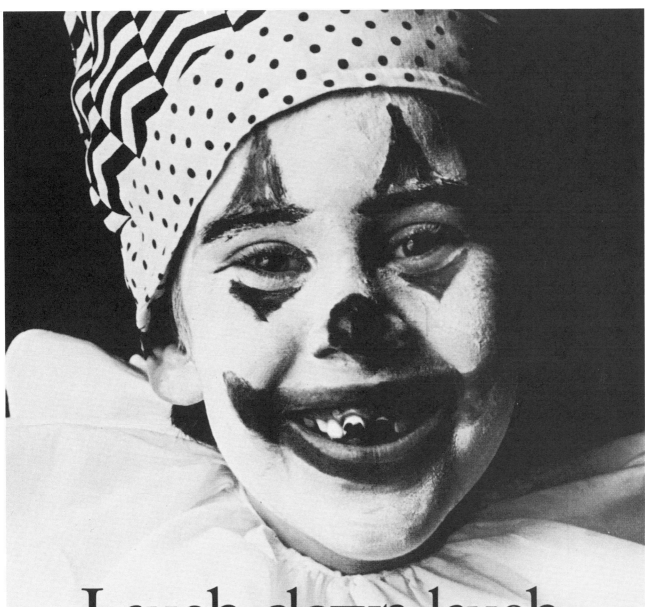

Some companies, notably manufacturers of detergent and fabric softeners use repetition of the product name to reinforce their brand preference. **Repetitive advertising** often repeats the product name six to ten times during a one-minute commercial. Companies that produce items that differ little from their competitors rely on repetitive advertising to "help" you remember that particular brand name.

Most ads simply provide useful information about the product. **Informative advertising** contains information about prices, guarantees, ingredients, and uses of the product. The ads local retailers put in the newspaper are generally of this type.

Recognizing the Product

Manufacturers are constantly concerned about whether or not consumers will remember their product's name or recognize it when it is placed alongside several others in the store. In order to make their product more easily recognized, producers design special labels with a distinctive trademark. The **trademark** is a symbol or design that can only be used by that particular company.

Another way to reinforce the product's distinctiveness is to use a slogan that people can remember. Crest toothpaste commercials advertise "fewer cavities with Crest" and the use of "fluoride to reduce tooth decay". Crest is an interesting example of a successful product in a highly competitive market. If you study the toothpaste tube, you will discover two registered trademarks, and a testimonial from the Canadian Dental Association on the brightly coloured, red, white, green, and blue package. These factors along with numerous testimonial television commercials ensure Procter and Gamble Company a large share of the toothpaste market.

1

2

3

Libby's first can label design for corned beef appeared in North America in 1875. The script "Libby's" (top) was adopted by Libby in Canada in 1912, and was last updated in 1965 (middle).

Now, after more than half a century of use, the script and pennant have been replaced on vegetable and fruit products by a bold new Libby's, with a dramatically different typeface (bottom).

52

Sales Promotion

Have you ever used a ball-point pen on which an advertising message has been printed? Many companies give away helpful items such as calendars, pens, matchbooks, or writing pads with their name on them. Sometimes local retailers will sponsor hockey or baseball teams by providing them with free uniforms. These are examples of sales promotion techniques. **Sales promotion** refers to things that a company does in addition to advertising in order to attract customers. Customers usually benefit directly from these activities.

Some producers use premiums to maintain customer loyalty. Premiums are items that are added to a product to promote its sale. Cereal boxes often have prizes inside. Some peanut butter jars become drinking glasses once the contents are used up. Detergent companies may include towels or dinnerware with their product and gasoline stations may advertise car washes with a minimum gas purchase.

Grocery stores use many promotion methods when competing with one another including contests, trading stamps, and redeemable coupons. Large department stores may offer discounts on merchandise to attract customers during normally slow sales periods. One of the famous annual discount sales is the Rexall Drug Company's "one-cent sale".

Selling the Product to the Customer

In most retail stores today, salespersons are available to assist you in making your purchase. The sales staff is considered so important that large companies train their sales personnel in the art of friendly, courteous service. The kind of service that the sales staff provides may determine whether or not a customer will return to that store in the future.

The "self-service" concept is becoming increasingly popular in the retail business. Supermarkets, record stores, drug marts, and gasoline stations have found that their costs can be reduced by allowing the customers to serve themselves. Quick-service cafeterias may offer self-serve food displays from which diners can choose their meal. Many high schools have adopted this method. When self-service outlets are properly designed, they have the advantages of lowering retail costs and of allowing a greater number of people to be served. The customers benefit by a reduction in price and by being allowed to proceed at their own pace.

Automatic vending machines are a type of self-service outlet that eliminates the need for a cashier. Many schools, factories, and public buildings have agreed to allow vending machine companies to instal them in their cafeterias. A variety of hot and cold food products can be purchased in this manner. Machines that dispense services are also popular. These include juke boxes, photocopiers, and money changers.

The Effect of Advertising on Our Economy

The main purpose of advertising is to presell goods and services to a large number of people and this plays an important role in our economy; effective advertising provides a way of expanding the economy by creating demands for goods and services. In turn, the continuing demand for products keeps factories and businesses operating by providing jobs for our large labour force. Without advertising, people would purchase less, which could cause many factories to close down and unemployment to rise. However, advertising also creates unnecessary consumer demands; consumers are not aware of a need for a good until they are surrounded by advertisements stressing the need or demand. Wise consumers will think for themselves and not be pressured into buying unecessary goods just because an advertising campaign tells them they cannot live without them.

UNIT C

MARKETING RESEARCH

Have you ever wondered why some people choose expensive-looking cars while other people choose sub-compacts? Have you ever noticed that some people choose to wear brightly-coloured clothes but others prefer darker, more conservative clothing? Businesses are concerned with questions like these. Because it is no longer difficult to manufacture goods of acceptable quality, the main problem facing producers today is finding customers to buy the product they make. Marketing research is the name used to describe methods of gathering information about the best ways of presenting products to potential customers.

Marketing a New Product

When a new product is being introduced to the public, a test market is sometimes used. A **test market** is an area in which a limited number of people are allowed, as an experiment, to purchase a product or service for a short period of time. During the experiment, researchers will interview the users to determine how well the product is liked. By limiting production, this research method may prevent a disastrous financial loss if the customers do not favour the new product. The first manufacturer of freeze-dried instant coffee used London, Ontario, as a test market for two years before promoting sales on a national scale.

The popularity of new kinds of services can also be determined with the same testing technique. An interesting computer service by Simpson-Sears was offered to a test market of 2000 people in Toronto. For several months, customers who owned a push-button telephone could use a special number and order catalogue items directly from a computer. Customers used the telephone keyboard to communicate with the computer, while the computer used recorded messages such as "What quantity do you wish?" to respond to the caller. Because Toronto has the most digital push-button telephones, this city provided the best potential testing market for this type of service. The response to the computer service was favourable, and may lead to greater application in the future as more people convert to push-button telephones.

Consumer Opinion

There are about thirty-five **research agencies** in Canada that conduct marketing research for other businesses. Among the services offered by these agencies are consumer surveys, advertising research, and studies on the effects of price and package changes.

Consumer surveys are methods of obtaining facts and opinions about products or services from customers. These surveys can be done by telephone, by mail, or by personal interviews. Have you ever received a telephone call from someone who is surveying what television shows you are watching? This is one way the famous "Neilsen ratings" rank television shows. Advertisers use the ratings to decide which television shows they should sponsor with their commercials.

Mail surveys are also popular because they are relatively inexpensive. The next time you are at a family restaurant, check the tables near the entrance for a mail survey. Restaurants use your opinions to improve their service. The main disadvantage of mail surveys is the low percentage of returned questionnaires.

Shopping malls are favourite places for researchers to conduct personal interviews. Sometimes they will set up comfortable environments where you can talk in private.

Some research agencies have "testmobiles", which they can park outside of stores to conduct comparison tests. The Pepsi Cola Company used this method to see if "Coke" drinkers could actually tell the difference between the two products. Many of these tests were filmed and used as commercials. Comparison tests are also found in grocery stores where a small table can be set up. Passing customers are offered free samples of items such as margarine, meat, cheese, and crackers.

Specific Market Appeal

Generally speaking, young people are not interested in advertisements for products such as luxury cars, carpets, or living-room furniture. Similarly, older people lack interest in ads promoting products such as chewing gum, motorcycles, or blue jeans. Technicians who create the ads know that the desires and needs of the buying public varies with age. Researchers find it useful to subdivide the population into several smaller groups such as those between twelve and nineteen years and those between twenty and thirty years. These groups are referred to as **markets**. Each group has similar needs and wants for products.

The **teenage market,** which includes all potential customers in their teenage years, is important to manufacturers. Producers know that teenagers represent a large-sized market and that many teenagers have money to spend from working at part-time jobs. Thus, many television commercials are specifically designed to reach this group of potential buyers. A typical commercial for the teenage market shows young actors actively involved, looking happy, and very popular as they use a particular product. You can, no doubt, recall television commercials of this kind. They will probably include products such as breath mints, chewing gum, soda pop, toothpaste, blue jeans, and record albums.

Once a commercial is completed, researchers may pay a group of ordinary people to sit and watch it for the purpose of commenting on it afterwards. The reactions of the sample group indicate whether or not the commercial will be successful. Advertising research is the name applied to studies of this nature. The role of **advertising research** is to investigate which ads best suit the market in which the producer is planning to sell the products.

Effects of Packaging and Pricing

Several years ago, a major supermarket performed a comparison study in packaging. A new shipment of potatoes was packaged in two different ways. The first method involved placing two kilograms of the vegetable into a plain, brown paper bag. The second method involved a transparent, plastic bag with a colourful label and the same amount of potatoes. Both bags were indentically priced. After a week, the manager observed that the plastic-bagged potatoes well outsold the ones in the paper bag. The manager then tried the same experiment the following week, but this time the price of the potatoes in the plastic bag was increased by thirty cents. At the end of the second week, the ones in the plain package still sold less!

Packaging clearly plays an important role in motivating consumers to purchase products. Many companies hire research agencies to study the effects of a proposed change in packaging. The agencies use surveys to discover the reasons behind consumer preferences. **Consumer preferences** refers to the choices consumers make when allowed to choose from several similar products.

Research agencies also conduct studies to determine the effect on sales when prices increase. Surprisingly, some surveys have indicated that people may choose a higher-priced product because of the "status" associated with the ownership of an expensive article, particularly if it is a widely advertised brand name.

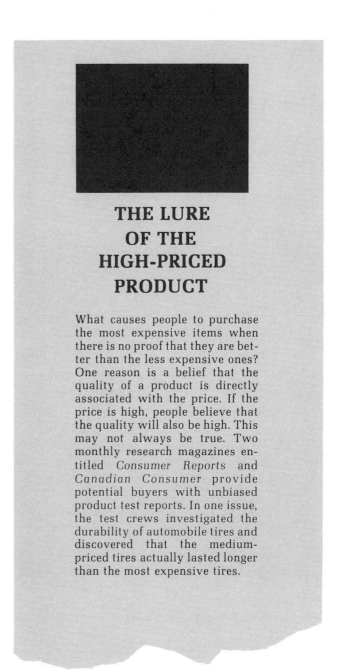

THE LURE OF THE HIGH-PRICED PRODUCT

What causes people to purchase the most expensive items when there is no proof that they are better than the less expensive ones? One reason is a belief that the quality of a product is directly associated with the price. If the price is high, people believe that the quality will also be high. This may not always be true. Two monthly research magazines entitled *Consumer Reports* and *Canadian Consumer* provide potential buyers with unbiased product test reports. In one issue, the test crews investigated the durability of automobile tires and discovered that the medium-priced tires actually lasted longer than the most expensive tires.

The Research Report

When researchers have completed their studies and have analysed the information, they must prepare a clear and meaningful report that producers can understand. A long, typewritten report can be quite boring unless it is illustrated by pictures, charts, graphs, or diagrams. Researchers have discovered several ways of preparing simple graphs that make their facts and figures easy to interpret. Some of the more popular types of illustrations include a line graph, a bar graph, a circle graph, or pie chart, and a pictograph.

55

The Line Graph

A simple type of diagram to draw, the line graph gets its name from a line that is drawn by joining several points on the graph. The points are plotted by using the values found along the horizontal and vertical scales.

The Line Graph

($ Sales in millions)

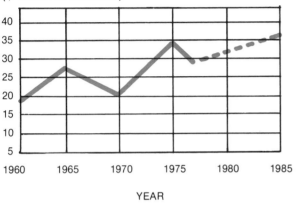

YEAR

This line graph illustrates the amount of sales (in millions of dollars) for each year, beginning in 1960. The dotted portion of the graph indicates an estimate of future sales.

The Bar Graph

The bar graph is easy to interpret. Each bar is a different length. By comparing the lengths of the bars, changes in values are easily seen. There are two types: the vertical bar graph and the horizontal bar graph.

The Bar Graph

($ Sales in millions)

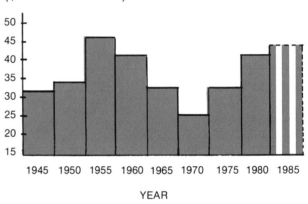

YEAR

This vertical bar graph shows a company's sales (in millions of dollars) every five years, beginning in 1945. The dotted bar indicates an estimate of future sales.

Circle Graph

The circle graph or pie chart has the shape of a circle divided into several pie-shaped sections. Usually, each section represents a percentage of a whole item.

The Circle Graph or Pie Chart

This circle graph, or pie chart, indicates by percentage the amount spent on marketing in each area. The total percentage of the parts must equal 100%.

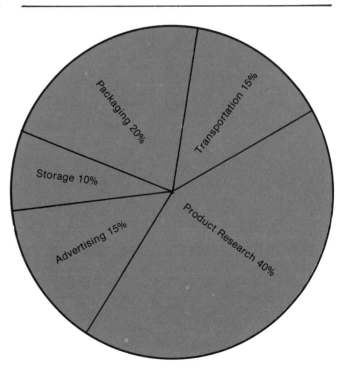

A pictograph is usually quite interesting to look at because little figures such as trees, people, or houses are used to represent quantities in the diagram. A line of five symbols, for example, would be of greater value than a line of four symbols.

The pictograph shows production for three months of the year. In this pictograph, each symbol represents 2000 (January's production was equal to 6000 cars). The half symbol in March represents less than 2000 units.

Pictograph depicting car production
Key: One Complete Symbol = 2000 cars

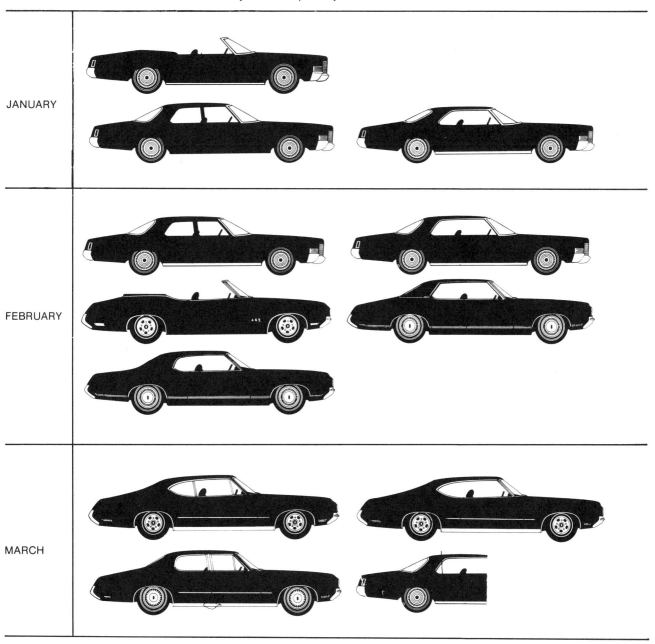

★★IN-PLANT AND ON-THE-JOB TRAINING★★

THERE ARE MANY JOBS IN THE OCCUPA-
TIONAL FIELD FOR WHICH THE EMPLOYER
UNDERTAKES TO GIVE THE NECESSARY TRAIN-
ING EITHER ON OR OFF THE PREMISES. THE
INSTRUCTION MAY VARY FROM A SHORT PERIOD
TO THAT OF A YEAR OR MORE UNDER THE
SUPERVISION OF QUALIFIED WORKERS. IN-
PLANT AND ON-THE-JOB TRAININGS ARE
INTENDED FOR SPECIFIC JOBS AND DO NOT
NORMALLY LEAD TO CERTIFICATION.

APPRENTICESHIP TRAINING USUALLY HAS A
LONGER PERIOD OF INSTRUCTION, COVERS A
BROADER AREA AND LEADS TO RECOGNITION
IN THE FORM OF CERTIFICATION.

IF YOU INTEND TO ENTER A CAREER
THROUGH IN-PLANT OR ON-THE-JOB TRAINING
YOU SHOULD GIVE CAREFUL ATTENTION TO THE
SELECTION OF COURSES THROUGHOUT YOUR
SECONDARY AND POST-SECONDARY PROGRAMS SO
THAT YOU WILL ACQUIRE THE ACADEMIC BACK-
GROUND PREFERRED BY YOUR FUTURE EMPLOYER
AS WELL AS THE BEST PREPARATION IN
SKILLS REQUIRED FOR YOUR CAREER.

WHILE A BACKGROUND OF COMMERCIAL AND
TECHNICAL SUBJECTS MAY ASSIST YOU IN
FINDING YOUR FIRST JOB, IT IS USUALLY
THE STANDARD OF ACADEMIC COMPETENCE,
PERSONALITY CHARACTERISTICS AND WORK
HABITS WHICH PLAY A MAJOR ROLE IN
ADVANCEMENT.

IT MAY BE HELPFUL FOR YOU TO SEE
YOUR GUIDANCE COUNSELLOR FOR MORE
DETAILS RELATIVE TO YOUR INTENTIONS.

★MARKETING TRAINING★

MANY OF THE LARGER SECONDARY SCHOOLS
IN THE PROVINCE OFFER MARKETING COURSES
TO STUDENTS THROUGH THEIR COMMERCIAL
DEPARTMENTS.

MOST OF THE COMMUNITY COLLEGES ALSO
OFFER FOUR AND SIX SEMESTER COURSES TO
THOSE STUDENTS HAVING A SECONDARY
SCHOOL GRADUATION DIPLOMA.

THE COSTS AT THE COMMUNITY
COLLEGES ARE THE NORMAL
COLLEGE FEES.

MARKETING PROGRAMS SHOULD BE AN ASSET
TO THOSE STUDENTS HOPING TO BE INVOLVED
IN SALES AND SALES PROMOTION CAREERS.

REVIEWING
YOUR BUSINESS VOCABULARY

Write the number of each definition.
Write the word that matches the definition number.

UNIT A

consumers, functions of marketing, market, marketing, marketing research, middlemen, product research, retailer, sales promotion techniques, wholesaler

1. The process of getting goods from the producer to the consumer.
2. The merchant who sells directly to customers.
3. A businessperson who buys products in large quantities from producers then sells them in smaller lots.
4. The general name for wholesalers and retailers.
5. Investigating ways of improving a product.
6. All the tasks performed by middlemen.
7. Items such as free samples, sales discounts, and bonus coupons.
8. A group of people with similar needs and wants for a product.

UNIT B

advertising agencies, emotional advertising, informative, repetitive advertising, sales promotion, sponsor, testimonial, trademark

1. The company that pays for the advertisements.
2. The term used when the name of the product is repeated many times during a commercial.
3. A helpful ad that informs consumers about such things as prices, guarantees, ingredients, and uses.
4. Business enterprises that provide advertising services for other companies.
5. An advertisement that uses television or movie personalities or athletes to promote a product.
6. A symbol or design that can only be used by one particular company.
7. Ads that appeal to human emotions such as fear, insecurity, or pride.
8. Things that a company does in addition to advertising in order to attract customers.

UNIT C

advertising research, consumer preferences, consumer surveys, pictograph, research agencies, teenage market, test market

1. Obtaining facts and opinions from customers about products and services.
2. Business enterprises that conduct marketing research for other businesses.
3. An area with a limited number of people who are allowed to purchase a product or service for a short period of time as an experiment.
4. Studies used to investigate which ads are best suited for a particular market.
5. All potential customers between the ages of twelve and nineteen.
6. The choices people make when allowed to choose between several similar products.
7. A type of illustration that uses symbols such as cars, people, or houses to represent quantities.

REVIEW QUESTIONS

UNIT A

1. Describe the two things that the word *market* can refer to.
2. What does the phrase "to market a product" mean?
3. Give an example of the simplest form of marketing?
4. Name the three methods of marketing. Include the steps involved in each one.
5. What important tasks do wholesalers perform in marketing?
6. Describe three tasks that a well-designed package can perform. Give three examples of a perishable product.
7. Why do stores have clearance sales?
8. Name three things that would determine the cost of transporting a product?
9. What is the "piggyback" method of transporting products?
10. To what does "containerization" refer?
11. Besides advertising, describe three other methods of "promoting" a product.
12. Explain the two types of research that companies may engage in.
13. Give three different methods of selling a product.
14. Even though self-serve stores are popular, why do other stores have salespersons.
15. Name five items that you could obtain through a mail order house.
16. One way of remembering the functions of marketing is to use the first letters of each word as a memory aid. They spell "M. PARTS". List the six functions using this memory technique.

UNIT B

1. What does "advertising media" refer to?
2. Name four different types of advertising media.
3. Why do some manufacturers use magazines rather than newspapers to advertise?
4. What type of business prefers to use the local newspaper to place their advertisements. Explain why.
5. Why is the "direct mail" technique popular?

6. What services do advertising agencies provide to other businesses.
7. Sponsors have a wide variety of advertisements that they can use to promote their product. Name three types of ads commonly used by sponsors.
8. Name two things that producers can use to help a consumer recognize and remember their product.
9. Explain what a premium is.
10. Explain three different kinds of sales promotion techniques.
11. Describe the two main methods that retailers use to sell merchandise.
12. What are vending machines?
13. State the benefits of the self-service style of selling.
14. What is the main purpose of advertising?
15. Why is advertising important to our economy?

UNIT C

1. What is the main problem many producers face today?
2. Why do some producers use a "test market" before distributing a product on a wider scale?
3. Name three services that research agencies offer other businesses?
4. Describe three ways by which consumer surveys can be carried out.
5. What is the advantage of using a mail survey? What is a disadvantage?
6. What is a "comparison test"?
7. Name four products aimed at the teenage market. What image do the actors in commercials for this market portray?
8. How do research agencies test the success of a commercial before it is actually aired on television?
9. Explain the statement "packaging plays an important role in motivating consumers to purchase products".
10. Name four ways of illustrating facts and figures in a report and state which, in your opinion, is easiest to interpret.

APPLYING YOUR KNOWLEDGE

UNIT A

1. Explain why consumers can obtain discounts at some stores during a seasonal changeover of merchandise.
2. Why do most producers prefer to sell their product to middlemen rather than directly to the consumer?
3. Although fruit and vegetables can be purchased at a supermarket, why do some people still insist on shopping at a farmer's market?
4. The results of market research are sometimes used in television advertising in order to show the "superiority" of one product over another. Describe an advertisement that includes market research.
5. Special storage and handling instructions can be found on many packages and boxes. Name three instructions of that nature.
6. The Canadian Pacific Railway Company operates several forms of transportation including ships, planes, trucks, and trains. Explain why the "containerization" method of shipping is suitable for that business enterprise.

UNIT B

1. Testimonial ads are often used on television. Describe one that you have seen on TV.
2. Who ultimately pays for advertising? Explain.
3. Businesses providing products or services are not the only ones who advertise. Most institutions and "helpful" agencies advertise too. Describe two kinds of institutional advertising you have seen.
4. Explain what is meant by the statement "Advertising may create artificial wants".
5. Subliminal advertising uses hidden messages or symbols in a regular advertisement. These messages are not seen consciously, but are recorded in our subconscious. The Canadian government has barred such advertising. Why is subliminal advertising undesirable?

UNIT C

1. Suppose your school cafeteria is thinking of introducing new lunch meals. Suggest how the supervisor could conduct marketing research to determine what meals would be most popular.
2. If you had to design an ad that would appeal to the teenage market, what features would you include with the product that would hold the attention of the viewer?
3. When Simpson-Sears allowed customers to place orders directly from a computer, they knew that some people would not use the service. Why would people not use it? Why do you think it had a favourable response in the test market?
4. What factors cause people to buy the most expensive items when there is no proof that they are superior to the less expensive ones?
5. Describe a television commercial that involves a comparison test. Why do some sponsors use this technique in their ads?

PROJECTS
AND PROBLEMS

UNIT A

Marketing Cases

1. Bill Lowell, a student at a local high school, is thinking of starting his own business of repairing old bikes and reselling them in his spare time. But he is not sure how to go about it.
   a. What things should Bill *research* first?
   b. How would you recommend that Bill *advertise* his completed bikes?
   c. Considering the other factors of marketing—*packaging, storage,* and *transportation*—what additional problems might he run into?

2. Janice and Jimmy Walker live on a small farm near a large city. The farm is situated on a side-road about five kilometres off the main highway and several kilometres from town. Because their mother makes terrific jams and apple sauce, they have decided, with their parents' consent, to attempt to sell some of the 100 jars of jam and sauce that they have stored in the basement at a selling price of $1.25 a jar.
   a. What would be the best way to go about selling them?
   b. What should they *research* about the situation first?
   c. What *transportation problems* will they have and how can they solve them?
   d. How should they go about *advertising*?
   e. What *packaging* or *storage* problems might they have?

3. Tony and Brad, two grade ten high school students have decided to run a *"helpers' service"* next summer in order to get extra spending money. They plan to do jobs such as cleaning basements, cutting the grass, and small painting jobs.
   a. What things should they *research* first?
   b. How should they *advertise* their service?
   c. What *transportation* problems might they have and how can they solve them?
   d. What *storage* problems may occur and how can they solve them?
   What additional problems do you think that they might run into?

UNIT B

1. Some businesses use the self-service method of selling. Name six businesses in your community that allow you to serve yourself.
2. Name five businesses that use salespersons to serve the customers. Explain why the sales staff are required for each situation.
3. Premiums are items added to a particular product to encourage customers to buy that brand. In column one, list five products that have premiums. In column two, list the type of premium found with each product.
4. Emotional advertising is one method of attracting customers. Write the letter of each phrase below. Beside each letter, match the emotion that the phrase appeals to according to the following classification: pride, fear, desire to be liked, insecurity.
   a. "I don't think all this caffeine is good for me."
   b. "Your breath may be the problem."
   c. "Important people own this car."
   d. "With these jeans you will be right in style."
   e. "Is your child's health important to you?"
   f. "Be the first one on your block to own this new motorcycle."
   g. "These are cavity-prone years."
   h. "Underarm wetness is a problem for some people."
5. Using magazines and newspapers at home, find one example of each of the following types of advertisements: testimonial advertising; emotional advertising; informative advertising. Fasten each of the ads securely to a separate page, labelling each one by its appropriate name.
6. Using magazines and newspapers at home, find ten examples of trademarks. Fasten each trademark securely to a page. Under each one, write the name of the product, and the name of the company that uses it.

UNIT C

1. Prepare a line graph. Label the vertical scale "Dollar Sales (in millions)"; label the horizontal scale "Year". Plot the following points:

1960	5 million	1975	25 million
1965	20 million	1980	28 million
1970	15 million	1985	30 million

   a. In which year were sales the lowest?
   b. How much were sales that year?
   c. In which year were sales the highest?
   d. How much were sales in that year?
   e. When should parts of the line graph be represented by dotted lines?

2. Prepare a bar graph. Label the vertical scale "Dollar Sales (in millions)"; label the horizontal scale "Year". Show the following figures in the form of vertical bars.

1945	35 million	1965	43 million
1950	40 million	1970	45 million
1955	55 million	1975	25 million
1960	50 million	1980	30 million

Group Projects

1. **Comparison Taste Tests**
   Comparison tests are often used to determine whether a customer can correctly identify a product by its taste.

   Each group is to plan a comparison taste test that they can demonstrate to the class. The idea is to have two or more similar products with their identity hidden from the class. Ask classmates if they can tell the products apart. Examples of products could include butter versus margarine; similar kinds of pop; similar kinds of chocolate bars; similar kinds of toothpaste or mouthwash.

2. **The Survey**
   Consumer surveys are important ways of finding out what products people like.

   Each group is to design a consumer survey to discover: which products are bought most, how often, which products are bought the least, and what products they would like to see made available. This survey should be based on products for the school cafeteria, the school marketing store, or the school book/supply store.

   Each member of the group must interview at least ten students, and prepare a research report. A bar graph or some other illustration should be used to show the difference in products demanded.

55

6

2^x

9900

4 Accounting

UNIT A
FINANCIAL PLANNING

A basic fact of life is that we cannot have everything we want. Our wants are great, but our income is limited and so we must make choices. As individuals, we attempt to make the most of our money and select the goods and services that give us the most satisfaction. But we can select only those that we can afford. All through life, therefore, our decisions involving our spending will determine the happiness we will experience.

Businesses must also face a basic fact of life. They wish to make as big a profit as possible, but they cannot produce all the goods or services they want to produce because they have limited amounts of money, workers, and buildings. Owners, like individuals, must decide what goods to produce to make maximum profits. They must decide where to sell their products, where to buy the raw materials, and how many employees to hire. These decisions determine the amount of profit businesses earn.

Governments face decisions just like individuals and businesses. Many citizens make requests for more pensions, more schools, more hospitals, more recreational facilities, and better roads. These same citizens also want governments to cut their personal taxes. Elected representatives have to decide what services to provide to give the total population the greatest happiness.

IN "HOCK" FOR EVERYTHING

John D'Alton, Staff Writer

Living on credit is a way of life for many Canadians. Some may even think it is the in-thing to do. And why not? People are subliminally seduced through various advertising techniques to buy a piece of the good life now and pay for it later.

This philosophy backfired for one local couple who will be called Jim and June in this article. The only thing that saved their future was the Guelph debt counselling service, which put them on the right track in family financing.

"The whole problem is that credit is too easy for most people to get. Those little plastic cards you get in the mail really give you a false sense of security. ... Strangely enough, there is little public education available to show people how to use credit cards and handle their personal finances."

With these comments both admitted getting caught up in the spending spree encouraged in our society. It was all too easy to pull out the credit card to buy something on impulse. They lived in this fashion for months. Jim and June were virtually in hock for everything–clothes, sporting goods, holidays, Christmas gifts, car parts, a new vehicle and accessories.

Jim and June realized they were sliding into trouble.

The real clincher came when Jim went to the bank to ask for a large loan to consolidate all his debts. His application was rejected because he was rated as a bad risk. The only thing Jim had going for him was a steady job and union protection.

"The situation was a constant source of worry. I felt as if I was working for nothing," Jim said.

As a result of all this June became depressed. Jim consulted with his doctor. He referred them to a marriage counsellor who straightened out their relationship. Jim also went to his banker and said if he didn't get some financial counselling he would have to declare bankruptcy. And this is how they found themselves at the debt counselling service in December 1976.

Their total debt was about $7000. Their use of two credit cards accounted for 33 per cent of this total. Monthly payments totalled $415, just over half of their monthly income.

"So as you can see by the time we paid off our debt and bought other necessities, we hardly had anything left over," June said.

Jim and June with counsellor Pat Liptrap worked out a more reasonable budget combined with a debt repayment plan. Their debts have been whittled down considerably and the monthly payments are much easier to live with. They have since overhauled their lifestyle and attitudes.

"I've learned to live without a credit card and am a lot happier for it," Jim said.

They now resist the consumer pressure inherent in our society through the conserver lifestyle they adopted. Self-sufficiency and self-reliance are their watchwords.

"The best advice I can give a young married couple is to establish their priorities and budget accordingly," June said.

"As your lifestyle changes, review your priorities. The main thing is to keep your communications open and work together to reach your goals."

Guelph Daily Mercury
March 1978
Reprinted by permission

Personal Money Records: Individuals and Families

Individuals and families work very hard to earn their income and many of them develop a **financial plan** that will help them get the most satisfaction from their money. Such financial planning involves the following four steps: estimating all **income**; estimating all **regular expenses**; setting a **savings goal**; estimating **variable expenses**. Let's study each step; first for a student and then for a family.

Individuals: Estimate All Income

Generally speaking, students earn very little money because they have less time to work, and are still learning the skills they need to earn a living. The usual sources of income for students are as follows: allowances from parents; irregular amounts from parents; family allowances; part-time jobs such as babysitting; working in stores, restaurants, service stations, etc.; full-time shifts in factories; sale of crafts; self-employment, such as lawn-cutting service; typing essays. It is easy to estimate accurately the income from some of these sources, such as allowances, and jobs with regular hours. The income from some of the other sources, such as sale of crafts, baby-sitting, and self-employment is more difficult to estimate. In these cases, one must check past records to help estimate for the future. The next step is to add the estimated income from all sources to give **total income**.

Individuals: Estimate All Regular Expenses

Many students have some expenses that occur regularly. Examples of **regular fixed expenses** are clothes, school supplies, school lunches, and presents. We know that these expenses will occur regularly, and we can estimate fairly accurately what they will cost. Regular expenses are commitments we make because they are very important to us. It is necessary for us to have school supplies for courses such as *Typing* and *Family Studies*. It is important to us to give presents to our family and friends for birthdays and other special events. These expenses, therefore, are the first claims against our income.

Individuals: Set a Savings Goal

Most of us want to get as much satisfaction from our income as we can. This means we must plan ahead. Since we cannot have all of everything we want, we must select some goals for ourselves and plan a way to achieve them. Since most of our goals cost money, sometimes a great deal of money, we must plan a savings goal to accumulate the necessary money. Some of our goals could include a stereo set, a trail bike, a special holiday, some expensive sports equipment, or a musical instrument. The achievement of the goal will give us more satisfaction or happiness. This is the real reason for saving and financial planning.

Individuals: Estimate Variable Expenses

Variable expenses are expenses that change over time. The expenses may occur only at irregular times or may change in size from time to time. For example, we usually buy hockey or skating equipment only in the fall and winter seasons. The cost of Christmas gifts occurs just once a year.

Variable expenses are also expenses that we can control. If we decide to set a high savings goal, we may have to limit our variable expenses. In some cases, we may decide to buy less expensive items or to delay the purchase for a month or even a year. If our savings goal is very important to us, we may eliminate some of our variable expenses. The important thing to remember is that we are making decisions based on our goals and on facts that we have gathered. These are the important concepts of financial planning.

Families and Financial Planning

Nearly all families make a financial plan. The format varies a great deal from family to family. Some keep a simple chart of their income, savings, and expenses. Others have a very detailed system of records that they follow weekly, monthly, and yearly. Most families use a simple record of monthly income, bills to be paid by cash and cheque, and up-to-date records of personal chequing and savings bank accounts. Most local bank branches will provide families with forms that will make record keeping very easy. Bank managers also have personnel to give advice to families who need help in financial planning.

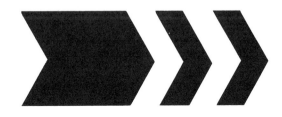

STEP 1: INCOME

Annual take-home pay $_____

Investment income $_____

Family allowance $_____

Other income $_____

Total annual $_____ income

Total weekly $_____ income (divide by 52)

Total monthly $_____ income (divide by 12)

(enter amount in the balance sheet at the bottom of the page.)

STEP 2: FIXED EXPENSES

	JAN.	FEB.	MARCH	APRIL	MAY	JUNE	JULY	AUG.	SEPT.	OCT.	NOV.	DEC.	TOTAL (12 months)
Rent:	$___	$___	$___	$___	$___	$___	$___	$___	$___	$___	$___	$___	$___
First mortgage													
Second mortgage													
Maintenance fees													
Heat/Light													
Other utility													
Telephone													
Insurance premiums:													
Life													
Homeowners'													
Auto													
Installment debt:													
Car													
Credit card													
Payments													
Savings:													
RRSP, RHOSP, etc.													
Vacations													
Auto maintenance													
Gas (auto)													
Tax:													
Property													
Automobile (license)													
Charitable donations													
Other fixed expenses													

TOTAL FOR THE YEAR $_____

WEEKLY "SET-ASIDE" (divide by 52) $_____

MONTHLY "SET-ASIDE" (divide by 12) $_____

(enter this weekly or monthly amount in the balance sheet at the bottom of this page)

STEP 3: EMERGENCY FUND

It is recommended that the Emergency Fund should represent two to three months total earnings.

Our Emergency Fund will be allowed to accumulate until it reaches $_____

Emergency Fund payments will be made weekly (divide by 52) $_____

Emergency Fund payments will be made monthly (divide by 12) $_____

(enter this amount in the family balance sheet at the foot of this page)

STEP 4: MONTHLY LIVING ALLOWANCE

Family groceries $_____

Clothing: Wife _____

Husband _____

Children _____

Laundry, dry cleaning _____

Entertainment: _____
movies, parties, gifts, eating out, liquor, tobacco, memberships, cottage

Hobbies and sports _____

Children's allowances $_____

Personal: _____
medical, dental, drugs, sundries, cosmetics

Pets (including veterinarian) _____

Transportation: taxi/bus _____

Other _____

Total monthly living allowance $_____

Total weekly living allowance $_____ (divide by 4)

(enter this amount in the balance sheet at the foot of this page)

FAMILY BALANCE SHEET

Our weekly/monthly income is (STEP 1) $_____

Our weekly/monthly "set-aside" amounts to (STEP 2) $_____

Our Emergency Fund payments are (STEP 3) $_____

Our weekly/monthly living allowance is (STEP 4) $_____

Add Steps 2, 3 and 4 and subtract from Step 1 $_____

This is the amount that is left for regular savings.

If your expenses are greater than your income you must go back over your estimates and find ways to trim expenditures and/or look for ways to increase your annual income.

The most important part of financial planning for families is involving all members of the family. Parents have the greatest involvement because they financially contribute the most to the family and usually have the largest expenses. Older children often contribute to the family income and often require large expenses for education, clothes, entertainment, and holidays. Younger children contribute little in the way of income but require expenses for clothes, food, holidays, and special furniture.

All members of the family who are old enough to contribute to family finances and are also able to understand the financial demands on the family should be involved in financial discussions. This situation makes it easier for all family members to support the decisions and helps prevent arguments over the family spending. Financial planning for a family involves the same steps as that for an individual, but usually there are more items in each step, and the amounts are larger.

Families: Estimate All Income

There are many possible types of incomes for a family but the most common are wages or salaries, fees, commissions, pensions, and interest and dividends. Many families have two incomes, but before a family includes both incomes to cover necessities, they should consider the security given by each job. Some jobs are seasonal in nature, and income from a seasonal job may be lost for part of the year. Workers in agriculture, fishing, and construction face this problem. A wife's income may be interrupted for family reasons. Since each case is differ-

ent, individual families must make their own decisions on the amount of income to actually consider for expenses.

There is usually a large difference between the income one earns and the amount taken home. Payroll deductions such as income tax, insurance, health plans, pension plans, social security, and union or professional fees can account for twenty to thirty per cent of the total income. A family should consider only the "take-home" or "left-over" pay to use for expenses and savings.

Families: Estimate All Regular Expenses

Families face many expenses some of which occur on a regular basis and in specific amounts. **Regular fixed expenses** would be payments for rent or mortgage, instalment loans, insurance premiums, and newspaper subscriptions. They are usually paid weekly, monthly, or yearly and in most cases the amount remains the same; so regular fixed expenses are easy to estimate.

Another group of expenses occurs regularly except that the amount varies each time the expense occurs. Such expenses, called **regular flexible expenses,** are telephone bills, food, clothing, house repairs, gifts, dental bills, and entertainment. We know these expenses are going to occur but are not sure of the exact amounts. Families have some control over the amount of these expenses, but usually cannot eliminate them or delay payment of them for long. However it is possible to practise thrift in this part of financial planning by shopping carefully for food, clothing, and gifts.

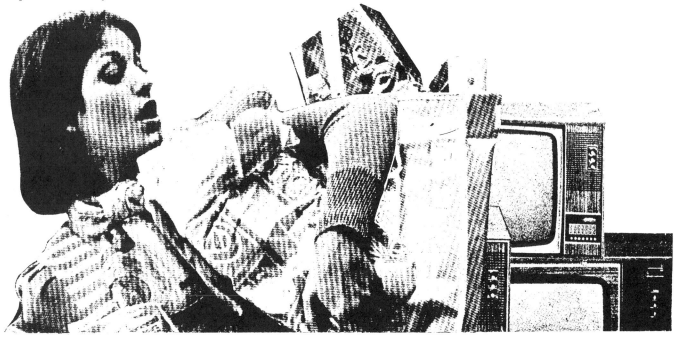

Families: Set a Savings Goal

Family goals are the things that families wish to achieve by working and playing together. These goals represent the interest and needs of all members of the family. Examples of such goals may be a new car, a vacation, a house, a larger T.V., new furniture, or college or university education for children of the family. To achieve these goals requires money which in turn requires a savings plan. If a family is going to save money, it means the family must do without other things it could buy with that money. This is the choice that any family has.

It is wise to include all members of the family in the setting of a savings goal. It is not only good training for children but with all members having some input into the financial plan, all members will want to achieve the savings goal.

Families: Estimate Variable Expenses

Variable expenses differ in both amount and time. In most cases it is impossible to estimate the exact amount of any expense and exactly when it will occur. Examples of such expenses are car repairs, new appliances and furniture, special gifts, vacations, and hobbies. These expenses are very necessary for a family. However, a family does have some control over these expenses.

In most cases they can be reduced or even postponed for a while if necessary. Purchases of new furniture can often be delayed. The purchase of a new car can be postponed though repairs for the old car may increase. It is possible to take a shorter vacation, or cut down on the expenses of a family member's hobby. Although it may be necessary for a family to reduce some of its variable expenses to meet its savings goal, as all family members agreed to the goal, they will understand and support the reduction of their variable expenses.

Families: Making It Work

Setting the family's financial goals and plans represents only the first step. The second step involves carrying out the plan, which requires the co-operation of each member of the family. One member of the family should be responsible for keeping a record of the income, expenses, and savings amounts. These amounts must be compared with the financial plan so that the family can see where adjustments in savings and spending must be made to achieve their financial goal.

how others spend their income

It may be interesting for you to have some indication of how other people spend their money. Because everyone's circumstances are different it is difficult to lay down hard and fast rules but statistics tell us that take-home pay is used as follows:

Shelter (renting or buying, including cost of operation)	28-35%
Household repairs and upkeep	2%
Food	23-30%
Clothing	8-15%
Transportation	10-12%
Health and personal care	5- 8%
Recreation	3- 6%
Insurance	3- 6%
Savings	3- 7%

making your budget balance

Naturally, you won't be able to make changes easily in fixed items such as shelter. But you can make adjustments with less difficulty in non-fixed items such as food, transportation, clothing and recreation. Some suggestions are offered below.

Planning menus and sticking to your shopping list will discourage impulse grocery buying. Public transportation and car pools are a means of reducing transportation costs. Savings in clothing costs can be made by taking advantage of sales. Women who can make their own and their children's clothing can achieve considerable savings. Entertainment and vacation costs can be reduced by taking advantage of free public events, when available, and by taking a camping holiday rather than a cruise. These are only a few suggestions which, although not changing your way of life greatly, can bring about reductions in living costs.

If you review your budget periodically, you can revise figures to reflect any change in circumstances. Obviously, any increase or decrease in income should be shown, as should changes in amounts expended or saved. What you choose to do when a final loan payment has been made, will depend on your personal financial plan, but increasing the amount you have allocated to saving and emergency reserve is frequently a good course of action.

Above all, don't worry about making changes in your plan. Budgets are meant to be flexible and beneficial, never burdensome.

tips on how to make your budget work

1. Keep your plan simple and flexible. The more convenient the system, the easier it will be to stick to the basic plan.
2. Be realistic in setting your goals and your estimates of income and expenditures.
3. Use an organized and efficient system to pay bills. A Personal Chequing Account should be an integral part of your budgeting system. It provides you with a record of your expenditures; you receive cancelled cheques to verify your records and to help you estimate for your next budget period.
4. Find a place to keep your records, incoming bills, etc.; valuable records and papers should be kept in a Safety Deposit Box.
5. Do not try to keep track of every cent.
6. Select a budget period which meets your needs and habits. For some people, a budget will be prepared every pay period; for others, a budget will be prepared and reviewed every quarter or semi-annually. Remember the amount of detail you include is up to you.
7. Develop a specific savings program to ensure that you don't just get by but succeed in your goals.
8. Consult your bank manager if you have any problems about your personal finances.

Budgeting is like any other skill. At first it is awkward and seems difficult but after a few attempts, it becomes easy and automatic. Good budgeting is a cornerstone on which a better and fuller life can be built.

UNIT B
THE BALANCE SHEET

We read earlier that the purpose of business activity is to earn a profit. This profit can be used to expand the business, increase the wages of employees, or passed to the owners as income for their own personal use. This unit and the next discuss the methods and financial statements used by businesses to record their actions as they strive to earn profits.

The two main statements used by business are the **balance sheet** and the **income statement.** The balance sheet shows the financial position of the business at a particular time. The income statement measures the profit or the loss of a business over a period of time. For example, a business would normally prepare a balance sheet on December 30 of a particular year. This would show the financial position of the business at that time. An income statement would be prepared to show the profit or the loss of the business over the next full year. Then another balance sheet would be prepared to show the new position of the business on December 30, one year after the last balance sheet. Financial statements are prepared by businesses for three main groups.

Business Managers or Owners

Business managers or owners need the statements to calculate the value of the business. This information, when calculated over a period of time, tells them if the business is growing. The owners also use the statements to compare profit earned in one year with another year. These statements also help the owners in planning business changes. Owners must decide if they should or can afford to expand, if they should stop producing one of their products, or if they should try to find a better way to produce.

Investors

Investors are the second group of people who use financial statements. These people often wish to buy part or all of a profitable business. This often helps the owners who may wish to retire, need money for personal reasons, or wish to try some other type of business. In any case, investors rely on the financial statements to give them accurate information on the financial position and profits of the business.

Government

The government is the third group that needs financial information on businesses. Businesses must pay taxes on their earnings, just as workers do. Government tax officials carefully check the financial statements to make sure the correct amount of tax is paid. Also, the government pays out grants to certain businesses, to help them grow in an area where jobs are needed, or to help them get established in a product line that is controlled by foreign business. The financial statements of a business help the government determine the correct amount of these grants.

As you can see, many people use financial statements, and there are many jobs and career opportunities for people interested in making decisions and who are accurate with figures.

The Balance Sheet

The **balance sheet** shows the financial position of the business at a particular time. It contains the names and amounts of three different types of accounts. The accounts are classed as **assets, liabilities,** and owner's **equity.**

ACCOUNTANT

ACCOUNTANTS COMPILE AND ANALYZE
BUSINESS RECORDS AND PREPARE FINANCIAL
REPORTS, MAKE COST STUDIES, AND
MAKE UP INCOME TAX RETURNS. PUBLIC
ACCOUNTANTS CHARGE BUSINESS FIRMS
A FEE FOR THEIR SERVICES. THEY MAY
WORK INDEPENDENTLY OR FOR AN
ACCOUNTANCY FIRM. INDUSTRIAL AND
FINANCIAL ACCOUNTANTS ARE CONCERNED
WITH THE BUSINESS RECORDS OF THEIR FIRM.
THEY MAY SPECIALIZE IN A NUMBER
OF AREAS -- AUDITING, ACCOUNTING,
BUDGETING AND CONTROL, TAXES,
OR SYSTEMS AND PROCEDURES.
PUBLIC ACCOUNTANTS WHO SPECIALIZE
IN AUDITING ANALYZE FINANCIAL
RECORDS AND GIVE AN INDEPENDENT, OBJECT-
IVE OPINION AS TO THEIR RELIABILITY TO
SHAREHOLDERS, CREDITORS OR OTHER
INTERESTED PERSONS. THEY MAY ALSO ADVISE
THEIR CLIENTS ON TAX MATTERS INVOLVING
INCOMES, ESTATES, PROPERTY, SALES, MIN-
ING, LOGGING, CAPITAL AND OTHERS. THE
COMPLEXITY OF TAXING STATUTES REQUIRES
PROFESSIONAL HELP. PUBLIC ACCOUNTANTS
ALSO PROVIDE MANAGEMENT WITH INFORMATION
FOR DECISION MAKING INVOLVING PRODUCTION
PLANNING, RE-ORGANIZATIONS AND MERGERS,
AND COMPUTER INSTALLATIONS. MANAGEMENT
ACCOUNTANTS EXAMINE AND EVALUATE BUSI-
NESS CONTROL PROCEDURES IN THEIR COMPANY
AND ARE CONCERNED WITH TAXES, BUDGETING,
INTERNAL AUDITING. THE DUTIES OF GOVERN-
MENT ACCOUNTANTS DEPEND UPON THE GOVERN-
MENT AGENCY IN WHICH THEY ARE EMPLOYED.
ACCOUNTANTS MAY BE IN PRIVATE PRACTICE
WITH ONE OR   ERS   Y AY
EMP   D BY

ACCOUNTANT TRAINING

STUDENTS PLANNING TO BE ACCOUNTANTS MUST
PASS EXAMINATIONS SET BY THE PROFESSION-
AL ORGANIZATION IN WHICH THEY WISH TO
BECOME A MEMBER--CANADIAN INSTITUTE OF
CHARTERED ACCOUNTANTS, THE SOCIETY OF
INDUSTRIAL ACCOUNTANTS, OR THE CERTIFIED
GENERAL ACCOUNTANTS ASSOCIATION. THESE
ASSOCIATIONS GENERALLY TRAIN PERSONS FOR
PUBLIC ACCOUNTING, COST ACCOUNTING, AND

GENERAL BUSINESS TRAINING

TRAINING FOR STUDENTS SEEKING A BROAD INTEGRATED PROGRAM IN THE FIELD OF BUSINESS IS USUALLY OFFERED IN 2 YEAR DIPLOMA COURSES AT COMMUNITY COLLEGES AND PRIVATE TRADE SCHOOLS.

THE FEES AT THE COMMUNITY COLLEGES ARE APPROXIMATELY $325.00 WHILE THE PRIVATE TRADE SCHOOLS ARE USUALLY OF SHORTER DURATION WITH FEES PROPORTIONATELY HIGH-

A SECONDARY SCHOOL GRADUATION IS THE NORMAL ADMISSION ENTRANCE REQUIREMENT. SOME ASK AS WELL FOR ENGLISH & MATHEMATICS.

A WIDE VARIETY OF SUBJECTS ARE STUDIED. SOME INSTITUTIONS HAVE A COMMON FIRST YEAR WITH OPTIONS IN THE SECOND YEAR OF ACCOUNTING, DATA PROCESSING, BUSINESS ADMINISTRATION AND MARKETING.

OCCUPATIONS RELATED TO MANAGEMENT AND ADMINISTRATION - TRAINING

THESE OCCUPATIONS REQUIRE A CONSIDERABLE BACKGROUND IN THE FINANCIAL AREA (ACCOUNTING, AUDITING, PURCHASING AND SALES PROMOTION).

THEY INCLUDE THOSE WHO REVIEW, ANALYSE AND IMPROVE BUSINESS AND ORGANIZATIONAL SYSTEMS. THERE ARE ALSO INCLUDED PERSONNEL AND LABOUR RELATIONS OFFICERS AND THOSE INVOLVED IN ENFORCING ADHERENCE TO REGULATIONS AND ADVISING ON STANDARDS AS WELL AS EXECUTIVE AND CORPORATE SECRETARIES.

WHILE THE ACADEMIC STANDARD IN MOST OF THESE OCCUPATIONS REQUIRE POST SECONDARY COURSES, (UNIVERSITIES, COMMUNITY COLLEGE, TRADE SCHOOL) A FEW MAY BE ENTERED FROM SENIOR SECONDARY PROGRAMS.

THESE OCCUPATIONS USUALLY REQUIRE MANY YEARS OF SUCCESSFUL EXPERIENCE IN THE AREA OF THEIR ACADEMIC COMPETENCE. PERSONALITY CHARACTERISTICS, IN WHICH THOROUGHNESS, RESPONSIBILITY AND DETAILED APPLICATION ARE EXHIBITED, ARE AN ASSET.

****

To help us understand these ideas and terms, we will study Pete's Pizza, an eat-in and take-out restaurant. In addition to serving his own customers with ready-to-eat pizzas, Pete also supplies two other restaurants with ready-to-cook pizzas.

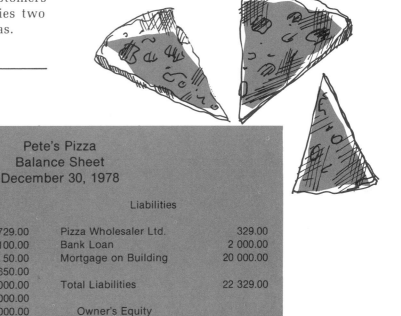

Pete's Pizza
Balance Sheet
December 30, 1978

Assets		Liabilities	
Cash	1 729.00	Pizza Wholesaler Ltd.	329.00
Joe's Place	100.00	Bank Loan	2 000.00
Sally's Snack Shop	50.00	Mortgage on Building	20 000.00
Supplies	650.00		
Equipment	8 000.00	Total Liabilities	22 329.00
Building	40 000.00		
Land	10 000.00	Owner's Equity	
		Peter Cantoni, Capital	38 200.00
Total Assets	60 529.00	Total Liabilities and Capital	60 529.00

Assets are things of value owned by a business. The assets for Pete's Pizza are cash, accounts receivable (the money that the other two restaurants owe him), supplies (cheese, tomato sauce, pastry, etc.), equipment (tables, chairs, ovens, cash register, counter), and land and building. This is a summary of Pete's assets.

Liabilities are the debts owed by business. Pete buys his supplies from Pizza Wholesaler Ltd. on a weekly basis and pays the following week. Therefore he always owes for one week's supplies. Three years ago he borrowed $5000 from the bank to buy equipment he needed. He has paid off $3000 of this loan and at present owes the bank $2000. There is also a $20 000 **mortgage** (loan) on the restaurant itself. This is a summary of Pete's liabilities.

ASSETS

Cash (including bank account)	$ 1 729.00
Joe's Place	100.00
Sally's Snack Shop	50.00
Supplies	650.00
Equipment	8 000.00
Building	40 000.00
Land	10 000.00
TOTAL ASSETS	$60 529.00

LIABILITIES

Pizza Wholesaler Ltd.	$ 329.00
Bank Loan	2 000.00
Mortgage on Building	20 000.00
TOTAL LIABILITIES	$22 329.00

Owner's equity represents the value of the business to the owner or owners. In this example, Pete's Pizza, Peter Cantoni is the sole owner; all the net value of the business belongs to him. We calculate the equity by totalling all the assets of the business and subtracting all the liabilities. In other words, the owner's equity (net value) of the business is the difference between the assets (things of value) and the liabilities (debts).

The Basic Accounting Equation

We have just developed the **basic accounting equation.** It shows the relationship among assets, liabilities, and owner's equity. The equation itself is that assets equals liabilities plus owner's equity. As long as we know the value of the assets and liabilities of a business, we can calculate the owner's equity. For example, Peter Cantoni's equity in Pete's Pizza is calculated by using this equation:

Assets		Liabilities		Owner's Equity
$60 529.00	=	$22 329.00	+	$38 200.00

Peter's equity in the business is $38 200.00.

The two sides of the equation must be equal. As long as we know the value of two of the terms we can calculate the value of the third term.

Preparing a Balance Sheet

A **balance sheet** is a formal financial statement. To produce a balance sheet in the proper format requires one to follow a set of rules. These rules cover the four main parts of the balance sheet: **heading, assets, liabilities, owner's equity.**

Heading

The **heading** identifies the business, identifies the statement, and indicates the date. The heading occupies three lines, and each item is centred.

Assets

The assets section starts with the title **assets** centred above the individual assets. The individual assets are listed in order of liquidity, that is, the accounts that are cash, or will soon be changed into cash are listed first. Each asset is listed by name and by amount. The individual amounts are added to give the total assets figure. Since this is a formal statement, every amount must be accurate to the exact cent (though our illustration has been simplified to round figures) and every amount must have a title to explain it. A single line under a figure indicates the figure is to be added to the figure(s) above it or is to be subtracted from the figure above it. A double line is used to indicate that all calculations are completed.

Liabilities

The liabilities section is very similar in format to the asset section. The term **liabilities** is centred above all the individual liabilities. The individual liabilities are listed in the order in which they are to be paid. Debts or loans to be paid in seven days are listed before those to be paid in thirty days. These usually include suppliers' accounts. Bank loans on instalment plans and mortgages are listed last. Each amount must have a total or name to explain it.

Owner's Equity

The **owner's equity** section is listed directly below the liabilities section with a blank line to separate them. The title, owner's equity, is centred above the actual statement of capital. The formal title for this account is Owner's Capital, and in our case would be Peter Cantoni, Capital. As the basic accounting equation indicates, the total of liabilities and owner's equity equals the total assets. To highlight this fact, it is customary to set the total assets and total liabilities on the same line.

UNIT C
THE INCOME STATEMENT

A business must earn a profit to remain healthy and alive. A healthy business, one that makes a reasonable profit, grows. This provides income for the owner, goods for the consumers, and jobs for the community. An unhealthy business, one that suffers a loss, has to decrease its operations and may even go bankrupt. Such an action results in no income for the owners, fewer goods for the consumers, and less jobs for the community. Healthy businesses are essential to our economy.

Business owners need financial facts to help them make decisions to keep their businesses healthy. The income statement indicates the financial health of a business and provides some of the facts business owners need to help them make wise business decisions. An income statement deals with the accounts that determine the net income of a business. These accounts involve sales or revenue expenses, and net income or net profit.

Sales, or revenue, refers to the income received by the business, for example, money paid by customers to a barber for hair cuts; value of tickets sold for a play or movie; money paid to the school cafeteria cashier for lunches; green fees for a golf course. In a large manufacturing business, the sales figure could represent income received from the sale of cars, planes, wheat, pulp and paper, fish, steel, and minerals.

The expenses of a business represent the activities and materials needed by a business to earn revenue. The most common expenses faced by

nearly all businesses are salaries, rent, electricity, telephone, and supplies. Other expenses occur for particular businesses; typing and postage are major expenses for companies selling through mail order offices; fuel, oil, repairs, and insurance are major expenses for taxi operators.

All the businesses referred to here provide services to their customers, but of course many businesses need to buy materials and change those materials into products to sell to their customers. For a business making furniture, this would include wood, cloth, springs, and nails. A bakery needs flour, sugar, water, and packaging materials. A farm business needs seeds, fertilizer, and livestock. Adjustments must be made to ensure that only the materials used to make the goods sold during the period are charged against the revenue. (These adjustments are made for you in the sample statements.)

Willson's Service Centre
Income Statement
For Six Months Ended June 30, 1978

Revenue		
Gasoline Sales	$120 000.00	
Parts Sales	30 000.00	
Repair Fees	60 000.00	
Total Revenue		$210 000.00
Cost of Goods Sold		
Gasoline	$ 90 000.00	
Parts	20 000.00	
Cost of Goods Sold		$110 000.00
Gross Profit		$100 000.00
Expenses		
Rent	$ 12 000.00	
Wages	15 000.00	
Supplies	20 000.00	
Utilities	2 000.00	
Equipment Repairs	8 000.00	
Advertising	3 000.00	
Interest Expense	4 000.00	
Insurance Expense	1 000.00	
Office Expenses	5 000.00	
Total Expenses		$ 70 000.00
Net Profit		$ 30 000.00

Joe's Lawn Service
Income Statement
For the Year Ended December 31, 1977

Revenue		
Total Revenue		$70 000.00
Expenses		
Rent	$ 8 000.00	
Wages	20 000.00	
Supplies	2 500.00	
Equipment Repairs	3 000.00	
Total Expenses		33 500.00
Net Profit		$36 500.00

Net income is the difference between **revenue** and **expenses**. The term **net income** is also known as **net profit**, or if negative, **net loss**.

Sales or revenue minus expenses equals net income

This is a simple equation but it is of major importance. The single figure, **net income**, indicates the health of the business, and also the living standard for the owner. In a proprietorship, or a partnership, this figure is the source of income for the owner. Since these owners do not receive a salary from the business, this figure represents their personal purchasing power.

In a manufacturing business, the cost of materials must also be taken from **revenue** to determine **net income**. This equation would be sales or revenue minus cost of materials minus expenses equals net income.

Preparing an Income Statement

The income statements for service and retailing businesses are quite similar. This unit explains the format for each type of business.

Service Business

Heading

The **heading** must identify the business, identify the statement, and indicate the period of time the business earned the net profit or loss.

Sales or Revenue

This sub-title is written at the left margin of the statement, below the heading. If the business has two or more sources of revenue, each source and amount would be listed separately and then totalled.

Expenses

This sub-title is written at the left margin below the total sales line. Each expense is listed individually and then totalled.

Net Income

The **total expense** figure is subtracted from the **total sales** figure to give the **net income**. The term **net income** (or net profit) explains or identifies the amount.

Retail Business

Heading

As for the service business, the **heading** must identify the business, identify the statement, and indicate the period of time the business earned the net profit or loss.

Sales or Revenue

This sub-title is written at the left margin of the statement below the heading. In most cases, retail businesses have revenue from many sources. For example, a business selling leather products may have sales from furniture, clothing items, and novelty items. The owner may wish to record sales from each area separately. In this case, each source and amount would be listed separately and then totalled to give **total revenue**.

Cost of Goods Sold

Businesses that sell goods in order to earn income must first buy those goods. Your local service station is a good example of this type of business. The service station must have gasoline, oil, and parts on hand to provide a service to its customers. These items, recorded in an account called **inventory,** are items the owner needs to sell in order to make a profit. To calculate a true profit for the period, the owner must record the costs for only that period. In other words, to find the profit for a month, the owner must use the revenue for that month and the costs of those goods sold during the month. The cost of the goods is subtracted from the revenue from selling the goods. This figure is called the **gross profit.**

Expenses

This sub-title is written at the left margin below the **cost of goods sold** section. Each expense is listed individually and then totalled.

Net Income

The **total expenses** figure is subtracted from the **gross profit** to give the **net income** or **net loss**.

A single line drawn under a figure indicates an addition or subtraction; a double line indicates calculations are finished.

REVIEWING
YOUR BUSINESS VOCABULARY

Write the number of each definition.
Write the word that matches the definition number.

UNIT A

financial plan, regular fixed expenses, regular flexible expenses, savings, variable expenses

1. The method by which people achieve a financial goal.
2. A plan that helps families get the most satisfaction from their money.
3. Expenses that occur on a regular basis and for particular amounts.
4. Expenses that occur regularly but in varying amounts.
5. Expenses that change over time and amount.

UNIT B

balance sheet, assets, liabilities, owner's equity

1. Items of value owned by a business.
2. The worth of a business to the owner.
3. A statement that shows the net worth of the business at a particular time.
4. Debts owed by a business.

UNIT C

income statement, revenue, expenses, net income, gross profit

1. The difference between revenue and cost of sold goods.
2. The income received by the business.
3. The difference between revenue and expenses.
4. The statement that indicates the financial health of the business.
5. The activities and materials needed by a business to earn revenue.

REVIEW QUESTIONS

UNIT A

1. Why can businesses not produce all they want?
2. What financial problems do our elected representatives face?
3. List the four steps involved in making a financial plan.
4. List four possible sources of income and four regular expenses for most students.
5. How are variable expenses and savings goals related?
6. Why should all family members be involved in financial planning?
7. What sources of income are common for families?
8. Explain the difference between regular fixed expenses and regular flexible expenses.
9. Why is it difficult to estimate variable expenses?
10. Why must a family compare its spending to its financial plan?

UNIT B

1. What is the purpose of the balance sheet?
2. What does the income statement tell the owner?
3. Name the three groups interested in financial statements and state each group's interest.
4. Explain the difference between assets and liabilities.
5. How is the owner's equity calculated?
6. What is the basic accounting equation?
7. How was owner's equity calculated for Pete's Pizza?
8. List the four main parts of the balance sheet.
9. In accounting, what is indicated by a single line under a figure? a double line under a figure?

UNIT C

1. What are the benefits of a healthy business, and the results of an unhealthy one?
2. What accounts are included in the income statement?
3. List five examples of expenses common to most businesses.
4. What equation is used to determine net income?
5. Why is net income important to the owner of a business?
6. Why is the cost of materials included in the income statement?
7. Why are different sources of revenue totalled?

APPLYING
YOUR KNOWLEDGE

UNIT A

1. List your amount and sources of income in the past two months.
2. List your regular expenses in the past two months.
3. List your variable expenses in the past two months.
4. Name two reasonable financial goals you expect to achieve in the next two years, and explain the steps you must follow to achieve those goals.
5. Discuss with an adult who has been working full time for a least three years, the problems encountered in setting a savings goal. Be prepared to make a short report to your class.
6. List at least ten expenses faced by most families, classifying each expense as a regular fixed expense, a regular flexible expense, or as a variable expense.

UNIT B

1. Why would a furniture store owner prepare financial statements?
2. Why would a farmer keep financial statements for personal use?
3. Why would a stockbroker be interested in the financial statements of Bell Canada?
4. Why would the federal government be interested in the financial statements of Ford Canada Ltd.?
5. List ten different assets of the largest business in your community.
6. List twenty different assets of your local school board.
7. Name the common assets and liabilities of a family.
8. Should a family prepare financial statements?

UNIT C

1. Name as many sources of revenue as you can for each of the following: baseball stadium; automobile sales business; movie theatre; golf course; hotel. Now list five major expenses for each business.
2. Using Joe's Lawn Service as an example, what happens to net income or profit when any expense shown can be reduced by $1000?
3. What advice would you give to Joe to help him increase his net profit?
4. Materials represent major costs for some manufacturing businesses. List five different materials used to produce each of the following products: car; television; hamburger; textbook; shoes.
5. Suppose each of these businesses, farmer, pulp and paper company, and auto parts manufacturer, earned an above average net profit last year. List three specific activities for each that the owners might do with the profit.

PROJECTS AND PROBLEMS

UNIT A

1. Many students continue their education beyond secondary school by attending university, college, a trade school, or an apprenticeship plan. Select one institution and find the following information: the tuition; cost of accommodation; cost of supplies; cost of transportation; any other costs; expected income upon graduation.
2. Many Canadians spend two to three weeks travelling sometime during the year. Select a place in Canada that you would like to visit for two weeks.
a. Prepare a financial plan that includes: transportation costs; accommodation costs; meal costs; special entertainment costs; special clothing or equipment, if necessary; any other special costs.
b. How would you earn the money needed to pay for the trip?
3. Furnishing an apartment or a house is a major expense for a young individual or a family just beginning housekeeping. Prepare a list of all the items and amounts needed to furnish an apartment or a house with a reasonable income.
4. Tom graduated from grade 12 last year with good training in auto mechanics. He has a full time job with a service station, working with a certified mechanic. Tom hopes to start his mechanic's apprenticeship in three months' time. He needs a car to travel to and from work, to attend apprenticeship school, and for personal use. He can buy a new car for $6000 or a used one with 80 000 km on it for $3000. What choice would you advise Tom to take? Why? Use financial facts to support your choice.
5. Alice's family is considering the installation of a swimming pool in the backyard. The cost is $7000. This will mean no more travelling holidays and a cut in clothing and entertainment budgets for the next three years.
a. What benefits will this project provide for the family?
b. What disadvantages will the family face?

UNIT B

1. Prepare a balance sheet for Alan Smith, using the following information. Assets: cash $850; investments $1000; car $6000; house $50 000. Liabilities: bank loan on car $2000; mortgage on house $20 000; capital: Alan Smith Capital $35 850. Use today's date.
2. Prepare a balance sheet for Betty's Boutique, using the following information. Assets: cash $1500; Joe Brown owes $75; George Blackwell owes $125; inventory $11 500; furniture and equipment $6000; building $60 000. Liabilities: owing to Tom's Supply $3000; owing to bank $5000; owing on mortgage $25 000. Use the basic accounting equation to calculate Betty Boswell's capital. Use today's date.
3. The corner store is a neighbourhood grocery, milk and confectionery store. Its accounts are as follows: cash $1200; bank loan $6000; equipment .$10 000; mortgage $30 000; the business owes Sam's Wholesalers $3500; Sally's Restaurant owes the corner store $700; building $55 000; inventory $24 000; delivery truck $6000. Prepare a balance sheet as of today's date for the corner store owned by Marion Miller.

UNIT C

1. Prepare an income statement for the month of January, 19 – for Peter Moss. The accounts are as follows: fees received $7000; salaries $2000; rent $400; advertising $100; delivery $200; utilities $75.
2. Prepare an income statement for six months ended June 30, 19 – for Monique's Beauty Salon. The accounts are as follows: fees received $32 000; salaries $8000; rent $1800; advertising $800; supplies $2400; utilities $1280.
3. Prepare an income statement for the year ended December 31, 19 – for Heston's Theatres. The accounts are as follows: rent $4000; advertising $6000; rental paid for films $35 000; janitorial services $8000; ticket sales $58 000; fees received for rental of theatre for meetings $5000; rental received for concession stand $4500.
4. Josie Alberghetti owns Alberghetti's Corner Store. She sells grocery and confectionery items. She owns her own building and all the furniture and fixtures. She is now 58 years old and would like to retire soon. Using the following figures for the past year, January to December, 19 – , prepare an income statement for Josie. Cost of goods for sale $60 000; taxes on building $1400; advertising $2000; delivery expense $1600; utilities $2600; sales of groceries and confectionery items $98 000. Would you consider buying Josie's Corner Store? Why or why not?

5 Computers

UNIT A
THE COMPUTER

One of civilization's most exciting achievements in the last thirty years has been the development of the computer. Interplanetary space travel, nuclear power, medical discoveries and improved office communication were made possible because of the computer's capabilities. The space crafts that travelled to the moon and the planet Mars were guided by calculations performed by an on-board computer. Even the training of the astronauts included computers hooked up to machinery that imitated actual flight conditions.

Computers have become an important part of our everyday living. Many retail stores use electronic computer devices called terminals, instead of cash registers. Banks have computer terminals with special printers for your bankbook, and cash dispensers on the outside wall of the building to allow banking twenty-four hours a day.

The tremendous quantities of paperwork, sometimes referred to as an "information explosion" has led businesses to rely on computers to handle the information quickly and accurately. When you consider that each day around the world over one thousand new books are being printed, and that scientific and technical literature alone amounts to sixty million pages a year, it's no wonder that computers are popular. Any machine that can help us cope with this quantity of data is greatly needed.

Information Processing

The computer is an information processing machine. **Information processing** refers to the handling of facts and figures to achieve a desired goal. For example, a large business with ten thousand employees, must keep track of each person's wages in order to calculate and print out their pay cheques on pay day. Imagine what it would be like if clerks had to calculate each amount separately, and write each cheque by hand. Using a computer, one person can do in *one* hour what a room full of clerks working manually achieve in one week.

Most of the routine paperwork jobs in a company can be handled by a computer. Information such as monthly sales, customer accounts, payments to suppliers, and amount of stock still in the warehouse are easily processed by a computer.

Parts of a Computer

The computer does several things extremely well. It performs many complex instructions quickly; it follows instructions step by step, repeatedly, without making a mistake; it stores millions of facts and figures easily locating them when you need them again.

The machine itself is not complicated. Outside, it has several buttons that operate it; inside are several panel with rows of plastic-covered "chips" containing miniaturized circuits. These tiny circuits (about half a centimetre square) can be designed to do different things such as adding, subtracting, comparing, or storing. This same type of circuit can also be found in digital watches, clocks, and pocket calculators, but the computer simply has more of them. The remainder of the computer might include such things as a cooling fan to keep the circuits from overheating, plus several items directing and controlling the flow of electricity.

Hardware

All of the electrical and mechanical parts that make up a computer are referred to as **hardware**. Hardware might include a keyboard, which is similar to a typewriter, a printer, a T.V. screen, a main processing area, and some device that can be used to store information for long periods of time, such as a magnetic tape unit, which uses tape similar to that in a cassette deck.

Software

All the instructions that make the computer operate in a required manner are referred to as **software**. The software might include a set of instructions called a compiler. A **compiler,** usually provided by the computer manufacturer, allows the computer to translate language instructions into electrical impulses so that it can operate the circuits. Then, when an answer is ready, the compiler can convert the impulses back into language again.

Other instructions, such as the steps needed to solve a problem, are provided by the person using the computer. For instance, if someone wants the computer to do a calculation, that person must tell the computer exactly how the calculation is to be done.

Five Features of Every Computer

Computers are available in various sizes from large systems that fill a room to portable desk models. There are even hobby kits you can purchase and assemble yourself for use at home. Computers are manufactured by several companies such as I.B.M., Honeywell, Hewlett-Packard, Burroughs, N.C.R., Control Data, Digital, and Data General. Regardless of their size and origin, all computers display five distinctive features–**input**, **processing**, **output**, **storage**, and **control**.

Input

Each computer has some method of allowing instructions and information to be fed in. One popular device is a card reader that translates holes or pencil marks on the computer card into electrical impulses for the computer to understand. Another method that can be used when speed is not so important is a keyboard much like that of a typewriter.

Processing

All the calculating, comparing, and handling of information is done in one main area called the **central processing unit** or **C.P.U.** This is the place where the electronic circuits are used to operate the whole computer.

Output

Once the processing is completed, the answer can be displayed in a variety of ways. The most commonly used method is to use a printer. When the answer to a problem appears on paper, it is called a **printout**. If a permanent copy of the answer is not necessary, a display screen similar to a television set can be used. The printing or charts on the T.V. screen, sometimes referred to as a **readout**, can be altered or cleared from the screen whenever the user wishes. The correct name for the screen is **cathode ray tube** or **C.R.T.**

A SIMPLE COMPUTER

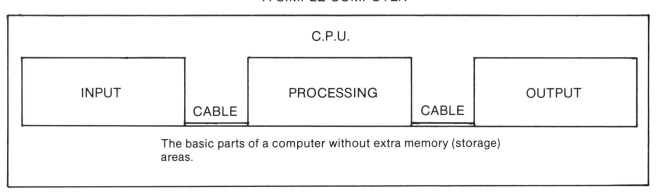

The basic parts of a computer without extra memory (storage) areas.

Storage

If you own a portable calculator, you know that when the power is shut off the numbers in the memory circuits are erased. The same thing is true of a computer and for this reason, some extra storage devices are often added to it. One storage device puts facts and figures on magnetic tape similar to those used in cassettes. Another method uses magnetic discs that resemble record albums to store information for future reference.

Control

This last function is important because it involves checking all the other sections to see that they are operating correctly. Sometimes, the control function is built in as part of the circuitry, such as the clear button on a keyboard. In other instances, the software instructions in the compiler check to see that each instruction given it makes sense. If you give the computer an incomplete command such as ADD 5 + (with the second number left out), the compiler would print out a message called an **error diagnostic** to let you know why it could not follow your instructions.

DIGITAL COMPUTER SYSTEM

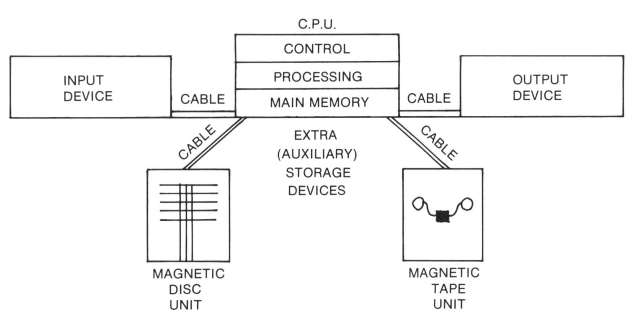

A complete digital computer system illustrating the three main types of circuits in the central processing unit. The diagram also shows two popular kinds of extra storage devices.

Computers Are Accurate

Research studies of accountants have shown that they tend to make mistakes as much as 15 per cent of the time while working on calculations. Computers, on the other hand, make less than one error in every ten thousand times or 0.01 per cent. The computer provides a strong advantage in working with numbers and most accountants now include training with computers along with their accounting courses. Mistakes are still made, however, by people who are using the keyboard or preparing computer cards. "G.I.G.O." is a phrase that often hangs in computer departments. The translation "Garbage In-Garbage Out!" reminds computer users to be careful while putting information into the machine; otherwise, the wrong answer will be printed out.

People Who Work With Computers

It is not unusual for large business firms and government offices to have their own computer department run by specially trained people. For example, one of the trained staff members could be a **systems analyst.** This person studies ways of

improving office routines involving the computer. For example, if a new type of customer's invoice (a bill) is needed, the systems analyst will study the required changes and then design the new form that will be used in the future.

The new design would then be given to another staff member called a **programmer.** The programmer converts the new ideas into short messages the computer can understand. These messages are then put on computer cards by a **keypunch clerk** or on magnetic tape by a **keytape clerk** or on magnetic disc by a **data entry clerk.** These people are skilled at using machines with a keyboard similar to that of a typewriter.

The information that these clerks prepare is then given to the **computer operator,** who loads the information into the computer and collects the printouts. This person is in charge of making sure that the computers operate correctly and without delay.

COMPUTER OPERATOR   (CLERICAL)
CONSOLE OPERATOR; DIGITAL-COMPUTER
OPERATOR.
OPERATES AND CONTROLS ELECTRONIC DIGITAL
COMPUTER TO PROCESS BUSINESS,
SCIENTIFIC, ENGINEERING, OR OTHER DATA:
SETS CONTROL SWITCHES ON COMPUTER AND
PERIPHERAL EQUIPMENT; SUCH AS, EXTERNAL
MEMORY, DATA COMMUNICATING,
SYNCHRONIZING, INPUT AND OUTPUT
RECORDING, OR DISPLAY DEVICES, TO
INTEGRATE AND OPERATE EQUIPMENT
ACCORDING TO PROGRAM AND DATA
REQUIREMENTS SPECIFIED IN WRITTEN
OPERATING INSTRUCTIONS. SELECTS AND
LOADS INPUT AND OUTPUT UNITS WITH
MATERIALS; SUCH AS, DISKS, TAPES OR
PUNCH CARDS AND PRINTOUT FORMS, FOR
OPERATING RUNS, OR OVERSEES OPERATORS OF
PERIPHERAL EQUIPMENT WHO PERFORM THESE
FUNCTIONS. SETS SWITCHES TO CLEAR
SYS...

COMPUTER BUSINESS PROGRAMMER TRAINING
  THE TRAINING OF PROGRAMMERS/ANALYSTS
FOR BUSINESS APPLICATIONS IS OFFERED
AT UNIVERSITIES, COMMUNITY COLLEGES,
AND PRIVATE TRADE SCHOOLS. HERE COURSES
ARE AVAILABLE IN COMPUTER SCIENCE AND
DATA PROCESSING. MANY UNIVERSITIES IN
THEIR BUSINESS ADMINISTRATION AND
COMMERCE PROGRAMS ALSO PROVIDE COURSES
AND OPTIONS IN COMPUTER METHODS.
ADMISSION REQUIREMENTS FOR THESE
PROGRAMS VARY WITH THE LEVEL OF THE
INSTITUTION WHERE SUCH COURSES ARE
OFFERED.

    COMPUTER TECHNOLOGY
PROGRAMMER, ENGINEERING AND SCIENTIFIC
  TRAINING MAY BE OBTAINED THROUGH
UNIVERSITIES, COMMUNITY COLLEGES AND
RYERSON.
  ENTRANCE REQUIREMENTS, TO UNIVERSITIES
ARE USUALLY A SECONDARY SCHOOL HONOUR
GRADUATION DIPLOMA WITH A BACKGROUND
IN MATHEMATICS AND SCIENCE, WHILE TO
COMMUNITY COLLEGES AND RYERSON ARE A
SECONDARY SCHOOL GRADUATION DIPLOMA
(GRADE 12) WITH MATHEMATICS AND SCIENCE
OF LEVEL THREE AND FOUR.
  THE PROGRAMS ARE USUALLY OF THREE

How Computers Started

The first electronic computer, called ENIAC, was designed in 1946 by two engineers at the University of Pennsylvania. It contained eighteen thousand vacuum tubes, eight kilometres of electrical wire, and had a mass of close to thirty tonnes. About the same time, a mathematician named John Von Newmann developed an idea that made computers different from any other machine. He found a way of storing all the instructions needed to solve a problem inside the computer. The machine could now do any problem simply by following its own stored instructions. This idea, known as the **stored program concept**, is used by all present-day computers.

By 1952, the Sperry Rand Company began mass production of the first series of computers for general use with a model called Univac I. Since that time, new models and techniques have been developed to improve the speed and accuracy of the machines. One noticeable change has been the miniaturization of the parts inside the Central Processing Unit. Instead of hot and bulky vacuum tubes, the C.P.U. now contains microscopic circuits that are light-weight and perform calculations in millionths of a second.

Many uses have been found for computers. Some of the most powerful computer systems available are being used by governments for such things as census-taking, taxes, welfare, space research, and military defence. Businesses have adapted the computer to perform routine office work, and to control machinery on assembly lines and in processing plants.

As the manufacturing trend towards smaller, lighter, and less expensive models continues, it may become commonplace for the average home-owner of the future to have his or her very own computer.

"Gee! my first computer date! I wonder what he'll be like?"

"Why did you turn off my power? I paid my bill. See? Here's my cancelled cheque."

UNIT B
COMPUTER APPLICATIONS

"HAVE A NICE TRIP." _____

Kit Murphy rested her elbow against the ticket counter as an Air Canada clerk keyed her name on the typewriter keyboard. Within a few seconds, the visual monitor displayed her destination, flight number, and departure time. The clerk then copied the information onto a plane ticket and handed it to Kit. "Thank you Mrs. Murphy, and have a nice trip." As boarding time was not for twenty minutes, Kit stopped at a 24-hour cash dispenser and slid her plastic identity card into the card socket. A message appeared in the viewing screen.

"Enter identity number."

Kit pressed the numbers 9 ... 2 ... 4 ... 3 ...

A second message appeared. "Select transaction."

She paused a moment to study the choices, then pressed the button marked "chequing account withdrawal". A third message appeared.

"Select amount."

Kit keyed in the numbers 5 ... 0 ... 0 ... 0 ... The computer clicked several times. Then, a drawer popped open containing two packages of crisp, new bills totalling $50. Kit put the money in her wallet along with the printed receipt for future reference.

As this story illustrates, computers are becoming widely used. Flight reservations and banking transactions are only two of the many computer applications available in Canada. **Computer applications** refers to the various situations to which the computer can be applied. Examples of these situations are found in business offices, factories, hospitals, schools, retail stores, and recently, in people's homes.

Computers in Business Offices

The computer is an excellent information processing machine. Because business offices have large amounts of information to be processed, the computer is well suited to the job. The computer can store large data banks of information about all their credit customers on storage devices such as magnetic tape or magnetic disc units. Each month, the head office will bring all the business transactions up to date, and send out a computer printout to each customer. In this way, credit managers of large companies always know how much each credit card holder owes the company.

One interesting feature about computers is that it is not necessary to be in the same room, building, or even the same city to use the computer. A special communication link can be arranged with a telephone or telegraph company that will transmit information back and forth between two distant places.

Teleprocessing, which means processing at a distance, is the name given to a situation in which one building has the computer while another simply has input and output devices. Input and output devices such as keyboards and printers are called **terminals** because they are the end point of a communication link. Several terminals can be hooked up to a large computer.

91

TELEPROCESSING

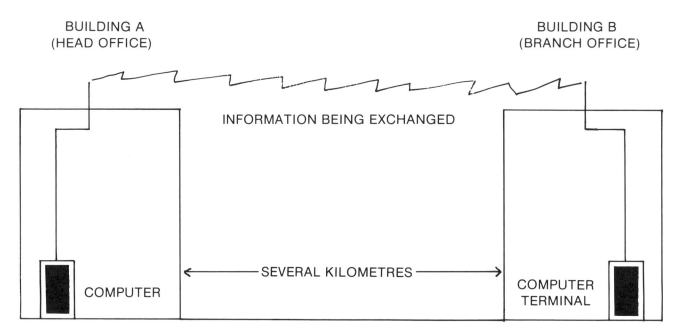

Banks and trust companies often have several "teller terminals" all connected to a large Central Processing Unit at the head office. The C.P.U., in this case, must be fairly large to cope with the large number of transactions being processed at the same time. If there are too many requests for information, the answers may take a minute or so to return. Perhaps you've noticed how slow the terminals respond in a bank on a busy Friday afternoon.

Computers That Operate Machinery

Some recently built factories use a combination of two types of computers to operate several machines on assembly lines and other places. This is referred to as cybernation. **Cybernation** is the control of automatic machines by means of a computer. Usually, very few people are needed to operate a factory with cybernation control.

This diagram illustrates how a main computer (digital) can control and operate a complete assembly line with the help of several control units called analog computers.

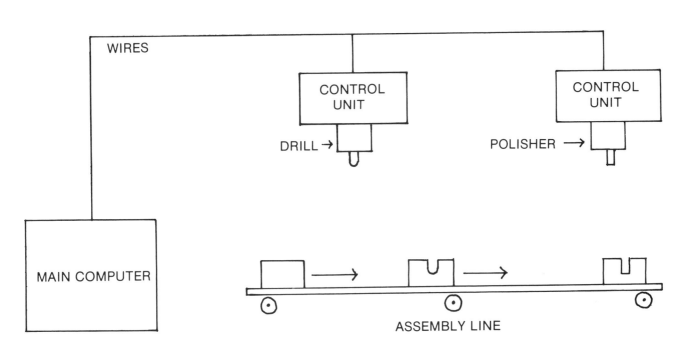

CYBERNATION

WIRES

CONTROL UNIT

DRILL →

CONTROL UNIT

POLISHER →

MAIN COMPUTER

ASSEMBLY LINE

Computer-Operated Assembly Lines

By 1985, assembly lines in newly built manufacturing plants will have a different appearance than those that exist today. The difference will be in the use of computers controlling machinery; robot devices, not human beings, will be placed along assembly lines.

Such a situation will be achieved by having a main computer give instructions to smaller computers placed along production lines. Each of the smaller devices will manipulate machines, such as drills, cutters, shapers, and moving facilities.

The advantage of this type of manufacture, known as *cybernation*, is that computers can operate non-stop over long periods of time without sleep, coffee, lunch breaks, and paid vacations; productive output will be greater and less expensive than current methods.

Manufacturers are predicting that new job skills will be needed. The demand for manual labourers and assembly workers will decline, while the demand for computer operators, systems analysts, engineers, administrators, computer, and machine repair personnel will increase.

Digest of Business News
Summer 1978

Computers Help Researchers

Computers have had an enormous impact on many kinds of scientific research. Advances in medicine and engineering research have been dependent on calculations and control devices computers have provided. Researchers may test out a theory by creating a computer model. A **computer model** is composed of a series of equations representing several ideas involved in a situation. By using several different values, the model is tested to see if it measures what the researcher wants. Engineers, for example, may want to find out how strong a bridge has to be before they actually build it. They consider all the things that would make the bridge heavy such as cars, trucks, asphalt, concrete, even a heavy snowfall. Once the mass of all these items is determined, they can assess how strong the bridge must be.

One engineer, while designing a Canadian university library, used a computer model to calculate the building's total mass. He needed this figure because the ground on which the building was to be erected could hold only a certain mass before compressing and sinking. Six months after the building's completion, the building started to tilt and

sink. The engineer was astonished! What had gone wrong? He checked his computer figures for several days before he discovered the answer. He had forgotten to include the mass of the two million books that were on the library shelves. The computer had given the right answer for the information it had been fed, but unfortunately, the programmer's values were incomplete.

Computer simulation is another way researchers estimate how something will work without actually building it. Car designers use a large visual screen operated by a computer to draw various car models. The designer uses a light pen to touch the screen. The pen sends out electrons that are sensed by the computer and then drawn as a line as the pen moves over the surface of the screen.

Airline pilots can be trained in on-the-ground simulators. The device is a realistic copy of a cockpit with operating dials and plane movements that respond to the steering wheel. A computer can be programmed to simulate actual flight conditions. Even such perilous occurrences as sudden storms, strong air currents, and engine failure can be simulated. With this device, training expenses are greatly reduced and pilot reliability increased.

Computers in Retail Stores

Have you noticed the electronic cash registers many large stores are now using? These devices have become popular because they can also act as a computer terminal. As a sale is recorded on the keyboard, the information can be processed by the C.P.U. Items such as total sales, sales by department, and changing inventory can be determined from the recorded information. Since this device is placed where the sale occurs, computer manufacturers call it a **point-of-sale terminal**.

Grocery stores can combine an optical scanning device that can read the U.P.C. (Universal Product Code) stripes on packages along with the terminal. The advantage of this device is that inventory can be kept track of automatically. The following morning, the computer can print out the items that need to be re-ordered.

Small Models for Home Use

Miniaturization has provided computer manufacturers with a transistor chip that can be used as a C.P.U. Because of its tiny size, this type of Central Processing Unit is called a **microprocessor**. The microprocessor and the circuitry are placed in the same container as the keyboard. With the addition of a television monitor and a cassette deck, anyone can have their own private computer for $500-$750.

Computer enthusiasts are using the computer for a variety of things: controlling the environment (heat, air conditioning, locking doors); recipe storage; writing books (without notepaper); budget calculations; practising at math, science, and language questions for school; diary entries; tax preparation; storing birthday and anniversary dates, Christmas-card lists; and computer games.

When you consider the wide range of applications the computer has, it is easy to see why it is considered to be one of our most useful inventions.

UNIT C

THE USE OF A COMPUTER TO SOLVE PROBLEMS

Have you ever watched a science fiction movie in which a computer was involved? *Star Wars,* for example, included two futuristic but friendly robots named "R2D2" and "C3PO". Each robot had a different design and a different model of computer inside to operate it. Another movie called *Close Encounters of the Third Kind* showed computers being used to analyse information about U.F.O.s, Unidentified Flying Objects. The information from the computers led the scientists to a place where they actually met "beings" from another planet. The computer systems depicted in science fiction movies often resemble some of the more powerful computers already available. The only thing missing in our present-day computers compared with film versions of their actions is the instructions that allow computers to perform a variety of different actions.

The computer is just a machine. Without step-by-step instructions, the computer cannot do anything. It does what it is told to do, nothing more. The preparation of instructions that allow a computer to draw pictures, play music, or imitate talking, is quite an art. But, with practice, most people can learn how to solve problems with a computer in a short span of time.

The Program

Some computers are provided with software, or instructions, by the manufacturer. This is helpful in a situation in which the problem is always the same. For example, a company with ten thousand employees that uses the computer to do the payroll each week is actually giving the computer the same problem ten thousand times, only with different values each time. The values used in a problem are referred to as the **data**.

The actual solution to the payroll problem only needs to be put into the computer once. The commands that tell the computer to print, read, or calculate something are called **instructions**. Together, the instructions and the data make up the solution to a problem. When this solution is converted into messages that the computer will understand, it is referred to as a **computer program**. The person who writes programs for a computer is called a **programmer**.

PROGRAMMER — WRITES THE → PROGRAM (SOLUTION) — INSTRUCTIONS / DATA

Steps Used to Solve a Computer Problem

Computers are excellent machines for following instructions. If you can tell a computer all the steps required to solve a problem, it can perform each step at speeds that equate each step to one-millionth of a second!

It is obviously important that your solution to the problem is carefully planned. To become skilled at programming, it is necessary to follow the same pattern plan each time you are confronted with a new problem. This pattern can be listed as a series of four steps, which are as follows:
1. Define the problem
2. Plan the solution
3. Code the solution into a computer language
4. Test the solution and correct if necessary.

Step One—Define the Problem

One way to make problems easy is to find out exactly what the problem requires, then write it down in the simplest way possible. This can be done in two ways. The first method is to reduce all the ideas needed to solve the problem down to one or two sentences. The second method, which is particularly useful if calculations are involved, is to represent the ideas in the form of an equation. Many programmers prefer the equation method because it is shorter and sometimes less confusing than sentences. For example, consider the two ways of expressing this problem.

Sample Problem
Donna Polinski put $650 into a savings account. The bank indicated that they would pay 8% interest on the deposit. How much interest would Donna make if she left it in the account for one year?

Sentence Method

Problem Definition	Data
Calculate the interest by multiplying 8% × $650.	Principal in savings account = $650
	Rate of Interest = 8%

Equation Method

Problem Definition	Data
I = (P)(R)	P = $650
	R = 0.08
	I = ?

Notice that the letters used in the equation method are the first letters of the words they represent. To represent the answer *interest*, the letter "I" is used. This trick helps the programmer remember later on what the letters mean.

Step Two—Plan the Solution

Once you have mastered the art of reducing a problem to its simplest form, the next step is to plan the solution. The solution is a list of instructions that the computer must follow step by step along with the data to be used in the problem

Computer programmers have discovered a way of planning that makes it easy to follow. They use a diagram called a flowchart. A **flowchart** is a diagram with special symbols that show the steps needed to solve a problem. Consider the following flowchart for the bank interest problem defined earlier in this unit.

FLOWCHART FOR THE BANK INTEREST PROBLEM

FLOWCHART SYMBOLS

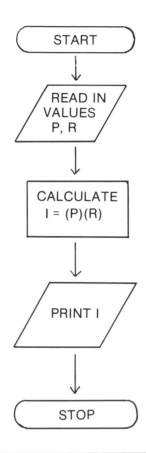

START

READ IN VALUES P, R

CALCULATE I = (P)(R)

PRINT I

STOP

The solution as indicated has only three instructions for the computer–READ, CALCULATE, and PRINT. The START and STOP symbols simply provide a beginning and ending for the diagram.

The way in which the steps are listed in a **flowchart** is similar to the design of a computer. As a result, the symbols are named after the various functions, such as input, or output, that the computer must perform.

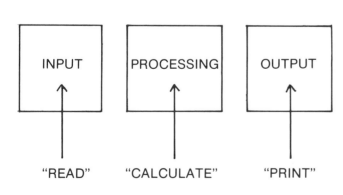

The TERMINAL SYMBOL. It is used to show the beginning and the end of a program.

The INPUT/OUT SYMBOL. This shape is used to show what letters or numbers are to be read into the computer and also what needs to be printed out.

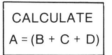

The PROCESSING SYMBOL. It is used to show equations and other information handling.

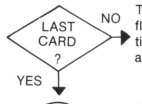

The DECISION SYMBOL. This flat diamond is used for questions that have two possible answers.

The STEP CONNECTOR. Two of these are needed to hop from one part of the solution to another.

The OFF-PAGE CONNECTOR. Two of these are needed to continue elsewhere when you run out of room at the bottom of the page.

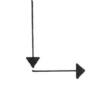

ARROWS AND ARROWHEADS. These are used to show which way the steps are to be followed. A good flowchart flows the same way in which a person reads, i.e., left to right and top to bottom (as shown).

Since most people draw in different ways, programmers use a stencil called a **template** that makes everyone's diagrams readable and similar in design.

Step Three—Code the Solution

Once the problem has been defined and a solution planned with a flowchart, the next step is to convert the steps listed in the flowchart into a computer language. A **computer language** is a short form style of listing instructions that can be understood by a particular computer. Some of the more popular languages that computers can understand are Hypo, Zap, Mini, ICL, Basic, Fortran, and Cobol. The first three languages use numbers to state both instructions and data; the last four use short English phrases.

A problem that requires three numbers to be added together might be flowcharted and coded as shown.

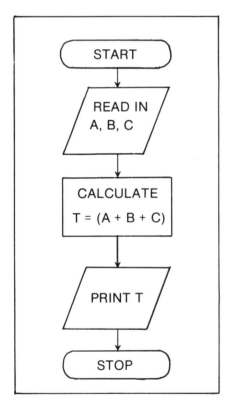

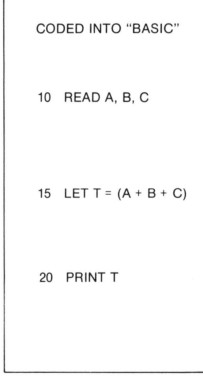

CODED INTO "BASIC"	CODED INTO "HYPO"
	000 05 100
10 READ A, B, C	001 05 110
	002 05 115
	003 03 100
15 LET T = (A + B + C)	004 03 110
	005 03 115
	006 02 200
20 PRINT T	007 06 200

PROBLEM: T = (A + B + C)

If you compare the **basic coding** (middle diagram) to the flowchart, you will notice that the instructions are in the form of English verbs that are easy to understand. The numbers along the left-hand side in **basic** are used to keep the instructions in order.

The **hypo coding** also follows the same pattern as the flowchart. Hypo uses only numbers to instruct the computer. It also takes more lines than the **basic** language to get the computer to solve the same problem.

100

Step Four—Test the Solution

In order to test the solution to see if it works properly, the programmer can do two things. First, the solution can be worked out using a pencil and paper to see if the answer makes sense. Second, the programmer can put the program into the computer and have the computer check it for errors. The solution can be entered into the computer in several ways. The information can be put on computer cards for the computer to read. There are two kinds of computer cards. The **mark sense card** records information with pencil marks. The **punched card** records information with holes. Another method of entering information is to use a computer terminal that allows a person to key in information by means of a panel that resembles a typewriter keyboard. If anything needs correcting, the computer will show you where and why on the printout. Once the solution is tested and corrected, your program can be used over and over again, using different values each time.

REVIEWING
YOUR BUSINESS VOCABULARY

Write the number of each definition.
Write the word that matches the definition.

UNIT A

central processing unit, computer operator, hardware, input device, output device, printout, software

1. All the electrical and mechanical equipment that make up a computer system.
2. All the instructions that make the computer operate in a required manner.
3. A machine used to load information into a computer.
4. The area of a computer that does all the calculating, comparing, and handling of information.
5. The person in charge of making sure that the computer operates correctly and without delays.
6. A machine used to visually display the computer's answer.
7. The name of the sheet of paper on which a computer prints answers.

UNIT B

computer model, computer simulation, cybernation, microprocessor, point-of-sale terminal, teleprocessing, terminals

1. Processing information at a distance.
2. Input and output devices, such as keyboards and printers.
3. The process of using computers to operate other machines.
4. A series of equations used to represent several ideas involved in a situation.
5. The use of a computer to imitate a real-life situation.
6. Electronic cash registers that stores can connect to a computer.
7. A tiny electronic circuit used in watches, calculators, and computers.

UNIT C

computer language, computer program, data, flowchart, instructions, programmer, template

1. The commands that tell the computer to print, read, or calculate something.
2. The values used in a problem.
3. A short form of writing that can be understood by a computer.
4. A diagram with arrows and special symbols used to plan the solution to a problem.
5. The person who plans and writes the solution to a computer problem.
6. The stencil used to draw flowcharts.
7. The whole solution to a problem including both instruction and data.

REVIEW QUESTIONS

UNIT A

1. In what two ways have computers been involved in space flight?
2. Name five routine paperwork jobs a computer can perform.
3. The computer does several things extremely well. In your own words, explain four of them.
4. Describe the inside of a computer.
5. Explain what a *compiler* is. What is it used for?
6. Name the five distinctive features that all computers display.
7. Name two methods of input.
8. Explain the difference between a *printout* and a *readout*.
9. What is a C.R.T. and what is it used for?
10. Why are extra storage devices usually attached to a computer?
11. Name two items that could be used to store information.
12. What does a systems analyst do?
13. What does a programmer do?
14. Who is John Von Newmann and for what is he famous?

UNIT B

1. Name three facts that an airport clerk processing a flight ticket can obtain from the visual monitor.
2. Name five items that businesses can use the computer to process.
3. Explain why it is not necessary to be in the same place as a computer in order to use it.
4. Why do bank computer terminals usually respond slowly on busy Friday afternoons?
5. State two reasons why a pilot training simulator is important to companies like Air Canada and Canadian Pacific Airline?
6. Cash registers in stores are changing. Explain.

UNIT C

1. Although the computer is capable of performing several tasks, it remains highly dependent. Explain.
2. What are the purposes of the two parts of a computer program.
3. Name the four steps to be followed when planning a solution to a computer problem.
4. Explain the two methods of reducing a problem to its simplest form.
5. In your own words, describe a flowchart.
6. Why do programmers use a template to draw flowcharts?
7. List four computer languages that use short English phrases to instruct the computer.
8. Explain two methods of testing the program once it is completed.
9. What is the difference between a mark sense computer card and a punched computer card?
10. Why do programmers sometimes save programs?

APPLYING YOUR KNOWLEDGE

UNIT A

1. Astronauts use an on-board computer when they are in space. For what kind of things would they use the computer?
2. Against which three people in a computer department could the acronymn G.I.G.O. be applied?
3. A company with 10 000 employees does not have a computer. It takes a clerk five minutes to do the calculations and the writing needed to prepare one cheque. If there are 20 clerks in the payroll department, how long will it take them to process pay cheques for all the employees? Calculate the answer first in minutes and then in hours.
4. If a computer could do the calculations and the printing of one cheque in three seconds how long would it take a computer to prepare 10 000 cheques? How much time would the company referred to in the previous question save if they used a computer?
5. Suppose that you wanted to build your own computer. For each of the following functions, name the device required to complete the computer: input; processing; output; storage.

UNIT B

1. Many banks have 24-hour cash dispensers on the outside wall of the building. Using functions of a digital computer–*input, output, processing, storage* and *control*, explain how each function is involved in a transaction.
2. Explain why the name CN-CP Telecommunications is an appropriate name for a telegraph company that also has microwave towers. Check the prefix *tele* in the dictionary.
3. Steve Austin, "the six-million dollar man" was originally described as a *cyborg*–part man, part machine. (Later the word *bionic* was used.) Study the definition for *cybernation* and explain why *cyborg* is a more accurate description.

4. If the U.P.C. stripes on a product label are used to record that item, name three things that the code must contain to make an order complete.
5. What makes *microprocessors* so important?

UNIT C

1. Besides solving problems, what else can an experienced programmer make a computer do?
2. Many science fiction movies portray the computer of the future as something quite frightening. Explain why people should not be frightened of it.
3. Most people believe that computers actually *solve* problems. Why is this not an accurate statement?
4. Which of the four steps in problem-solving are concerned with planning?
5. Study one of the flowchart diagrams in the text. Why is it referred to as a *flowchart*?
6. Read the following problem, then reduce it to its simplest form using first the sentence method, then the equation method.

    Jackie Ratkowski put $450 into a savings account. The bank pays 10% interest on deposits. If Jackie left the money in the bank for one year, how much interest would she have earned?

PROJECTS AND PROBLEMS

UNIT A

1. Write each of the following computer-related actions. Beside each one, identify them as examples of either *input, output, processing, storage,* or *control.*
a. Ten numbers being added together.
b. Information being keyed in on a typewriter keyboard.
c. A sheet of paper on which the answer is being printed out.
d. A list of words being put on magnetic tape.
e. The operator makes an error and the computer orders a correction.
f. A deck of computer cards being read into the computer.
g. A list of names in alphabetical order.
h. An answer appearing on the viewing screen.
2. Write each of the following job descriptions. Beside each one, identify the computer person who would do that particular job.
a. A person who converts ideas into written messages the computer can understand.
b. A person who uses a machine to punch holes into computer cards.
c. A person who runs the computer.
d. A person who uses a machine to put information on magnetic tape.
e. A person who studies ways of improving office routines involving the computer.
3. Using magazines such as Reader's Digest, Newsweek, Time, Weekend Magazine, or any others, and newspapers at home, find five examples of stories and pictures that involve computers. Write a brief explanation, in your own words, about each item.
4. Obtain from your teacher a "mark sense card" that uses pencil marks to record information. Using a pencil, or a hard, flat surface, code your name on the card leaving a space between your first and last name.

UNIT B

1. Cash dispensers on the outside wall of a bank are capable of doing several things for you, even though no bank teller is present. List six different banking transactions that it can perform.
2. Large aircraft often have an automatic pilot mechanism that can be used to control the plane while the pilot relaxes. The automatic pilot is actually a combination of computers. Name three things the computer must constantly check in order to keep the plane safe and on course.
3. Imagine that you are sitting in a satellite 200 km above the earth with just a computer to keep you informed of what is happening. Name five things that you would like the computer to keep track of for you.
4. Since computers, with the help of some control devices, can be used to monitor and operate anything electrical name five things in your school that a computer could watch and operate. (The control panel will be placed in the head janitor's office.)
5. Imagine you have a computer in your bedroom. It has a small T.V. screen, a printer, and a typewriter keyboard with a microprocessor inside. If you could only enter things by using the typewriter, describe how you would set up the following: special calendar dates–for birthdays, parents' anniversary; questions to be used to study for a computer test (answers as well); a daily diary. In addition to describing how you would do each section, write up an example of how it would look.

UNIT C

The text relating to Unit C is meant as an introduction to flowcharting for those students whose business course does not include an introduction to the computer. The following problems are for those students whose course does include computer applications. However, questions 1a, 2, 4 and those asterisked under the titles *Flowcharts with Decisions,* and *Decision and End-of-File Problems* should be teacher-directed before students attempt the questions that follow.

1. For each of the following problems, define it using the equation method whenever possible, then flowchart the steps needed to solve each one. In the left-hand column, under the head "problem definition", define the problem. In the right-hand column, under the head "data", supply the data. Centre your flowchart under the two columns.

   a. Solve $\dfrac{X + Y}{Z}$ where   X = 65
   Y = 25
   Z = 5

   b. Solve $\dfrac{A + B + C}{D}$ where   A = 40
   B = 25
   C = 85
   D = 15

   c. Solve $\dfrac{(A)(B)}{C} - D$ where   A = 10
   B = 15
   C = 5
   D = 2

2. Peter Brown purchased a stereo set worth $350. The store calculated the interest at 18% per year. Flowchart the solution that would print out the dollar amount of interest.

3. Joan Whittiker purchased a car on credit for $5500. The bank calculates her interest at 12% and added it to the loan. Flowchart the solution that would calculate and print only the final total.

4. Find the *net pay* for an employee whose rate is five dollars an hour and who works forty hours per week. Weekly deductions are $35. Note: Net Pay = (Rate × Time) — Deductions.

5. Charles Babbage put $150 into a term account at the local trust company. They promised to pay him 10% interest each year. Show the solution that would calculate and print two things: the dollar amount of interest; the total balance in his account by the end of the year.

6. Susan Clark wanted to calculate the average of her term marks. Flowchart the solution that would print out her average.

Her term marks.

Math	65	English	69	Science	71
Business	75	Physical Ed.	83	Geography	72
French	64	History	78		

Flowcharts with Decisions

These problems include a decision symbol that asks if there are any more values. This is needed because several different calculations must be performed and printed out. The decision symbol, in these problems, is used to see if the file (list of values or words) is completed. When it is used for this purpose, the decision symbol is called an END-OF-FILE check.

*1. List of Workers
The manager of a company wants the computer department to prepare a printout of the company's two hundred workers. There is a separate computer card for every employee. Each card contains the employee's number, and name. Flowchart the solution that would print both items for all two hundred employees.

2. List of students and marks
A teacher wants a printout of all the students in her business class and their year-end mark. Flowchart the solution that would read in each student's record card which contains the *student's name* and *subject mark* and have both items printed out for the whole class.

3. Payroll Cheques
The owner of a large business wishes to use a computer to print out the pay cheques for all his employees. He uses the formula: *net pay = gross pay — deductions* to calculate the amount of each cheque. Flowchart the solution that reads in the employee's name, gross pay, and deductions, and prints a cheque containing the employee's name and net pay. There are 150 employees.

4. Class Average
There are thirty-five students at Albright High School in the computer studies class. Read in each student record card which contains *student name* and *subject mark*. Find the class average and have it printed out.

Decision and End-of-File Problems

These next problems have two or more decision symbols in them. One of the decisions is used to select from a list only the names or numbers desired by the programmer.

*1. Baseball Draftees
For every baseball player eligible to be drafted, a card has been prepared that shows the Name and Position of that player. The Toronto Blue-jays are looking for a first baseman. Flowchart the solution that reads the cards and prints out only a listing of players who play first base.

2. Honour List
There are 1250 students at Glendale. The office has a card for each student containing the student's number, code (1 — female, 2 — male), and average mark. Print out a list of girls only who have obtained an average of 80% or better. The list should contain both student number and average.

3. Criminal Record
The Stoney Creek Police Station wants a list of those criminals in the computer records that have been convicted of theft. The tape being read in (one record at a time) contains *name, offence,* and *conviction date.* The offences are listed as T (theft), A (arson), and H (homicide). The list should only contain the name and conviction date of those who were arrested for theft.

4. Positive Output
You have a deck of cards with three variables on each card–A, B, C. Calculate A + B , but print only the positive answers.

6 Communications

UNIT A

BUSINESS COMMUNICATES

Ask classmates to turn to a particular page in this textbook or to perform some other simple task. Check to see that they have correctly completed the task. If they have, you have just successfully communicated. Communication is a simple process and most of us take everyday communications for granted. Generally, we are able to successfully communicate our thoughts, ideas, and questions to others, but sometimes we do not say exactly what we mean, or other people misinterpret what we say. When this happens, we have a breakdown in communication and it can cause problems. Because businesses must communicate with many people both within and outside of the business, there are many chances for breakdowns.

Communications has four ingredients. First, something is to be communicated–a message, an idea–something that one person wants others to understand. This information is commonly in the form of words or numbers. Artists "communicate" when they paint a picture or create a sculpture. Composers communicate when they write a piece of music.

Information is delivered or transmitted by a sender, a person who wishes to make the communication. The person to whom the information is transmitted is called the receiver. In the situation when you asked classmates to perform a simple task, you were the sender, and they were receivers. The information you transmitted was the request to perform the task. A salesperson trying to sell a product to a customer is the sender, the customer is the receiver. Most communications are two-way in that both persons spend part of the time sending information and part of the time receiving it.

Finally, there must be a method of transmitting the information. This method is called a medium (plural "media"). When we speak to other people, the communication medium we use is our voice. When we write a letter to a friend, the printed words form the medium. These are the two primary media used in businesses. The voice can be transmitted by telephone or intercom, on a tape recording, or "live and in person". Printed words can be presented in different forms. Senders and receivers are people. The methods used to communicate are the media.

Communications can be simple. When a supervisor in an office asks a secretary to "be more polite to customers when speaking to them on the telephone", there is one sender, one receiver, one medium, and a simple message. When ten managers meet for several hours to prepare a report for the owners of the company, there are several senders, perhaps thousands of owners if the business is a corporation, a complicated report (the information) and more formal media–perhaps an attractive brochure delivered by mail or courier. This type of communication is more complex.

"ARE YOU RECEIVING ME?"

The way in which the information is expressed is important in both voice and print communications. We use our language to help us to describe our thoughts and ideas to others. If John calls something that travels on a road with four wheels, carrying people at various speeds, a "car", but Janet has never heard the word "car", or seen a "car" before, she will have trouble trying to visualize what John means. The one simple word "car" is used by us as a code to conveniently describe a particular thing. Imagine trying to explain what a "car" is to someone who has never seen one before and who doesn't know what a "wheel" is, or an "engine", or a "road".

This brings us to an important principle of communication. The *words* we use have no meaning of their own; only *people* have an understanding of what a word means. If a person has never heard the word "car", they have no meaning for that word–they will not understand a communication that uses the word "car". The English language is a difficult one to learn because many English words represent several different meanings. On an oral level, the context tells the receiver the sender of the message said this: "There must be a way to find where I made a mistake". But on a written level, words that have similar pronunciations have different spellings and different meanings. The sentence expressed orally makes no sense when expressed on paper in this fashion: "Their mussed bee a weigh two fined wear eye maid a mist steak."

Although the communication process is simple to understand, problems are created when we do not communicate clearly. It is desirable that we develop our language skills and become aware of the conventions and rules used to help us to communicate effectively. Spelling, grammar, and pronunciation help us to make sure our message is understood. When people do not use correct language, communication problems develop. Courses in Business Communications and Business English and Correspondence are offered in many high schools. They strive to improve students' skills in both verbal and written communications.

In a typical business, thousands of communications are made daily. Memos and letters are sent and received, people speak to each other on the telephone, in person, in an office, and in meetings. Communicating is a necessary part of living; we all need to communicate successfully.

JOHN WILEY & SONS CANADA, LIMITED

22 Worchester Road, Rexdale, Ontario, M9W 1L1, Tel. 675-3580 Telex 06-989189

SHIP TO:
EXPÉDIÉ À:

SOLD TO
VENDU À

Mr. R. Williams,
Halton Board of Education,
Box 5005,
Burlington, Ontario
L7R 3Z7

SHIPPED VIA
EXPÉDIÉ VIA   CN EXPRESS

CUSTOMER NUMBER CUST. NO.	NO. DU CLIENT TERR. NO.	SHIP TO	EXPLANATION	F.O.B. F.A.B.	REXDALE		TERMS DATE TERMES DATE			SPECIAL INSTRUCTIONS		INVOICE DATE DATE DE LA FACTURE			INVOICE NO. NO. DE FACTURE
							MO	DAY	YR			MO	DAY	YR	
0090	3005			NET 60	DAYS/JOURS		09	08	78			09	08	78	G7946

ORDER NO. NO. DE COMMANDE	SHIPPED EXPEDIE	NOT SHIPPED PAS EXPEDIE	EXPL	PRODUCT CODE ARTICLE NO.	DESCRIPTION	SUBJ. CODE	SUGG. LIST PRICE PRIX COURANT	DISC. %	NET AMOUNT MONTANT NET
49763	150			C19940	Daw You the Consumer		9.75	20	1,170.00
	40			C99848	Culliford Typing Book		9.75	20	312.00
		20	2	C99795	Preshing Business 2nd			20	
	75			C29757	Murphy Law		11.95	20	717.00
		50	2	C99794	Murphy World of Business			20	
	50	150	1	C02384	Jarman Pursuit Justice		9.75	20	390.00

TOTAL	SHIPPED EXPEDIE	265

ALL ITEMS EXEMPT FROM FEDERAL & PROVINCIAL SALES TAXES.
TOUS LES ARTICLES SONT EXEMPTES DES TAXES DE VENTE FÉDÉRALE ET PROVINCIALE.

EXPLANATION
1 OUT OF STOCK WILL SUPPLY APPROX 2-4 WEEKS
2 IN PRESS - BACK ORDERED
3 NO CANADIAN RIGHTS - ORDER CANCELLED
4 OUT OF PRINT - ORDER CANCELLED
5 OUT OF STOCK - ORDER CANCELLED
6 IN PRESS - ORDER CANCELLED

EXPLICATION
1 SUIVRE D'ICI À PEU PRÈS 2-4 SEMAINES
2 EN IMPRIMERIE — À SUIVRE
3 NOUS N'AVONS PAS LES DROITS AU CANADA
4 EPUISE — COMMANDE ANNULÉE
5 STOCK EPUISE — COMMANDE ANNULEE
6 EN IMPRIMERIE — COMMANDE ANNULEE

PACKING & DEL.
EMBELLAGE ET LIVE.

PAGE 1 OF 1

TOTAL   2,589.00

INVOICE FACTURE

PLEASE RETURN A COPY OF THIS INVOICE WITH REMITTANCE OR WITH RETURNS TO ENSURE PROPER CREDIT
S.V.P. RENVOYEZ UNE COPIE DE CETTE FACTURE AVEC VOTRE REMISE OU AVEC RETOUR POUR ASSURER UN CRÉDIT EXACT

JOHN WILEY & SONS CANADA, LIMITED No. 1585

22 WORCESTER ROAD, REXDALE, ONTARIO M9W 1L1 (416) 677-5080

TO Miller Services,
45 Charles Street East,
Toronto, Ontario
M4Y 1S6

SHIP TO Wiley Publishers of Canada Limited,
22 Worcester Road,
Rexdale, Ontario
M9W 1L1

DATE	TERMS	ACCOUNT NO.	VIA	F.O.B.	P.P.D	COLL	DATE REQUIRED
June 30, 1978	60 days	PO300	Mail				July 21, 1978

ITEM	QUANTITY	DESCRIPTION	UNIT PRICE	AMOUNT
		PLEASE SUPPLY THE FOLLOWING. SUBJECT TO THE CONDITIONS STATED.		
		Project #307 World of Business		
	2 cartoons	Uluschack	$35.00	$70.00
	1 photo	56023 – Sides of Beef in Wholesale		35.00
	1 photo	68-2670 – Cars being shipped by truck		35.00
	1 photo	F2610M – Flames/burning timbers		35.00
		Use: Editorial inside		
		1 time reproduction rights.		
		TOTAL		$175.00

TERMS
1 ACKNOWLEDGE RECEIPT OF THIS ORDER. CONFIRMING PRICES AND DELIVERY DATE.
2 NO SUBSTITUTIONS OR CHANGES WILL BE ACCEPTED UNLESS AUTHORIZED BY US.
3 WE RESERVE THE RIGHT TO CANCEL THIS ORDER IF SHIPMENT IS NOT MADE IN QUANTITIES AND AT PRICES AND DELIVERY SHOWN.
4 SALES TAX LICENCE NUMBERS ARE APPLICABLE WHEN SHOWN.

DIVISION MANAGER
DEPT. MANAGER
Mary Mochuen

COMPANY OFFICER

PURCHASE ORDER

VENDOR

Internal and External Communications

There are two basic types of communications in businesses. **External communications** are those messages transmitted from people in a business to people outside it. Information exchanged among people within a business is called **internal communications**.

External Communications

Information must be exchanged between businesses and many other organizations and individuals. Probably the most important from the point of view of a business are those that take place between a business and its customers. All businesses strive to have effective communications with customers: if they do not, lost sales and decreased profits result. Personal sales visits, telephone calls, letters, advertisements and catalogues are some of the ways in which businesses communicate with their customers. An invoice (the bill sent to a customer after a sale has been made) is a good example of effective communications. A customer who calls a business on the telephone, and gets cut off, or is spoken to discourteously will be annoyed and may place the order with a competing business. Poorly designed advertisements are not read; salespersons who cannot speak clearly or in a pleasant manner do not have many sales.

Businesses communicate with other businesses, particularly suppliers. Again, depending on the situation, several media can be used. Many businesses sell their products and services only to other companies and have no business with the general public.

Governments and businesses exchange information frequently in that businesses must collect and pay taxes to governments. To ensure these collections are accurate, governments hire auditors to check on the clarity and completeness of tax records. Governments also pass laws affecting the operation of businesses, and these laws must be communicated to the businesses. Minimum Wage, Unemployment Insurance, and Canada Pension Plan laws are examples of these. It is estimated that business executives spend approximately one third of their time making sure that government laws and regulations are carried out.

Internal Communications

In large businesses, thousands of people work together to produce the goods and services the business sells. To operate a modern business smoothly, there must be clear communications among the people who work in it. Many types of information must be transmitted daily. If the communications are not clear and understandable, time and energy is spent trying to clarify what was meant, and in explaining repeatedly the same information. For a business to operate efficiently, everyone working in the organization must have a clear idea of what they are expected to do. One of the problems facing many businesses is caused when employees do not know what is expected of them.

Letters, reports, and memoranda outlining procedures, routines, and requirements are common in businesses. Meetings are often called for the purpose of communicating information important to the operation of the company although some people seem to believe, erroneously, that the pay cheque is the most important type of communication between a business and the people who work in it.

Information Processing

The information used in all businesses can be divided into two categories–data and words. Data refers to numerical and financial information, and is linked to the accounting function of business. The other type of information processing is called word processing, which is discussed here.

The Manager's Desk

Let us take a look behind the scenes in a modern business. We are in the office of the manager of a local manufacturer. On the desk are several piles of paper. Facing the manager today are nine letters. Four are from customers requesting attention to various problems, three are from suppliers, and two are from government tax auditing departments. There are seven telephone messages, one telegram, three memos from other managers in the office, and the month-end financial report from the accounting department. In another neat pile are seven letters and one report that the manager dictated yesterday that now require proof reading and a signature.

People in businesses spend much time communicating. It is a natural process, and must be done well if problems are to be avoided. The modern office exists to make sure that communications both within and out of the business are made effectively and efficiently. The office is the communications centre for a company. Successful businesses are those that communicate well and a modern office contributes to good communications.

POOR COMMUNICATION

"My boss just doesn't seem to understand me," said Carol. "She never takes the time to listen to my suggestions. I could save the company time and money, but no one will listen!"

At least half of good communication is effective listening–not just hearing the words and nodding the head, but trying one's hardest to understand the meaning intended by the sender.

A good way to develop listening skills is to learn to paraphrase. When someone says something, say it in your own words, just to check that you understand. Try this exercise the next time you listen to a speaker or a newsbroadcaster. When the speaker makes a statement, paraphrase it in your mind. This forces you to concentrate on what is being said, and to "think" about it. Be selective and listen for the main points–often not everything that is said is important. The skill requires a bit of practice, but can make you a better listener.

113

UNIT B

BUSINESS PROCESSES WORDS

The English language has thousands of words. Words are the tools we use to help us communicate our thoughts and ideas to others. Words in the English language can be either spoken or written. Most of the world's languages are the same in this respect although there are a few African and South American tribes that have only a spoken language.

We say that people communicate effectively when the meaning the receiver understands from the message is the same as the meaning the sender intended. Communication problems occur when there is a difference between what was intended and what was actually understood.

In this unit we examine written communications in business, word processing. There are four basic activities carried out in the processing of words: recording information, transferring the information to paper, transmitting the information, and storing information.

Recording Information

When an author (the originator of a written communication) wants to communicate in writing, the ideas and thoughts can be recorded in several ways. The method chosen depends on the purpose for which the communication is intended and on the types of procedures and equipment available in the office.

An author may choose to write a message directly on paper. For personal notes, this is quite convenient. However, if the information is to be read by others, the communication will probably be improved if it is typewritten. Because they are paid to do other things, most managers do not type their own correspondence. Businesses find it more efficient to give the job of typing to specialists—secretaries, stenographers, and dicta-typists. Because they are highly trained, these specialists complete the work faster, more accurately, and at less cost than the author.

Some authors still write out all of their material in long hand and give it in that form to their secretaries. For most communication tasks this is inefficient, as it wastes valuable time. Today's managers are being encouraged to learn **dictation skills**.

Stenographic Dictation

Stenographers are people who have mastered the valuable skill of **shorthand**. Shorthand is a method of taking down spoken words in short form. To learn it, one must learn a new "written" language. While the author speaks, a stenographer records the information on a pad. To the untrained observer, most shorthand looks much like chicken scratches on a page, but the stenographer can take this abbreviated work, and type up the intended correspondence from it. A trained stenographer can take down

Forkner Shorthand   **Pitman Shorthand**

information in shorthand at 100 to 120 words per minute. This is much more efficient than taking down dictation in long hand-most people average approximately 15 to 20 words per minute this way.

Machine Dictation

Several machines have been invented to permit an author to record on some type of magnetic tape, a communication electronically. The first such machine was invented by Thomas Edison over one hundred years ago. Modern dictating machines are simply sophisticated tape recorders available in many makes and models. Much of the information in this book was initially recorded using portable dictation equipment.

Many large businesses have installed centralized **PBX dictation systems**, which permit authors to use the telephone to dictate directly into a central recording unit. PBX stands for Private Branch Exchange. This type of system allows users to dictate in the office, at home, or in a distant city, by simply dialing a special telephone number. By having a pool of typists to transcribe from the central recording unit, correspondence can be completed very quickly-often before the author returns to the office.

1978-04-28

Mr. G. A. Jones,
Production Manager,
Andco Canada Ltd.,
4398 Service Road South,
Burlington, Ontario.
L7R 3P2

Dear Mr. Jones:

I want to introduce you to our new series of industrial lubricants. We have developed a full line of top quality products, and our prices are very competitive.

Enclosed is a brochure that outlines the specifications for our lubricants.

I'm planning to be in Burlington on Wednesday, May 24. Could I see you in your office at 9 a.m. to determine your requirements and answer any of your questions?

My secretary will call in a few days to confirm an appointment. Thank you for your interest.

Yours sincerely,

Jack Johnson,
Marketing Manager.

Executives still fighting dictation systems —

"It's hard to teach an old dog new tricks", but executives must learn to use modern dictating equipment if they are to keep pace with changes in business. Manufacturers of dictation systems eagerly point out that costs alone should force executives to change to the new electronic equipment. The cost of a business letter (executive's salary, secretary's salary, equipment and supply costs) is decreased by $4.00 a letter if a dictating machine is used instead of a secretary taking shorthand.

An executive who drafts a report in long hand averages fifteen words a minute-average dictation speed is seventy-five words a minute. It just isn't efficient to use two people's time instead of one. With dictation equipment, letters and reports can be recorded at any time, not just during normal working hours, when the secretary is on the job.

But although arguments strongly favour a switch to dictation equipment, there is still resistance. Executives don't want to take the time to learn a new technique, and many are frightened by the new electronic gadgetry. Status is the biggest barrier-there is prestige in having a private secretary.

Although most secretaries seldom use their shorthand skills in the office, 50% of prospective employers are still looking for secretaries with shorthand training.

Although it takes only a few hours to learn how to use the new equipment effectively most colleges and universities do not include dictation skills in their training programs for future executives. However, manufacturers are willing to fill the gap by providing on-the-job training to customers.

As salaries of secretaries continue to climb, more and more companies need to make the switch to dictation equipment.

Digest of Business News
Spring 1978

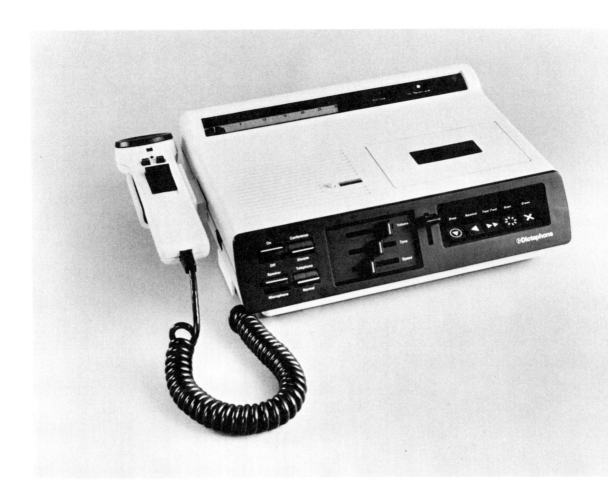

Transferring Information to Paper

After desired communications have been recorded, the next step is to transfer them to the printed page. The most common types of office communications are letters, memoranda, reports, and minutes. Generally they are typed in a form easy to read by skilled secretarial employees. The typewriter is, of course, the most common type of office machine.

In many businesses, managers are assigned personal secretaries or share a secretary with one or two other managers. Other companies use a stenographic pool and managers call upon a centralized group of stenographers and typists.

Word Processing Environments

Several equipment manufacturers are encouraging large businesses to centralize their office functions, and to instal technologically advanced new equipment such as the PBX dictation systems referred to earlier. These systems combine the keyboard of an everyday standard typewriter with a computerized memory system, and a high-speed printing ability. Rather than retyping letters and reports containing errors in the first draft, corrections are made electronically.

A word processing system combines some of the features of the one manager-one secretary arrangement or stenographic pool. In word processing environments, the recording and transferring of information to paper is accomplished centrally by highly trained **word processing operators.** Administrative assistants are assigned on the basis of one assistant for every three or four managers; they perform the non-stenographic functions of secretaries for this group of managers. These might include arranging meetings, taking minutes, answering the telephone, making travel arrangements, answering correspondence, making appointments, and preparing statistical reports.

Transmitting Information

Once communications have been transferred to paper and proofread, it is then necessary to send them to the intended receivers. This may be accomplished using several types of systems including mail, special courier, delivery services, telegraph, and telex.

In the 1980s it is likely that businesses will begin using electronic mail. Several systems are currently being studied. With the proper equipment attached to telephones it is possible to transmit written

information using telephone lines. The advantages of electronic mail are that mail can be delivered instantly to the intended receivers, without worry that it will be lost or delayed. Many large businesses now have computers that "talk" with one another–they transmit information using telephone lines. Some experts suggest that private individuals, you and me, will eventually have electronic mail service in our homes.

Storing Information

It is a common business practice to keep copies of important written communications for it is often necessary to refer to letters and reports written several months or even years ago. All businesses use some type of information storage system. Filing cabinets are common fixtures in most offices.

Large businesses, with volumes of information to store, often use microfilm or microfiche systems. These systems can store several pages of information on a small "photograph", which can be viewed on a special viewer. Using these systems results in substantial savings for a business because renting or buying office space to store large file cabinets is expensive. Because several copies of some types of information may be necessary, modern offices have automatic copying and duplicating equipment. In the future it is likely that much information will be stored on computer systems.

Information Processing and Word Processing

An information processing system has three basic components: input, processing, and output. Word processing systems have the same components. Words and numerical data are both information. Input to a word processing system is normally accomplished using some type of dictation equipment. The words are processed by a typist and some type of automatic typewriter. The output is the finished copy–the letter, memorandum, or report. It is very important that businesses process words effectively and economically. The modern office is designed to do just this.

UNIT C

BUSINESS COMMUNICATIONS AND YOU

How are you affected by business communications? Businesses communicate with you every day. Communication is such a simple process that we often take it for granted. How many times have you communicated with business today? Every time you see or hear an advertisement from a business, the business is communicating. They are attempting to inform you about their products and services, and to entice you to buy them. This form of communication is explained in the Marketing chapter.

Every time you enquire about a product or make a complaint to a business, you are communicating. These are examples of external communications. Many of you, because you will work in businesses, will also be involved in internal communications. Many of you will be employed in business offices, in one of the many occupations available there.

Office Occupations

Did you know that the biggest single group of workers in Canadian businesses are office workers? There is always a demand for trained individuals to work in these important occupations.

If we examine the people working in a typical business office, we will see a mixture of individuals with different backgrounds, education, skills, and responsibilities. Some people working in the office will have less than a high school education, others will have several university degrees. Some perform repetitive jobs, like filing, others deal with complex situations requiring decision-making and problem-solving skills.

It might seem strange that office workers form such a large part of modern businesses for office workers do not contribute directly to the production of a company's goods and services. Rather, the office worker exists to perform many background services required to operate a business. Office workers support the production activities of businesses. Let us examine some of the **support services** provided by these workers to their businesses.

Businesses are people. People expect to be paid for the services they perform and therefore **payroll** departments exist to make sure that employees receive their wages and salaries. Most employees have deductions from their basic pay–pension plans, unemployment insurance, union dues, hos-

pitalization, dental plans, taxes, and charitable donations. Calculating the payroll for a company with many employees is quite complicated and large businesses use computers to assist them. Payroll departments cannot afford to make mistakes. Nothing makes an employee madder than to be paid less than he or she is entitled. While the employee may not object to too much pay, this type of error is costly to a business.

Keeping track of the finances of a business is the responsibility of the accounting department. There are several different types of jobs requiring various levels of skills available in large departments. These are discussed in more detail in the chapter on accounting. Modern offices employ numerous **clerical employees**–secretaries, stenographers, typists, file clerks, mail clerks, and several others.

Specialists in data processing are employed by large businesses to operate the computers and other equipment necessary to process large volumes of information.

Most businesses also have a **personnel department** to co-ordinate the hiring of the many kinds of workers required in a modern business. Personnel workers also keep accurate records of the employees.

Much office activity goes on behind the scenes in a modern business and no one has found a way yet of deleting the office function in business. Even businesses with one employee normally have some type of office. Businesses depend on offices to perform the many services required to ensure smooth operation and as most of the work in offices involves business communications you can see why communications is important to business.

Education for Office Work

How many courses in your own school will help to prepare you for office jobs? Most high schools have extensive programs to train students who wish to develop typing, secretarial, and clerical skills. Accounting and data processing courses introduce the student to the financial activities of businesses. Courses in economics, law, and consumer studies provide a good general background for students who want to work in modern offices.

```
*********************************************
```

YOU HAVE INDICATED AN INTEREST IN
                    PAYROLL CLERK

        PAYROLL CLERK   (CLERICAL)
        COMPUTES WAGES AND POSTS WAGE DATA TO
        PAYROLL RECORDS:
        COMPUTES EARNINGS FROM TIME SHEETS AND
        WORK TICKETS, USING CALCULATOR, OR
        COMPTOMETER. OPERATES POSTING MACHINE
        TO COMPUTE AND SUBTRACT DEDUCTIONS; SUCH
        AS, INCOME TAX, UNEMPLOYMENT AND OTHER
        INSURANCE, UNION PAYMENTS AND BOND
        PURCHASES. ENTERS NET WAGES ON
        EARNINGS-RECORD CARD, CHEQUE STUB AND
        PAYROLL SHEET. COMPUTES WAGES FOR
        EMPLOYEES WORKING ON BONUS, COMMISSION,
        OR PIECEWORK SYSTEMS.
        MAY KEEP RECORDS OF SICK LEAVE, PAY AND
        NON-TAXABLE WAGES. MAY DISTRIBUTE PAY
        CHEQUES TO EMPLOYEES OR TO DEPARTMENT
        HEADS, SETTLE PAYROLL DISPUTES AND BE
        DESIGNATED ACCORDINGLY,
        PAYMASTER

        FOR RELATED CAREERS CONSULT THE MASTER
        LIST UNDER THE MINOR GROUP-------------- 413

THESE TRAININGS SUPPORT PAYROLL CLERK

            ACCOUNTING CLERK TRAINING
        THIS TRAINING IS GIVEN IN A 2 OR 3 YEAR
        DIPLOMA PROGRAM AT CAAT & RYERSON LEVEL,
        OR IN SHORTER COURSES AT PRIVATE BUSI-
        NESS COLLEGES, IN ONE OF: ACCOUNTING,
        GENERAL BUSINESS OR BUSINESS ADMINIS-
        TRATION.
        *ADMISSION REQUIREMENTS: O.S.S.G.D.
        (27 CREDITS). SOME SCHOOLS RECOMMEND
        ENGLISH LEVEL 4, MATHEMATICS LEVEL 3
        AND 4.
          TUITION FEES VARY DEPENDING ON WHETHER
        TRAINING IS OFFERED AT CAAT OR RYERSON
        LEVEL. HIGHER FEES ARE CHARGED FOR THE

A Typical High School Business Education Program

1st Year	2nd Year	3rd Year	4th Year
Typing	Typing	Office Procedures Shorthand	Office Procedures Shorthand
		Business Communications	Business Communications
Introduction to Business	Data Processing	Data Processing	
	Accounting	Accounting	Accounting
	Business Mathematics	Business Mathematics	
		Marketing	Marketing
			Consumer Studies
			Canadian Law
			Economics

REVIEWING
YOUR BUSINESS VOCABULARY

Write the number of each definition.
Write the word that matches the definition number.

UNIT A

data processing, external communications,
information, internal communication, media,
medium, receiver, sender, word processing

1. The person who initiates a communication.
2. The method by which a communication is transmitted.
3. A memorandum from a manager to her employees.
4. Communicating financial and numerical statistics.
5. The mail, telephone, telex, and television.
6. Inputting, processing, and outputting words.
7. Advertisement, commercials, etc.
8. The person for whom a message is intended.
9. Written or oral expressions of ideas and thoughts.

UNIT B

author, dictation, machine dictation, PBX
dictation system, secretary, shorthand,
stenographic pool, word processing operator

1. Short form method of writing down words.
2. A centralized machine dictation system using the telephone.
3. Specialists who operate automatic typewriters.
4. Recording information on magnetic tape.
5. The verbal expression of thoughts and ideas.
6. A stenographer skilled in shorthand.
7. A centralized office system in which managers do not have their own secretaries or assistants.
8. The originator of a communication.

UNIT C

clerical, deductions, payroll, personnel,
support services

1. Secretaries, typists, and file clerks.
2. The department that ensures employees are paid the correct amount of money.
3. Taxes, hospitalization premiums, union dues, etc.
4. Payroll, accounting, and personnel departments.

REVIEW QUESTIONS

UNIT A

1. What are the four ingredients common to all communications?
2. List three voice and five print media.
3. Name three kinds of internal and three kinds of external communications.
4. What is the communications centre for a business?
5. Name five different types of communications that a typical manager deals with daily.

UNIT B

1. Why is it not common for managers to type their own work?
2. Why are managers being encouraged to learn dictation skills?
3. What is the difference between stenographic dictation and machine dictation?
4. Who normally performs the processing function in a word processing system?
5. What is a PBX dictation system? How does it differ from other systems?
6. Why do some managers resist using dictation equipment?
7. What is the most common type of office machine?
8. Explain what is meant by a word processing environment.

UNIT C

1. Give three examples that show how you communicate with businesses.
2. List four support services commonly provided by offices.
3. Name five different jobs common in offices.
4. What types of activities are accounting and bookkeeping employees engaged in?
5. What is the largest category of employees in Canadian businesses?
6. State four typical payroll deductions.

APPLYING
YOUR KNOWLEDGE

UNIT A

1. Draw a diagram illustrating the relationships among the four parts of communications.
2. Name three possible causes of poor communications in a business; suggest a solution for each.
3. Can people communicate without a written or verbal language? Think up a simple message, and try to communicate it to a classmate without using language.
4. Draw up a two-column table with the headings *internal communication, external communication*. Classify the following examples in the proper columns: minutes of a meeting of supervisors; a pay cheque; an invoice; a notice about the coffee fund; a sales call on a customer; a meeting with the boss; a telephone call from a customer; a purchase order; a job application.
5. Collect examples of seven different types of print communications used in a business. Be able to explain the information given on each one.
6. Name three different types of communications a business would have with governments.

UNIT B

1. Explain by specific examples how the purpose of a communication determines how it is processed in an office.
2. What functions can automatic typewriters perform that standard typewriters cannot?
3. Research and explain how the telex system works.
4. Draw up a three-column chart that clearly shows the types of input, processing, and output activities common in word-processing environments.

UNIT C

1. Name three important characteristics office workers should have. Why?
2. Name four duties performed by secretaries.
3. Examine the courses of study for several other courses offered in the Business Education Department in your high school. Which one appeals to you most? Why? What types of jobs will this course help to prepare you for? (Your teacher will provide you with the courses of study you want to see.)
4. Ask your parents to tell you what types of deductions are made from their pay cheques. Which is the largest deduction?
5. Clerical jobs must be performed accurately with attention to detail. Explain why you think that accuracy is so important. Do you feel that you could do this kind of work?

PROJECTS AND PROBLEMS

UNIT A

1. Arrange to interview a person who works in a business office. Find out from them three or four different types of communication problems that they have experienced while working in the office. Try to get specific examples of these problems. Explain what you would do to improve the communication in each case.
2. Arrange to visit a business manager, or your school principal, and ask them to show you a typical day's communications. Record the number and types of different communications; report the results to your class.
3. Discuss the statement: "As the size of a business increases, the number of communication problems increases."
4. Write a one-page essay on the topic: "Effective Communications–The Key to Successful Businesses."

UNIT B

1. Research the average costs of producing a business letter in an office. What are the components of this cost? What can be done to decrease these costs?
2. Have a classmate dictate a passage from this textbook to you for five minutes. Take down the information in long hand, so that you can read it. At the end of five minutes, calculate the number of words you have taken down. Calculate the number of words per minute.

   Invite the shorthand teacher in your school to come to class, to take down the same information, only in shorthand. Again calculate the number of words per minute achieved by the teacher. Have the teacher explain the advantages of using shorthand.

3. Draw up a chart that clearly shows the advantages and disadvantages of using direct dictation, stenographic dictation, and machine dictation.
4. Have your teacher bring dictation machines to class. Experiment by dictating a letter of complaint to a business whose product has dissatisfied you. In a class discussion, summarize the principles of effective dictation.
5. Research four common copying and duplicating methods used in offices. Compare them on the basis of cost, quality, and speed.

UNIT C

1. Examine the *Help Wanted* section of your local newspaper. How many office type jobs are listed? What percentage of the total number of jobs listed are office type jobs? How many of these jobs do you have sufficient education for? How many of these jobs can be performed by high school graduates? Select three office jobs in which you have an interest and bring the advertisements to class.

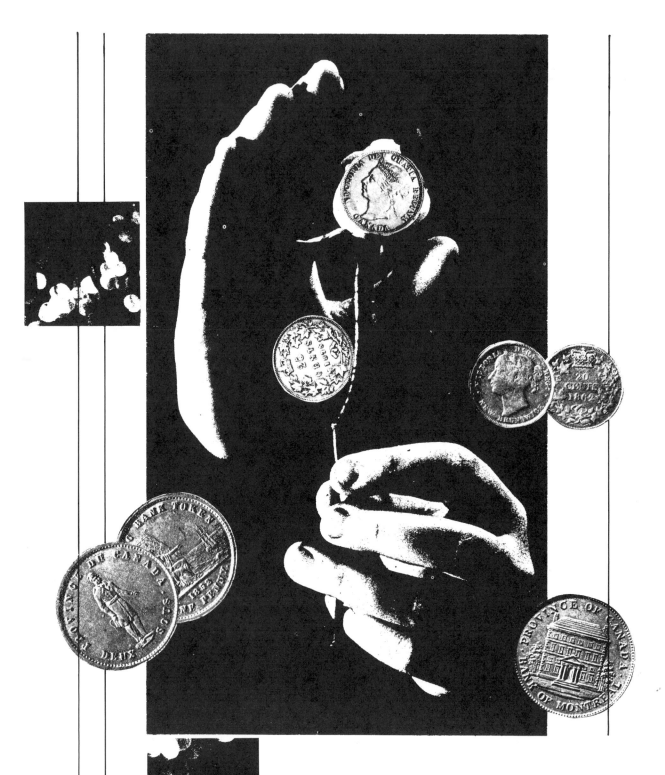

7 Money and Banking

UNIT A
MONEY—ITS MEANING AND VALUE

Money is something all of us like to have. You and everybody else use money when you buy something and without it, Canada's economy could not operate. Yet many people do not really understand much about money. For this reason, it is important both to understand how money developed and its functions in a modern economy.

How Money Developed

Hundreds of years ago, people traded different types of goods with their neighbours and with one another. A baker might trade loaves of freshly baked bread with a farmer for some milk and vegetables. A fisherman might trade some of his catch of fish to a carpenter in return for work done on the fisherman's boat. This exchange of goods or services by trading was called bartering.

Bartering

Bartering was an acceptable way of doing business as long as both parties could agree on the worth or value of their goods. But how many loaves of bread were a farmer's milk and vegetables worth? How many fish were equal to the value of the time spent by the carpenter repairing the fisherman's boat? As more people bartered, it became more difficult to find people who wanted the goods that you had available to trade. It was difficult to place fair value on the different products and also bartering was a very slow process.

Bartering was successful as long as the two parties willingly accepted each other's goods or services without any problems. But as society grew larger, it became clear that something new was needed, something that would be accepted by everybody in exchange for goods and services. That "something" is money.

CITY MERCHANTS BARTER GOODS

"What do you want for this bracelet?"

"Oh, it's worth about a set of strings."

"Done."

This sort of wheeling and dealing is common to a group of Kingston merchants who dabble at bartering, the oldest system of exchange—and one that's been staging a comeback.

"Bartering makes a lot of sense, if you can work it out," according to Bram Fisher, proprietor of the Scarecrow restaurant. "I've got a bartering system myself, with a few other friends in town."

One of those friends, Gary Mullen, who owns Renaissance Music, said, "We do it all the time." He trades this way mainly with the Scarecrow, Silver Threads, and Tara Natural Foods.

"It's a great system ... when I want some shirts or pants or something I go up there ... and then they come here and they do the same thing."

Mr. Fisher said he sees only one drawback to the system, "... if one person runs a service that's worth a lot on the marketplace and yours isn't worth much on the marketplace ..., it's hard trying to give something of equal value to them."

Jim Lyon, of Tara Foods, who barters with Printed Passage Books and Carrigan Printing and Copying as well as the three businesses mentioned, said, "it's not really the ideal system of bartering", since they have to keep track of what's been traded, instead of "taking up a bag of oats" to pay for other goods.

At Tara, they also trade with individuals who can offer goods or services. A man from Queen's University who makes posters for them is 'paid' in food.

A Toronto-based firm is promoting a different sort of bartering—an inter-business arrangement, with trading recorded by means of a plastic credit card. Robin Weatherstone operates Tradex International, a year-old bartering group that is spreading country-wide and now has about four hundred members, trading both goods and services. Members have access to legal and dental services, an accountant, many repair businesses, and even a mortician, as well as a range of goods.

"Instead of actually having people plunking down tires for suits, we operate on a system of debits and credits", he explained. One credit equals one dollar.

People are, in effect, buying a

What Actually Is Money?

Money is something that is generally acceptable in exchange for goods and services. Animal skins, beads, cattle, stones, tobacco, even playing cards were some of the earliest forms of money used in North America. Any item acceptable to members of a society could be used as money.

Before coins were introduced, lumps of precious metals were the medium of exchange; these had to be assessed for mass and purity before they were exchanged, which was a cumbersome process. In time, coins were introduced–lumps of precious metals of fixed mass and purity guaranteed by an official stamp. **Coins,** similar to the ones we use today, were first introduced around 700 B.C. The first known **paper money** was used in China around A.D. 1400. The use of paper money and coins created the need for people to change and handle this money; such people were our first bankers.

The Need for Paper Money

During the seventeenth and eighteenth centuries, trade increased considerably. With increased trade, there was an increased need for more money. During the eighteenth century there were no major discoveries of precious metals to make more coins. In addition, the **Industrial Revolution** produced a large number of new goods for purchase. Money was needed to build more factories, to pay the workers, and to buy the goods produced. When coins became scarce, **paper currency** came into use.

By the nineteenth century, paper currency was being used in most countries and as time passed, people more willingly accepted paper money instead of precious metal coins. As people gained **confidence in paper money,** it became more widely

used. Today, paper money is wholly acceptable. Society has confidence in its value in that it enables us to buy the goods and services we need and want.

Forms of Money

Today, the two **major forms of money** used in Canada are coins and paper money, and cheques. These are the common forms of money used in most other countries in the world. The coins and paper money we use are our **currency.** All currency is issued under the control of the federal government. Coins are produced–minted–at the **Royal Canadian Mint** in Ottawa and Winnipeg. The **Bank of Canada** in Ottawa issues the paper money in circulation in Canada.

1. French Régime in Canada, 5 sols, 1670, silver coin. (first coin issued for use in Canada).

2. French Régime in Canada, 3 livres, 1749, card money. (one of the earliest types of Canadian paper money).

128

3. Merchants note, 30 sous, 1837.

4. International Bank of Canada, $2, 1858.

The Use of Cheques as Money

Cheques represent a large part of everyday business. A cheque is an order telling a financial institution to pay a certain amount of money to another person or business. Anyone who writes a cheque should have enough money to pay it. If money is not available, that person is guilty of a crime. Cheques are used as money because most people and businesses are prepared to accept them in return for goods and services. Employers often pay their employees by cheque. Many of you probably pay your bills by cheque. Governments pay for nearly everything by cheque. It is much easier and safer to pay by cheque than to carry around large amounts of currency.

The Winnipeg Mint is the most modern and efficient mint in the world. It produces nearly four million coins a day for various countries.

Legal tender is the lawful money that can be accepted by people and businesses in Canada. Legal tender in Canada consists of:

- Bank of Canada notes (paper currency)–up to any amount
- Silver coins–up to $10.00
- Nickel coins–up to $5.00
- Copper coins–up to $0.25
- Gold coins of Canada, Great Britain, and the United States.

When coins are taken to a financial institution, they should be rolled in coin wrappers or **"Penny Pinchers"**, re-usable plastic coin clips. These clips are colour-coded in four sizes and hold the number of coins normally rolled in paper coin wrappers. The Royal Bank of Canada was the first bank to introduce these convenience devices to their customers in the spring of 1978 to end what was, for many people, the nuisance of paper wrapping coins.

Each type of coin requires a different number of coins for a complete roll.

Coin	Number of Coins	Value of Roll
Quarters	40	$10.00
Dimes	50	$ 5.00
Nickels	40	$ 2.00
Coppers	50	$ 0.50

Most businesses ignore the requirements of legal tender and accept larger amounts of coin than the legal limit; so long as they feel the payment will be good, that is, collectible. Credit cards, money orders, United States coin and bills, even postage stamps are used and accepted for payment in Canada. And although cheques represent a large part of everyday business, they are *not* legal tender.

Forms of tender, larger than the legal requirements and cheques, do not have to be accepted. Retailers have the right to refuse a cheque as payment for goods and services in that it is not legal tender.

The Functions of Money

Our money has several functions, each of which is important. For many of us money is often something that lets us buy what we want. But money is much more than a medium of exchange. It represents a standard of value, a store of value, and a standard of future payment.

Medium of Exchange

Money makes it possible for you to obtain the goods and services you want without having to trade or barter for them. Suppose that you want to buy a record album and the only thing you have to trade is your time and services as a babysitter. This will be fine if the owner of the record store has children for you to babysit. If this is not so, you will have to look around to find a store owner who needs your services in exchange for the album you want. Without money, it could take you a long time to get that album you want. With money, you can buy the album at any store that sells it, and the store owner can use the money you provide to buy goods from other people. Money is the medium through which most daily business transactions occur–it is the **medium of exchange.**

Standard of Value

Money is the basis most societies use to determine the value of goods and services. Supposing you had found a record dealer willing to trade you a record album for your babysitting services. Both of you would then have to decide how many hours you'd have to babysit in return for the album. The owner wants ten hours of your time for the worth of the album, but you feel five hours is a fair trade. It is difficult to determine the worth of one item in terms of another, and this is just one of the reasons bartering is seldom used today.

With money, the value of all goods and services is measured in a term common to all: this is the **price** of the item. By using money as a **standard of value,** we all know how many babysitting hours equal an album. Money compares or measures the value of one item against another.

$3.00 an hour wages	for	eight hours of work	equals	one $24.00 blouse or shirt

Store of Value

Money is a **store of value** when we use it to save for the future. In the days of bartering, goods like fruit, vegetables, milk, and other perishable items had to be traded immediately. But money can be stored indefinitely. It need not be spent immediately.

Money allows you to purchase a record album whenever you want it. You might decide to wait two weeks before buying it for then the store will be holding a big sale; by waiting, you save $2.00 on its purchase. You have stored or saved the value of your money for this future want. Your money was, therefore, acting as a store of value.

Standard of Future Payment

The final function of money is acting as a **standard of future payment.** When you borrow money from a financial institution, you repay the money with interest at a future date. Suppose you want to buy a new five-speed bike for $125.00. You need the bike for your part-time work as a delivery clerk at a local store. You have saved $25.00 so far, leaving a balance of $100.00 to be paid. The store owner says you can pay $100.00 plus interest of $10.00–a total of $110.00 to be paid over the next ten months. You will pay the store owner $11.00 each month for ten months, at the end of which time you will have fully paid for the bike. Your money has thus served you as a basis or standard of future payments.

The Purchasing Power of Money

Money's true value is its **purchasing power**-what it will buy. Our purchasing power is represented by the amount of goods and services our dollars buy. We work to earn money to give us this purchasing power.

The paper used in printing currency is not worth much itself as paper. Our "silver" coins-nickels, dimes, and quarters-do not contain silver any more. The precious metal content of our coins is worth less than the actual value of the coins. For example, there is just a few cents worth of metal in a quarter. Our money is worth something only because all of us accept it as a value that means the same thing to everybody-two nickels equal one dime; four quarters equal one dollar. Ten ten-dollar bills equal one hundred dollars, and so on.

Money is a convenience. It is small, light, and easy to carry and store. The coins last a long time. Worn or torn paper currency can be easily exchanged at banks for new money. Our money is readily accepted by most people.

Our Changing Purchasing Power

Although money serves as a standard of value, the value of our money changes. The value of a dollar does not remain the same from year to year. The five dollars in your pocket or purse today will buy much less than it did when your parents were your age. You may have heard your parents say that a dollar does not go far any more, and this is true. What they were able to buy for thirty or forty cents costs a dollar to buy today. We need not even return to your parents' teens; five dollars today buys less for you than it did last year.

The purchasing power of our dollars changes as prices for goods and services change. An increase, infrequently a decrease, in the price of a single product does not greatly affect our overall purchasing power. For example, every winter Canadians pay more money for fresh fruit and vegetables in the supermarket. These food products must be imported or brought into Canada from the southern United States and other foreign countries. Our weather is too cold for growing many fruits and vegetables during the winter months. This increases our costs for fresh produce.

"I thought I'd better spend it before the dollar depreciates any more."

Inflation

When the prices of most goods and services increase or decrease, there is a very definite change in our overall purchasing power. A period of generally rising prices is **inflation**. A general decrease in prices is **deflation**. In recent years, inflation has been far more of a problem for consumers and governments than deflation.

Income and Inflation

During a period of inflation, each dollar you have buys less and less; more money is needed to buy goods and services. If prices double, your dollar buys only half as much. Between 1971 and 1977, prices in Canada rose sharply and reduced most people's purchasing power. In 1977, $1.67 was needed to buy what cost $1.00 in 1971.

If your income increases during a period of inflation, you may not suffer too much. But if the inflation rate in Canada is ten per cent and your salary or wage increases by only six per cent, your income is not keeping up to the price increases. Your purchasing power is less each time prices increase. People with **fixed incomes**, such as retired people receiving pensions, suffer most during an inflation.

Savings and Inflation

Besides reducing people's purchasing power, inflation affects people who save money. Your money is not serving as a good store of value. The dollars you are saving buy less and less as prices rise. If savings accounts earn six per cent interest each year and prices rise by five per cent each year, your savings are really earning only one per cent per year. Inflation, naturally, hurts people who save money for

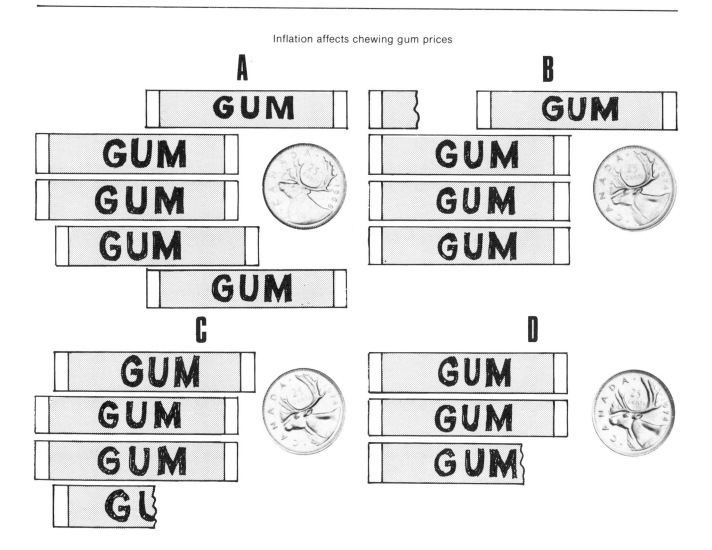

Inflation affects chewing gum prices

their retirement. As prices increase, their savings buy less and less. The result is reduced purchasing power with savings during retirement.

Borrowing and Inflation

Lenders and financial institutions also suffer during inflation. This is because loans are repaid with dollars worth less than when the money was first borrowed. Your parents borrow $6000 from a bank to purchase a car. If prices increase over the next few years, your parents will pay back the loan with dollars that buy less than the dollars they borrowed. Your parents have benefited from this inflation. The lender–the bank–suffers for the repayment dollars it receives do not have the same buying power as the money lent to your parents.

Causes of Inflation

People differ on why inflation occurs. There are many theories for its causes. One simplistic theory is that prices increase if there are not enough goods and services to meet the demand for them. Most people have jobs and have a regular income. This gives them adequate purchasing power. When there is a shortage of goods and services, many people do not appear to object to price increases. If they want the goods and services, they pay the required prices. But should prices continue to increase, employees will naturally demand higher wages to prevent a lessening of their purchasing power. Higher wages makes available even more money for buying goods and services. If there is an increase in the amount of money available to spend, there needs to be a similar increase in the production of goods and services. If there is no production increase even more inflation results.

Easy-to-obtain credit often produces similar effects. If financial institutions make too many loans, there is more money available for consumers to spend. The problem arises when there are not enough goods and services to meet this demand.

Government spending is also blamed for causing inflation. The money governments pay to people through various programs (pensions, family allowances, and other health and welfare plans), puts more money into the economy. If governments spend more money than they receive in taxes, they go into debt. This is called **deficit spending**. Governments must then borrow money. This extra money poured into the economy can increase prices and so cause inflation.

Controlling Inflation

There is no one single best solution for controlling inflation. If one simple solution existed, all government leaders would use it. The main reason for controlling inflation is to keep the value of our currency stable. But this is a difficult thing to do.

Governments attempt to play a major role in controlling inflation. They try to reduce spending by decreasing the public's demand for government goods and services. Every year millions of dollars are spent by all levels of government for highways, transportation, new buildings, office supplies, salaries, and so on. Much of our **public debt** can be reduced by governments controlling expenditures in these areas.

Governments attempt to control inflation by increasing taxes. Taking money from consumers this way means that consumers will have less money to use for their purchases. Tax increases are not popular with consumers as they have less money to spend. Thus, governments do not often use tax increases to control inflation for it is possible they will lose peoples' votes in the next election.

If interest rates are increased making credit borrowing more expensive, consumers are discouraged from buying expensive items. When loans are more costly, consumers and businesses often delay their spending.

Consumers can also voluntarily decide not to buy goods. Governments often attempt to persuade consumers to practice "voluntary restraint" and reduce their spending without government interference. If enough people stopped buying goods and services, a slowing effect on price increases might result. But unless large numbers of consumers are prepared to delay their spending, this is not thought of as a too effective method of controlling inflation.

The Anti-Inflation Board

In an effort to control inflation, governments can pass laws to control wages, salaries, and prices. In October, 1975, when inflation was running at twelve per cent annually and unemployment was high, the federal government established anti-inflation measures under the supervision of the Anti-Inflation Board.

These guidelines imposed controls on large corporations, unions, and workers. Ceilings were established for wage and salary increases for most Canadians. Companies were allowed to raise prices only to cover increased costs of producing their products. Any legitimate price increases were limited to once every three months. Jail terms of up to five years and fines from $200 to $10 000 were established for anyone defying the guidelines.

Between 1975 and 1978, inflation was reduced somewhat in Canada. However, by the spring of 1978 the rate of inflation was still higher than the four per cent that the federal government had hoped would exist by then. In April, 1978 the anti-inflation controls were removed. To prevent a return to high rates of inflation, prices and wages were to be monitored by government agencies, primarily the **Economic Council of Canada** to ensure that increases were reasonable and non-inflationary.

Deflation

Inflation is a period of generally rising prices. Deflation is a period of generally decreasing prices. This decrease results in more purchasing power as your dollars will buy more goods and services. However, deflation is not as good for the economy as we might think. Periods of serious deflation are usually bad for a country. Business firms fail and go out of business; unemployment is high and government action often becomes necessary. This involves cutting taxes, lowering interest rates, and increasing government spending. This additional money in the economy for spending should increase production of goods and services. But in common with the rest of Western society, Canada's economic history reveals more inflationary periods than deflationary ones.

UNIT B
SAVINGS AND INVESTING

Some day you may want to buy a new ten-speed bike, an electric guitar, a winter holiday in Florida, even a used car. These are things that are expensive, and you will need to save part of your income to be able to meet these needs. Borrowing money is the alternative.

Savings is the difference between the money you earn and the money you spend. During your lifetime, you will likely earn several hundreds of thousands of dollars, and how much of this will be saved will be up to you. It does not take a lot of money to begin saving money. No matter how little money you earn, it is wise to form the habit of saving some money each time you are paid. Starting to save while you are young gets you into the habit of saving as a regular part of your financial planning.

The Goals of Saving

The goals of saving are either short-term or long-term. Short-term savings goals are usually intended for the purchase of a not-too-expensive item within a short period of time. For example, perhaps you've been saving money since September to buy a pair of cross-country skis, poles, and ski boots for $95.00 at the annual after-Christmas sale at your local ski shop.

A long-term savings goal requires saving for a year or more for the purchase of an expensive item. For example, you and your family decide to spend your winter holiday in Mexico or the Caribbean as an escape from a cold and snowy Canadian winter. Since this trip will cost a few thousand dollars, money will have to be saved for a long time before you go south. Other examples of long-term goals are saving money to buy a car, a colour television, to pay for a college or university education, or to make the down payment on your first home. People save money for many different reasons. Some of these are examined below.

Emergencies

An accident or serious illness to the breadwinner in your family could cause sudden and unexpected expenses. There would be a reduction in money available to your family if the breadwinner was unable to work for some time. Suppose the company

or business employing the breadwinner in your family closes permanently as it is losing money and can no longer stay in business–another unexpected expense. Insurance exists as protection against risks like these but it does not always equal the losses. Suppose your five-year-old car needs $1500 worth of repairs to make it safe for the road. Should you spend this much money on an old car, or should you consider buying a new car? The amount of your savings, if you have any, may determine the decision you make. Savings would certainly help you or your family meet expenses during an emergency period. This is what is meant by the maxim "saving for a rainy day".

Future Needs and Security

Parents often save money to help pay for your educational expenses after you finish high school. Older people save to provide them with extra income for their retirement years. They set aside money during their working years to give them future financial security when they retire.

Many people save money to pay for their short and long-term goals. These are needs and wants like a new stove and refrigerator, a family holiday, or a new car. It is much easier to save if you have a specific goal in mind. Any time that you think of spending the money that you have in your savings, remember your savings goal.

Peace of Mind

Knowing that they have money saved for unexpected emergencies, opportunities, and future needs gives many people peace of mind. This sense of security and satisfaction, knowing that there is a sum of money saved, is a comfortable feeling.

The Amount in Savings

In the 1960s and early 1970s, financial experts recommended that families should have savings equal to three or four months' income. Saving ten per cent of your income was another suggested guideline. Unfortunately, with inflation and high unemployment, such guidelines are difficult to accomplish. Recommendations like these are not as realistic as they once were since many families today are spending first and then saving, if there is any money left over to save. Two married people who are both working and who have no children may have a greater total income than a married couple with one working parent and two children, although it is not necessarily true that the couple with children have the greater financial responsibilities.

What is true is that a couple with children do have additional responsibilities. But the childless couple may have a higher standard of living because of their combined salaries and so they have purchased a more expensive car, take two vacations a year, and eat out more regularly because both of them work. Their total financial responsibilities can be just as high as the family although their expenses are quite different.

The amount you should save is something only you alone can determine. If you want to save money for a winter vacation that will cost $2000 and you have a year in which to save, you will need to save about $40 a week. If you don't have a particular goal to save for, save as much as you can each week or each month. But don't plan your savings so tightly that you are unable to meet your regular, basic expenses. Any money that you can save is better than none at all.

Personal Savings Accounts

There are several different ways in which people can save money. It can be invested in stocks and bonds as explained later. It can also be deposited in a savings account in a financial institution. You can have a personal savings account in your own name which gives you full control over the account. A joint account is often opened in the name of two or more persons, usually a wife and husband or parent and child. During the lifetime of each individual, each of them may deposit and withdraw money from the account. Savings accounts are easy to open and use.

Different types of savings accounts are available in the different types of institutions. But all savings accounts operate in much the same way. Chartered banks, trust companies, and credit unions are the main savings institutions in Canada.

Opening a Savings Account

Opening a savings account is a simple matter. The steps involved in opening such an account are similar in all savings institutions. A $1.00 minimum is usually all the money that is needed to open an account.

Let's assume that Stephen Pundyk, a Grade 9 student, earns $10.00 a week minimum from cutting grass in the summer and shovelling snow in the winter. He decides to open a savings account in one of the bank branches in his community. Someone at the bank needs certain personal information about him, such as his name, address, telephone number, and occupation. Some institutions only require the customer's name, account number, and the customer's signature. Steve would list *student* as his occupation. This information is recorded on a signature card. (If you are going to open a savings account, it is important to sign this card with the signature that you use all the time as it is your identification to the bank.) Anyone can deposit money in Steve's account but he is the only one able to withdraw or take money from it. With his signature on file, the bank can check it against the signature on cheques and withdrawal slips before money is withdrawn from his account.

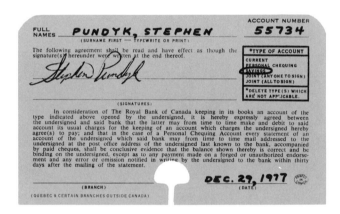

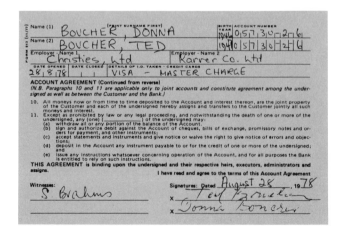

HERMAN

"I wanna open a joint-account with someone who's got plenty of dough."

138

Steve can do two things with his savings account: deposit money and withdraw money. Each time that he (or anyone else) deposits money, a **deposit slip** must be completed. It shows the amount of money being deposited in the account. The bank keeps this slip as a record.

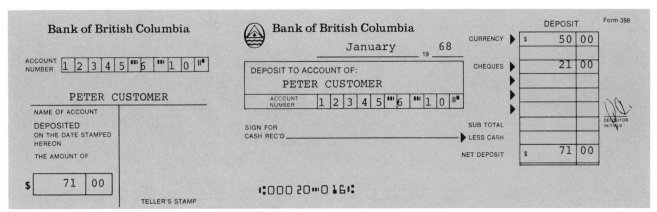

Steve is given a **passbook** by the bank, which is his record of his bank account. Each time he deposits or withdraws money from his account, his passbook records the transactions. Each account at the bank has a different number; this number usually appears on the front of each passbook.

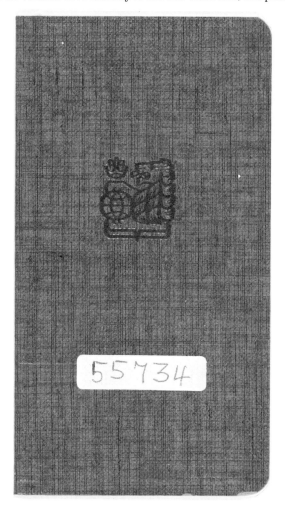

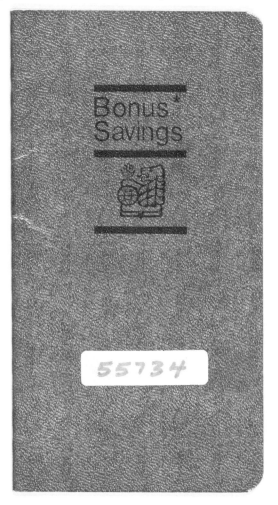

Steve wants to withdraw $5.00 from his savings account to buy a school yearbook. To do this, he must fill out a **withdrawal slip** and sign it. This order allows the bank to pay him the amount of money he wants to take out. Like the deposit slip, the withdrawal slip is kept by the bank for its records. The amount of the $5.00 withdrawal is then recorded in Steve's passbook, leaving him a new balance of $20.00.

Steve is also able to write cheques on his account, although his account is primarily used for saving money. Handling and processing cheques is a major concern of banks. Canadians pay more than three-quarters of all their bills by cheque. For this reason, banks charge a fee or **service charge** for the privilege of writing cheques. Some banks allow customers one free cheque every three months for each $1 of quarterly minimum balance, and cash withdrawals are free in all banks. Each additional cheque costs twenty cents in most banks. Because Steve can use his account for making deposits, withdrawing money, and writing cheques, it is called a **regular** or **chequing savings account**.

Benefits of Savings Accounts

Savings accounts in financial institutions have many benefits: they earn interest on your money, the money is protected, and it can be withdrawn easily.

Savings Accounts Earn Interest

Money deposited in a savings account earns money. This additional money or **interest** is the money that the savings institutions pay you for the use of your money and the money of the other depositors. Much of the money that is deposited in savings institutions is available for **loans** to people wanting to borrow money.

The rate of interest that people receive for the money they have deposited differs from institution to institution. Rates also rise and fall with economic conditions in the country.

There is also a difference in the number of times a year that the institution pays the interest to you. Some institutions pay **semi-annually**, twice a year. Other institutions pay **quarterly**, every three months. The practice followed for calculating interest varies. The more often interest is paid, the

CIBC'S *signature verification system* compares signatures thus reducing fraud and increasing customer service. The system also produces account information.

greater the return on the money in an account.

Procedures for determining the amount of money on which the interest calculations are made vary. One method is to pay interest on the lowest or smallest amount of money in the account during a specified period. Other institutions pay interest on the average amount of money in the account during the specified period. The federal government is suggesting that financial institutions begin to consider calculating interest daily and crediting it to the account quarterly. As you can see, it is wise to compare the interest rates and the method of calculation before deciding which institution offers the best deal.

Savings Are Insured

Savings accounts are protected and guaranteed. Deposits are protected in chartered banks and trust companies to a maximum of $20 000 for each account held if the institutions are members of the **Canada Deposit Insurance Corporation.** The savings institutions pay for this insurance thus guaranteeing depositors' accounts to the maximum amount stated. Credit union deposits are guaranteed dollar for dollar by the provincial credit union organizations.

The Liquidity of Savings

An important feature of a savings account is that it can usually be withdrawn on demand. If you have such an account and need cash in a hurry, you can usually get it right away from a regular savings account. However, to prevent a drain or a "run" on the banks' money occurring at any one time, banks *can* require fifteen days notice of withdrawal of all or any part of the amount in a person's account. This seldom happens, especially for small or reasonable amounts of money. Funds that can be withdrawn quickly and easily are said to be **liquid.** A savings account is a very liquid asset in that you can withdraw money quickly and without notice most times.

Other Savings Plans

With a regular savings account, similar to the one Steve opened, you can make deposits, withdraw money, and write cheques on the account at any time. Because of this, the savings institution must have enough cash available at all times to meet the withdrawal and payment requirements of their depositors. This reduces the amount of money that the institutions have for loans and so, naturally, the interest rate paid on regular savings accounts is usually not as high as a true or straight savings account.

Savings institutions have other types of savings plans to encourage saving money with them and to help people reach different goals. These other savings plans include non-chequing savings accounts, term deposits, retirement savings plans, and home ownership plans.

Non-chequing Savings Accounts

As the name of this account suggests, it allows people to make deposits and withdraw money but not to write cheques. The money saved stays put until needed. Some banks refer to this type of account as **bonus** or **true savings.** Since this account is strictly a savings account, the interest rate is higher than the interest paid on regular savings accounts with cheque-writing privileges.

Term Deposits

Term deposits are a good savings plan for amounts of money that you won't need for some time. You agree to leave your money with the savings institution for a fixed term or period of time. The term is usually for one to five years, although it can be for a short a time as thirty days. The rate of interest depends on the amount of money deposited and the length of time of the deposit. If you must withdraw your money before the end of the agreed-upon term, you will receive a lesser amount of interest. Some savings institutions will *not* allow you to withdraw your money early, while others will charge a special fee.

Home Ownership Savings Plans

Many people who want to buy a house find it difficult to save enough money for a down payment. A **registered home ownership savings plan (RHOSP)** is a plan to help people save for this purpose. RHOSP was introduced by the federal government to assist people to purchase a home in today's inflated economy. RHOSPs are sold by banks, trust companies, and credit unions.

Any Canadian resident, eighteen years of age or over, married or single, who does not own or have any interest in any property used as a dwelling house may establish an RHOSP. In 1978 you could contribute up to $1000 a year to a lifetime maximum of $10 000. The life of an RHOSP is limited to twenty years from the time it is established. Money may be withdrawn at any time within that period of time in one lump sum. You are entitled to have only one RHOSP in your lifetime. Once you have ended your plan, you can never establish another one.

This special savings plan is registered with the federal government and is tax deductible from income. In 1978, two people, each contributing their $1000 limit for ten years, with added interest earned, could save close to $30 000 for a down payment and purchase of a home. And all of this money is completely tax free when used as a down payment or put towards the construction of a home.

143

Registered Retirement Savings Plan

The **registered retirement savings plan (RRSP)** was also introduced by the federal government. It allows Canadians to defer, until a later time in life, paying tax on part of their income while building up a savings fund for their retirement.

There is an overall limit of twenty per cent of earned income for everybody, except that people who contribute to a pension plan where they work are limited to a maximum of $3500, less their contributions to their employer's plan. For example, if you have contributed $1600 to a pension plan through your employment, you can contribute up to an additional $1900 toward the purchase of an RRSP. Self-employed people or those not members of an employee pension plan can have a contribution limit of up to $5500. You can save money now, paying no tax on the money paid into the plan until much later in life.

Until 1978, if the plan was used the way for which it was designed, the money in the plan had to be taken out some time before or on reaching the age of seventy-one and used to purchase a **life annuity** from an insurance company. An annuity provides regular income for the rest of the holder's life. Many retiring people choose an annuity that pays them a certain guaranteed number of dollars each month for as long as they live. Annuities are discussed in greater detail in Chapter 10.

Two new options that provide more freedom in choosing how to invest RRSP savings were introduced in the spring federal budget in 1978: investment of RRSP savings into a new **fixed-term annuity** designed to provide benefits to age ninety and investment of RRSP savings into a new, self-administered **Registered Retirement Income Fund (RRIF)**, which allows increasing payouts each year to more or less meet inflation. Any institutions that now provide RRSPs are permitted to provide these new investment plans, and transfer to them must occur between the ages of sixty and seventy-one. This increased competition for the savings dollar is expected to provide better rates of return for the holders of these plans.

Investments

When people save money in a savings institution, interest is earned and the money is well protected against loss. But, as you read earlier, during inflationary periods, this money loses value in terms of its purchasing power. When people invest money, the original investment can increase or decrease. For example, if you had a bushel of wheat and stored it away for future use, it would be a *savings*.

However, if you planted that wheat and it produced more wheat, it would be an **investment**.

Investing has two major advantages over savings: there is often a higher **rate of return** and a chance of making a profit, and investments may grow in value in periods of inflation while savings remain the same or lose value. But, there is one major disadvantage of investing; there is an **element of risk**. While savings are secure and protected in savings institutions, investments can be reduced if the investment fails. In fact, it is possible to lose some or even all of the money invested. Thus, investors look for reliable and safe sources where money can grow slowly and steadily and where the risk involved is limited. Three principal forms of investment are the purchase of Canada Savings Bonds, stocks, and corporation bonds. Each of these investments and their different characteristics are examined below.

Canada Savings Bonds

A Canada Savings Bond is a printed promise by the government of Canada to pay the purchaser of the bond a certain sum of money plus interest on a definite future date, the **maturity date**. By purchasing such a bond, you are actually lending money to the government. Provincial and municipal bonds are also available for purchase, but Canada Savings Bonds are the ones most commonly purchased by many Canadians from banks, trust companies, credit unions, stock brokers, and investment dealers.

Canada Savings Bonds have been issued annually since 1946 between October 1 and mid November by the federal government to provide a safe, secure investment that earns reasonable rates of interest for Canadians. These bonds are available in denominations of $100, $300, $500, $1 000, and $5 000 up to a total purchase limit of $15 000.

There are several definite advantages of purchasing Canada Savings Bonds as an investment. They are instant cash as they can be cashed in or **redeemed** at any time at which time you receive the full or **face value** of the bond plus the interest earned up to that date. This is a useful feature if money is needed quickly to meet an emergency. Each fall when the new series of Canada Savings Bonds is issued, many **bondholders** redeem their bonds if the interest rate features on the new series is better than that on the previous series.

Another advantage is that these bonds can be purchased through **payroll deduction**-a small amount of money is deducted from each pay cheque until the value of the bond has been reached. This is of benefit to those people who find it difficult to save money. Finally, Canada Savings Bonds are a good investment for people prepared to accept the safety and reasonable return on bonds in exchange for not having to worry about the money they have invested.

A Choice of Bonds

Since the fall of 1977, Canada Savings Bonds are available in two forms; the regular interest bond and a new compound interest bond. The **regular interest bond** automatically pays the bondholder interest each November 1. There is a choice of receiving interest by cheque or by a direct deposit into the holder's chequing or savings account. This type of bond comes in denominations starting at $300.

The **compound interest bond** re-invests the earned interest automatically, so that interest is earned on interest after the first year. Interest is payable only at maturity or when the bonds are redeemed. Using the Canada Savings Bonds dated November 1, 1977 as an example, the compound interest bond increases in value as follows at an average annual interest to maturity of 8.06 per cent.

Nov. 1	Value	Nov. 1	Value	Nov. 1	Value
1978	$107.00	1981	$135.63	1984	$171.77
1979	115.81	1982	146.76	1985	185.81
1980	125.34	1983	158.78	1986	200.97

Thus, if left to maturity, a $100 bond will grow to $200.97 in just nine years. This type of bond is available in a minimum denomination of $100.

When you purchase Canada Savings Bonds, you are required to provide your **Social Insurance Number,** which acts as a single lifetime account number for you whenever you purchase these bonds. It is an accurate identification number to provide you with better and faster services.

Investing in Business Corporations

Business corporations often need to raise money to increase production, expand the size of their operation, to introduce new products to the marketplace, and so on. Small sums of money can be borrowed from financial institutions while large sums of money can be obtained from the sale of two forms of investment **securities;** shares of stock and corporate

bonds. Thousands of Canadians purchase these investments and provide the necessary funds to assist the growth of Canadian corporations.

Corporate Bonds

People buying **corporate bonds** are lending money to corporations and become the **creditors** just as the people buying Canada Savings Bonds are lending money to the federal government. **Bonds** are a definite promise to repay, at some future date, money borrowed by the corporation issuing them. For the use of this money, the bondholders receive a **fixed rate of interest** payable regularly each year. For this reason, bonds are **fixed-income investments.** The interest rate is determined by the reputation and credit rating of the corporation issuing the bond and by the general interest rates that exist in Canada at the time of issue. Bond interest rates must be high enough to attract serious investors and to provide them with a reasonable return on their investment.

Most corporate bonds have a face value of $1000, although some are issued for smaller and larger amounts. Interest is calculated on the bond's face value. For example, the Ontario Hydro bond with a value of $1000 pays interest of $46.25 twice a year until the bond matures on January 6, 2004. **Interest coupons**, each bearing a different due date, are attached to the bond. As each date arrives, the holder can clip off the coupon and redeem it for $46.25 or keep all the coupons attached to the bond and then cash them in when the bond is redeemed. If bondholders want their money back before the bond's maturity date, they can sell them on the market at current prices. This **market value** may be more or less than the bond's original face value. This value depends on what other investors are willing to pay for the bonds. As such, they are a little less **liquid** than savings accounts and Canada Savings Bonds. Although some bonds change in price, such changes are generally slight. People, who purchase corporate bonds, generally do so for the regular interest income rather than for highly profitable investments.

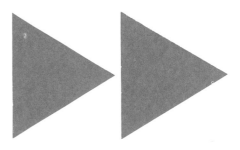

145

$1,000

$1,000

A
AU3-K
00000

A
AU3-K
00000

Ontario Hydro
SPECIMEN

9-1/4% BOND SERIES AU3 DUE JANUARY 6, 2004

(SUBJECT TO PRIOR REDEMPTION)

THE FIRST PAYMENT OF INTEREST ON THIS BOND IS FOR THE PERIOD FROM MARCH 10, 1977 TO JULY 6, 1977 AND THEREFORE THIS BOND UNTIL AFTER JULY 6, 1977 MAY ONLY BE EXCHANGED FOR OTHER BONDS OF SERIES AU3 ON WHICH THE FIRST PAYMENT OF INTEREST IS FOR THE SAME PERIOD OF TIME.

CUSIP 683078 AV 1

GUARANTEED AS TO PRINCIPAL AND INTEREST BY THE PROVINCE OF ONTARIO

ONTARIO HYDRO (hereinafter called the "Corporation") for value received hereby promises to pay to the bearer on the 6th day of January, 2004, or on such earlier date as this Bond may be redeemed in accordance with the provisions for redemption hereinafter set forth, on presentation and surrender of this Bond, the sum of

ONE THOUSAND DOLLARS

in lawful money of Canada at any branch of any Chartered Bank in the Province of Ontario or in any of the Cities of St. John's, Halifax, Charlottetown, Saint John, Quebec, Montreal, Winnipeg, Regina, Calgary, Edmonton, Vancouver or Victoria, Canada, at holder's option, with interest thereon from the 10th day of March, 1977 at the rate of Nine and one-quarter per centum (9-1/4%) per annum payable half-yearly in like money at any of the said places, at holder's option, on the 6th day of January and the 6th day of July in each year of the currency of this Bond on presentation and surrender of the interest coupons hereto annexed as they severally become due.

The Corporation shall have the right at its option to redeem the Bonds of this Series AU3, either in whole or in part, in advance of maturity, on any interest payment date on or after the 6th day of January, 1997 at the places where and in the money in which the said Bonds are expressed to be payable, upon payment of the principal amount thereof together with interest accrued thereon to the date of redemption, and upon giving previous notice of such redemption by advertisement once in at least one City in each of the Provinces of Canada in a daily newspaper of general circulation published in such City, such notice to be advertised as aforesaid at least thirty (30) days before the date fixed for redemption. In the event that less than all of the said Bonds shall be redeemed, the Bonds to be redeemed shall be chosen by lot in such manner as the Corporation may deem equitable, and for the purpose of redemption and selection for redemption, each Bond of a denomination greater than $1,000 may be deemed to consist of the appropriate number of units of $1,000 each and any part of the principal amount of such Bond comprising one or more of such units may accordingly be selected and called for redemption. In the event of the selection for redemption of a portion only of the principal amount of any coupon Bond, payment of the redemption price of such portion will be made only upon surrender of such Bond with all unmatured interest coupons attached in exchange for a coupon Bond or Bonds of this Series for the unredeemed balance of such principal amount, with all unmatured interest coupons attached. In the event of the selection for redemption of a portion only of the principal amount of any fully registered Bond, payment of the redemption price of such portion will be made only upon surrender of such Bond in exchange for a fully registered Bond or Bonds of this Series for the unredeemed balance of such principal amount.

This Bond is subject to the Conditions endorsed hereon which form part hereof.

This Bond is issued under the authority of The Power Corporation Act, Revised Statutes of Ontario, 1970, Chapter 354, as amended, and of an Order of the Lieutenant Governor in Council.

IN WITNESS WHEREOF the Corporation has caused its Corporate Seal and the engraved facsimile signature of its Chairman or Vice-Chairman or President to be affixed hereto and this Bond to be duly signed by an Authorized Signing Officer of the Corporation and to be dated the 10th day of March, 1977.

GUARANTEE BY THE PROVINCE OF ONTARIO
BY VIRTUE OF THE POWERS CONFERRED BY THE LEGISLATURE OF THE PROVINCE OF ONTARIO AND OF AN ORDER OF THE LIEUTENANT GOVERNOR IN COUNCIL, THE PROVINCE OF ONTARIO HEREBY GUARANTEES TO THE HOLDER FOR THE TIME BEING OF THIS BOND AND TO THE HOLDER FOR THE TIME BEING OF ANY OF THE COUPONS ATTACHED THERETO, DUE PAYMENT OF THE PRINCIPAL OF THIS BOND AND OF THE INTEREST THEREON ACCORDING TO THE TENOR OF THE SAID BOND AND OF THE COUPONS ATTACHED THERETO.

Treasurer of Ontario

Chairman

Authorized Signing Officer

B A BANK NOTE OTTAWA

Ontario Hydro $46.25 JAN. 2004
SPECIMEN AU3-K
COUPON NO F54

Ontario Hydro $46.25 JULY 2003
SPECIMEN AU3-K
COUPON NO F53

Ontario Hydro $46.25 JAN. 2003
SPECIMEN AU3-K
COUPON NO F52

Ontario Hydro $46.25 JULY 2002
FORTY-SIX 25/100 DOLLARS
SPECIMEN AU3-K
COUPON NO F51

147

Shares of Stock

People buying **shares of stock** become part owners or **shareholders** of the corporations selling the stock. In large corporations there may be thousands of shareholders who, as part owners, are eligible to share in the company's profits. In some small companies the stock may not be for sale to the general public but owned instead by the people who founded the company.

Many corporations issue two kinds of stock: common and preferred. **Common stock**, the type most frequently issued, gives purchasers the right to attend shareholders' meetings and to vote on company matters. Purchasers hoping to influence company policy are likely to purchase as much common stock as possible and as much as they can afford since each share equals one vote. **Preferred stock**, as the name suggests, gives purchasers certain advantages or preferences. Once the company's expenses have been paid from its profits, the board of directors of the company may declare or vote to pay a **dividend**–a portion of the profits–to the shareholders. The main advantage to preferred shareholders is that they receive a dividend for each share of stock earned before any dividends are paid to the common shareholders.

The payment of dividends increases the value of the stock and because of this, many people will want to invest their money in the corporation. In a good business year, the rate of dividend paid to common shareholders may be greater than the fixed rate paid to preferred shareholders. In a poor year, the dividend paid to common holders may be much less or even nothing at all. Thus, dividends paid the common shareholders vary each year depending on the company's earnings and profits. There is, therefore, less risk in preferred stock since prices tend to be more stable and dividends fixed, but there is less chance of big gains in years of high profit.

Another advantage to preferred shareholders is that if a corporation went out of business and the inventory, equipment, and other assets were sold, the preferred shareholders would get back the value of their investments before the common shareholders. All people who purchase both common and preferred shares in corporations are liable only for the amount of money they invest if the company goes out of business. For example, if you had purchased ten shares at thirty dollars each, you would only lose that $300 if the company fails and nothing else. This is an example of **limited liability**; your liability is limited to the limit or extent of your investment.

The Stock Exchange

The **stock exchange** provides a convenient marketplace for the buying and selling of shares of stock. There are several stock exchanges in Canada, the major ones located in Toronto, Montreal, and Vancouver. The stock exchange brings buyers and sellers of stocks together so that both parties can do what they want. Stocks are often listed on more than one exchange.

Before a person can buy and sell stock at a stock exchange, that person must be a member and have purchased a **seat** on the **exchange**. Anyone who wants to buy a seat must purchase it from someone who already owns one. Individuals purchasing a seat, if one is available, are usually members of an investment firm that buys and sells stock for their customers. These seats entitle the holder and representatives, the **"floor traders"**, to trade stocks on the floor of the exchange.

The actual sale of shares takes place between **stock brokers** who act as agents of the owners of the stock. People wanting to sell shares of stock contact stock brokers in their communities, telling the brokers what they have to sell. The brokers have bought the privilege of dealing on the floor of the stock exchange and thus contact their floor traders. These traders walk around the floor of the exchange shouting the prices of the different stocks they have to sell. Other traders, acting for people who want to buy, have the prices they are willing to pay for stocks. When the buyer and seller agree on a price, a sale is made. These sales usually occur at the **trading posts** on the floor of the exchange. A large **ticker tape** records the transaction and also lists current prices of all listed stocks.

Once the two traders reach an agreement, they contact their respective offices indicating that the sale and purchase have been completed. It is usually easy to buy and sell shares of stock because buyers and sellers are easy to find. Since stock brokers are providing a service, they charge a **commission** for both buying and selling.

The current prices of the more common and popular stocks are listed in most daily newspapers. These stock quotations usually list the highest price paid for the stock during the current year, the lowest price during the year, the number of shares traded each day, the highest and the lowest price paid for the stock that day, and the last or closing price of the stock that day.

Other Investments

Real estate is another common form of investment, and this involves the purchase of a home or a piece of property. Putting money into your own or someone else's business is another way of investing. Investing in your future is a very personal kind of investment.

The Wise Investor

Investing involves putting money to work in a safe and reasonable manner to earn additional money in the form of interest, dividends, or profit. Before you invest, check the following criteria:

- safety of the investment
- assurance of income (the interest or dividends you expect to receive)
- liquidity (the ease of converting the investment into cash)
- growth of investment (the chances of the investment increasing or decreasing).

Investing money has its risks and rewards. Comparison shop for an investment just as you would for goods and services to be a wise consumer.

149

UNIT C

BANKS AND
OTHER FINANCIAL INSTITUTIONS

Most people use the services of a bank, trust company, or credit union. These are the main **financial institutions** in Canada today. To use these institutions effectively, you should have some understanding of them and their services. Then you will be able to use them to good advantage.

Financial institutions are essential to our economy. They accept deposits, encourage savings, and safeguard your money. They provide loan money to individuals and businesses, and they allow business transactions to be handled by the writing of millions of cheques every day. This unit will examine these basic functions and other available services in greater detail. Since there are about 7600 bank branches all across Canada, most of the discussion will focus on the Canadian banking system. It is the system with which you are probably most familiar.

The Early Years of Canadian Banking

Unit A described the development of the money system from bartering to the acceptance of paper money. The beginnings of trade and commerce created a need for banks as it became difficult to barter any longer.

The first bank in Canada was established by a group of merchants in Montreal in late 1817. This bank accepted deposits and made loans. It later became the Bank of Montreal or, as its advertisements now state, the First Canadian Bank. By the time of Confederation in 1867, thirty-five banks were operating in Canada. Since 1867, new banks have been established and others have **merged** or joined together. For example, the Bank of Commerce (established in 1867) and the Imperial Bank of Canada (established in 1875) merged in 1961 to form the Canadian Imperial Bank of Commerce. Similarly, the Bank of Toronto (1871) and the Dominion Bank (1856) formed the Toronto Dominion Bank in 1955.

Today, the Canadian banking system consists of eleven chartered banks with their head offices and thousands of branches across the country. Some of today's banks were originally established under other names. The Merchant's Bank of Halifax, established in 1869, became The Royal Bank of Canada in 1901.

In order of chronological establishment, Canada's chartered banks are: Bank of Montreal, The Bank of Nova Scotia, Toronto Dominion Bank, The Provincial Bank of Canada, Canadian Imperial Bank of Commerce, The Royal Bank of Canada, Bank Canadian National, The Mercantile Bank of Canada, Bank of British Columbia, Canadian Commercial and Industrial Bank, and Northland Bank. The last two banks were established in 1976.

The Chartered Banks of Canada

Bank of Montreal
P.O. Box 6002
Montreal, Quebec
H3C 3B1

Toronto Dominion Bank
P.O. Box 1
Toronto Dominion Centre
Toronto, Ontario
M5K 1A2

Canadian Imperial Bank
 of Commerce
Commerce Court
Toronto, Ontario
M5L 1A2

Bank Canadian National
Place d'Armes
Montreal, Quebec
H2Y 2W3

Bank of British Columbia
1725-Two Bentall Centre
Vancouver, B.C.
V7X 1K1

Northland Bank
1200 Home Oil Tower
324 8th Avenue S.W.
Calgary, Alberta
T2P 2Z2

The Bank of Nova Scotia
44 King Street West
Toronto, Ontario
M5H 1E2

The Provincial Bank of Canada
221 St. James Street West
Montreal, Quebec
H2Y 1M7

The Royal Bank of Canada
P.O. Box 6001
Montreal, Quebec
H3C 3A9

The Mercantile Bank of Canada
P.O. Box 520
Montreal, Quebec
H3C 2T6

Canadian Commercial and Industrial Bank
1801 Toronto Dominion Tower
Edmonton Centre
Edmonton, Alberta
T5J 2Z1

Source: The Canadian Bankers' Association

Organization of Branch Banking

All banks in Canada receive a **charter**, or authority to operate, from the federal government. Each of the eleven chartered banks has a **head office** in one of Canada's large cities. Head offices determine bank policy. Connected to head office are the thousands of different bank branches spread all across Canada. Most of the main business of banking, accepting deposits and making loans, is done at the branch level. Canadian banks have also established branches in more than forty foreign countries. This is why our banking system is called a **branch banking system**.

You are probably aware of new bank branches opening in your community. There is strong competition among the chartered banks to be the first one to open a branch in a new area or to provide service to a new economic development. Because of this, there are now branches serviced by air inside the Arctic Circle. A branch bank was opened in Leduc, Alberta, the day after the first producing oil well delivered its first supply of oil. Some remote towns and villages along the north shore of the Gulf of St. Lawrence are serviced by ship. Even mobile trailers have been used to provide banking services for construction workers and settlers in remote areas.

Because many Canadian banks contain the name of a province or a city in their titles, some Canadians believe that our banks are owned and operated by the provinces or cities in the name of the banks, but this is not so. All of Canada's chartered banks are business organizations, owned by people who have bought shares of stock in the bank to become part owners. There are about 196 000 **shareholders,** and more than ninety-four per cent of these shareholders are Canadians. More than twice as many Canadians today own bank stock compared with ten years ago.

In the United States banks operate under a **unit banking system**; each bank is a separate operation, locally owned and operated. U.S. banks offer basically the same services as Canadian chartered banks, but the unit banks are not part of a unified national system.

Advantages of Branch Banking

Our branch banking system provides residents of small communities everywhere in Canada with the same services that residents of the largest cities have. And this is done at no extra cost to the residents in the small communities. It would be too expensive for a U.S. unit bank to open in a small or remote community, and residents of the United States are, therefore, not as well served by their

151

banks as Canadians. In Canada, bank branches provide the financial contact between small communities and the big cities.

Another advantage of the Canadian banking system is that a bank can **diversify** or spread out its loans to reduce risk. Since branches are located in areas of different economic conditions, a crop failure in Saskatchewan or a poor fishing supply in Nova Scotia will not affect the bank too seriously. If one branch is in need of money to meet emergency situations, head office is able to come to its aid. The branch banks support one another; the full resources of each bank stand behind every branch.

Each branch, no matter how small, is fully supported by the expertise and services of the bank's head office. Specialists in many different areas service the branches. For example, each branch manager has the authority to grant loans up to a certain limit, usually about $50 000, without referring the loan application to head office. If such a referral is necessary, personnel in head office handle the request quickly and efficiently.

Finally, branch banks provide an excellent training ground for men and women interested in banking careers. New employees will usually begin work in a branch bank, often in their home town. After a period of time there, he or she will be transferred to another branch in another part of the country to gain experience and knowledge of the concerns and economic conditions existing in that area. Each transfer and promotion leads to increased responsibility within the banking system.

CCDO(A) ★ BRANCH BANK MANAGER ★
PLANS, ORGANIZES, DIRECTS AND CONTROLS
THROUGH SUBORDINATE MANAGERS OR SUPER-
VISORS, BANKING ACTIVITIES IN HEAD
OFFICE DEPARTMENT, REGIONAL TERRITORY OR
BRANCH OF CHARTERED BANK.
PERFORMS SEVERAL DUTIES, APPLYING
SPECIALIZED KNOWLEDGE OF BANKING
ACTIVITIES.
ENSURES ESTABLISHED OPERATING POLICIES
AND PROCEDURES ARE CARRIED OUT IN
RESPECT TO: ACCEPTING OF DEPOSITS FROM
THE PUBLIC, MAKING OF LOANS FOR BUSINESS
AGRICULTURE AND CONSUMER REQUIREMENTS,
SELLING OF SECURITIES, DEALING IN
FOREIGN EXCHANGE, PROVIDING OF SAFE-
KEEPING FACILITIES AND RECEIVING AND
PAYING OUT OF CASH. ADVISES BANK CLIENTS
REGARDING INVESTMENT AND OTHER MONETARY
AFFAIRS AND SOUND BUSINESS PRACTICES.
APPROVES GRANTS OR DECLINES LOANS TO
BANK CUSTOMERS WITHIN LIMITS LAID DOWN
BY HEAD OFFICE. ENSURES THAT SUFFICIENT
COLLATERAL IS HELD REGARDING AUTHORIZED
LINES OF CREDIT. STUDIES ORGANIZATION,
OPERATION AND FINANCIAL BACKGROUND OF
LOCAL INDUSTRIES TO BE IN A POSITION TO
ASSESS ANY FUTURE REQUESTS FOR LINES OF
CREDIT. DEVELOPS AND RECOMMENDS PLANS
FOR NEW FORMS OF LENDING ACTIVITY OR
PROGRAM EXPANSION. INVESTIGATES AND
SETTLES CUSTOMER COMPLAINTS REGARDING
SERVICE, AND PARTICIPATES IN VARIOUS
COMMUNITY ACTIVITIES TO PROMOTE SERVICES
OFFERED BY BANK.

★BANK MANAGER TRAINING★
STUDENTS MAY APPLY FOR TRAINING WITH A
MINIMUM OF GRADE 12 OR 13 BUT BANKS ARE
NOW LOOKING FOR THE GRADUATE FROM THE 2
AND 3 YEAR BUSINESS PROGRAMS AT CAAT,
THE BUSINESS ADMINISTRATION GRADUATE IN
FINANCE AND/OR MARKETING FROM RYERSON AS
WELL AS THOSE WITH UNIVERSITY TRAINING.
THE BANK TRAINING IS GIVEN IN A TWO TO
THREE YEAR DEVELOPMENT PROGRAM WHERE THE
STUDENT ACTS AS ACCOUNTANT AND TAKES
BANK TRAINING COURSES. A STUDY PROGRAM
IS SPONSORED BY THE CANADIAN BANKERS'
ASSOCIATION. THIS COURSE IS OFFERED AS
AN EVENING (EXTENSION) PROGRAM AT MOST
UNIVERSITIES AND AT A FEW COMMUNITY
COLLEGES.

Regulation of Banks: The Bank Act

In 1867, the Canadian constitution, the British North America Act, gave the federal government control over such things as currency and coinage, the issue of paper money, and banking and the establishment of banks. This guaranteed that all banks in Canada would operate under similar rules to create a unified banking system.

In 1871, the first *Bank Act* was passed. This was the first permanent legislation regulating banks and banking across Canada. Since 1871 there have been ten major revisions of the *Bank Act*, the last in 1978. Every ten years, the *Bank Act* is re-examined in great detail by Parliament. There have been a few occasions in which it has been necessary for Parliament to extend the existing Act to allow more time to examine the legislation before revising it. Such detailed revisions keep the *Bank Act* up to date and allows it to meet the current needs of society and the business community.

The *Bank Act* contains the rules and regulations under which the banking system operates. It outlines the procedures for opening new banks, the minimum amount of money required, how mergers are effected, and other details of what banks are allowed and not allowed to do. It also describes the reports that banks must regularly make to the federal Minister of Justice and to the Inspector General of Banks, an official in the federal finance department. Procedures are outlined for at least one yearly examination of each bank's head office records; bank branches are inspected on a regular basis too.

The Bank of Canada

Many of you will have heard of the Bank of Canada. It is not one of the eleven chartered banks, and it offers no direct services to the general public. It is owned by the federal government and is responsible for keeping Canadian business conditions stable.

The Bank of Canada is Canada's central bank. All the chartered banks have regular dealings with it. The *Bank Act* requires that each of the eleven chartered banks deposit a certain percentage of their customers' deposits on reserve with the Bank of Canada. This guarantees the chartered banks a certain amount of ready cash to meet the unexpected needs of their depositors.

The central bank also issues the paper money in circulation in Canada. You will see "Bank of Canada" printed on all of our Canadian bank notes. This bank also controls the supply of money and credit in Canada. With this control, the Bank of

Canada has a major influence on Canadian economic and banking policies.

Finally, the chartered banks use their deposits with the central bank to settle accounts among themselves. This is the reason why the Bank of Canada is called the "banker's bank".

Other Financial Institutions

Although the chartered banks are the financial institutions with which Canadians are most familiar, there are other institutions that are important to the Canadian economy.

Trust Companies

Trust companies provide many of the services provided by the banks–savings and chequing services and the lending of money–and they are often referred to as "near banks". In addition to these banking services, trust companies specialize in handling such personal and business financial affairs as the purchase and sale of real estate, the administration of estates, and the settlement of the will of a deceased person. Partly because of the fees charged for these special services, trust companies are sometimes able to pay depositors a slightly higher interest rate than banks do on their savings accounts. Trust companies are usually open for longer hours during the week and on Saturday morning too, and their savings account business has increased as a result of this customer convenience.

Trust companies receive their right to operate from either the federal or provincial government. Depositors' savings are protected just as savings are protected in the chartered banks.

Credit Unions

Credit unions are similar to banks and trust companies in that they receive deposits, lend money, and offer a chequing service in some of their branches. Interest is paid on money deposited, and loans are available at reasonable interest rates competitive with other financial institutions. The chequing service depends on the size of the credit union and the availability of full-time rather than volunteer staff.

However, there are major differences between financial institutions. Banks and trust companies are owned by shareholders while credit unions are owned by their members–a group of people with a common bond or interest who agree to pool and share their resources as a service for each other. The common bond is usually members of a church or lodge group, employees in a business, or even members in a community. Credit union services are available only to its members and their families.

Provincial legislation gives credit unions the right to operate and establish maximum rates of interest and interest rates. Since credit unions are non-profit organizations, any profits earned by the credit unions are returned to members in the form of **dividends** or **rebates** at the end of the year.

Savings and Chequing Programs

Unit B outlined the procedures for opening a savings account and described the two main types of savings accounts; chequing savings accounts and non-chequing savings accounts. Most Canadians have at least one savings account in one of Canada's financial institutions. Between 1967 and 1977 the number of personal savings accounts increased from 13.5 million to just over 23 million.

Two other common types of bank accounts are the personal chequing account and the current account. The **personal chequing account** is designed as a simple, economical account for paying personal and household bills by cheque. Some institutions refer to this account as a **true chequing account.**

Since chequing accounts are not intended for saving money but rather for paying bills, interest is not paid on the money in the account. (Many people nowadays open a true chequing account for payment of monthly bills and a true savings account for saving money and earning interest.) **Service charges** are charged for cheques and withdrawals against true chequing accounts, but the fee is lower than that charged on true savings accounts. The current charge is sixteen cents to twenty cents for each cheque or withdrawal. Instead of receiving a passbook, customers receive a **monthly statement** and their cancelled cheques each month. The returned statement provides customers with a record of everything that happened to their accounts during the month and should be checked against personal records for accuracy. The **cancelled cheques** are cheques that have been written by the customers and have been paid by the bank. These cheques are valuable receipts and are evidence that the bills have been paid. A cancelled cheque is proof of payment because a person or business cashing the cheque must sign it on the back before cashing it. This signature is called an **endorsement**

Current accounts are mainly intended for business use and for writing large numbers of cheques. The Students' Association in your school probably uses a current account. As with true chequing accounts, no interest is paid on these accounts. Monthly statements and cancelled cheques are returned to the business or organization every month, and service charges are also made.

The Writing of Cheques

People write cheques to transfer money from their bank accounts to another person or business. All financial institutions provide standard, printed cheque forms for their customers. **Personalized cheques** with the customer's name and address are available for a small fee. Cheques with pictorial scenes from across Canada can also be obtained. (In 1977, Canadians wrote about 1.6 billion cheques for goods and services worth $2.7 trillion.) However, legal cheques can be written on anything, as long as certain basic essentials appear. Financial institutions have accepted such things as a roofing shingle, the hide of a cow, an envelope, and a two-foot piece of white spruce as valid cheques.

ORDER FORM   Important! Order Immediately to maintain a continuous supply of cheques

My name and address to appear as follows:

NAME *PETER CUSTOMER*

ADDRESS *1111 SAMPLE STREET*   APT NO

CITY/TOWN *ANYTOWN*   PROV *BC*   POSTAL CODE *V1L 4N4*

TELEPHONE (if desired) *715 0111*

Please process my order for cheques and charge the cost to my account.

Signature _____   Date _____

🔺 **Bank of British Columbia**
999 WEST PENDER
VANCOUVER, B.C.

Cheque style required*	Style of Wallet*	Quantity
☒ Panorama scenics	☒ White Brocade	☒ 200 (standard quantity)
☐ Ornata designs in blue ☐ green ☐ apricot ☐	☐ Aztec Orange ☐ Western Calf ☐ Florentine ☐ Cameo ☐ Morocco	or
☐ Security colour of paper _____	☐ Lizagator ☐ Voreila ☐ Elephant	☐ 400 ☐ 600 ☐ 800 ☐ 1,000

Standard bank cheques may be obtained by enquiring at your branch
*Wallet illustrations on reverse side
Print order in ☒ English ☐ French

Personal Cheque Printers   Personal Cheque Printers
6032-103rd Street   or   3470 Gardner Court
Edmonton, Alberta   T6H 2H7   Burnaby, British Columbia   V5G 3K6

Fill in this form completely and mail to Personal Cheque Printers. Your order will be returned prepaid via Mail.

⑈000 20⑈0 16⑈

156

Essentials of a Cheque

When you write a cheque, you will notice the words "Pay to the order of ———— ". The name of the person or business to whom the cheque is written appears in this space. That name is the **payee** on a cheque. This name should be written at the extreme left side of the cheque, followed by a line to fill in any remaining blank space. It is important to spell the payee's name correctly so that there will not be a difficulty in later cashing the cheque.

If you want to withdraw money from your bank account, you can write a cheque by filling in your own name or making it payable to "Cash". As cheques to "Cash" can be cashed by anyone, it is very important to cash them quickly before they are misplaced or lost. When cashing such a cheque, you will have to sign or endorse it on the back.

Another essential that must appear is the name and branch location of the financial institution so that the payee's bank will know from which institution the money is coming. The name of the institution is the **drawee**, and this information is usually pre-printed on the cheque forms.

All cheques must be **dated**, and this includes the day, month, and year. (Many institutions will not accept cheques that are over six months' old because they are too old. For this reason, cheques should be cashed promptly.) Some people postdate their cheques, but this is not always a good idea as it is easy to forget about them. **Postdating** means putting a future date on a cheque. Suppose you can purchase a pair of slacks that you have wanted for a long time at a low sale price. You buy the slacks today, April 20, and you date the cheque for April 30 when you get paid for your part-time job. If the retail store attempts to cash the cheque before April 30, the bank should refuse to cash it as you will not have enough money in your account until pay day. The bank should refuse to cash it even if there is enough money in the account. A cheque is not valid until or after the date written on it.

All cheques are written for some **amount** of money. The amount must appear in both numbers and words on the cheque. The figures should begin close to the dollar sign to prevent people from adding more numbers in front of the true amount. The amount in words should be written as far to the left as possible, followed by a line to fill in the blank space. This prevents people from adding another word or **altering** the amount of the cheque.

Make certain that the amounts in figures and in words are the same. If the amounts do not agree, the amount in words is the one that will be paid. However, in most cases, financial institutions will not cash a cheque if the amounts are not similar.

The last essential on a cheque is the signature of the person writing the cheque. This person is the **drawer**. The drawer's name appears on the bottom right-hand line of a cheque and should be identical to that person's signature on the signature card held at the bank.

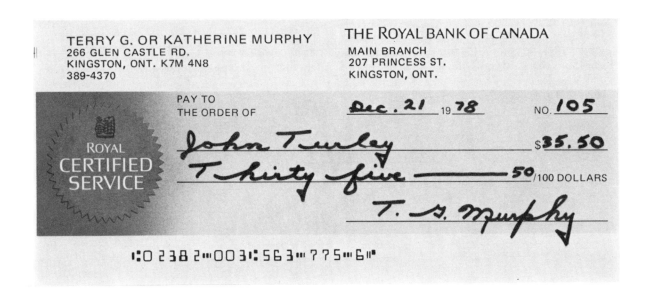

Cheque-writing Reminders

All cheques should be typed or written in ink as cheques written in pencil are too easy to alter or change. If you make an error in writing a cheque, never erase the mistake. One alternative is to destroy the cheque and write another, or if there is only one small error, draw a single line through the mistake and write the correct item by the error, initialling the change. This tells the bank that the change is legitimate and was made by you, the drawer.

Remember *never* sign a blank or an incomplete cheque. A **blank cheque** is one with no details filled in. A signed blank cheque can be filled in with any name and for any amount by anyone finding it and cashed by that person. Because you have actually signed the cheque, it will be cashed by the bank.

Stopping Payment on a Cheque

When a cheque you have written is lost, stolen, or contains an error, you, as the drawer, do not want to see that particular cheque paid from your account. You can notify the institution immediately that you want a **stop payment** made on the cheque.

First telephone the bank, giving them the details of the cheque. This does not officially stop payment, but it does delay payment of the cheque until you fill out a proper request stop-payment form at the bank. This form requires the date the cheque was written, the number of the cheque, the payee's name, the amount of the cheque, and your signature as the drawer. A fee is usually charged for this service.

If payment of the cheque has been stopped because it was lost, another cheque should be issued to replace it. The second cheque should be given a new date and number to distinguish it from the original and to avoid confusion at the institution.

Certified Cheques

Sometimes a business will request payment by **certified cheque,** a cheque for which the payment is guaranteed to the payee in advance by the financial institution. Dance bands at school dances often want to be paid by certified cheque. Real estate sales are another example of transactions requiring certified cheques.

The drawer makes out the cheque in the regular manner and then takes it to the institution to be certified. Once the teller has determined that there is enough money in the account to cover the cheque, the cheque will be stamped "Certified" or "Accepted" by the bank. The amount of the cheque will be immediately deducted from the drawer's account and held in a special account until payment has been made later to the payee. When the certified cheque is finally cashed, it is returned to the drawer along with the other cancelled cheques at the end of the month.

Endorsing Cheques

Before cheques can be deposited into an account, cashed, or transferred to another person, they must be endorsed. An **endorsement** is the payee's signature on the back of the cheque. It is proof that the payee has received payment for the cheque or given it to a third party. The endorsement should appear at the left end of the back of the cheque for easier and more efficient handling by the bank employees. The two main types of endorsements are blank and restrictive.

A **blank endorsement** is the most common type and requires only the signature of the payee. A cheque with a blank endorsement can legally be cashed by anyone who holds it. As a result, a blank endorsement should not be used until you are ready to cash or deposit the cheque.

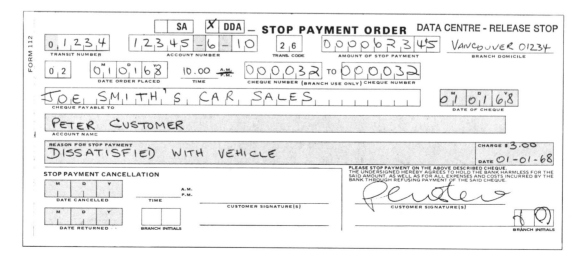

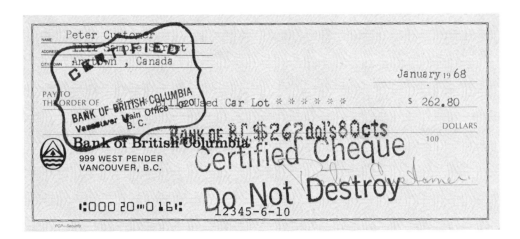

A **restrictive endorsement** limits what can be done with the cheque. When such an endorsement is used, the cheque may be used only for that particular purpose. The most common restrictive endorsement is "For deposit only to the account of ..." above the signature of the payee. Another person finding the cheque cannot do anything with it other than to deposit it into the payee's account as its use has been restricted or limited by the endorsement. Business organizations often use this type of endorsement.

The Cheque-clearing Process

Canadians are among the biggest users of cheques in the world, second only to Americans. Between 75-80 per cent of all business transactions in Canada are currently handled by cheque. Present predictions are that by 1980 Canadians will be writing at least two billion cheques every year. Every business day millions of cheques are deposited or cashed by individuals and businesses. The process that occurs from the time a cheque is written until it is paid is known as the **clearing system**.

This diagram traces the process of clearing a cheque written by Bob Pesowsky on his Royal Bank account in Dartmouth, Nova Scotia, to a mail order company in Edmonton, Alberta.

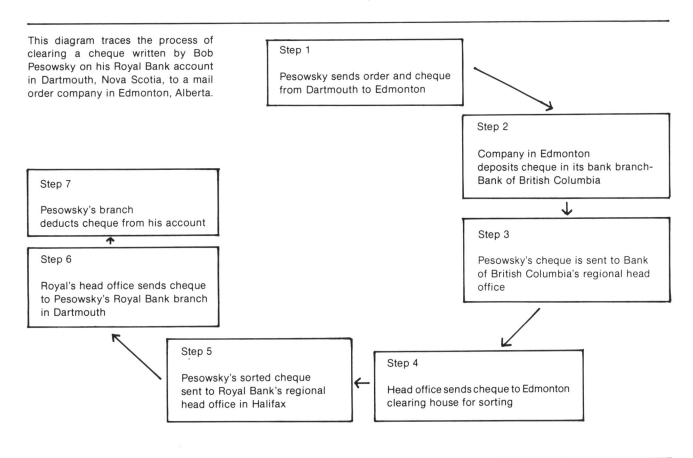

Step 1

Pesowsky sends order and cheque from Dartmouth to Edmonton

Step 2

Company in Edmonton deposits cheque in its bank branch- Bank of British Columbia

Step 3

Pesowsky's cheque is sent to Bank of British Columbia's regional head office

Step 4

Head office sends cheque to Edmonton clearing house for sorting

Step 5

Pesowsky's sorted cheque sent to Royal Bank's regional head office in Halifax

Step 6

Royal's head office sends cheque to Pesowsky's Royal Bank branch in Dartmouth

Step 7

Pesowsky's branch deducts cheque from his account

Clearing is the process used by banks for the settlement of balances among themselves every business day. All cheques are sent to the bank's main branch or regional head office. Cheques are sorted, bundled for clearing, and returned to the branches if they are drawn on the same bank. Cheques drawn on other banks are exchanged at one of the banks, acting as a clearing house. Representatives from each bank meet daily to exchange cheques drawn against their bank. No money exchanges hands among the banks because each one keeps an account and any differences are handled by a bookkeeping entry. Then, these cheques are returned to the individual bank branches for further processing.

The accuracy and speed that cheques move through the clearing process is evidence of its efficiency. From the time you first write a cheque to the time it is returned and deducted from your bank account, it has passed through several stages, has been fed through computer systems, and has been handled by many people. Most cheques today can be processed across Canada within a few days. This has become possible with the introduction of magnetic ink character coding, computer terminals in most branches linked to central computers, and increased use of different kinds of electronic equipment.

Magnetic Ink Character Recognition (MICR)

On the lower left-hand side of most cheques you will see a group of coded numbers printed in special ink. This encoding line is magnetized when the cheque is processed through an electronic sorting machine, and cheques are correctly sorted by the names of the individual banks. MICR is also "read" by the banks' computers to deduct the amount of the cheque from the customer's account. Most banking forms now have MICR coding on them.

The first group of characters, Encoding I, contains the name of the bank branch–the first five numbers–and the name of the bank–the next three numbers. The symbols on either side of the numbers and the dash in the middle are necessary for the sorting process so the cheques can be returned to the banks on which they are drawn. The next group of characters, Encoding II, identifies the customer's specific account number. These first two groups of numbers are usually preprinted on customers' cheques.

The last group of characters, Encoding III, contains the amount of the cheque and is added later by the bank after the cheque has been cashed. This encode always consists of ten digits, and zeros are always added to the left of the amount to provide for ten digits. The second and third set of digits enables the computing equipment to up-date the customer's account.

Other Financial Services

Canada's financial institutions provide many different services for individuals and businesses. Following are some of the more important services provided by most of these institutions.

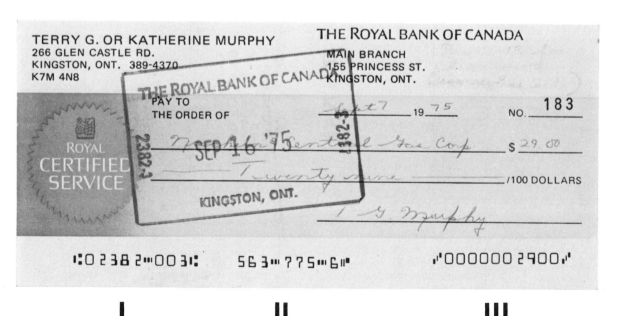

Loans

One of the major services provided by these institutions is lending money to businesses, farmers, fishermen, individuals, governments, and other public services. The loans range in size from millions of dollars to government and industry to a few hundred dollars for consumer needs. Advertising tells consumers the benefit of borrowing from one institution instead of the other, and new consumer lending policies are constantly being created to attract customers. For example, there has been a rapid growth in the use of consumer credit since the early 1950s. Banks now supply over sixty per cent of all outstanding consumer credit. The various sources and costs of loan credit are discussed in greater detail in Chapter 9.

Safety Deposit Boxes

Safety deposit boxes are used to protect a person's important documents and valuables. Items such as birth certificates, stocks and bonds, insurance policies, coins and jewellery, and home ownership papers are kept in these boxes. They are kept in well-guarded vaults, and only the person renting the box or a person legally named by the renter can open it. Two keys are required to open the box–one is the key always kept by the bank, the other is the customer's key. The rental rate for these boxes varies according to the size of the box, but the cost is very reasonable.

Money Orders

Many retailers will send goods ordered by mail immediately if a money order is enclosed as payment. Like certified cheques, a money order is almost always guaranteed to be good. Money orders can be purchased at banks, trust companies, and at the post office.

Money orders may be purchased for up to a maximum amount of money, plus a small service charge; money orders bought from banks are usually available for larger maximum amounts. The order is completed in triplicate–the main copy to be sent for payment, the second copy to be kept by the sender as a receipt, and the final copy to be kept by the issuing organization for its own records. The issuer fills in the amount of the money order, while the sender completes the remainder of the information–the name of the payee, the date, and the sender's own name and address.

Travellers' Cheques

When you are travelling, you should not carry large amounts of money with you. Credit cards may be used in many places if you want to charge your purchases and pay for them at a later time. If you want to pay as you go, it is wise to purchase travellers' cheques. They are convenient to use and will be replaced if they are lost. They are issued in amounts of $10, $20, $50, and $100. When you buy travellers' cheques, you are required to sign each one in the presence of the person selling them to you. When you later cash each cheque, you must sign it again in the presence of the person cashing it. These two signatures must match before the cheque will be accepted. Because it is difficult to forge or alter travellers' cheques, they are readily accepted throughout the world.

Overdrafts

Even careful depositors occasionally write cheques for more money than in their accounts. Anything over the total in your account is an overdraft. For example, if you write a cheque for $250 and your bank balance is $240, your account is overdrawn by $10. In such cases, the bank will mark your cheque, "Persuant to clearing regulations, this item may not be cleared again unless certified", and send it back to the payee's bank. This N.S.F. (Not Sufficient Funds) cheque is said to have "bounced". Because of the expense of processing N.S.F. cheques, most financial institutions will charge a fee of $2.00 to $3.50 for an overdrawn cheque. Some banks, however, have special card service plans that permit depositors to write cheques in excess of their account balances up to a maximum limit and if the overdrawn amount is paid within a short period of time.

Credit Cards

Several of the banks offer two of the major credit card plans–Visa and Master Charge. Bank credit cards are making inroads into the retail store and travel and entertainment services markets at the expense of cash, cheques, and private company credit card plans, such as American Express. One of the reasons for this is that bank cards are issued free of charge, once the person's credit card application has been approved. The use of bank credit cards is increasing between twenty-five and thirty per cent each year. In 1978 there were over six million Visa cardholders who spent nearly four billion dollars while Master Charge, which started several years after Visa, had over two million cardholders who spent nearly one billion dollars on goods and services. Visa is available from the following banks: the Commerce, Royal, Nova Scotia, Toronto-Dominion, and the Canadian National. Master Charge is issued by the Bank of Montreal and the Provincial Bank of Canada.

Combination Service Packages

Package plans, in which the banks provide a range of services for a flat monthly fee, are one of the most recent services provided by banks and other financial institutions. These plans do away with separate charges on day-to-day banking services and allow you special reductions on other banking services, all for a set monthly charge of two or three dollars for the total package.

The services provided differ slightly from bank to bank, and this is the reason for the different

CHARGEX
APPLICATION FORM

Chargex cards are issued only through these five banks. Please check the bank of your choice.

PLEASE PRINT IN BLOCK LETTERS

☐ CANADIAN IMPERIAL BANK OF COMMERCE
☐ THE BANK OF NOVA SCOTIA   ☐ BANK CANADIAN NATIONAL
☐ THE TORONTO-DOMINION BANK   ☐ THE ROYAL BANK OF CANADA

Last Name	First Name	Initials	Telephone No.	Social Insurance No.	No. of Cards Required 1 ☐ 2 ☐
No. and Street name (specify St., Ave., Rd., etc.)		Apt. No.	☐ Single ☐ Separated ☐ Married ☐ Divorced ☐ Widow(er)	Date of Birth Month Day Year	Spouse (first name)
City	Province	Postal Code	At present address ☐ Own ☐ Rent $____ ☐ With parents per month	No. of Dependents (excluding spouse)	Driver's License No.

Previous Address (if at present address less than 2 years)	How Long?

Employer—Name and Address	Telephone	Occupation	How Long?	Gross Monthly Income $
Previous Employer (if with above less than 2 years)	Telephone	Occupation	How Long?	Gross Monthly Income $
Spouse now employed by—Name and Address	Telephone	Occupation	How Long?	Gross Monthly Income $
Name and Address of Nearest Relative not living with me				Relationship

REFERENCES	Bank	Branch	☐ Loan $ ☐ PCA No. ☐ Savings Acct. No. ☐ C/A No.
	Home: Financed by		$ $ $
	Auto: Year and Make	Financed by	—Estimated Value—$ —Amount Owing—$ —Monthly Payment—$

Other Loans (Credit Cards, Dept. Stores, Finance Co's etc.)	Name	Address	$ $
	Name	Address	—Amount Owing—$ —Monthly Payment—$

I, the undersigned, hereby certify the above information to be true and, if this application is accepted, request Chargex card(s) be issued to me, and renewals or replacements thereof from time to time. In connection with such issuance, renewal or replacement, the undersigned authorizes and consents to the receipt and exchange of credit information and agrees to abide by the terms of the issuing bank's Cardholder's Agreement. Use of such card shall evidence receipt of such Cardholder's agreement.

DATE_____ APPLICANT'S SIGNATURE **X**_____

monthly charge. Among the basic services included in the package at most banks are personalized cheques, overdraft protection, no service charge for money orders and travellers' cheques or for payment of service and utility bills, cheques cashed at any branch, unlimited chequing privileges without the normal service charge, a Master Charge or Visa card, a safety deposit box at some banks, and a preferred rate on personal loans. These plans are good for people if they take advantage of the benefits included in the package.

Banking by Mail

If you find it difficult or inconvenient, because of time or distance, to get to the bank, most banks make it possible to **bank by mail.** Special deposit-by-mail forms are available for mailing to the banks in special envelopes. By mailing your funds promptly, you reduce the danger of loss or theft. It is safe to send cheques in the mail, but any cash should always be sent by registered mail.

After-Hour Depositories

Many bank branches provide **twenty-four-hour depository service** for customers who can't get to the bank during regular banking hours. This service is especially useful for business people who can make night deposits at the end of their working day. For a small yearly fee, customers receive a canvas bag with a lock and a key and another key for the depository located outside the bank. The deposit slip is filled out, placed in the bag with the deposit, and dropped through the depository slot. The deposit is handled by the bank staff the next day, and a copy of the deposit slip is given back to the customer as proof of receipt of the deposit when the night deposit bag is returned.

Automatic Banking Services

These automatic services fall into three categories: cash dispensers, automatic teller machines, and automated television banking. These services are available in some branches in Canada's largest cities.

The **cash dispensers** provide bank customers holding specially issued cards with the opportunity to withdraw money from their accounts twenty-four hours a day. They can get money from their accounts after normal banking hours and on weekends. Cash dispensers are also a convenience as cardholders are able to withdraw money without having to go into the bank branch itself. There has been a recent trend towards people using these units more frequently during banking hours.

Automatic teller machines (ATM) combine the cash withdrawal features of the dispenser units along with most other personal banking features. Customers receive a special magnetically striped card and a personal identification code number. If somebody finds your card and tries to use it, the transaction cannot be completed without your code number. After the third incorrect try, the machine will retain the card until you claim it later at the bank.

This card enables customers to obtain instant cash, to make deposits at any time, and to transfer money from one bank account to another. Utility bills and loan payments can be paid conveniently. Customers receive a printed receipt after each completed transaction. ATMs provide customers with a convenience day and night, weekdays, weekends, and on holidays, without waiting in line. Bankette and Instabank are among the trade names used by banks to identify their ATMs.

In late 1976, The Royal Bank of Canada introduced another type of automated banking at its branch in Toronto's Royal Bank Plaza with the first **TV Banking** installation in Canada. The customer speaks directly to the teller or by private telephone for complete privacy. The teller is located elsewhere in the building. A capsule is used to send the transaction between the customer and the teller. TV Banking is very fast and easy to use, and it is the latest development in the rapidly changing world of automatic banking services. All of these new services are part of the movement toward an **Electronic Funds Transfer System (EFTS).**

Electronic Funds Transfer System (EFTS)

Mechanization of banking processes is inevitable in future years as the job and the cost of processing cheques and other paperwork increases every day. The changeover will occur gradually. Many banking officials suggest that it may be 1990 before most Canadians are as willing to have a transfer of funds handled electronically as they are now to have it done by cheque or cash.

The computer systems used vary from bank to bank, but all of them have a central computer installed in the regional or head office, and on-line teller computer terminals in most branches. Some terminals update customers' passbooks, which are inserted in the top of the terminals. Other terminals provide printed output for bank reports and customers' bank statements from the central computer.

There are several advantages of computerization of banking. Bank transactions are speeded up, and human error is reduced as the computer makes all arithmetical calculations. Your account is up-to-date at all times and as more terminals are installed in bank branches, you will probably be able to withdraw money at any bank branch. Branches with automatic teller machines enable you to withdraw money at any time of the day or night. Finally, the tedious and time-consuming bookkeeping and balancing functions are speeded up and completed with greater accuracy by computers.

However, there is one main disadvantage. Power failure and mechanical problems place computers on "down time" or not working. Tellers are unable to update your passbooks or give you your present bank balance because manual records are disappearing in branches as the transition to computers continues.

Furthermore, cheques and cash will never completely disappear. Cheques will be needed for expensive transactions, such as the settlement payment on the completion of a home purchase, and cash will be needed for small-value transactions, such as the purchase of a chocolate bar or a newspaper. Also, some Canadians will never accept the concept of EFTS, just as there are some people who never use a credit card. Thus, the move towards EFTS will be gradual as banks are not going to instal expensive computer networks if customers do not want them. The introduction of new computerized banking services is determined not by what banks can offer Canadians but by what Canadians decide they want banks to provide for them.

REVIEWING YOUR BUSINESS VOCABULARY

Write the number of each definition.
Write the word that matches the definition number.

UNIT A

barter, cheque, currency, deficit spending, inflation, legal tender, medium of exchange, money, price, purchasing power, standard of value, store of value

1. A country's coins and paper money.
2. Something acceptable as a medium of exchange.
3. An order to a bank to pay a certain sum of money to another person or business.
4. What money will buy.
5. To trade one product or service for another.
6. A period of generally rising prices.
7. Value of an item expressed in terms of dollars and cents.
8. A function of money when it is saved for future needs.
9. A function of money that relates to the price of an item.
10. Occurs when government spends more money than it raises in taxes.
11. Lawful money of a country.
12. Another function of money.

UNIT B

bond, dividend, interest, investment, joint account, liquidity, market value, maturity, passbook, redeem, savings, signature card, stock, term deposit

1. Price that securities will bring at any given time.
2. Difference between the money you earn and the money you spend.
3. An account used by two or more people.
4. Bank's record of the transactions in a bank account.
5. Evidence of ownership in a corporation.
6. Customer's record of the transactions in a bank account.
7. Ease with which assets may be converted into cash.
8. Liability of a corporation.
9. Share of corporation's profit paid to stockholders.
10. Price paid for the use of money over a period of time.
11. Money deposited for a specific period of time.
12. Money put into something for the purpose of earning income.
13. Date on which the face value of a bond is to be repaid.
14. To exchange for cash.

UNIT C

branch banking, cancelled cheque, certified cheque, charter, current account, drawee, drawer, encoding, endorsement, overdraft, payee, personal chequing account, postdating, unit banking

1. Government authority to operate a bank.
2. Account intended for business use.
3. Account intended for payment of personal and household bills.
4. Person or business to whom a cheque is payable.
5. Person making and signing a cheque.
6. Name of bank and branch on a cheque.
7. Cheque guaranteed as to payment.
8. Cheque written by you and paid by the bank.
9. To write a cheque for more money than you have on account.
10. Putting information into a code or plan.
11. Canadian banking system.
12. American banking system.
13. Signature of person cashing a cheque.
14. Putting a future date on a cheque.

REVIEW QUESTIONS

UNIT A

1. What is bartering? Give two examples of how it operates.
2. List two reasons why bartering is an awkward system for conducting business.
3. What is money? What were some of the early forms of money?
4. What are the two major forms of money used in Canada today?
5. Who controls the issue of all currency in Canada? Where are coins minted in Canada?
6. List three reasons why cheques are the most widely used form of money today.
7. What is legal tender in Canada?
8. How does money serve as a medium of exchange?
9. How does money act as a store of value?
10. What is meant by the purchasing power of money?
11. List three reasons why money is considered a convenience.
12. What is the difference between inflation and deflation?
13. What groups of people suffer most during an inflation and why?
14. What is deficit spending?
15. Why was the Anti-Inflation Board established? When did it begin and end?

UNIT B

1. By giving two examples, distinguish between short-term and long-term savings goals.
2. List three reasons why many people have a planned savings program.
3. Why might two or more people open a joint account?
4. What kinds of information are recorded in savings account passbooks?
5. List three benefits of having a savings account in a financial institution.
6. Why do financial institutions pay interest on money deposited in savings accounts?
7. Why is there a difference in the interest rate received on a regular savings account and a true savings account?

8. What are RHOSPs and RRSPs?
9. Why are Canada Savings Bonds considered a good investment?
10. What is the difference between a regular interest and a compound interest Canada Savings Bond?
11. What is the main difference between a corporation bond and a share of stock?
12. Why are bonds called fixed-income investments?
13. What is the difference between common and preferred stock?
14. What does having a seat on the stock exchange enable a person to do?
15. Outline the four basic objectives to consider before investing money.

UNIT C

1. What is a chartered bank? How many of them exist in Canada?
2. What is the difference between the branch banking and the unit banking system?
3. List three advantages that the branch banking system offers to Canadians.
4. What is the *Bank Act*? When was it last revised?
5. In what major way does a credit union differ from a bank and a trust company?
6. What is a cancelled cheque? What possible use is it to you?
7. Explain the details for stopping payment on a cheque.
8. What is the difference between a blank and a restrictive endorsement?
9. What is meant by the clearing system?
10. What is Magnetic Ink Character coding? What use is it?
11. List four main services that banks provide besides accepting deposits and making loans.
12. Explain the meaning of EFTS.
13. What are two advantages of computerized banking? List the major disadvantage.
14. Why will the use of cheques and cash never disappear completely in Canada?

APPLYING YOUR KNOWLEDGE

UNIT A

1. To what extent is bartering used today for conducting business? Give an example of its present-day use.
2. What standard was used by different societies to determine which items were used as money?
3. Why did paper currency come into common use in the eighteenth century?
4. What major problem is overcome between consumers and businesses when money serves as a standard of value?
5. If the paper used to print our currency is worth so little, why are our dollar bills worth so much?
6. What determines the real value of our money? Why is this so?
7. How might you not suffer too much as a result of price increases in a period of inflation?
8. Explain the meaning of the statement: "During a period of inflation, money is not a good store of value."
9. If prices begin to rise rapidly, why don't consumers simply refuse to buy the goods and services?
10. Why is there no one single best solution for controlling inflation?

UNIT B

1. Explain what is meant by "saving for a rainy day".
2. Why is it wise to begin saving money while you are young?
3. Some people save money in a cookie jar or under their mattress. Why are these not good forms of saving?
4. It is much easier to save when you have a purpose or goal for saving. What goals might you and your friends have that would make you save? List as many reasons as possible.
5. Why does a period of inflation reduce the purchasing power of your savings?
6. Why are savings guidelines from financial experts no longer as realistic as they once were?
7. Why does a savings account grow even when you don't deposit any more money it it?
8. Why did the federal government introduce two new options in 1978 to provide more freedom in choosing how to invest RRSP savings?
9. Why do many Canadians arrange for regular payroll deductions to purchase Canada Savings Bonds?
10. What factors determine the interest rates that corporations establish for their bonds?
11. Why do most corporation bonds pay a higher rate of interest than Canada Savings Bonds?
12. What factors might influence you to purchase common stock, rather than preferred stock, of a particular corporation?
13. When you purchase stock in a corporation, what is meant by "limited liability"?
14. Why do banks seldom require a depositor to provide fifteen days' notice before withdrawal of funds? When might such notice be required?
15. Why are corporate bonds considered a more secure investment than common stocks?

UNIT C

1. Why are banking services so important to your community and to you as an individual?
2. What is the Bank of Canada, and why is it called the "banker's bank"?
3. Why are trust companies called "near banks"? In what ways are they similar? In what ways do they differ?
4. What is meant by postdating a cheque? Why is it not a good idea to do this?
5. Why do banks charge depositors for writing cheques on their accounts?
6. Why is each of the following a bad practice to follow:
   a. writing a cheque payable to "Cash"
   b. signing an incomplete or blank cheque
   c. cashing a cheque for a stranger.
7. Assume you have just opened a small retail business and now want to open a bank account for your store. What type of account would you likely open and why?
8. What is a certified cheque? Under what circumstances might a cheque need to be certified?
9. Explain in detail the routing of a cheque from the time it is written until it is returned as a cancelled cheque to the depositor.
10. People rent safety deposit boxes for storing items of value. List at least five articles that people might store in these boxes.
11. Why should you always require an endorsement on a cheque that is being transferred to you?
12. Why has the use of Visa and Master Charge credit cards increased so much in recent years?
13. Why are you required to have two signatures on travellers' cheques before cashing them?
14. Why are travellers' cheques better and easier to use than personal cheques when travelling away from home?
15. Why might the combination service package plans offered by the chartered banks not be a good investment for all customers?

PROJECTS AND PROBLEMS

UNIT A

1. Many magazine and newspapers contain regular articles and columns about money, inflation, and the economy. Look at some recent articles and choose three of them that deal with current economic events. Read the articles and report to the class on the importance of the articles you selected. Summarize the content of the articles for your presentation. As a class, prepare a bulletin board display of your material.

2. Statistics Canada issues a set of figures each month known as the **Consumer Price Index.** It is often called the cost-of-living index. The index measures the changes in prices for a large number of items from food to services. The result is a useful indicator of the rate of inflation over the years. This statistic measures the change in the purchasing power of the dollar.

   By examining the Canada Year Book, economics texts, encyclopedias, or other general reference texts in your school or public library, prepare a report that covers the following points:

   a. the group of items used to calculate the index
   b. how the index is calculated
   c. the purpose of the base year
   d. the value of the price index to consumers
   e. the change in the index from the current base year to now.

   Construct a line graph to show the changes in the index between the base year and now.

UNIT B

1. Obtain a copy of a newspaper that contains a listing of stocks traded on one of the Canadian stock exchanges. Choose any five stocks that interest you and find answers to the following questions:

   a. What was the high and low price for each stock today?
   b. How many shares were traded today?
   c. Find out the high and the low price for each stock so far this year.

d. Follow the stock price for one month for two of your choices and then plot the price changes on a line graph at the end of that time.
e. Can you explain why the price changed as it did?

2. Prepare a chart of the Comparison of Financial Institution Savings Plans for the current month and year. The following questions will provide you with the necessary information to prepare the chart:
a. What is the current rate of interest paid on your regular savings account; your non-chequing savings account.
b. What is the name of your non-chequing savings account plan?
c. On what basis is interest calculated?
d. How often is it calculated? How often is it credited to the customer's account?
e. Do you accept term deposits for less than one year? If so, what is the minimum period of time, and what is the minimum amount of money accepted for deposit?
f. What is the current rate of interest on these deposits?
g. What is the current rate of interest on term deposits of one to five years?

UNIT C

1. One of the advantages of the branch banking system is that it provides an excellent training ground for men and women interested in banking careers. Visit at least one bank in your community and prepare a list of at least ten jobs observed during your visit. Interview the people holding these positions and determine: responsibilities of the job; education needed; possibility of advancement; beginning salary. Prepare a report for the class on job opportunities available in Canadian chartered banks.

2. Visit two banks in your community or a bank and one of the other financial institutions and determine: what customer services are offered; which services are most popular with customers and why; what charges, if any, are required for these services. Prepare a report for the class and a bulletin board display of services available.

8 Consuming

UNIT A

WISE SPENDING AND THE CONSUMER

When people buy and use goods and services, they are **consumers**. What have you bought or used so far today? Possibly you purchased bus tickets to get to school or bought a snack or a lunch in the school cafeteria this morning. Such regular activities are part of your role as a consumer.

All of us are consumers. You, your parents, relatives, and your friends regularly buy food, clothing, magazines, appliances, and other items. Most of us use some of the services provided by the telephone and electric companies, the public transportation companies, the airlines, and the railroads.

When consumers spend their money, they like to obtain **value** and get their money's worth. This requires careful shopping and wise spending. Quality, price comparisons, life of the products, safety, and reliability are all factors that need to be considered by wise consumers.

Needs and Wants

Consumer choices are usually the result of needs or wants. **Needs** are the things we must have for basic life and survival like food, clothing, and shelter. **Wants** are things we would like to have for pleasure and comfort. Our needs must be paid for before we satisfy our wants.

But how do we keep our needs and wants separate? Is a family car a need or a want? Most families need a basic compact or intermediate size car for daily transportation. Extra features like leather seats, air conditioning, and a stereo tape deck are wants that give satisfaction and pleasure to the driver and passengers.

It may be necessary for your mother to wear a new pant suit to work, but she does not need a $250 Paris fashion designer's creation—unless she's a model. Fresh fruit is necessary for a balanced diet, but expensive imported fruit in the wintertime is probably not. You need some new clothes to protect you against rain and snow. But clothes purchased for you just for you to be in style are more likely wants than needs. A basic pair of blue jeans or corduroy slacks is probably a need for most students. To pay several extra dollars for a particular company's label or design for style or status is more a want than a need.

Decision-making by Consumers

Consumers are constantly making choices when they buy and use goods and services. There was a time once when all consumers had to do to know something about the products they were buying was to ask the butcher, the baker, or the store owner. This is no longer possible in today's marketplace.

Today's consumers must make more choices than ever before. For example, a person shopping for food today must be able to evaluate and choose from over 8000 items in a typical large supermarket. As more choices become available, it becomes more difficult to make wise choices. Before consumers get their money's worth, they need more information to make good choices.

Think about some of your more recent purchases and consider your answers to the following questions:

Was that item available for sale last year or two years ago?

Have you ever purchased the item before?

If so, how did you hear about the item?

Where did you get the information to help you make your decision?

Did you have enough information to make a wise choice?

Influences on Consumer Decisions

All of us depend on certain **sources of information** in making choices. All of us buy products for different reasons. Surveys and statistics provide businesses with information about total sales. But surveys alone do not help Burger King, Red Barn, Wendy's and A. & W. compete with McDonald's in the fast food hamburger business. Businesses need to know why consumers choose one product over another. Why did your parents buy a Chrysler instead of a Ford, General Motors, or American Motors product when they purchased their new car? Or why did they purchase an imported car? Knowing how and why consumers make these choices is very important to business. The reasons why consumers make the choices they do are the **motives for buying**.

Motives for Buying

Part of becoming a better and more satisfied consumer is understanding why certain purchases are made. Any decision to buy a product is based on two main factors: the consumer's needs and wants; the **qualities of the product**–brand, dependability, package label, and price.

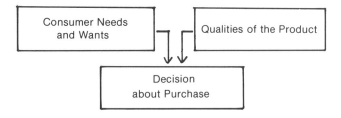

Imagine that you are considering the purchase of a portable typewriter for your personal use. If you were asked why you were buying a particular kind, your answer would likely be based on good sense and reason. The typewriter is a variety of metal and plastic parts assembled and packaged in an attractive case or cabinet that is pleasing to look at. It has a brand name of a particular manufacturer that has a reputation for making dependable and safe products of quality. Finally, it has a **price** that reflects a good and fair value. The qualities of a product are reflected in brand names and dependability, package and labels, and the price.

Brand Names

Many consumers buy only one particular brand of a product because that **brand name** has proved satisfactory and provided good value in the past. Do you and your friends drink Coke or Pepsi? Do you and your family use Crest, Colgate, Closeup, Pepsodent, Aquafresh, or some other brand of toothpaste? Why did you make the choice you did? Do these name brands indicate a certain standard of quality? Were these brands purchased because they were advertised the most? Consumers often believe that brand names guarantee quality. This may or may not be true. It is true that manufacturers attempt to maintain a standard of quality in their brand name products. However, sometimes the most well-known brands that people buy are the most heavily advertised products. They are well-known only because of their advertising campaign–they are not necessarily the best available brand on the market. Brand names, therefore, are not always a reliable buying guide.

Store Brands

Many stores sell products under their store or **private brand** labels. The quality of **store brand** products is often as good as that of nationally advertised brands. Can you really tell the difference between Red Rose, Salada, or Tetley tea compared with Dominion, Loblaws, Miracle Mart, and Woodward's store brand teas? Buying store brand products usually results in savings as these items are sold at lower prices than nationally advertised brands.

Advertising

Advertising plays an important role in influencing consumer choice. It often provides useful information about the products. It also creates a demand for an advertised product or service. The effects of advertising on consumer choice is discussed in the chapter on Marketing.

Price

Price is probably the main consideration that determines what products consumers buy. When consumers shop for bargains, they are price-shopping and often buy in quantity to save money. Some consumers believe that the higher the price the better the product. Prices also serve as **status symbols**. Some consumers are more interested in bragging about how much or how little they paid for a product than in the product itself. This desire to impress others with a purchase is called **conspicuous consumption**.

Sales and Prices

Retail stores reduce their prices at the end of a season. The stores want to clear their shelves for new merchandise, and this is the main reason for the sale. Some sales occur seasonally. Every January and August are the **"white sales"** in which sheets,

pillow cases, and towels are available at sale prices. Boxing Day, December 26, is the first day on which Christmas cards and wrapping paper go on sale. Many people buy their next year's cards and paper at these greatly reduced prices. Cars are usually available at reduced prices in the summertime just before next year's models arrive in late September. But with this type of sale, choices are limited as you must take whatever is available. These sales are **clearance** or **end-of-season sales. Promotional** or **special sales** occur when a manufacturer or retailer wants to promote or display a new product. Such a sale is intended to get people into a store to buy the product. This is often done when a manufacturer of a new perfume or cologne wants to introduce a new fragrance. If you are satisfied, the manufacturer hopes you will return to the store for future purchases.

Sales provide good value for consumers who plan for them in advance. Sales are good value too for consumers who really need a sale's item at the time of a sale. Sales are not good value for persons who make unnecessary purchases simply because of low sale prices.

Packages and Labels

Consumers used to be able to check the quality of products by examining the product itself. That system had its advantages, but it also exposed foods and perishable goods to handling and dirt. This is not possible much any more except when you buy fresh fruit and vegetables. **Packaging**

keeps food clean and makes shopping more convenient. The label on the package contains considerable information for the consumer.

Labels include information on how to use the product. Clothing labels often indicate instructions for washing and cleaning. Packages that contain harmful substances are required to have warning symbols on the containers. Canned goods labels contain a food grade and a listing of the ingredients of the product. Federal government legislation regulates the types of information that must appear on labels and packages. Consumer protection legislation is examined in greater detail in the next unit.

Although packages are used as an advertising and marketing medium, they are important in protecting, transporting, and storing a product. If a particular product looks worn from constant handling on the shelves of a store, consumers will not buy the item. **Durable packaging** will keep a product looking good for as long as it is on the shelf. Toothpaste, for example, is a product that is constantly criticized for its bulky packaging. However, toothpaste can be too easily squeezed out of shape on the shelves and takes on a worn and used look from handling. It is also difficult to shop and store the tubes unless they are boxed. And it would be almost impossible to stack the tubes on a shelf and expect them to stay in place if they were not boxed.

Universal Product Code

As you have probably noticed, most prepackaged grocery goods and magazines now contain a series of vertical bars and numbers, printed directly on the products. These markings are the **Universal Product Code (UPC)** and are applied to the products directly by the manufacturer. The UPC is *not* the result of any government legislation but is a system of product identification that has been chosen by the Grocery Products Manufacturers of Canada and by suppliers of packaged meat products. The first five numbers and black bars identify the manufacturer. The second set of five numbers and

the store. The computer matches the product to the price and the item and sends this information back to the cashier's register. The price is flashed on a display panel at the checkout desk for the consumer to read. The same information is printed on the cashier's sales slip, and a detailed sales slip is given to the customer.

Advantages of UPC

The scanners mean faster customer movement through checkout counters, and the resulting speed of checkout should overcome one of consumers'

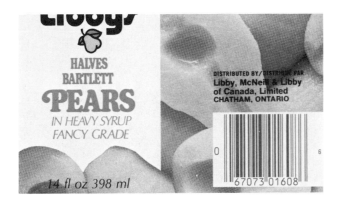
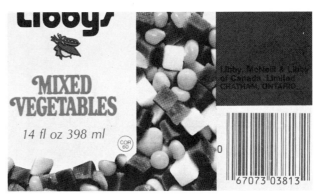

bars identifies the product–its name, size, colour, flavour, and so on. In most systems the UPC does not include the price of the product. As major grocery stores move towards computer-operated checkout systems, the grocery industry developed UPC to improve the efficiency of store operations.

How UPC Works

The clerk passes groceries with UPC markings over an **optical scanner**. The scanner reads the code and sends this information to a computer elsewhere in

main complaints about supermarkets, namely, long and time-consuming line-ups. The detailed information that is listed on cash register tapes will be helpful to consumers in reviewing their purchases after leaving the store and in budgeting for future food shopping bills.

Since cashiers no longer punch in prices on a cash register, there is a reduction in price-recording error for the computer supplies the prices. This eliminates both errors made by the cashier in entering prices on the cash register, as well as situations in which the price falls off a product and the cashier has to guess at the price.

Checkout features

178

The main advantage is that there should be fewer out-of-stock items since the computer will be able to keep accurate inventory records for each product as it is purchased. Supermarkets will know in an instant how much of a particular item has been sold and how much is left in stock. As well, the computer provides an analysis of which items are selling in a particular store so that the assortment of merchandise and space allocation on the shelves can be better customized to the needs and wants of the consumers in a particular store. This inventory analysis benefit is thought to be great enough to offset the great expense of installation of such a computer-operated system.

When UPC scanning equipment was first introduced in the United States, consumer reaction was somewhat negative in those stores that did not continue to mark individual prices on each product for consumers to see. Consumers like to see prices marked on products for price comparisons and to be aware of price increases.

In Canada, the Retail Council of Canada has asked both the federal Department of Consumer and Corporate Affairs and the Consumers' Association of Canada to conduct research regarding consumer attitudes towards the use of UPC and "prices off" shopping. Industry feeling is that the issue of price removal is best satisfied in a free market situation in which consumers are able to choose between a conventional supermarket and a "prices off" store.

Metrication and the Consumer

Metrication is a word that describes the change from the imperial system of weights and measures (feet, pounds, miles) to one based on the metric system (metres, grams, kilometres). By the end of 1980, Canada will be primarily a metric country. This changeover began in 1970 when a report, the *White Paper on Metric Conversion in Canada* prepared by the federal government, recommended that Canada "get in step" with the rest of the world. A result of that report was the establishment of Metric Commission Canada, whose main responsibility is to plan and coordinate the conversion.

Metric Units for Everyday Use

Physical Quantity	Unit	Symbol	Relationship
Length	kilometre	km	1 km = 1000 m
	metre	m	1 m = 100 cm
	centimetre	cm	1 cm = 10 mm
	millimetre	mm	10 mm = 1 cm
Volume	cubic metre	m³	1 m³ = 1000 L
	litre	L	
	millilitre	mL	1 L = 1000 mL
Mass	tonne (metric ton)	t	1 t = 1000 kg
	kilogram	kg	1 kg = 1000 g
	gram	g	1 g = 1000 mg
	milligram	mg	

Maritime Tel and Tel promotes metric

Starting in April of this year, the yellow pages of 600 000 telephone directories in Nova Scotia and Prince Edward Island will contain an insert (above) on metric conversion in the telephone industry. This public service is made possible through the cooperation of Metric Commission Canada, who provided the reproduction copy, and Tel & Tel, who runs the ad free of charge. G.E. Miller, staff supervisor of Coin and Directory at Tel & Tel, says the company is promoting metric generally. "For instance", says Mr. Miller, "all plans for cable and switching will be devised in metric in the future". Maritime Tel & Tel has made a commitment to be totally metric by 1980, thereby joining the rest of the world in the use of SI.

Reasons for the Change

The *White Paper* noted that most of the countries in the world that Canada traded with were already using the metric system. At the time, only the United States, Australia, and New Zealand still used the imperial system, and today each of these countries has begun to adopt the metric system. Export trade would be much easier with the other metric countries if Canada also followed the metric system.

Another reason for the change is that the metric system is a much easier system to use than the imperial system. There are only a few base units; all other units have been derived from these base units. The different magnitudes of units are based on multiples and sub-multiples of ten, which is easier to teach and to learn. There is also a direct relationship between the units of length, volume, and mass.

Signs of the Conversion

Canada's conversion has been taking place since the early 1970s. One of the first changes occurred in the reporting of weather forecasts and reports. Following is a list of major weather elements and the units used for reporting them:

Elements	Reporting Unit
Temperature	degrees Celsius (°C)
Speed of wind	kilometres per hour (km/h)
Visibility, distances	metres, kilometres (m, km)
Rainfall	millimetres (mm)
Depth of snow	centimetres, metres (cm, m)
Pressure	kilopascals (kPa)

During 1977 and 1978 speed limit signs on highways in all provinces changed to kilòmetres per hour. New automobiles are equipped with metric speedometers. Metric decals are available for pasting over the miles per hour speedometers on older cars.

Benefits of Metrication to Consumers

Consumers obtain considerable benefits from the metric packaging of food and other products. The number of container and package sizes is reduced in number. Price comparisons are easier to calculate in metric sizes. Some food products are still labelled in both the imperial and metric systems. Where the package was originally measured in imperial, the metric equivalents are exact conversions and turn out to be rather awkward numbers; for example, 10 oz. equates with 284 mg, which reduces the

simplicity of metric multiples and sub-multiples of ten. But more and more packages are being converted and sold in round numbers. Sugar, toothpastes, snack foods, hot cereals, ice cream, pet foods, and salt were among the first products to appear in round metric masses.

Using the metric system is an easy task for you. Many of you have studied the metric system in public school. Your parents may be reluctant to accept the changes as people tend to resist changes in habit. There is only one way of learning the metric system. That is by actually measuring and working with it. You can assist your parents in this effort and help them THINK METRIC.

Know What You Want

Consumer protection legislation can guarantee that goods sold meet certain requirements. But consumers need to use available information about

Price Differences in Childrens' Toys from Three Catalogues

General toys	Consumers	Sears	Shop-rite
WAKE-UP THUMBELINA	$17.75	$20.99	$19.99
BABY COME BACK	17.75	19.99	19.93
BABY BABY	4.97	5.99	5.96
BABY ALIVE	17.99	21.99	18.99
BABY ALIVE NURSERY CENTRE	9.97	12.99	10.94
HOLLY HOBBIE RAG DOLL	4.97	6.99	5.33
SUPERSTAR BARBIE	5.45	6.99	5.83
SUNTAN TUESDAY TAYLOR	8.60	9.49	9.67
HOLLY HOBBIE PLAY OVEN	10.65	13.99	10.96
SPIROGRAPH	5.99	7.99	6.97
THE BIONIC WOMAN	10.49	12.99	11.97
JAIME'S WARDROBE	9.97	9.99	9.97
SIX MILLION DOLLAR MAN	9.45	12.99	10.88
OSCAR GOLDMAN	10.65	12.99	11.97
STRETCH ARMSTRONG	14.65	17.99	15.88

The Whig Standard, Kingston
November 21, 1977
Reprinted by permission

products and services before making their purchases. Decide what you want to buy *before* you go shopping. If you do not have a list or a plan in mind when you go shopping, you may forget something and have to return later for it. Without a plan you are more likely to see an item in a store and buy it on the spot. This is called **impulse buying**. Buying without planning or thinking can be very costly.

Comparison Shopping Saves Time and Money

Most goods and services are available from more than one retailer. Comparing the price and the quality of goods in different stores can be a time and money saving exercise before you go shopping. If the price is almost identical in all stores, the store nearest you or the one that you know the best is probably a wise choice. If there is a fair difference in the price, the cheaper goods are often not the best buy because they do not last as long as more expensive items generally do.

The more you know about the items you intend to buy, the better a shopper you are. As a result of your **comparison shopping** in the catalogue and newspaper advertisements, you will avoid impulse buying and will know where to obtain the best buys. The telephone can also be used for comparison shopping in advance of your purchases.

The Need for a Conserver Society

Demands on both consumers and business are changing in today's marketplace. Our diminishing resources will mean a change in the way we live and in what we buy. Canadians must be concerned with the conservation of our resources. Canadians must change from a consumer society to a "**conserver society**".

Consumers are as much to blame for our diminishing resources as the business community. Consumers have demanded luxury and convenience products and packaging—TV dinners, canned soft drinks, luxury cars—without much concern for cost or waste of natural resources. Lacking consumer demand, these products would not be manufactured.

As members of a conserver society, we should all drive smaller cars with more efficient gasoline consumption; we should encourage the use of car pools; we should make better use of public transit; we should conserve fuel; we should insulate our homes; and we should make certain that we buy goods and services that are energy-efficient.

In 1977, the **Science Council of Canada** reported that home insulation has a large potential in saving energy resources. If three-quarters of Canadian homes were insulted by 1987, the Council suggested that the energy saving would be almost forty million barrels of oil annually.

Recycling garbage and waste ensures that expensive resources are used several times before being discarded. Nearly all packages become solid waste within one year of the purchase of products. Thirty-five per cent of all solid waste is packaging material. Thus, packaging is the single largest portion of solid waste. Ways to recycle solid waste are being examined carefully by manufacturers, consumers, and governments.

Consumers should be persuaded to purchase products that may cost more but will last longer and will be of better quality and have several uses. Encouragement of recycling and new approaches to packaging should be immediate goals of a conserver society.

UNIT B
CONSUMER AID FROM GOVERNMENT

In spite of wise shopping by consumers, many of us may still buy unsafe or faulty products. Misleading advertising may have caused us to make poor choices. Because problems still exist in the marketplace, governments have become involved in protecting consumers. Governments aid consumers by passing laws and setting up organizations to help consumers. Being familiar with these laws should help make all of us better consumers. We will know if we are getting our money's worth when we purchase goods and services. We will also be aware of our rights and responsibilities as consumers.

Federal Government Protection

There are several federal agencies that are directly involved in consumer protection. The ones that have the greatest effect on us as consumers are Consumer and Corporate Affairs Canada, Agriculture Canada, and the Health Protection Branch of Health and Welfare Canada. Each of these agencies is described in more detail below.

Consumer and Corporate Affairs Canada

Consumer and Corporate Affairs Canada, established in 1967, has two main functions: to represent consumer interests and to regulate business. It was one of the first national government departments in the world to be set up to handle consumer problems. The department's employees and inspectors investigate consumer complaints and concerns in areas such as hazardous products, textile labelling, misleading advertising, and consumer packaging and labelling. The department has established regional or district offices in all provinces to serve and assist consumers more effectively.

The Handling of Consumer Complaints

In 1968, the department set up a complaint-handling service, **Box 99,** in Ottawa to assist consumers with complaints about the marketplace. The box number was chosen as a name for the service because it was easier to remember than a department address. In its first year of operation, Box 99 received about 4000 complaints and requests for assistance. By the mid 1970s, about 100 000 complaints and inquiries

were being received annually. When a complaint is received by Box 99 officials, they can only discuss the problem with the company or persons involved. Box 99 has no legal authority to take legal action under federal control. All that can be done for provincial or local problems is to refer these problems to another agency to deal with them. As a result of these concerns with Box 99, Consumer and Corporate Affairs Canada is shifting the emphasis from Ottawa to their **regional offices** across Canada. All letters being sent to Box 99 are being handled at the regional level in an attempt to help consumers deal with the marketplace more effectively.

Hazardous Products Act

The **Hazardous Products Act,** passed in 1969, was the first major consumer legislation under the authority of Consumer and Corporate Affairs Canada. It was necessary as children were suffering injuries from dangerous products and unsafe toys. Some products, bleaches, polishes, and cleansers, are hazardous to both children and adults because they contain chemicals that are harmful to people. These products are necessary in homes, but people should be warned of the possible dangers if they are not used properly.

This law also lists certain very dangerous products that cannot be advertised, sold, or brought into Canada from another country. The law also requires that warning labels must appear on any household products that are possibly dangerous to consumers.

Warning statements and basic first aid information in French and English must appear on the labels. Many products must also have child-proof tops with instructions in both languages on how to open and close them.

Product Testing

Since 1969 Consumer and Corporate Affairs Canada has continued the **testing** of **products** that might be dangerous to consumers. These test results have been used to set up safety standards for such things as children's car seats, baby rattles and soothers, and baby cribs. Products that do not meet these standards must be removed from retail stores.

FOUR SYMBOLS TELL THE KINDS OF HAZARDS:

POISON　　　　**FLAMMABLE**　　　　**EXPLOSIVE**　　　　**CORROSIVE**

THREE SHAPES TELL THE DEGREES OF HAZARD:

DANGER　　　　　　**WARNING**　　　　　　**CAUTION**

The octagon danger symbol means the product could kill you; the diamond warning symbol means the product could make you very ill; the triangle caution symbol means the product could make you ill or hurt you in some way.

When the symbols and shapes are put together, they make twelve combinations that can appear on hazardous products.

More than one combination can appear on hazardous products.

Textile Labelling Act

The **Textile Labelling Act,** passed by Parliament in 1970, went into effect in 1972. The Act deals with the labelling, sale, and advertising of consumer textile articles. Two years were needed for manufacturers to prepare the required labels and identification of the textiles as the law specifies.

Years ago most textile articles were made from **natural fibres** of cotton, linen, silk, or wool. Since then technology has resulted in the creation of **man-made fibres** such as nylon, rayon, and polyester. The many different combinations of artificial and natural fibres presented problems of identification and understanding for consumers. Dry cleaners also faced the problem of not being certain of the best method for cleaning textiles.

Requirements of the Act

The *Textile Labelling Act* requires manufacturers to put labels on nearly all articles made from fibres. This means that almost everything that you buy made of fabric will have a label that tells you the name of the fibres used in the fabric and the amount by percentage of each fibre in the product. You will then know exactly how much of which fibres were used. Fibres must be identified by their family names and not only by trade names or the nicknames that manufacturers give the fibres. For example, if the fibre is polyester, the label will say so. It is easier for you to recognize the fibre if you know its family name.

The label also identifies the manufacturer by name and address or by an identification number. If only a number is used, you can obtain the name and address of the manufacturer from Consumer and Corporate Affairs Canada, or from one of its regional offices across Canada.

Care Labelling of Textiles

The mandatory or compulsory *Textile Labelling Act* tells consumers what their fabrics are made of. The voluntary **care labelling** system tells consumers how to take care of their fabrics. A series of coloured symbols has been created since they are easier to understand than words. The symbols indicate washing, bleaching, drying, ironing, and dry cleaning procedures. The system includes additional symbols that indicate such things as water temperatures for washing, iron temperatures, and methods of cleaning.

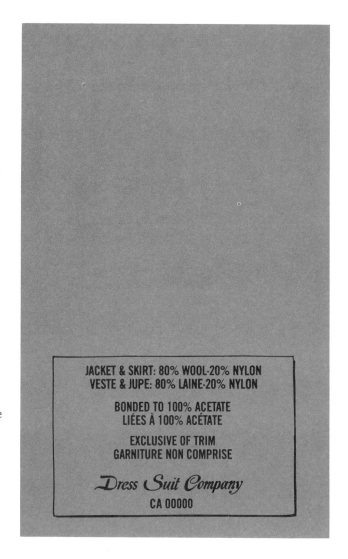

JACKET & SKIRT: 80% WOOL-20% NYLON
VESTE & JUPE: 80% LAINE-20% NYLON

BONDED TO 100% ACETATE
LIÉES À 100% ACÉTATE

EXCLUSIVE OF TRIM
GARNITURE NON COMPRISE

Dress Suit Company
CA 00000

What the Symbols Mean

The symbols appear in the traffic light colours of red, amber, and green. Red indicates that the procedures should not be used. Green indicates that the procedures are safe and to go ahead. Amber indicates that they may be used with care. The symbols clearly indicate what procedures are necessary to keep an article in clean and wearable condition. They also indicate what care methods should not be used. Many manufacturers supply cleaning and care instructions with their products. However, many consumers either lose these instructions or throw them away. This problem does not exist with the care labels as they must be permanently attached to the products. Although care labels are a voluntary program, many textile products carry these labels. They are a very useful source of consumer information.

For your laundry area.
This is what the symbols mean:
Voluntary Care Labelling of Textiles

WASHING   **BLEACHING**   **DRYING**   **IRONING**   **DRY CLEANING**

Stop	Be careful.	Go ahead.
●	●	●
RED	AMBER	GREEN

Do not wash.

Machine washable in warm water.

Machine washable in hot water.

Hand washable in lukewarm water.

Do not bleach.

Use chlorine bleach as directed.

Tumble dry medium-high.

Tumble dry low.

Dry flat.

Hang to dry soaking-wet.

Hang to dry.

Do not iron or press.

Iron medium.

Iron high.

Do not dry clean.

Dry clean low.

Dry clean.

Consumer Packaging and Labelling Act

The Consumer Packaging and Labelling Act provides a detailed set of rules for the labelling and packaging of most consumer products. This law enables consumers to make more informed choices when they purchase packaged goods. The Act, passed in 1971, was effective by March, 1976. The law came into effect gradually so that manufacturers could make the necessary label changes required under the law.

The Need for Such a Law

Before this law many consumers felt that packages did not contain enough useful information about the product. If you were unhappy with a product and wanted to complain to the manufacturer, you could not find a name and address anywhere on the package. If you were allergic to certain **food additives**, you often could not find a list of the **ingredients** or contents of the product. With the passage of the *Consumer Packaging and Labelling Act*, this information is available to consumers.

Requirements of the Act

According to federal legislation, labels on packages must contain the following information:

A list of ingredients in descending order by their proportion or mass. This tells you, for example, whether a can of beef stew contains more beef than potatoes or gravy.

The identity of the product in French and English and an indication of the net quantity in the old imperial and the newer metric units. Quantities will be totally metricated by the early 1980s.

The name and address of the company responsible for the product. This information can appear anywhere on the package except the bottom. It must be complete enough for the post office to deliver a letter that you might want to write about the product.

The **"durable life date"** of the product for all prepackaged foods with a durable life of ninety days or less, except for fresh fruits and vegetables. This durable life date is the date after which the maker estimates the food may not be at its best in terms of quality. However, this does *not* mean that the product is no longer any good. It still may be consumed after that date without any problem.

A **"best before"** date must also appear in both languages with the durable life date. The year is required only when it is needed to make the statement clear to consumers. This would occur when the durable life extends from December of one year to January of the next as this example shows:

BEST BEFORE/MEILLEUR AVANT   79   01   05.

If such a statement appeared on a loaf of bread, this means that the loaf could be expected to remain fresh until January 5, 1979. The months of the date marking are: JA = January; FE = February; MR = March; AL = April; MA = May; JN = June; JL = July; AU = August; SE = September; OC = October; NO = November; DE = December.

Reduction of Package Sizes

In the past it was very difficult for consumers to make price comparisons between different sizes of the same product and between different products. This was because of the large number of sizes in which products were packaged. For example, in the late 1970s there were some sixty-four sizes of biscuit and cookie packages available to consumers.

The *Consumer Packaging and Labelling Act* provides one way of dealing with this problem of too many sizes of packages. New regulations now require the **standardization of package sizes**. These sizes were arrived at through the combined efforts of consumer, industry, and government representatives. Since 1971, Consumer and Corporate Affairs Canada has already reduced the large number of package sizes for toothpaste, shampoos, skin creams, lotions, and snack foods. Under the Act package sizes for biscuits and cookies will soon number fourteen in a mass range from 60 g to 1 kg. The reduction of the number of sizes and products in metric units enables consumers to make better-informed choices when they make price comparisons.

Misleading Advertising

The **Combines Investigation Act** is the main federal law of general application covering Canadian media advertising. Other federal laws outline specific advertising offences. The *Food and Drugs Act* lists a number of diseases for which no person can advertise a treatment or cure. The *Consumer Packaging and Labelling Act* makes it an offence to advertise or label any prepackaged product, including beer, wine, and cider, in a misleading manner. The *Hazardous Products Act* makes it an offence to sell, bring into Canada, or advertise certain hazardous products.

In 1975, the *Combines Investigation Act* was amended to protect consumers even more. Services as well as goods are now subject to fair business regulations. Thus, **service industries** such as insurance and real estate agencies and funeral homes are now brought within the full scope of the Act. The inclusion of services under the Act reflects the growing importance of this type of business in the Canadian economy.

The Act contains provisions for misleading advertising, promotions, and deceptive marketing practices. Violations of these provisions are criminal offences and may result in conviction on indictment or summary conviction. **Summary conviction** or minor offences can result in fines up to $25 000 or imprisonment for one year or both. Conviction on

indictment or more serious offences can result in a fine at the discretion of the court or to imprisonment of five years or both.

In December, 1974, Consumer and Corporate Affairs Canada published its first *Misleading Advertising Bulletin*. This bulletin, published quarterly, contains articles and other information relating to various aspects of the marketing practices provisions of the Act and as well, lists people and firms convicted of misleading advertising practices. The bulletin is sent quarterly to those who have requested that their names be placed on the mailing list as well as to the media, Members of Parliament, and Senators.

The Health Protection Branch of Health and Welfare Canada

The **Health Protection Branch of Health and Welfare Canada** is concerned with matters that represent a possible danger to the health of consumers. It is responsible for the protection of the public from unsafe food, drugs, and cosmetics. The branch is also responsible for truthful labelling and the sanitary packaging of food, drugs, and cosmetics. The *Food and Drugs Act* and the *Narcotic Control Act* are the two major federal statutes regulated by the branch.

The Food and Drugs Act

The first **Food and Drugs Act** was passed in 1920. A later Act, passed in 1953, provides the legal authority for food and drug control in Canada today. The purpose of the law is to protect the public from injury to health and from fraud and deception in relation to food, drugs, and cosmetics. **Food** means any article manufactured, sold, or represented for use as food and drink, and any ingredient that can be mixed with food. **Inspectors** for this branch check buildings, plants, and warehouses where foods are stored or processed. They also examine the conditions under which drugs are processed, manufactured, tested, and packaged.

It is unlawful to sell any cosmetic product that can cause injury to a consumer's health when the product is used according to the directions on the label. Labels must tell what the products are for and how they are to be used. Ingredients must be listed so that consumers are aware of items that might cause possible skin irritation or other medical problems.

In 1973, the Health Protection Branch was responsible for the publication of the first survey of the nutritional health of Canadians, *Nutrition Canada.*

Agriculture Canada

One of the most important consumer services provided by Agriculture Canada is food grading and standards. Today there are grades for butter, cheese, skim milk, powder, eggs, fresh and processed fruits and vegetables, honey and maple syrup, poultry and meat. Foods are graded according to federal and provincial standards established by law. If the food products are moving across provincial or international boundaries, they must meet federal grades.

Other functions of Agriculture Canada are to inspect farm products (feeds, seeds, fertilizers, and pesticides), to safeguard crops and livestock from disease and insect pests, and to research agricultural problems.

Food Grading and Inspection

Most processed fruits and vegetables are sold by grade in Canada. Imported fruit and vegetables must meet federal grade standards if grades are established for the products. They are not permitted to carry the word "Canada" as part of their grade name when sold in their original containers. The name of the country from which the goods came must appear on the labels.

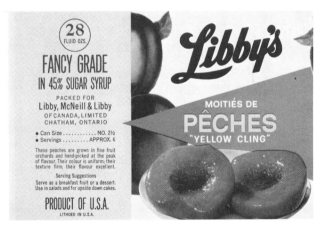

Processed fruits and vegetables are graded on flavour, colour, tenderness, maturity, shape, size, and freedom from defects. The basic grades are Canada Fancy, Canada Choice, and Canada Standard. Processors grade their own products. Federal inspectors check the accuracy of the grading.

The sugar added to canned or frozen fruit must be declared on the label as a percentage of syrup or as dry sugar. When fruits and juices are packed without sugar, the words "No Sugar Added" or "Unsweetened" must appear on the labels, except for apple juice. Some canned vegetables, such as peas or beans, may be graded and marked with a size, or marked "Assorted Sizes" or "Mixed Sizes" if ungraded as to size.

Meat is inspected by a veterinarian for wholesomeness at the slaughterhouse. Approved meat is stamped or labelled with the official inspection mark. It means that the food meets the high standards established for human consumption.

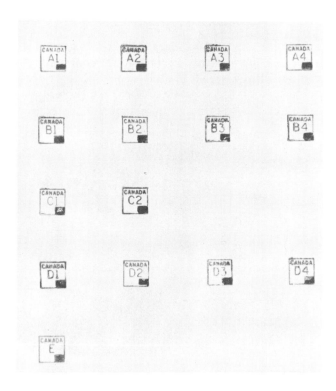

steers. Classes 1 to 4 are divided according to muscle development and quality, with Canada D4 having the lowest proportion of lean meat to bone. Grade standards have also been established for veal and lamb, and the meat carcasses are grade-stamped for consumer acceptance. Pork is not sold by grade in retail stores but is graded for producer payment only.

Grading of Meats

Grading is done by a federal meat grader. Beef is sold by grade usually. A beef carcass contains one major grade stamp and a series of ribbonlike marks in a colour grading. The ribbon brand indicates quality grade and fat level for Canada A in red ink. Canada A1 has the minimum level of fat and A4 has the highest. Canada D is from mature cows and

The main beef grades available in stores.

Grade	Colour of ribbon brand mark
Canada A, Classes 1-4	red
Canada B, Classes 1-4	blue
Canada C, Classes 1-2	brown
Canada D, Classes 1-4	black

Poultry must be graded for sale in retail stores in most major Canadian cities. The grade name appears inside a maple leaf symbol, which is prominently indicated on a metal breast tag on fresh poultry or printed on the bag for frozen poultry. A different colour indicates each grade. The grades are Canada Grade A (red), Grade B (blue), Utility (blue), and Grade C. Canada Grade C is not available in retail stores. In addition, turkeys, ducks, and geese must be marked "young" or "mature".

Eggs are sold by grade in all provinces. The grade marks must be shown on cartons and displays in retail stores. The three grades available in retail stores are Canada A1, Canada A, and Canada B. Canada A is the grade most usually available in retail stores. The three grades indicate the quality of the egg: do not confuse markings with size. Canada A1 and Canada A eggs are available in a range of sizes from Extra Large to Peewee.

The higher the grade, the more expensive the product is likely to be. Like processed fruit and vegetables, meat grades only indicate such things as flavour, tenderness, and juiciness. Food grades are not an indication of food value.

Provincial Consumer Protection

All ten Canadian provinces have consumer affairs departments dealing with consumer complaints and problems that come under provincial control. Although most merchants are fair and honest in their dealings with consumers, a few are not. Problems sometimes arise between buyers and sellers, and borrowers and lenders because one or both parties are not aware of their rights and responsibilities. Therefore, laws have been passed by provincial governments that regulate dealings between these parties.

Provincial legislation differs from province to province and because of this, it is difficult to provide details of each province's legislation. All provincial departments publish booklets and pamphlets that are available free of charge. These publications outline the highlights of the different consumer laws each province has.

Consumer Protection Acts

All provinces have passed *Consumer Protection Acts* that contain similar types of protection for consumers. Credit purchases and credit advertising must **disclose,** that is, show, the total amount of credit charges in dollars and cents and as a true annual percentage rate of interest.

Itinerant or **door-to-door sellers** must be licensed by most provinces. Licensing helps protect consumers from illegal and misleading sales schemes. The law provides a **"cooling-off period"** in which consumers may cancel in writing contracts signed with such salespersons. It does not usually apply to sales between buyers and sellers made at the seller's place of business. The cooling-off period differs in each province. In some provinces, the cooling-off period is outlined in the province's *Direct Sellers Act.*

Trade Practices Act

British Columbia was the first province to pass this type of legislation in 1974. Since then, Alberta has passed the *Unfair Trade Practices Act* and Ontario the *Business Practices Act* in 1975. Prince Edward Island passed a *Business Practices Act* in 1977. Similar legislation is in progress in Manitoba and Newfoundland. These Acts clearly outline what constitutes unfair or **misleading business practices.** If a contract involved any of these unfair practices, the consumer has certain rights, including the right to cancellation in some cases. It is also against the law to take advantage of people who cannot protect their own interests because of age, sickness, or a poor understanding of the language.

Such laws protect not only the consumer but also the reputable business community from dishonest business people.

Good Laws Need to Be Publicized

Laws are of little use if the people affected by them do not know about them. Publicity is necessary to achieve this purpose and so governments advertise to make people aware of the ways in which they are affected by the new laws. The British Columbia government sent a sixteen-page booklet, *The Trade Practices Act and You,* to every household in the province to publicize its legislation. Decisions under the *Trade Practices Act* are also publicized periodically by the Enforcement Report. Newspaper advertisements containing the main points of new laws appear in daily and weekly newspapers. Radio and television commercials also outline highlights of government legislation.

Saskatchewan Consumer Affairs

the Consumer Products Warranties Act

Answers to questions about the Saskatchewan Consumer Products Warranties Act.

Q. What is a Consumer Product?

A. A consumer product is any new or used item ordinarily used for personal, family, or household purposes. Some products bought by farmers and fishermen for use in their operations are also considered as consumer products.

Q. Are there any exceptions?

A. Yes. Products sold between private individuals, goods intended for resale or for business purposes, or goods sold by a trustee in a bankruptcy, a receiver, a sheriff, or by an auctioneer are all excluded from the Act.

Q. Who receives protection from the Act?

A. All persons who buy consumer products from a retail seller, as well as persons who get the product from the original purchaser, receive the protection provided by the Statutory Warranties. Non-profit organizations who purchase consumer products, and farmers and fishermen who buy products for use in their business, also receive these Statutory Warranties.

Q. How does the Act look after my interests?

A. Whenever you buy a consumer product from a Saskatchewan retailer, you will receive several basic warranties known as Statutory Warranties that provide you with a minimum standard of protection. These warranties are considered by the Act to be given to you by the retail seller and the manufacturer.

Q. What are the Statutory Warranties I am entitled to receive?

A. • You should be able to enjoy ownership of the goods without fear of undisclosed mortgages, liens, or other claims against them.
• The product must match its description.

• The goods must be of acceptable quality.
• The goods must be fit for specific purposes stated by you as well as for their usual purpose.
• If you purchase a product based on a sample, then the product must match the quality of the sample and must be free from defects.
• The goods must be durable for a reasonable period of time.
• Spare parts and repair facilities must be available for a reasonable period of time (not necessarily within the Province).

Q. What does "acceptable quality" mean?

A. A product has the quality and characteristics that consumers can reasonably expect taking into account such things as the price and description.

Q. What does "reasonable durability" mean?

A. The product must last for a reasonable length of time taking into account the price and description as well as how the product has been used and maintained.

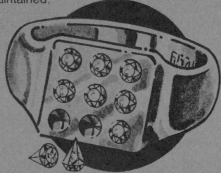

Q. What am I entitled to if the product fails to meet the Statutory Warranties?

A. If something is substantially wrong with a product and it cannot be repaired, you may reject the product and recover your purchase price less a deduction for use from the retailer or manufacturer at fault.

If the product is faulty but can be repaired, then the Act says that you are entitled to have the goods repaired at no cost to you. If, after a reasonable period of time, the seller has failed to fix the product, you can have the repair work done elsewhere and recover your costs from the seller.

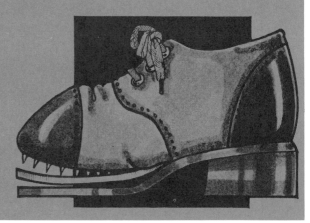

Provincial Consumer Affairs Departments

Department of Consumer Services
Parliament Buildings
Victoria, British Columbia
V8V 1X4

* 7 days

* **Length of
Cooling-off
Period**

Department of Consumer and Corporate Affairs
9915-108 Street
Edmonton, Alberta
T5K 2G8

*
4 days

Saskatchewan Department of Consumer Affairs
Box 3000
Regina, Saskatchewan
S4P 2K1

*
4 days

Consumers' Bureau   * 4 days
307 Kennedy Street
Winnipeg, Manitoba
R3B 2M7

Consumer Protection Bureau
Ministry of Consumer and Commercial Relations
555 Yonge Street
Toronto, Ontario
M4Y 1Y7

*
2 days

Consumer Services Bureau
Box 998
Halifax, Nova Scotia
B3J 2X3

* 5 days

Consumer Services Bureau
Box 32
Fredericton, New Brunswick
E3B 5H1

* 5 days

Department of Provincial Secretary
Box 2000
Charlottetown, P.E.I.
C1A 7N8

* 7 days

Consumer Protection Bureau
800 Place d'Youville
Quebec, P.Q.
G1A 1L8

* 5 days

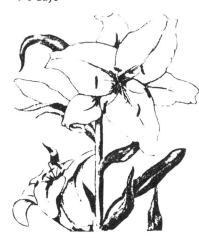

Department of Consumer Affairs
Box 999
St. John's, Newfoundland
A1C 5T7

* 10 days

197

UNIT C

CONSUMER AID
FROM PRIVATE ORGANIZATIONS

In the last unit you read about government legislation to help protect consumers. There are many private organizations and groups that offer protection to consumers too. There are also many sources of consumer information that help provide answers to basic buying questions. This unit examines some of these private organizations and sources of consumer information that are available to help consumers get their money's worth when they make choices in the marketplace.

Consumers' Association of Canada

The Consumers' Association of Canada, commonly known as the CAC, began in 1947. The CAC is a voluntary, non-profit organization that protects, represents, and educates consumers. CAC is a national organization with an increasing number of local branches and consumer action committees in all provinces. Current membership is about 105 000 and still increasing.

CAC has four main objectives:
To present consumers' views to the federal, provincial, and municipal governments and to provide a channel of communication between government and consumers.

To study consumer problems and make recommendations for their solution to industry, labour, and agriculture representatives.

To unite the strength of consumers to improve the standard of living in Canadian homes.

To obtain information on consumer goods and services by conducting research and tests, and rating products on the basis of their quality.

These test results are available in the *Canadian Consumer/Le Consommateur Canadien* published in both French and English editions every two months. This magazine can be purchased at most newstands or by subscription. It also contains buying guides, news reprints of consumer interest, and an analysis of government consumer legislation. It is an excellent source of information for all Canadian consumers.

The test results sometimes indicate that the very best buys are not always the national brand name products. Thus, reading these results will help families save money when making certain types of purchases. No product is accepted from a manufacturer for testing. All items tested are purchased by CAC members just as any shopper would buy them. These items are then sent to the headquarters of CAC in Ottawa for testing. No advertising appears in the magazine, and no funds are accepted from any industry or trade association which guarantees that the test results are fair and honest.

Many federal and provincial consumer protection laws were passed because of pressure exerted by the CAC. For example, the *Hazardous Products Act* included studies and tests done by the CAC on poisonous and dangerous substances in the home and garage. The *Consumer Packaging and Labelling Act* was composed of nearly fifty resolutions from CAC to the government over a period of eight years.

The main sources of CAC's income come from membership fees (about sixty per cent) and from an annual grant from the federal government. Because CAC is independent of agriculture, government, and industry, it is an important impartial, or fair voice, for all Canadian consumers.

Better Business Bureau

In fourteen of the major cities in Canada, Better Business Bureaus have been formed to provide information to consumers on local business firms. Each local bureau is a non-profit organization supported by membership fees from area businesses. All of the bureaus are joined together into a national network through the national office, the Better Business Bureau of Canada, located in Toronto.

The main purpose of the BBB is to improve business and consumer relationships by effective communication and action. Each bureau keeps detailed files on businesses in its area. These files provide the necessary information on the performance and dependability of a particular business. This includes a record of complaints by consumers

YOUR BETTER BUSINESS BUREAUS
ACROSS CANADA

Mr. E.G. Molloy, General Manager
BETTER BUSINESS BUREAU OF NFLD. & LABRADOR
P.O. Box 516
St. John's, Newfoundland A1C 5K4

Ms. Ann Janega, Manager
BETTER BUSINESS BUREAU OF NOVA SCOTIA
P.O. Box 2124, 1708 Granville Street
Halifax, Nova Scotia B3J 3B7

Mr. Maurice Guerin, General Manager
BUREAU D'ETHIQUE COMMERCIALE DE QUEBEC, INC.
475, rue Richelieu
Quebec City, P.Q. G1R 1K2

Mr. Roger Nadeau, Executive Vice-President & General Manager
BETTER BUSINESS BUREAU OF MONTREAL, INC.
1155 Dorchester Blvd. W.
Montreal, P.Q. H3B 2H5

Ms. Edith Huggins, General Manager
BETTER BUSINESS BUREAU OF OTTAWA & HULL, INC.
71 Bank Street, Suite 503
Ottawa, Ontario K1P 5N2

Mr. Paul J. Tuz, President & Chief Executive Operating Officer
BETTER BUSINESS BUREAU OF METRO TORONTO, INC.
321 Bloor Street East, Suite 901
Toronto, Ontario M4W 3K6

Mr. Dan MacDonald, General Manager
BETTER BUSINESS BUREAU OF HAMILTON & DISTRICT
170 Jackson Street East
Hamilton, Ontario L8N 1L4

Mr. Joe Amort, Manager
BETTER BUSINESS BUREAU OF WINDSOR & DISTRICT
500 Riverside Drive West
Windsor, Ontario N9A 5K4

Mr. John Mounstephen, Manager
BETTER BUSINESS BUREAU OF WATERLOO REGION
354 Charles Street East
Kitchener, Ontario N2G 4L5

Mr. Cedric A. Edson, Manager
BETTER BUSINESS BUREAU OF METRO WINNIPEG, INC.
365 Hargrave Street, Room 204
Winnipeg, Manitoba R3B 2K3

Mr. Wm. H.J. Stutt, President
BETTER BUSINESS BUREAU OF EDMONTON & NORTHERN ALBERTA
600 Guardian Building
10240 — 124th Street
Edmonton, Alberta T5N 3W6

Mr. David S. Oakes, Manager
BETTER BUSINESS BUREAU OF CALGARY, INC.
630 — 8th Avenue S.W., Suite 404
Calgary, Alberta T2P 1G6

Mr. Vincent E. Forbes, Executive Vice-President
BETTER BUSINESS BUREAU OF THE MAINLAND OF B.C.
100 West Pender Street, 12th Floor
Vancouver, B.C. V6B 1S3

Mr. W.D. Tindall, Executive Vice-President
BETTER BUSINESS BUREAU OF VANCOUVER ISLAND
P.O. Box M37, 635 Humboldt Street
Victoria, B.C. V8W 1A7

against the firm and the manner in which the complaints have been settled. This information is available to consumers upon request. With this information, the consumer can decide which business to deal with.

Before making any business dealings with a firm or person with whom they are not familiar, consumers are advised to check with the nearest Better Business Bureau. With their connections with similar bureaus in the United States, the Canadian Better Business Bureaus can provide information on a wide variety of businesses throughout North America. It is important to remember that the BBB only provides the information. It is not their function to recommend a product, service, or company.

The BBB also publishes a series of free or inexpensive fact booklets on a large number of goods and services. It provides consumer information through radio and television announcements, and by having speakers available to appear at business, public, and school functions.

Mediation and the BBB

Handling consumer complaints is another service provided by the BBB. In doing this, it recognizes that there are two sides to such disputes. When the BBB receives a complaint from a consumer, the business and the consumer are put in touch with one another to solve the problem. If there is no solution, the complaint is placed in the company's file. It is then reported to callers asking about the company's reputation.

Another alternative to settling the problem is available at some of the Bureaus. If both parties agree, the BBB will appoint an independent **mediator**, or third party expert, to hear both sides of the dispute. All of these experts are volunteers. The hearing is informal and private and there is no charge to either party. After hearing both sides, the mediator gives a decision to the parties. The decision can be completely in favour of one party or split between the two. This plan is an alternative to legal action.

Canadian Standards Association

The **Canadian Standards Association** or CSA is an independent not-for-profit organization that tests a wide variety of products, including plumbing goods, hockey helmets, face masks, and electrical appliances; so they can be safely used by consumers. CSA is financed from annual fees from any person or organization that wants to become a member. The other main sources of revenue are the fees charged to manufacturers when they submit their products for testing and certification and the sale of standards.

The volunteers who sit on CSA committees have developed over 1200 national **standards** for different products. A standard is a required level of safety, and performance in some cases, that products tested by CSA must meet. Most of CSA's standards do not indicate the efficiency of the product. The standards are developed by committees of volunteers drawn from all groups in society, such as manufacturers, consumers, university professors, and governmental representatives. All ideas from the committees are considered, and standards are the result of agreement among the members.

One of CSA's main concerns is in drawing up standards for electrical safety, especially against electrical shock and fire hazards. Their standards have no legal force, but governments often pass laws based on CSA standards. For example, all electrical products offered for sale in all ten provinces must be examined and certified by CSA before being sold.

A manufacturer submits a product to CSA for testing, and pays a fee for this service. CSA engineers examine and test the product against the standard for that type of product. If the product meets the standard, the manufacturer is able to apply a CSA **certification mark** to the product before it is sold. Most consumers look for the CSA mark before buying new products as it is an important piece of consumer information. More than 9 000 new products are tested by CSA each year. Over 10 000 companies participate in the CSA certification program.

CSA's headquarters and main testing facility is located in Rexdale, a suburb of Toronto. Regional offices and smaller testing facilities are located in major cities across Canada. Products manufactured outside of Canada and intended for sale in Canada are tested by agencies around the world.

CSA publishes a small pamphlet, *CSA and the Consumer*, four times a year. This publication provides consumers with an insight into the type of testing, products being tested, and the procedures for updating, revising, and improving standards. This informative publication is available free of charge from CSA headquarters to organizations, educational institutions, and others for bulk distribution.

Other Consumer Testing Organizations

Consumers' Union is a nonprofit American organization that tests various products and services in their private laboratories. The test results are then rated and reported each month in *Consumer Reports*. This magazine is available by subscription, at most newsstands each month, and in many school and public libraries. Products are rated as acceptable or not acceptable. Extra good buys and values are marked as "best buy". Besides product ratings, the magazine contains articles of general interest to consumers.

Consumer Reports carries no advertising and the ratings are critical and honest, even of leading manufacturers whose products do not meet the test standards. Each December an annual buying guide is published, which is an excellent and inexpensive source of consumer information for any family or person planning major purchases.

Consumers' Research also tests and rates various consumer products in their laboratories. Products are rated as recommended, intermediate, and not recommended. The test results are published each month in *Consumers' Research Magazine*. This magazine is not as well known in Canada as *Consumer Reports* as it is not for sale at Canadian newsstands.

Both testing organizations are very useful to consumers. This is because all of their tests are independent and are reported by brand name. It would cost too much money to test every brand of a particular product. Thus, only major brands are tested. *Consumer Reports* even includes some Canadian products now in their testing because of the large number of Canadian readers. Both magazines publish a product-test index once a year for easy reference. To maintain their critical and objective testing evaluations, neither organization allows manufacturers of products to use the test results in their product advertising.

Business Organizations

Many business organizations now publish consumer information available free of charge or at a small cost to consumers. This is a public service that more companies are following these days to help increase consumer awareness.

Most of the chartered banks publish free booklets that provide useful consumer information. The Royal Bank of Canada is the publisher of *Your Money Matters*. This free booklet discusses family money management, sources of credit, savings and investings, buying a car, and insurance and pensions. The Canadian Imperial Bank of Commerce has three very practical booklets available: *Buying a Car*, *Buying a House*, and *Personal Financial Planning*. The Bank of Montreal has met the increased awareness of women in money matters by publishing *Money-What Every Woman Should Know*. The other chartered banks have booklets on banking and banking services available to their customers. All of the banks also publish monthly newsletters on subjects of economic concern, general interest, and personal relations.

Household Finance Corporation (HFC) began their consumer education information program many years ago. They publish a series of booklets outlining various ways in which consumers can more effectively manage their money. The series of booklets include such topics as *Your Automobile Dollar*, *Your Food Dollar*, *Your Recreation Dollar*, *It's Your Credit-Manage It Wisely*, and several others that cover the major areas of personal and family finance. All of these booklets emphasize sound planning and careful shopping as the basis of wise money management. These booklets are available at a small cost from any office of HFC.

Provincial and local credit unions provide a series of booklets and free loan films to make consumers aware of the services they provide. Lists of available sources of consumer information can be obtained from your nearest credit union.

The Canadian Life Insurance Association, representing one hundred and thirty insurance companies, has prepared a wide variety of materials that provide consumer information. These items include films, filmstrips, and many different booklets dealing with insurance and money management problems of young people and families. *This Business of Life* is a detailed guide to life insurance for Canadian consumers. *Family Money Manager* is a do-it-yourself guide for sensible spending and saving. *What Will Your Career Be in Business?* is a very useful aid in providing you with some ideas about the many different types of careers in the business world. These publications are only a few of the many available from this association.

The Insurance Bureau of Canada is an organization of property and casualty insurance companies. Their concern is to improve communications with governments and the consumers and to distribute consumer information about general insurance. Their main publications are *Car Insurance Explained* and *Home Insurance Explained*. These two booklets are written in easy-to-understand question and answer form so that the average consumer will be able to understand these complex issues.

This list of materials is by no means complete. It does indicate the wide variety of business organizations that are providing free or inexpensive assistance to help consumers become more informed. However, some materials provided by business are mainly a sales promotion for that firm and are not very useful as consumer information. As a result, it is important to make sure that the facts in these materials are correct and free from a particular **bias** or one-sided point of view.

Specialized Magazines

Some magazines are published to provide information to help consumers make wise, informed choices. *Changing Times,* an American publication, is one such useful magazine. It is available by subscription only. It contains no advertising at all, and it compares the quality of competing products fairly and honestly. This magazine also contains considerable information on such things as types of insurance, money management, home buying, cars, energy conservation, and many other items of general interest to consumers. This magazine is a much more general consumer information magazine than *Consumer Reports* and *Consumers' Research Magazine.*

Another general interest publication is *Money.* It is available each month at newsstands or by sub-

scription. *Money* contains many interesting articles for consumers. Because this is an American magazine, a few of the articles have little use for Canadian consumers. Careful reading of the other articles will save consumers money and help them make wise choices.

Chatelaine, a Canadian magazine, is a general interest magazine that contains articles dealing with money management, legal concerns, food and health advice, and some specific consumer columns such as "Cash Flow". It is published each month and is available by subscription or at newstands.

Automotive, stereo equipment, and boating magazines provide specialized information written by experts. These magazines are very informative if you are buying the particular product they describe. They are not intended to provide articles of general interest.

Finally, nearly all magazines contain advertising. By looking at different advertisements for products, consumers can obtain answers to some basic buying decision. Advertisements also can inform consumer about new products on the market.

Newspapers

Newspapers, like magazines, publish various types of consumer information. Many consumer columns appear in newspapers throughout Canada. These columns discuss such topics as money management, buying fresh and frozen foods, nuitrition, how to care for different types of home products, and many other items of general interest to consumers. Much of the information that appears in magazines and newspapers is very useful. Many consumers cut out these articles and file them for future use. By doing this, they will have the information available when they need it. This would be a good habit for you to begin now.

Most newspapers contain stock exchange listings. From these charts you are able to see if the price of a stock you may have purchased has increased or decreased. You are also able to find the value of the Canadian dollar in relation to the American dollar, the English pound, the French franc, the German mark, and the foreign currencies of other major countries. This is very useful information if you are planning a trip to one of these foreign countries.

Some large city newspapers also contain special columns that help consumers with their problems. These "Probe" or "Action Line" columns provide answers to consumer concerns, and they assist consumers in obtaining satisfaction with manufacturers or retailers for unsatisfactory products.

Consumers contribute to their misfortune

It isn't legislation that the consumer needs. It is education, as consumers are by and large the authors of their own misfortune.

This was the opinion of panelists at a general discussion sponsored yesterday at Queen's University Law Student Society. Panelists included Donald Goudy, Registrar of the Consumer Protection Bureau of the Provincial Ministry of Consumer and Commercial Relations; Barry Craig, a journalist on leave from the Toronto *Globe and Mail;* and Gordon Sanderson, a writer with the *London Free Press.*

The three men spoke about consumer problems and found that education is needed now to protect the consumer.

Mr. Craig mentioned the case of an Alberta car dealership where it was proved and publicized that staff had been turning back the speedometers on the cars. The publicity they received actually increased sales. "People began to assume that these people were cleaned up and wouldn't dare do it again. But many companies aren't the least intimidated by the threat

of legal action," said Mr. Craig. Mr. Sanderson said consumers are often very lazy. "People don't want to read the fine print on the fire insurance policy until their house is on fire," he said, but added that the problem is not only the fault of the consumer. "The ethics of business are at an all time low ... business knows consumer protection better than the consumer–it's a very unfair marketplace."

Mr. Goudy pointed out that many consumers are gullible and lazy, but it is also true that they are trusting and they assume that others will act as they would.

Ontario's *Business Practices Act* is quite specific in outlining more than twenty subtle ways in which a business could deceive a consumer. "What is needed now is education," said Mr. Goudy, "but it would do little good to send out special booklets and buy advertising space in newspapers to advise consumers of their rights for public memory is short, and it would be forgotten three days later."

It is difficult to help consumers

by advance information because it is often not until they are right in the middle of things that they will realize they have been defrauded, said Mr. Craig.

The panel called for more awareness and scepticism on the part of the consumer. "If you go by a store which advertises a sale of items up to 70 per cent off, why not go into the store and say "show me something that is 70 per cent off!" said Mr. Sanderson.

In a question period the panel was asked how consumers can find out before they shop which are the best merchants to deal with. Many cities have a Better Business Bureau, which can furnish the consumer with statistics on complaints against certain local companies. Cities that do not have access to a BBB could contact the nearest Chamber of Commerce or local branch of the Consumers' Association of Canada.

The Whig-Standard, Kingston
February 7, 1975
Reprinted by permission

Radio and Television

Many local radio stations have set up "Hot-line" phone-in programs. They allow people to hear both sides of a consumer problem. Such shows can help settle local consumer problems by presenting the problem to the merchant involved.

The **Canadian Broadcasting Corporation** (CBC) and the **Canadian Television Network** (CTV) investigate major consumer problems on their public affairs programs. Fraudulent selling practices, food nutrition surveys, product testing, and wise shopping tips are among the kinds of information presented each week.

As you have read, there are many sources of private help and consumer information available to consumers. There is no one best source of information. The more information consumers have available to them, the better chance they have of making a good decision. Thus, a guide to wise shopping is, where possible, to consider several different sources of consumer information. This reduces or eliminates the possibility of your making a costly mistake.

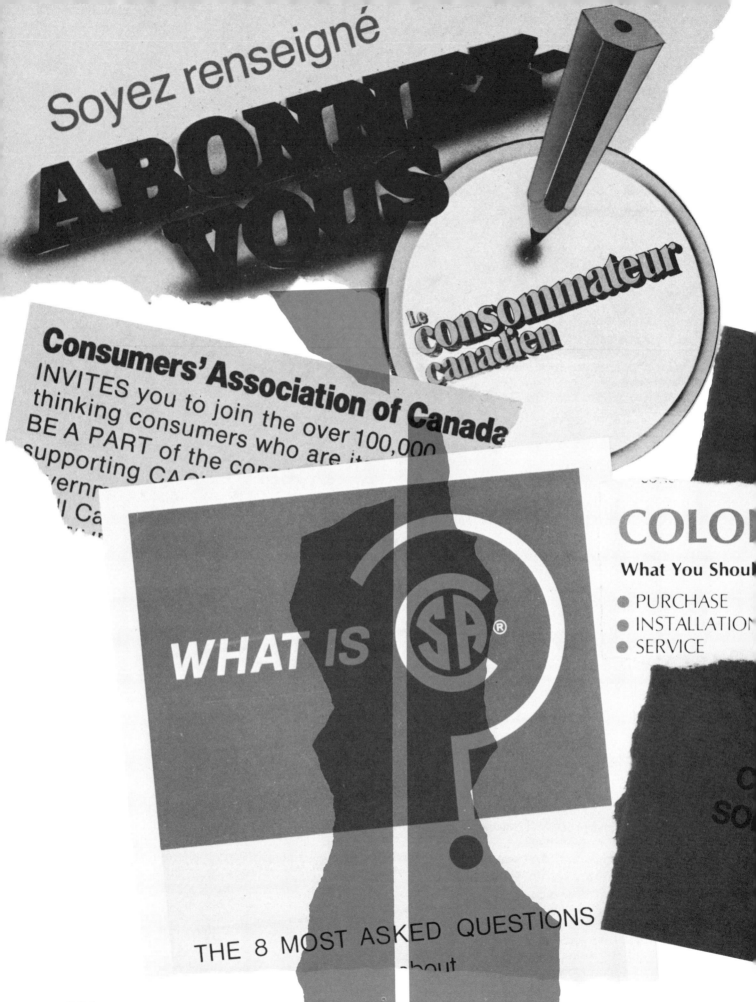

Soyez renseigné

ABONNEZ-VOUS

Le **consommateur** canadien

Consumers' Association of Canada

INVITES you to join the over 100,000
thinking consumers who are it
BE A PART of the con
supporting CAC
vernm
l Ca

WHAT IS ⒞⒮⒜®

COLO

What You Shoul

● PURCHASE
● INSTALLATION
● SERVICE

C
SO

THE 8 MOST ASKED QUESTIONS
about

BETTER
BUSINESS
BUREAU
OF CANADA

BBB

BUREAU
D'ET...
COM...
DU ...

BBB

CSA ®

CONSUMER TIPS ON
BAIT AND
SWITCH

bait

switch

BETTER
BUSINESS
BUREAU
OF CANADA

BBB

BUREAU
D'ETHIQUE
COMMERCIALE
DU CANADA

BETTER
BUSINESS
BUREAU
OF CANADA

BBB

Join us,

You can't afford
not to....

TV

About

BBB

Facts

ABOUT

L'ÉCHANGE

Parfois vous échangez une voiture d'occasion
contre un autre véhicule d'occasion.
Nous l'avons dit, le contrat ....
des ...ast-to-Coast network
...with

DELINES
FOR
NTABLE
CATIONS

BUYI...
CAR...

REVIEWING
YOUR BUSINESS VOCABULARY

Write the number of each definition.
Write the word that matches the definition number.

UNIT A

brand name, clearance sale, conspicuous consumption, consumer, impulse, label, motive, need, promotional sale, want

1. Person who purchases a product or service for personal use.
2. Something that people would like to have for pleasure or satisfaction.
3. Something that people must have to exist.
4. Trade name of a national manufacturer or well known producer.
5. Placing of certain items on sale to clear them out for new stock.
6. Sale to get consumers to visit the store to buy a certain product.
7. Buying goods without thinking or planning in advance.
8. Something attached to a product that describes its contents or how to use it.
9. Purchase of goods for the sake of impressing others.
10. A reason for doing something.

UNIT B

Agriculture Canada, care labelling of textiles, Combines Investigation Act, Consumer Packaging and Labelling Act, cooling-off period, Hazardous Products Act, Food and Drugs Act, full disclosure, Textile Labelling Act, Trade Practices Act

1. Law passed in 1969 to warn consumers about possible dangers from harmful household goods.
2. Law dealing with the labelling, sale, and advertising of consumer textile articles.
3. Voluntary labelling scheme that tells consumers how to treat their fabrics.
4. Law requiring an ordered list of ingredients of food products appear on the label of food containers.
5. Principal federal law that deals with misleading advertising.
6. Provides for inspectors to check the sanitary conditions in buildings and plants where foods are processed.
7. Responsible for grades and standards of food products.
8. Time within which consumers may cancel in writing contracts made with door-to-door sellers.
9. Provincial law outlining unfair or misleading sales practices between consumers and sellers.
10. True annual cost of credit in dollars and cents and as a true percentage rate of interest for credit.

UNIT C

advertising, Better Business Bureau, Canadian Standards Association, certification mark, Consumers' Association of Canada, Consumers' Union, newspaper, standard

1. Tries to settle valid complaints between retailers and consumers.
2. Puts its certification mark on certain products that meet their test standards.
3. Source of consumer information but is used mainly to sell goods and services.
4. Consumer buying aid that indicates a product has been tested for safety.
5. Level of safety that must be met before tested products can be certified.
6. One of the best local or area sources of consumer information.
7. Publisher of the *Canadian Consumer*.
8. Publisher of *Consumer Reports*.

REVIEW QUESTIONS

UNIT A

1. What is a consumer? List five items that you might buy as a consumer.
2. Why should people try to be wise consumers?
3. List four factors that should be considered by wise consumers when buying a product?
4. What is the difference between a need and a want? List four needs and four wants for you and your family.
5. What two factors affect most consumer buying decisions?
6. Does a brand name product guarantee the quality of a product?
7. What is a store brand product? How do these products compare in price to brand name products?
8. What is conspicuous consumption? List some products that you or your family may have purchased for this reason.
9. Explain the difference between end-of-season and special sales. Provide an example of each type.
10. Besides the obvious use of packages for advertising, packages do have some very practical and necessary functions. List three reasons why most goods are packaged.
11. What is the Universal Product Code? List two advantages of the UPC to the supermarket industry.
12. What benefits will adoption of the metric system have for Canadian consumers?
13. Why should consumers comparison shop before they go shopping?
14. What is a conserver society? Why should Canadians be moving in this direction?
15. What changes in buying patterns and living standards should consumers be encouraged to follow in the next ten years?

UNIT B

1. What are the two main functions of the Department of Consumer and Corporate Affairs?
2. What is the purpose of Box 99? What are three major concerns that consumers have for Box 99?
3. Why was it necessary for the federal government to pass the *Hazardous Products Act*? When did it become law?
4. Explain the meaning of the warning symbols that represent hazards on product labels.
5. What is the main purpose of the *Textile Labelling Act*? When was it passed, and when did it become law?
6. By law, what information must appear on fabric labels?
7. Explain the meaning of the care labelling symbols that may appear on fabric and textile products.
8. What is the main purpose of the *Consumer Packaging and Labelling Act*? When did it become fully effective?
9. Outline briefly the basic information that must appear on package labels in Canada.
10. Explain the meaning of the term "durable life date" as it applies to food products.
11. How has the *Consumer Packaging and Labelling Act* affected the size and number of packages available?
12. What are the main concerns of the Health Protection Branch of Health and Welfare Canada?
13. Describe the main protection that consumers receive from the *Food and Drugs Act*.
14. What kinds of protection do consumers receive from the provincial *Consumer Protection Acts* and the *Direct Sellers Acts*?
15. Why is it necessary for governments to publicize new laws?

UNIT C

1. How can private groups and sources of consumer information help consumers?
2. What are three of the main objectives of the Consumers' Association of Canada?
3. What kinds of information can consumers find in the *Canadian Consumer*?
4. From what two main sources does the Consumers' Association of Canada receive its income?
5. How is the Better Business Bureau organized?
6. How does a Better Business Bureau handle a dispute between a retailer and a consumer?
7. Explain how a mediator may settle a consumer complaint referred to a Better Business Bureau.
8. What is the main function of the Canadian Standards Association?
9. What does a CSA certification mark on a home appliance tell a consumer?
10. What kinds of information can consumers find in *CSA and the Consumer*?
11. How do Consumers' Union and Consumers' Research help consumers?
12. Why can consumers be sure that ratings from Consumers' Union and Consumers' Research are honest and unbiased?
13. List four examples of the kinds of consumer information available from various business organizations.
14. Name three private sources of consumer product information.
15. What types of consumer information are published in local newspapers?

APPLYING
YOUR BUSINESS KNOWLEDGE

UNIT A

1. Have you and your family purchased any products recently that did not meet your needs? If so, why didn't they meet your needs? Could you have avoided this problem?

2. Many consumer wants are the result of wanting to be in fashion or style. What items have you purchased recently for this reason? Were these wise choices? Why or why not?

3. Custom and style sometimes influence consumer choices. List three examples of purchases that consumers make for these reasons. Are they wise or unwise choices?

4. Are there any advantages to buying name brand merchandise? Why do many people prefer brand names to store brand products?

5. In what ways does advertising play a part in influencing consumer choice? Is the large amount of advertising really necessary and helpful to consumers?

6. Buying goods on sale may result in either a wise or an unwise choice being made by consumers. With examples, describe when the purchase of sale items provides good value and when it does not provide good value.

7. What information can consumers obtain from product packages and labels that may be useful in making wise consumer choices?

8. Is comparison shopping of prices and quality worth the time and effort? List examples of when it is worthwhile and when it is not. Give personal examples of how comparison shopping resulted in your making a wise choice.

9. Prepare a list of six principles of wise buying that you would recommend to a friend that should be considered before making any consumer purchase.

10. "Moving to a conserver from a consumer society doesn't mean sacrifice and a no-growth economy, but sanity and selective growth. The public has to learn that conserving society's resources is not a sacrifice but an act of sanity." (Science Council of Canada Report, September 1977.) Explain the meaning of this statement. Do you agree with it?

UNIT B

1. What is meant by the statement "Consumers must be honest and must be prepared to accept their responsibilities in the marketplace"?

2. Why do you think symbols rather than words were chosen to represent hazardous products on labels? Why were traffic sign shapes chosen to indicate the degrees of hazard?

3. Why was two years needed from passage to full implementation of the *Textile Labelling Act*? Was this a reasonable and necessary length of time?

4. Although the care labelling of textiles is a very useful source of consumer information, it has received criticism from many people. What is the main criticism of this program?

5. Why is it necessary for labels to include the use of additives in food?

6. How does the reduction in the number of package sizes for products make it easier for consumers to make better informed choices in the marketplace?

7. Why is it necessary for all provincial governments as well as the federal government to pass consumer protection legislation?

8. Why are provincial trade or business Acts useful to business people as well as to consumers?

9. If there were no misleading advertising or deceptive sales schemes, would there be any need for consumer protection legislation?

UNIT C

1. Why do you think *Canadian Consumer, Consumer Reports,* and *Changing Times* do not contain any advertising?
2. Why do you think these three magazines do not allow manufacturers to use their product test results in their product advertising?
3. Of the sources of consumer information discussed in this unit, which is the most informative for you and your family? Why is this so?
4. The main purpose of the private organizations discussed in this unit is to provide information to consumers. Do you feel this information is needed? Why or why not?
5. Why are more and more magazines these days publishing articles that provide information to consumers?
6. Why do you think manufacturers are willing to pay a fee for the testing of their products to obtain a CSA certification mark?
7. Why do so many consumers consult *Canadian Consumer* and *Consumer Reports* before making major purchases?
8. Why are so many businesses making consumer information publications available free of charge or at a small cost to their customers? Do you think this is a good idea?
9. What kinds of useful information can be obtained from advertising?
10. Discuss the role of the news media as sources of consumer information.

PROJECTS AND PROBLEMS

UNIT A

1. Visit one of your area's supermarkets or large department stores and investigate the manner in which advertising and promotions and displays are designed to exploit the impulse-buying tendencies of consumers. Carefully examine labels, packages, colours, location of the products on the shelves, lighting, and so on in terms of their effect on consumer buying impulses.

   Interview the manager and ask him or her what products are new in the business within the last two years and how have they been received and accepted by consumers. Determine to what extent packaging and advertising is used to sell the product. Prepare a written or oral report for the class on your investigations.

2. Select four products of different types in which you or your family are interested; for example, shampoos, automobiles, cassette recorders, a record album, and so on. For each item:
   a. determine the best time, if any, to purchase the item
   b. compare prices for the item at three different stores
   c. collect any information available about the item, before you go shopping for it
   d. determine the place where you will purchase the item.
   Prepare a report on your findings, indicating why you made the decisions that you did.

UNIT B

1. In a group of a maximum of four, choose a certain product such as facial tissues, shampoos, fruit juices, toothpaste, cereals, and so on. Compare the packaging and labelling. Make a chart showing the kinds of the product you are investigating with a list of the information given on the label. Does the labelling disguise the product, or does it create an impression that the product has different ingredients from those listed? Does all of the required information required by the law appear on the label? Is the print easy to read? Are the illustrations on the labels and packages misleading? Is the name of the manufacturer clearly identified? In your opinion, which are the best and the poorest labels? Give reasons for your choices.

UNIT C

1. Read a recent issue of *Canadian Consumer* or *Consumer Reports* and prepare a report of a product test of your choice. Your report should indicate:
   a. type of product tested
   b. nature of the tests that were conducted
   c. most significant results by brand name
   d. apparent relationship, if any, between price and quality.
2. In small groups, discuss the people, places, and informational publications that commonly provide consumer information, advice, and aid. From the discussions and group research, prepare a *Dictionary of Consumer Aid and Information* that would be useful to a person who knows little or nothing about consumer information and protection. List names and addresses, telephone numbers if possible, and the types of problems handled by each resource person or organization named. Distribute your dictionary to fellow students and staff.

9
Credit and Personal Finance

UNIT A
CREDIT AND CREDIT ACCOUNTS

"Will that be cash or charge?" is a common question asked by salespersons at most retail stores. The question itself is simple, but the answer leads to a very complex set of conditions. If the answer is *charge,* then the customer becomes not only a buyer of goods or services but also a borrower of money. Conversely, the business becomes a seller of goods or services and a lender of money.

Many people use credit. Canadians buy billions of dollars worth of goods and services every year on credit. This situation greatly affects consumers, businesses, and the economy. Credit, generally, allows consumers to buy more goods and services now than they could without it. Businesses sell more and the extra production means more jobs are available for workers. Credit, therefore, can be supported as a means of increasing our standard of living. But credit can be a two-edged sword. Used wisely, it can help us: used poorly, it causes us financial difficulty.

What Is Credit?

Credit is a privilege that allows us to purchase something now and pay for it later. We can buy records, sweaters, radios, cars, even candy on credit. Most gasoline purchases and car repair bills are made on credit. Most houses are heated by oil, gas, or electricity purchased on credit. Telephone, hydro, and water bills are received by us after the services have been used. Some local grocery stores still allow neighbourhood residents to buy on credit. These examples prove that credit is around us at all times and touches nearly all Canadians. And in all cases, it allows us to buy and use something now and pay for it later.

Why Consumers Use Credit

Consumers use credit for many reasons, but the following three are the most common.

Convenience

Most consumers find credit convenient for regular shopping as well as for special purchases of some expensive items that are purchased every five to ten years. Using credit to buy items of clothing, gasoline, and restaurant meals allows consumers to shop while carrying very little cash. Consumers can take advantage of special sales by using credit. It is much easier and safer to use credit on trips and holidays than to carry large amounts of cash. Many consumers buy expensive items such as cars and furniture on credit because they feel they should pay for the item as they use it.

Emergencies

Consumers often experience unexpected expenses that can be very costly. An emergency such as a major car, house, or appliance repair often occurs when individuals do not have enough cash to cover the expense. The best answer to such a situation is often credit. Paying on credit, that is spreading the expense over a longer period of time, usually means less of a financial problem to the family.

Forced Savings

Many individuals have difficulty saving money. The money that should have been saved for a long-term goal is spent on items of little value. People who cannot save for an item that will increase their standard of living buy on credit. An example of such an item is a car. By using credit, people are forced to make payments and after two or three years they have paid for the car completely. In some cases, the payments are automatically deducted from their pay cheques or bank accounts.

Disadvantages of Credit

Using credit has two main disadvantages and although consumers are usually aware of the disadvantages they feel that the benefits are great enough to overcome them. The two disadvantages of credit are interest costs and impulse buying

Interest Cost

When we use property that belongs to someone else, we expect to pay for that privilege. For example, we pay rent for an apartment or a kilometre fee for the use of a car. The same idea applies to money. If we borrow or rent money from someone or a business, we must pay a fee. This fee is called **interest**. It is usually expressed as a percentage of the loan. Sometimes this interest rate, the percentage fee, is quite high. This cost may overcome the advantage one might be receiving if buying a large item at a discount. Also, when we repay the loan, the interest must be paid. This means that we have less to pay for other things.

Impulse Buying

Credit allows us to increase our purchasing power in the short run. It can give us a feeling of having extra money to spend. Also, we don't see the actual cash going out of our hands. This often results in our being tempted to buy more or more expensive items than we would if we had to pay in hard cash. We don't always think about the need to pay for the item later, plus its interest. This situation results in many consumers buying items that are not really needed: **impulse buying** keeps many families in debt and paying large interest sums.

Types of Accounts

Most stores offer retail credit. For them credit is a means of competing against other like stores. Most retail store plans fall into one of three categories.

Regular Credit Account

The **regular credit account** has a thirty-day time limit. If the account is paid off in thirty days, there is no interest charge. If the goods are unsatisfactory, it is very easy to return credit goods during the thirty days. At the end of the thirty-day period, the buyer must either pay the account in full or the amount will be transferred to a revolving credit account. Customers often use a major credit card that services many different stores to purchase goods on this type of account.

Revolving Credit Account

The **revolving credit account** allows a customer to buy any number of goods on credit as long as the total value does not exceed the individual's credit limit. This limit is established by the business giving the credit. It is based on the individual's ability to repay and previous credit experience. The limit may range from $100 to $1000 for the average customer. The business requires that the customer make regular payments on the debt, usually monthly. The minimum payment is based on the amount of the total debt, usually five to ten per cent. Customers can pay more than the regular minimum and so reduce the total interest that must be paid. The interest is charged on the total debt and is calculated monthly. The interest rate is usually 1½% per month or 18% per year. However, some businesses may charge as high as 2% per month or 24% per year. Major credit cards are often used to operate revolving credit accounts. Consumers use this type of account to buy gasoline, clothes, small appliances, meals, hotel accommodations, and sports equipment among other things.

Instalment Accounts

Instalment accounts are used to buy more expensive items such as cars, large appliances, furniture, and recreational goods. A repayment plan is drawn up in the form of a **conditional sales contract** for each purchase. The contract covers a particular time period, i.e., twelve, twenty-four, or thirty-six months. A fixed payment is required each month. A very important part of the contract concerns the

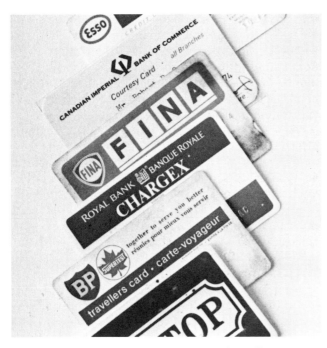

ownership of the item purchased. The seller retains ownership until the final payment is made. The buyer may use the item but he or she does not own it until the contract is paid in full. If the buyer defaults on any payment, the seller usually has the right to demand all payments immediately, or he can repossess the item (meaning the item is returned to the seller). In practice, if a payment is missed, the buyer and seller can usually make a new contract or the seller may allow the buyer to make up the missed payment at a later date.

The above three retail credit accounts are usually available where the items are offered for sale. Ready availability of credit is often used by businesses to help increase sales. Retailers can benefit from the use of credit in two ways: it increases their sales to help earn profit and they can also earn interest on the loans, earning even more profit for the business. A wise consumer will look at both the item and the credit plan with its interest charges before buying.

Consumers can also consider a **cash loan.** A cash loan can be made at financial businesses such as banks, trust companies, credit unions, and finance companies. Consumers with good credit ratings can usually borrow money from these sources at an attractive interest rate, and then go shopping with cash to buy the item they need. Although finance companies' rates are not attractive, they may be the only place where a young person can get a cash loan. This situation allows the consumer to shop for the best value item and the best credit terms to suit his or her particular situation.

UNIT B

SOURCES OF CREDIT

Credit is important to the Canadian economy. It is used by consumers, businesses, and governments. Consumers use credit to buy houses, cars, furniture, clothes, meals, vacations, telephone services, and just about any other good or service you can name. Businesses use credit to buy plants, land, offices, equipment, and raw materials. Governments use credit to buy offices, equipment, schools, hospitals, and to build roads, airports, water reservoirs, and recreation areas.

This wide use or demand for credit has resulted in many businesses offering credit as a service to their customers. Many businesses such as banks, trust companies, and credit unions, make credit the major part of their business. When businesses offer the same good or service for sale, the result is competition and this is the case in the credit market in Canada. Competition has created many different credit plans with many special features. This unit explains some of the basic features of the most common credit sources and plans. This information will help you select the right plans and sources for your future credit needs. There are two main types of credit that individuals and families use; **sales credit** and **cash credit**.

Sales Credit

Sales credit is used by businesses selling goods or services. The credit is usually granted at the checkout counter or the cash register. In most cases, the buyer simply uses a credit card or asks that the sale be put on a charge account. The purchase of large items, like a chesterfield suite, a motorcycle, or a car, requires the completion of an instalment contract in the sales manager's office.

Many large department and chain stores, Eatons, The Bay, Sears, and Canadian Tire Corporation, offer their own company credit plans. These companies issue their own credit cards to their customers, which are used to record the purchase of items directly on to a thirty-day or revolving charge account. The possession of the card gives "on the spot" credit approval. The seller must send monthly statements to the customer indicating the amount owing last month, new items purchased,

any payments made on account, and the new balance. These plans are very convenient but also rather expensive if used longer than thirty days. For example, the credit cost is usually 1½% to 2% per month on the unpaid balance. This figure represents a charge of 18% to 24% per year, which results in a substantial increase in the price of goods or services.

Department stores are not the only business offering this type of service. Possibly the most common issuers of the credit card plans are gasoline companies. All major gasoline companies allow credit card purchases of fuel, parts, and repairs. Many restaurants and motels associated with major gas station chains allow credit card purchases of meals, accommodation, confectionery items, and entertainment on the same card. The services of many ski lodges and summer resorts also fall into the same category.

Another type of sales credit that has proved very successful over the last few years is the universal credit card plan. Examples of these are Visa, Master Charge, and American Express. Many retail outlets of many kinds offer this service. A card holder of this type of plan can use the same card in a variety of stores. The store owners send the records of the purchases to the office of the universal credit card plan. The computer in this central office sorts out all the purchases that belong to individual consumers, and sends them statements including all their purchases for that month. Purchasers send one cheque to the credit card company to pay for the items. The credit card company then sends the necessary payments to all the stores that allowed the credit card purchases.

This plan is very convenient to consumers. It allows them to make many credit purchases in many different stores with just *one* card. Consumers receive an itemized statement every month and can pay off the monthly bills with just one

WHICH CARD DO YOU PREFER?

cheque. The plan also helps many businesses, especially small businesses. Most small businesses cannot afford to finance and operate a credit department. The universal credit card plan allows them to add this service to their businesses. Since credit buying is a basic fact of Canadian living, this plan has allowed many small businesses to remain competitive with larger businesses.

Cash Credit

Cash credit is the second main type of credit. Cash credit is represented by cash loans made to individuals on the basis of their credit rating. The borrowers use this money to buy consumer goods and services, to pay off other debts, or to invest. Interest rates vary, the time to repay varies, and the size of each repayment can be negotiated.

Canada's Chartered Banks

One primary function of Canada's banks is to make loans. Because interest on loans is the main source of income for banks, Canada's banks are very anxious to lend money. Also, our banks compete against one another to lend money to individuals. These two conditions have resulted in the banks creating many different features in loans. However, loans fall under three categories.

Mortgage Loan

Most homes in Canada are purchased on credit. The buyers pay a down payment of cash from their own savings and borrow the rest of the money. This type of loan is basically a long-term instalment loan, except that the home does belong to the purchaser. The loan is repaid over the next twenty to thirty-five years. The home itself is used as collateral or security for the loan. This type of loan is called a **mortgage loan**. Banks provide many of these loans for Canadians.

Instalment Loan

Many individuals and families borrow money from banks and other financial institutions to buy cars, furniture, and appliances. After the individual selects the particular item he or she wishes to purchase, he or she makes an appointment with the loan officer of the bank. The loan officer and the individual decide on the arrangements for the loan to pay for the item. These arrangements include the amount of the loan and the size and number of payments to repay the loan. After these arrangements are settled, the money is usually transferred to the customer's account. The customer then goes back to the store and purchases the item paying the store owner with a cheque. The bank usually requires that the item purchased by the loan is used as collateral or security for the loan. The interest rate is higher than that of mortgage loans.

Demand Loan

The most flexible of all loans is the **demand loan**. This type of loan is made by the bank to a customer on the strength of the customer's character and signature. The money can be used for any purpose decided by the customer. This may be buying new goods or services, to pay off other debts, or make investments. Interest is charged and paid monthly on the unpaid balance. Repayment on the loan may be made monthly or paid in a lump sum. The interest rate is approximately the same as that for mortgage loans.

Trust Companies

Trust companies are closely related to banks in the services they provide to customers and provide loans on the same basis as banks.

Credit Unions

Credit unions are organized on a co-operative form of business organization. Like trust companies, they offer loan arrangements very similar to those of the banks. However, only members of the credit union can have loans from the credit union. This condition requires borrowers to buy a share of the credit union. To become a member in a credit union, it is necessary to buy one or more shares in the credit union.

If the credit union has a profitable year, that is, its interest income is larger than its interest expense and other expenses, the profit is paid back to the members. The amount paid to any member varies with the size of the loan. This profit paid to members, called a **rebate,** actually lowers the interest cost to the borrowers.

Consumer Loan Companies

The consumer loan companies provide consumers with cash that is used for credit purchases. Most of the loans are of the instalment type. The interest rates vary with the credit rating of the individual borrower. The interest rates are usually higher because the consumer loan companies are willing to accept higher credit risks than would be accepted by banks, trust companies, and credit unions. These higher credit risks result in more defaulted payments and losses to the consumer loan company.

Life Insurance Companies

Some life insurance policies, such as endowment and ordinary life, have a cash-value feature. This means that some of the premium is for protection of the policy holder, and the rest is for a savings program. These savings build up over a period of time. The insurance companies use these savings to make mortgage loans and cash loans. Any individual who meets the insurance company's credit requirements, can acquire a mortgage loan. However, only policy owners can obtain cash loans. Also, the amount of the cash loan cannot usually exceed 95% of the policy's cash value. The interest rate is usually lower than that charged by other financial institutions.

UNIT C

GETTING AND KEEPING CREDIT

We have learned many of the uses of credit and where we can get credit. In this section, we will learn the procedure of credit approval, the basis of credit approval, and some of the special factors that involve the use and cost of credit.

Usually the first time an individual uses credit is also the first time the individual learns anything about credit. Often the lesson is quite expensive. Before an individual has had time to study all the terms and conditions of the credit agreement, he or she has been "pressured" into signing the contract by a salesperson using special selling techniques, or the consumer can over-respond to his or her own impulse and status-buying motives. In either case, the consumer can end up signing an agreement without knowing all the commitments or all the costs involved. Learning and using the information in this chapter may save you thousands of dollars in your lifetime.

Procedures for Granting Credit

Most stores or businesses granting credit follow the same procedure. It is a simple three-step procedure. The first step in a credit purchase of a large size is completing a credit application form. This form is a record of personal and financial facts of the potential borrower. The purchaser, who is also the potential borrower, must give information regarding name, address, occupation, employer, income, item to be purchased, other credit payments and debts, and other data that affects the credit decision. As one would expect, as the size of the loan increases, the lender requires more detailed information.

The second step in the procedure is an investigation of the applicant by the lender. If this is the applicant's first credit request, the lender, via a credit bureau, may have to contact the employer to check the information regarding the individual's occupation, work record, and income. The lender may also check the data regarding residence, bank account balances, and ownership of assets. As you can realize, this checking takes time, and the purchase can be delayed a day or two. If the applicant has purchased on credit before, especially from the same lender, the information can be checked very quickly. More information on this step and the role of the credit bureau is discussed later in this unit.

The third step involves the evaluation of the application by the lender. In most department stores, this is the job of the credit manager. In most banks, trust companies, and credit unions, the evaluation is the job of the manager or assistant manager.

Establishing a Credit Rating

Three factors are used to evaluate a credit application. These factors are **character**, **capacity**, and **capital** and are called the three C's of credit. The lender will check the information in the credit application on the basis of these three factors and will then rate the application according to the credit policy of the business. If the rating given the application meets the standard set by the business, the application is approved and credit is granted. If the rating is below the acceptable standard, the application will be rejected.

Character

Character concerns an individual's personality, but when the term *character* is used in credit evaluation, it means **financial personality**. The lender must know if the borrower can hold a regular job for a reasonable amount of time. The lender also wants to know how reliable the borrower has been at that particular job; whether or not the borrower has a particular job skill; whether he or she is willing to accept financial responsibility, how long he or she has lived at the same address; where he or she previously lived; if he or she has a bank account. The answers to these and other related questions should give the lender some idea of the borrower's reliability and intention to repay the loan. For the first-time borrower, the answers to these questions are the first financial-personality look that a lender takes of a borrower.

Capacity

Capacity refers to the financial ability to repay a debt and is the most important factor in establishing a credit rating. A borrower who has great intentions regarding repaying a debt, but not the financial ability to do so has little capacity, little financial ability. Naturally, financial ability refers to both income and expenses and a lender must consider the borrower's present income level, how long the job will last, whether or not the job pays a regular income, and if there is a second income. For large loans, a second income from a part-time job or from an employed spouse can be used to determine the ability to repay.

The lender also wants to know the major expenses of the borrower. Only by considering the income and the expenses such as food, rent or mortgage, car, household bills and other loans can the lender calculate how much is left to repay this new debt. If the amount is sufficient, the application may be approved. If not, the application will be rejected.

In some cases, especially for first time-borrowers, the lender will ask the applicant to have somebody co-sign the loan. This means a second person, often a relative or good friend, also signs the repayment contract. If the lender cannot repay the loan, then the co-signer is responsible for making the remaining payments. The lender will sometimes only approve an application from a first-time borrower if the co-signer is already an approved borrower. A co-signature reduces the risk for the lender.

Capital

Capital is the third factor used in evaluating an application. In this sense, capital means the financial value or worth of the applicant. The things that make up this capital include a house, car, furniture, appliances, savings, investments, insurance policies, and other personal effects. The lender will look at the total value of these things in two ways. First, if the applicant has a large capital investment, the lender may view this as wise money management. Second, a large capital is viewed as a potential source of repayment if the borrower cannot repay the debt from income. In some cases, the lender will even require the borrower to list some of the possessions as collateral for a cash loan. This means the possessions act as security for the loan. If the borrower defaults on payments, the collateral is taken and sold to pay for the loan. Capital is a very important factor to consider in evaluation of a credit application.

Keeping a Good Credit Rating

After an individual has built up a good credit rating, it is important that this record is maintained. We all know how easy it is for a poor test result to hurt an average mark or a record in a particular subject. So it is with a credit rating. As soon as a borrower fails to live up to the repayment terms, his or her credit rating is damaged. If this happens often, it results in an unacceptable credit rating and it is likely that the next loan application would be rejected. A good credit rating is established by paying credit responsibilities, i.e., repayments, as they fall due. But periodically, a borrower is not able to make a payment when it is due. There may have been an emergency; an unexpected expense or possibly a temporary loss of income. The wise borrower will contact the lender and explain the situation. The result may be to extend the loan repayment period, thus legally skipping the present and/or next few payments, or to draw up a new agreement with better terms for the borrower. Meeting and solving the problem this way will protect a good credit rating.

Protecting Your Reputation and Credit Rating

How much do you think people have to do with your credit record and your reputation? Perhaps more than you've realized.

The Ontario Consumer Reporting Act provides for the registration of consumer reporting agencies and those persons employed in investigating personal information for consumer reporting purposes.

The Act requires responsible conduct from businesses that gather, store, assemble or use credit and/or personal information.

While you may or may not agree with the principle of having files compiled on you, the Consumer Reporting Act covers you against the misuse of the information, or just plain inaccurate information.

Credit as well as personal reports are used extensively by most lending institutions. In addition, many employers, companies and landlords use reporting agencies to obtain personality background profiles.

Let's say you've decided to buy a new car and your loan application has been turned down. The loan manager has a report revealing information unacceptable for his firm to extend you credit. Now you're faced with not buying the car, or, if you can get credit elsewhere, probably paying a much higher rate of interest as a marginal risk.

If you are turned down in a credit application as a result of a report that has been compiled about you, the loan firm is required to tell you the name and address of the source agency. That agency is obligated to disclose your file to you, if you write requesting an appointment for that purpose. If an error has been made, the reporting agency has to send out a corrected version to anyone who received the incorrect report.

The Act clearly provides for significant fines for people and companies that refuse to correct any misinformation.

This is only an example of what can happen. If you have some questions that were not answered here, write. Remember, your credit rating is your responsibility and it's up to you to protect your reputation.

Ontario Ministry of Consumer and Commercial Relations

Reprinted by permission

221

CASH FLOW

Debt Management

Betty Lee

Records kept by the Canadian Credit Institute show that approximately 85 per cent of men or women who borrow cash, buy on time or use other kinds of deferred payment plans are meticulous about meeting their financial commitments.

Of the remaining 15 per cent, 10 per cent are bad managers, bad apples or simply compulsive shopaholics. Five per cent are the victims of genuine misfortune—layoffs, family emergencies or health problems. Records also show that almost all of the debtors in question will eventually pay up. But it is because they were delinquent in the first place that society has its collection agencies and bailiffs.

The story of an unpaid bill can vary from creditor to creditor (sales finance companies are quicker to react than, say, banks or professional groups) and debtor to debtor (if past performance has been exemplary, the bill could be temporarily overlooked as "forgetful"). Normally, though, reminder notes will start winging their way within a few days after payment is due, and if these semi-polite signals fall on deaf ears, there will probably be follow-up telephone calls. It's possible that "extended terms" might be arranged at this stage. But if all such nudging tactics fail, the war against the debtor begins.

(A debtor is the individual who is legally responsible for payment. According to law, a husband is responsible only for necessities such as rent, food and clothing bills incurred by his wife, although he can be sued for the payment of nonessentials if the creditor can prove he was present or consenting at the time credit was pledged or a sale was made. A woman—married or single—who holds credit accounts in her own name, of course, must pay the tab or face the consequences. But watch out for salespeople or finance company managers who insist that a husband and wife *both* sign a contract. If one defaults, the other must pay.)

Some companies—notably retail stores—simply dump a sour credit problem into the laps of their own collection agencies. Others employ private firms that charge the creditor a percentage of the account if it can be coaxed from the delinquent.

If merchandise happens to be involved, goods can be repossessed without court order under the Conditional Sales Act, then held for 21 days while the debtor figures out what to do about it. Should the bill payment come through, goods are returned and the entire unpleasantness is presumably forgiven and forgotten. If payment is still outstanding, the goods will be sold and the debtor can be sued for the difference between the proceeds and the debt. In most cases, though, creditors will bypass repossession (the cost of picking up the stuff, holding it and selling it is too steep) and launch legal proceedings.

Suing can be a harrowing experience for those in trouble with debts. A creditor first asks a provincial small claims court or a county court to issue a writ or summons. This is really a way of asking the delinquent to settle up now and avoid any more nasty hassles. If the delinquent fails to respond within 10 days of the writ being served, a judgment in default is signed by the court and the creditor can either (a) garnishee the debtor's wages (b) execute or (c) ask the court to issue a judgment summons.

The garnishee order is the first likely arm-twister to be tried—the attachment of take-home pay to a limit of 30 per cent for a married debtor or even 100 per cent if the delinquent is single. The order lasts for one pay only but the law allows the creditor to reapply. And to reapply again and again, to the predictable disgruntlement of employers.

Execution orders are invariably requested when the creditor knows the debtor is unemployed and therefore an unlikely candidate for garnishment. Under an execution, a delinquent's automobile and other personal possessions can be seized, although the law allows the debtor to keep $1,000 worth of what he or she owns. A judgment summons can be issued when the creditor cannot either garnishee or flush out any worthwhile assets. The delinquent is summoned into court for questioning and the judge decides about his or her ability to pay. If there is no appearance or if payment is not made according to order, the court can then issue a "show cause" summons. If the debtor will not or cannot explain, he or she can be jailed for contempt.

So what are the ways out of the mess for the debtor?

Well, the first route (which too few delinquents seem to take) is through communication with creditors before the wrangles with collection agencies and the courts even begin. If it looks as though bills are going to fall behind, a letter or letters explaining the problem and asking for 30 days to work out a solution *should* fall on receptive ears. At this stage, though, debtors should stick to their guns and make sure the solutions are strictly their own (a realistic plan for budgeting and repayment is a must). Visits to the offices of creditors for friendly talks can easily end up in "refinancing" deals that will cost the debtor a packet.

If things have gone beyond the 30-day stage or if even that ploy has failed, the delinquent will clearly have to try different strategies to stay out of trouble. In cases of real hardship, it's possible that a creditor might be persuaded to suspend interest charges while debt principal is cleared. But this is only a partial solution to the problem. Before the writs start to arrive, in fact, it's best for desperate debtors to investigate the help offered through social agencies and the law.

British Columbia, Alberta, Saskatchewan, Manitoba, Prince Edward Island and Nova Scotia, for example, all have adopted Part 10 of the federal Bankruptcy Act, which allows debtors to consolidate their commitments under Orderly Payment of Debt provisions. Basically, OPD is a court-administered debt pool plan, which allows the delinquent a reasonable amount of cash-from-income for current expenses and divides the rest among creditors. Most personal debts can be included in an OPD consolidation with the exception of mortgages, taxes and alimony payments. Interest charges on other debts are reduced to five per cent a year and, because the debtor is under the protection of the court, garnishees are prohibited and unsecured goods (that is, those not secured by chattel agreements or sales contracts) cannot be seized. Actually, it is rare that even secured merchandise is repossessed under OPD, anyway.

OPD is administered in a haphazard kind of way, but enquiries should be addressed to provincial consumer affairs departments or debt assistance bureaus. These agencies should be able to direct debtors to an OPD clerk-sheriff who can answer questions concerning consolidation applications.

In Quebec, somewhat the same kind of consolidation-repayment system exists under the LaCombe law. Ontario has not adopted OPD, but debtors–within certain income and debt-load restrictions –can apply for consolidation through Small Claims Court referees. Or they can ask for help from a local credit counseling bureau that will examine the tangle, intercede with creditors, plan a budget and repayment schedule and ladle out the funds.

Counseling and debt assistance bureaus will also advise whether a debtor should go the extreme route to voluntary bankruptcy. These days, the federal government (through its Department of Consumer and Corporate Affairs) will help debtors "wipe the slate clean" for a fee of $50 (it costs at least $500 to hire a private trustee). But even though the aid is federal, prospective bankrupts are subject to provincial laws.

What does the province of residence say, for example, about debts (alimony, necessities, court fines?) that are exempt from the bankruptcy? Can the insolvent keep a house, car, household furniture, tools of trade? Or must these assets be sold? Can, indeed, the bankrupt survive the psychological trauma of a sometimes prolonged action?

Most important, has he or she learned–at last–enough about debt management to keep out of the same mess in the future?

Chatelaine, March 1978
Reprinted by permission

The Credit Bureau

Businesses would normally spend a lot of time checking loan applications but for a separate type of business that specializes in this type of work. The business is called a credit bureau. The credit bureau is a business that keeps the credit records of all people who borrow in a particular region.

The credit bureau works for lenders and they pay a fee for this service. Here's how the system works. Suppose Herb Hyman wants to buy a car for $6000 on credit. Jill Hanes, the salesperson, is uncertain about Herb's ability to repay the loan. After the application is completed, Jill contacts the credit bureau to check the information on the application and any other pertinent information in Herb Hyman's file. Since the credit bureau keeps up-to-date credit information on the borrowers, this service is a great help to Jill as she evaluates the application.

Any borrower who has a record on file with a credit bureau can ask to see the file. As you can imagine, a single credit bureau may have thousands of files and records, and mistakes can occur. Individuals have the right to check the information in their files and ask that errors, if any, be corrected. Every individual should periodically check his or her file to ensure that correct information is available to evaluate loan applications.

Credit and Women

Many women are in Canada's labour force. Often, they are using their income to buy their own homes, cars, furniture, and other items. Credit can be a very important financial asset to single women and they should build up a good credit rating as soon as possible. Married women should also establish a separate credit rating. This rating may be a very important item if there is a sudden family break-up through separation, death, or divorce. Credit bureaus allow husbands and wives to set up separate files and will also consider both files when a major credit purchase is made from combined income.

Credit Costs

Credit is a service and lenders must spend time checking and evaluating loan applications. Businesses, sometimes, must borrow money to pay their present suppliers because their own customers are going to pay later. And, of course, some borrowers do not pay on time or at all. When this happens, the business will attempt to repossess the item or items, or turn the account over to a collection agency. The collection agency will contact the borrower and try to arrange for repayment of the loan. This procedure may involve a court case. Repossession of the item refers to the seller actually taking back ownership of the item and returning it to the store. This procedure may also require a court decision. The costs of repossession or the use of a collection agency are covered by the interest charged on the loan and vary from one lender to another.

Granters find few abuse credit and only 2% try to beat system.

By ANGELA BARNES

Eighty-five per cent of all debtors use credit properly at all times; another 10 per cent have credit problems only because of unforeseen events such as sickness or unemployment.

Only 5 per cent of all debtors use credit unwisely, and possibly only 2 per cent are out to take the system, says Hazel Wilson, president of the Credit Grantors Association of Canada. The credit industry cannot get at that 2 per cent of debtors through credit education, she said.

The 3 per cent who use credit unwisely by accident rather than design are probably in the low-income bracket and supporting a family on an income that covers just the necessities, but they are trying to stretch their income to include new cars and trips to Hawaii, for example–things that they see other people doing.

Mrs. Wilson said it is not necessarily the fault of the credit granter when such people over-extend themselves financially. Some people object to being asked about their indebtedness and so they do not disclose all their debts when they apply for further credit.

Although the credit industry is not to blame for people's credit problems, it does try to see they do not encounter such problems and if they do, it tries to help them. A key way the industry can help is through credit education–teaching people to handle their finances intelligently, showing them the pitfalls they can get into if they are not careful, she said.

(Credit education by employees of association members stresses that credit is good–if used properly.)

Employees of member companies are involved in groups that help with credit education in secondary schools among other places. In some cases, the companies ask to be permitted to go into the schools; in other cases, they are invited.

With the secondary schools, the industry's program of credit education is directed at the Grade 10 level. The reasoning is that if the companies waited any longer, those who turn out to be poor credit users might not be in school anymore.

Mrs. Wilson said credit education at an even earlier stage might be beneficial and credit granters would be ready to help if they were asked. But they have not been because, generally, budget-ing and money management courses do not start until the high school level.

Representatives of the industry will also address any group that asks them to do so, including church groups and women's community groups.

The association would like to get more involved in the community financial counselling programs being set up by provincial governments. Credit granters can add something to those programs that civil servants cannot, Mrs. Wilson said.

If the credit problems are severe enough, the financial counselling service will set up a budget for the person and work out a plan for repayment with the creditors. In Alberta, the interest rate applicable to those repayment plans is 5 per cent a year, she said.

The creditors are obliged, if they think the plan fair, to go along with it. In fact, it is usually in the creditor's interest to go along with the plan since the alternative would be to declare personal bankruptcy.

The Globe and Mail, Toronto
May 7, 1977
Reprinted by permission

CREDIT CLERK   (CLERICAL)
EXAMINES AND PROCESSES APPLICATION OF
INDIVIDUAL APPLYING FOR LOAN OR CREDIT:
INTERVIEWS CUSTOMER AND VERIFIES CREDIT
REFERENCES AND OTHER INFORMATION, SUCH
AS NAME, ADDRESS AND WHERE INDIVIDUAL
IS EMPLOYED. DETERMINES CREDIT LIMIT
BASED ON APPLICANT'S ASSETS, CREDIT
EXPERIENCE AND PERSONAL REFERENCES.
SUMMARIZES, IN PRESCRIBED FORM,
INFORMATION CONCERNING LOAN OR CREDIT
APPLICATION AND EXTRACTS PERTINENT DATA.
  PASSES THIS INFORMATION TO APPROVING
AUTHORITY. MONITORS FLOW OF CREDIT
APPLICATIONS TO ENSURE ADHERENCE TO
LINES OF CREDIT AUTHORIZED BY APPROVING
OFFICER. KEEPS RECORD OF CREDIT
TRANSACTIONS AND PAYMENTS AND ACCEPTS
PAYMENT OF ACCOUNTS. COMPUTES INTEREST
AND PAYMENTS, USING ADDING AND
CALCULATING MACHINE. ISSUES CREDIT CARD
TO CUSTOMER FOR USE AS IDENTIFICATION
WHEN PURCHASING ARTICLES TO BE CHARGED
TO HIS ACCOUNT. KEEPS RECORD OF CARDS
REPORTED LOST, CHECKING OFF NUMBER ON
CUSTOMER'S ACCOUNT, AND REISSUES NEW
CARDS.

FOR RELATED CAREERS CONSULT THE MASTER
LIST UNDER THE MINOR GROUP--------------- 413

THESE TRAININGS SUPPORT CREDIT CLERK

CREDIT OFFICER TRAINING
THERE ARE MANY PROGRAMS OFFERED AT THE
COMMUNITY COLLEGE LEVEL, AT PRIVATE
TRADE SCHOOLS AND AT UNIVERSITIES, BOTH
THROUGH DAY AND NIGHT CLASSES WHICH MAY
BE ADVANTAGEOUS TO THOSE WANTING TO WORK
IN THE CREDIT FIELD FOR BANKS, FINANCIAL
INSTITUTIONS, INDUSTRIES, ETC.
  GOOD FINANCIAL COURSES ARE OFFERED AS
WELL THROUGH THE COMMERCIAL DEPARTMENTS
OF THE SECONDARY SCHOOLS BOTH IN DAY
AND NIGHT CLASSES.
  THE USUAL COMMUNITY COLLEGE TUITION FEE
IS APPROXIMATELY $325.00 PER YEAR WHILE
THAT OF RYERSON IS ABOUT $528.00 AND
UNIVERSITIES OVER $700.00.
  THE ADMISSION TO COMMUNITY COLLEGES AND
RYERSON IS USUALLY A SECONDARY SCHOOL

REVIEWING
YOUR BUSINESS VOCABULARY

Write the number of each definition.
Write the word that matches the definition number.

UNIT A

credit, instalment account, regular credit account, revolving credit account

1. An account used to buy more expensive items.
2. The term that allows us to purchase something now and pay for it later.
3. An account on which there are no interest charges for thirty days.
4. An account that allows a customer to buy up to the total value of the customer's credit limit.

UNIT B

cash credit, consumer loan company, demand loan, instalment loan, mortgage loan, rebate, sales credit

1. A loan given by a bank to cover the cost of large items.
2. A long-term loan usually given to a consumer buying a house.
3. Items businesses allow consumers to charge to a credit card or charge account.
4. A loan made to a customer based on character and signature.
5. A cash loan made to an individual.
6. The profit made by a credit union and paid to its members who have loans with the credit union.
7. A financial company whose interest rates on loans are generally higher than other financial situations.

UNIT C

credit application, character, capacity, capital, credit bureau

1. A business that keeps credit records of all borrowers in a particular region.
2. A record of personal and financial facts about the potential borrower.
3. The financial ability to repay loans.
4. An individual's financial personality.
5. The financial value or worth of a loan applicant.

REVIEW QUESTIONS

UNIT A

1. What is credit and what advantages result from its use?
2. Name five items commonly bought on credit.
3. What is "forced savings"?
4. Explain clearly why credit must have an interest charge.
5. Explain the term "impulse buying" and state how it can be harmful.
6. Why do stores offer credit?
7. What are the characteristics of a regular credit account?
8. Explain the operation of a revolving credit account.
9. What items are usually purchased on instalment credit accounts?
10. Who owns an article purchased on an instalment credit contract?
11. How does a store benefit from the use of credit?
12. Why should consumers consider a cash loan from a financial institution?

UNIT B

1. Name three groups in the Canadian economy that use credit.
2. Why do businesses offer credit to customers?
3. Name two main types of credit used by families and individuals.
4. What stores offer their own credit plans?
5. What are the advantages of a universal credit plan to the store owner? to the consumer?
6. What are the most common items purchased on mortgage loans?
7. Explain the procedure of getting an instalment loan.
8. What are the differences between a bank loan and a credit union loan?
9. Who can obtain cash loans from insurance companies?

UNIT C

1. Why is a person's first experience with credit often an expensive one?
2. How can learning about credit now save you money in the future?
3. What is the first step in the procedure of granting credit?
4. List at least five items of information that must be stated on a credit application.
5. What are the three "C"s of credit?
6. What items are involved in evaluating a person's character as it relates to credit?
7. How does capacity influence a credit application?
8. What items would an individual list to indicate personal capital?
9. Why should a borrower protect a good credit rating?
10. What should a borrower do if he or she is unable to make a loan payment?
11. What is the purpose of a credit bureau? Explain how such a bureau operates.
12. Why should individuals check their own file in a credit bureau?
13. Why should both married and single women establish a good credit rating?
14. How does one build a good credit rating?

APPLYING YOUR KNOWLEDGE

UNIT A

1. How does credit affect the number of jobs available for Canadians?
2. Give a specific example of credit as a "two-edged sword".
3. List three goods or services that you used today that were purchased on credit.
4. Many consumers confuse impulse buying with buying on credit for convenience. Explain this statement.
5. Joe said that he bought a car for $6000 on credit because he could not afford to pay $4500 cash. How can he explain this situation as an advantage of using credit?
6. Name five items that are often purchased on impulse. Where are these items usually placed in the store?
7. Why do many consumers feel that buying on a regular credit account is a good way of getting a full guarantee?
8. How is credit helpful to both consumers and business owners?

UNIT B

1. List ten items not mentioned in the text that are purchased by consumers on credit.
2. List ten businesses in your community offering credit plans to consumers. Note any special features of some of the credit plans.
3. Explain why a small store would use a universal credit plan.
4. What benefits would a consumer on holiday receive from the use of a universal credit card?
5. A manager of one of Canada's largest banks stated that "a bank is a consumer's best one-stop credit shop". Explain what is meant by this statement.
6. What benefits does a credit union give to its members that a bank does not give to its customers?
7. Why should a consumer shop for credit?

UNIT C

1. Why would a lender want to know personal information, such as address, employer, occupation, and income of a credit applicant?
2. John says he does not need a good credit rating because he intends to pay cash for all his purchases. Is this a good idea? Why or why not?
3. Joe has a steady job and owns his own car. Three of this friends have graduated from high school and started working at construction jobs. They have all decided to purchase new cars. Because they are first-time borrowers, they ask Joe to co-sign their loans. Should Joe co-sign the loans for his friends? Why or why not?
4. A good credit rating is as good as money in the bank. Explain this statement.
5. Explain how credit bureaus are a benefit to both businesses and consumers.
6. Tom has an excellent job. He and his wife Anne own two cars, their furniture, and rent an apartment. They have saved a small down payment for a house. Since Tom has an excellent credit rating, Anne feels that she does not need to establish a credit rating. Do you agree with her thinking? Why or why not?

PROJECTS AND PROBLEMS

UNIT A

1. List the names of five businesses in your community that sell goods on credit. List the type of credit account or accounts that they offer.
2. List the names of five businesses in your community that sell services on credit. List the type of credit account or accounts they offer.
3. Make a list of at least five different items that would be purchased on a regular credit account, a revolving credit account, and an instalment account.
4. Some consumers say they buy on credit because they get better service from the retailer. Why would retailers give credit customers better service than they would give to cash customers?

UNIT B

1. Compare cash credit to sales credit on the basis of convenience and cost.
2. Many travellers say that a universal credit card is a necessity for their business. List as many points as you can to support this statement.
3. Credit is a very important part of economic activity. Write a short note on the advantages of credit to business and consumers.
4. Many different people are involved in activities that involve the granting of credit. List as many job titles and duties of people with careers in credit business as you can.
5. There are five hundred employees in the Avetone Chemical plant. They have decided to form their own credit union branch in the plant. What advantages and disadvantages would this operation give the employees?

UNIT C

1. The Harris family who have a small income and own a small house have a better credit rating than the Torrance family who have a large income, and own a large house and a cottage. How do you think this situation occurs?
2. Individuals have many different attitudes towards the use and the abuse of credit. The following statements express a variety of these attitudes. Explain why you agree or disagree with each statement.
   a. I don't use credit. I pay cash or don't buy.
   b. I always use credit. Why pay now, when I can pay later.
   c. Credit should be used to buy things that last a long time.
   d. I buy on credit but only on a thirty-day regular charge account.
   e. A credit card is a ticket to bankruptcy.
3. Joan had a cash loan from her bank for $2500 to help pay for a used car. The loan required payments on a monthly basis for two years. Ten months after the purchase of the car, Joan had a major unexpected repair bill for $300. After paying the repair bill, she did not have enough money for the next bank payment. What should she do now? Why? Can the bank help her?
4. The following chart represents the loan terms of one of Canada's chartered banks. The first column represents the size of the loan.

Amount of Loan	Monthly Payment	Monthly Payment
	12 months	36 months
$2500	$222	$ 82
5000	443	165
7500	670	254

Calculate the total amount in monthly payments and the total interest for each of the following loans.
   a. A $2500 loan for 12 months; for 36 months.
   b. A $5000 loan for 12 months; for 36 months.
   c. A $7500 loan for 12 months; for 36 months.
5. Refer to question 4 above to answer the following:
   a. How does interest cost affect purchasing power?
   b. Suppose the $7500 loan for 36 months was for the purchase of a car. If Marie could pay cash for the car, what could she buy with the money she would save on interest by not using credit?

10 Insurance

UNIT A

INSURANCE–PROTECTION AGAINST RISK

Every day you, members of your family, and businesses face different types of **risks.** Every time you cross a street or are riding your bike, you could be involved in an accident with a car. If your mother or father is involved in an accident or becomes ill suddenly, there may be no income for a period of time to meet family expenses for food, clothing, and shelter. You may know of someone whose house or place of business has been destroyed by fire or flood. All of us are constantly exposed to such risks throughout our lifetime.

Risk can be reduced by careful planning. Regular medical checkups reduce the chance of serious illness from a sudden heart attack or other crippling disease. Riding your bike on the correct side of the road and following proper safety rules reduces your chance of being injured and being hospitalized. A business or a home can be protected against certain risks or damage by the installation of burglar alarms, smoke detectors, and sprinkler systems. But no matter how careful you are planning against personal economic or property losses, such losses never are completely eliminated. Most losses are not expected; they cannot be planned for in advance. Some losses are so large that many people are unable to pay for them from their regular income and savings.

Sharing the Risks

Most people purchase **insurance** as a protection against personal or business loss. By sharing a risk with a large number of people, insurance is the major means of reducing possible loss of property or earning power. Assume you are one of a hundred people who are members of a neighbourhood recreation centre. During the weekend, there is a serious fire in the centre that results in $10 000 damages to the building and its contents. If this were your own private centre, the loss would have been entirely yours. However, if all one hundred members had earlier agreed to share the cost of any possible damages equally, all of you would only have to contribute $100 each to cover the losses caused by the fire. The loss suffered by each individual is therefore much less.

When people **pool** their money or **resources** in this way, they share an economic risk. Naturally, this

sharing does not eliminate the risk or prevent it from occurring in the future, but it does spread a loss over a large number of people because not all of them will suffer a loss at the same time. This type of protection is provided by insurance companies; the different plans they provide allow large groups of people to share various economic risks.

How Insurance Works

When people purchase any type of insurance (life, automobile, property, health), they contribute a sum of money on a regular basis to a fund to protect them against some possible future loss. Your mother pays money to insure her car against theft or damage from an accident. If these risks do not occur, the insurance company keeps the money. But should either of these risks occur, the insurance company pays for the loss or damage from the fund of money it has collected from others like your mother who are in the same insurance plan. Payments from the fund are only made to those who actually suffer damage or loss.

For example, consider the case of David Phippen's sailboat, which was completely destroyed when fire gutted the building in which his and other boats were stored for the winter. Without insurance, Mr. Phippen would have to pay the complete cost of a replacement sailboat himself. With insurance, he—and other boat owners who had purchased property insurance—would have received payment to cover this loss from the common fund of the insurance plan. If each of two hundred boat owners had paid $200 for insurance, there would be $40 000 in a central fund to cover possible losses. The $2 000 necessary to replace Mr. Phippen's sailboat would be paid from this fund. The sharing of risk by spreading possible future losses over a large number of people is the main purpose of buying insurance.

Main Types of Losses

The most serious loss is the death or **disability to work** of the principal wage earner in the family. In addition to the economic loss, the family undergoes an emotional loss too.

Losses also occur to a family or person's property. These losses can be permanent—total destruction of a home or car by fire, flood, or explosion. Less severe is loss caused by property damage. Whatever the type of loss, you and your family should consider which one is the most important to you and determine what protection through insurance is needed.

Purchasing Insurance

Each year millions of Canadians purchase some type of insurance. The kinds of insurance purchased depends on the amount of money people can afford for the different types of insurance coverage and the possible risk of loss against which they need to protect themselves. Two parties are involved in the purchase of insurance: the person purchasing insurance—**the insured**; and the insurance company—**the insurer**.

There are many different kinds of insurance plans that a person might consider buying. Life insurance and car insurance are probably the most common types purchased by most people. Home and property insurance is increasing as more and more families want protection against possible losses such as fire and theft, and nearly all families have some form of health insurance because of increased medical and hospital costs.

Insurance companies will sell protection against almost any type of loss that you can imagine. In

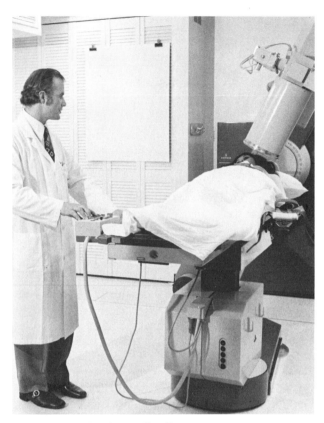

Cardiovascular Investigation

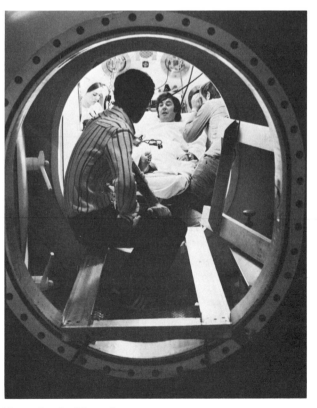

Hyperbaric Chamber

232

the 1940s Betty Grable, a Hollywood actress and dancer, insured her legs for one million dollars. In 1977, Eddie Shack, former Toronto Maple Leaf hockey player, insured his nose for one million dollars as part of a promotional campaign for Pop Shoppes, a national soft drink firm. Musicians insure their voices; fashion models their faces and hands. Because these items are unusual would-be losses not shared by many other people, the cost of such an insurance plan is very expensive for the insured.

The Language of Insurance

A person or business-the insured-purchases protection against risk of a loss from an insurance company, the insurer. If the company has a representative acting on their behalf, this person is **an agent**.

When insurance is purchased, an **insurance policy** is prepared. The policy with all its details is a legal agreement between the insured and the insurer. It describes the kinds of risks covered and not covered by the policy. It also states the **term** of the contract or the period of time over which the insurance protection exists. Any conditions that could lead to the cancellation of the insurance are also included.

For the protection offered by the insurance company, the insured pays money on a regular basis-usually once a year or once a month. The payment is the **premium**. All premiums covering like plans are pooled. This money is available to pay for any losses suffered by an insured individual. Such a statement of loss is a **claim**.

The Cost of Insurance

The level of risk in a situation is the main factor determining the cost of your premium. But just how do insurance companies afford the assumption of risks that people could encounter? The study of losses that have occurred in past years helps determine what an insurance company will have to pay for insurance losses this year. For example, millions of cars drive on Canada's highways daily. Most of these cars have some form of car insurance. Annually, drivers pay an amount of money for insurance but many never claim against it if they are not involved in an accident. It is the money of those who do not have claims that allows an insurance company to pay a large part of the repair bills of those **policyholders** with loss claims. All drivers share the risk. From past figures, an insurance company determines what insurance rates will be in effect this year.

Again, studies of past years provide guides as to the number of homes that might be vandalized, the number of deaths that might occur, the number of employees who will need medical attention, and the approximate cost to the insurance company of these losses. These studies determine what premiums will be charged.

An insurance company is the same as any other large business operation providing a service. Basic costs must be paid each month: salaries to employees, heating and electrical expenses, equipment and supplies, and the rental of office space or the purchase of an office building. Insurance premiums cover these basic expenses as well as providing for claims.

Finally, some of the money paid by insured persons as premiums is invested in stocks and bonds, real estate, and home ownership mortgages. Some of the money is lent to holders of insurance policies who want to borrow money. The reasons for making these investments are to provide a reserve fund to draw from when claims are greater than expected in a given year and to build up reserve funds to draw from when claims increase as expected in future years; for example, in life insurance where risk of death increases with age.

These main factors-expected claims, expected expenses, and expected investment yield or return-are then considered by the officials of the insurance company. From their study the insurance premiums are set for the next year. These rates will differ from one company to another. As a result, it is very important to identify the losses that you might suffer and then shop around for proper insurance protection.

Career Opportunities in Insurance

The Canadian life insurance industry numbers approximately one hundred and sixty companies. They provide a variety of services to almost twelve million policyholders. These services include life insurance, and health, accident, and sickness coverage. Because of the number and different sizes of insurance organizations, a variety of career opportunities is available. Over 47 000 people work in the life insurance industry today.

An **insurance agent** is probably the person most people think about first when considering a career in life insurance. The agent is the person who represents the insurance business in its daily contacts with policyholders. But insurance offices require managers, general office workers, and claims officers. The **claims officer** is responsible for the approval and payment of benefits from policies. Many clerical positions-secretary, file clerk, receptionist–are also needed. Bookkeepers and accountants keep accurate records of the company's finances.

With accounting procedures becoming more technological, experts in the computer field are necessary. Insurance companies are a major user of computer services in Canada. Computer operators, programmers, systems analysts–all these positions are available in the computer section of an insurance company. A **computer programmer** is the liaison between the **systems analyst**–the person who applies the computer to a problem, and the **computer operator**–the person who operates the programmed problems through the computer.

Insurance companies must also maintain a good public image–they must have an enviable trust-worthy image. People are therefore required to work in advertising and public relations departments. Artists are also needed to design information booklets for consumers, company guides, and newsletters, and marketing specialists who try to determine peoples' needs; so that products and policies are available for those needs.

Specialists called **actuaries** are essential: they prepare data on which insurance premiums are based. The actuary measures insurance risks and then calculates how much people will have to pay in premiums for coverage. For people interested in law, there are positions in the legal department. Every insurance policy is a legal contract and must meet the conditions of federal and provincial laws.

UNIT B

LIFE AND HEALTH INSURANCE

As you have read, insurance is protection against loss. The biggest losses to a person or family are loss of life and the loss of income resulting from the death of the insured person, usually the **breadwinner** or main earner of income in a family.

Everyone expects to live a long, healthy life. Modern science and medicine have found cures for many diseases and have lengthened life expectancy. But suppose that something unexpected happens to you, such as a serious illness or an accident. You might not be able to work and would have no income to pay your bills. Your savings may have to be used to meet your expenses. Your comfortable lifestyle would be greatly altered. Death also comes to all of us sooner or later.

Life and health insurance provides a means to provide family financial security and a means to protect families against accidental losses. Health insurance can help pay the hospital and medical bills while a person is unable to work. Life insurance replaces family income cut off by the death of the family's breadwinner.

Life insurance is an important source of personal and family security for most Canadians. According to the Canadian Life Insurance Association, more than twelve million Canadians own life insurance policies. Today the average amount of life insurance owned in every Canadian household exceeds $36 000. That is more than double the amount owned in 1966. Canadians own more life insurance per person than people in any other country in the world.

The Basis of Life Insurance

Everybody's needs are different, and these needs are constantly changing. That is why there is such a wide range of life insurance plans available today. All of these choices make life insurance seem a complex matter for many people. Yet, the basic principles of life insurance are quite simple to understand.

In making your future financial plans, you have two choices in dealing with death. You can gamble that you will live and keep earning and saving long enough to complete your financial plans. Or you can share the financial risk by pooling your money with a large number of other people. The purchase of life insurance involves a large number of people

each paying a premium on a regular basis to an insurance company that provides individual protection against loss of life or income. Such personal protection would be very expensive for any one person if the sharing of the risk did not occur. Premiums are collected from this large group of insured people, and the losses of a few are paid from this fund of money.

Calculation of Premiums

Insurance companies have statistics available to them that indicate the probability of death during the coming year for people at various ages. These statistics or **mortality tables** indicate for different ages the number of expected deaths in the year and the number of years people are expected to live after they reached that age. There are different types of mortality tables–for males, for females, and for different types of insurance. New tables are developed regularly as mortality or death rates change over the years. Improvements in medical care are one of the main reasons for longer life expectancy.

Assume that statistics indicate to insurance companies that six out of every 1000 people who are forty-six years of age will die each year. But, nobody knows for certain who the six are that will die or the 994 that will live. To protect themselves against this risk, all of the 1000 people will contribute to the fund. Money from this fund will be shared by the families of those six people who die during the year.

Because the cost of premiums is partly based on the risk of dying, an important consideration for insurance companies is a person's age. The younger you are, the lower the cost of life insurance since you are not a big risk at a young age. A person's chance of dying in the next year increases as he or she gets older. If you had to buy your insurance each year, the cost to you would be very expensive in your older years. In fact, you might not be able to afford to purchase insurance at those ages, just when the risk is highest. For this reason, life insurance is often sold on a **level premium basis.** This means that policyholders pay more in the earlier years of the policy than the cost of the protection and less in the later years than the cost of protection at older ages. The result is that the cost of the insurance is averaged out over the years so that you are paying the same premium each year.

Statistics give insurance companies an idea of how much money will be needed for them to pay claims during a given year. An amount is added to allow for operating expenses such as the cost of keeping records, issuing policies, paying employees, and a profit margin. Part of the premium is set aside in a **reserve fund** to help pay for claims in later years when the premium is insufficient to meet the rising cost of the claims. The total charge for insurance is then divided among the policyholders according to how much risk each one faces. This charge then represents the premium each insured person must pay for insurance protection.

Classes of Life Insurance

Life insurance is divided into two main groups—**individual and group insurance.** Individual life insurance is an agreement between one person and a life insurance company. Group insurance is insurance provided to a group of persons under a contract between the insurer and an employer or other persons. Group insurance is usually purchased by an employer, who may share the cost of insurance with the employee, for the benefit of employees. Many families purchase both forms of insurance in establishing their program for financial security.

Sources and Uses of Income of Canadian Life Insurance Companies 1975.

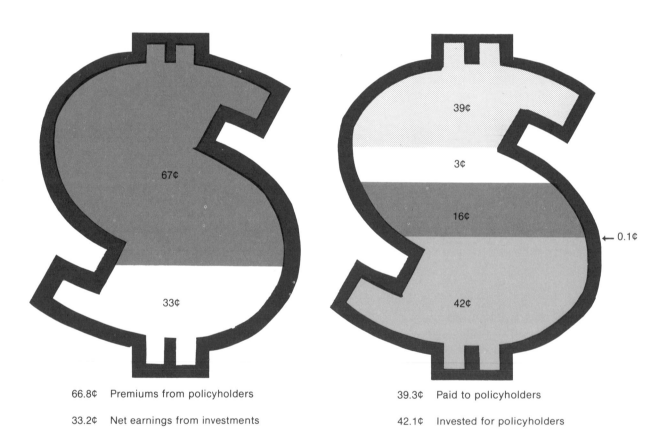

66.8¢	Premiums from policyholders
33.2¢	Net earnings from investments
$1.00	Total

Sources: Reports of Superintendent of Insurance, Ottawa; C.L.I.A.
Reprinted by permission

39.3¢	Paid to policyholders
42.1¢	Invested for policyholders
2.7¢	Taxes
15.8¢	Operating expenses
.1¢	Shareholders*
$1.00	Total

236

Individual Life Insurance

Many different kinds of individual policies are available, and insurance can be purchased to meet an individual's specific needs. People's lives constantly change: some people are raising families, some are buying homes. The wide choice of policies enables insurance agents to set up programs to meet people's present and future needs, goals, and family responsibilities.

Before an insurance company issues an individual policy, the agent will ask for specific information to learn more about the health of and type of work done by the prospective purchaser. Insurance companies will want to charge a higher premium to people who are not in good health since they are bigger risks. You may be required to have a medical examination as part of the application for life insurance.

Your type of work or occupation also affects the cost of your insurance. If your daily work is dangerous, you will probably have to pay a higher premium for insurance. A person who works underground in a mine has a more dangerous job than a clerk in an office. The mineworker pays more for insurance as the job involves a much greater insurance risk than an office job.

Group Life Insurance

Group life insurance is issued to a group of people under one policy. Under a group plan, all members of the group who want to be insured can usually be insured. Individual members receive a certificate stating the amount of their coverage. The amount of insurance is often based on the amount of salary. For example, your premium payments may insure you for twice or three times your salary. Group insurance sales represent about fifty-seven per cent of life insurance owned in Canada. This is up from forty-seven per cent in 1970.

One benefit of group insurance is that a medical examination is seldom required before you can be insured. This means that some people who might not be able to purchase individual life insurance are able to purchase group insurance at reasonable cost. Group insurance is temporary and ends when you leave the company or when you retire, although sometimes it continues for a reduced amount after retirement. Typically though it provides the option to purchase individual insurance from the insurer without undergoing a medical examination.

Naming the Beneficiary

Policyholders have the right to name the person or persons who will receive the proceeds or benefits from the policy. The person named is the beneficiary. A father often names his wife or children as beneficiaries, although just the wife is most common. It is possible for policyholders to change the name of the beneficiary if they want to but the insurance company must be informed of the change immediately. It is wise to write them about this change so that there is signed proof from you in order to avoid any problems that might later arise.

Life Insurance Owned, by Type of Insurance (000 000 omitted)

End of Year	Individual	Group	Total
1900	$ 431	$ —	$ 431
1910	856	—	856
1920	2 580	77	2 657
1930	6 010	482	6 492
1940	6 310	731	7 041
1945	8 894	1 070	9 964
1950	13 614	2 615	16 229
1955	20 271	6 353	26 624
1960	32 128	14 739	46 867
1965	45 243	28 832	74 075
1970	62 845	55 977	118 822
1971	66 674	63 268	129 942
1972	72 414	72 762	145 176
1973	78 822	84 470	163 292
1974	87 673	100 998	188 671
1975	98 224	121 688	219 912
1976	111 140	146 012	257 152

Sources: Reports of Superintendent of Insurance, Ottawa; C.L.I.A.
Reprinted by permission

PART 2 of Application to

THE EMPIRE LIFE INSURANCE COMPANY

Kingston, Ontario

If the life to be insured is to be examined this entire form shall be completed by the medical examiner; otherwise questions 1 to 7 shall be asked by the soliciting agent.

Statements by applicant concerning child to be insured

1. Full name of life to be insured .... Date of birth .... Place of birth ....

   Occupation .... Sex .... Does he reside with his parents? .... (If not, explain fully)............................

2. **FAMILY RECORD**

Parents		LIVING		DEAD				
		Ages	Condition of health	Ages	Cause of death	How long ill	Date of death	Previous health
Parents	Father							
	Mother							

Number	Living	Dead						
Brothers								
Sisters								

3. Has any member of the family of the life to be insured ever suffered from tuberculosis, cancer, epilepsy, insanity, heart disease or hereditary disorder.

4. Has the life to be insured now, or ever had:	Yes or No	Date Mo. Yr.	Duration	Nature of condition disease or injury	Severity or complications	Name and address of medical attendant
(a) Measles, scarlet fever, diphtheria or whooping cough?						
(b) Asthma, pleurisy, tuberculosis, habitual cough, rheumatism, heart disease, kidney trouble, mental impairment or epilepsy?						
(c) Any illness, disease, injury or operation other than as stated above?						
(d) Any deformity, disability or other condition such as spinal curvature, lameness, rupture, paralysis, impairment of vision or hearing?						

5. (a) Medical attendant of life to be insured: Name............................ Address ....

   (b) When was life to be insured last attended by this doctor? .... Reason? ....

6. Exact height?　ft.　in.　Exact weight?　lbs. Did you measure him?　weigh him?　Gain in weight in past year?　lbs.

7. Is the life to be insured now in good health?

I hereby declare that the above answers and statements are full, complete and true, it being understood and agreed that they are material to the risk and form part of the application and consideration for the insurance applied for and I hereby authorize any physician, medical practitioner, hospital, clinic, the Medical Information Bureau or other medical or medically related facility, insurance company or other organization, institution or person that has any records or knowledge of the above mentioned child to give to The Empire Life Insurance Company or its reinsurers any and all information about him/her with reference to his/her health and medical history and any hospitalization, advice, diagnosis, treatment, disease, ailment or condition. I consent to medical examination of the life to be insured if required by the Company. A photocopy of this authorization shall be as valid as the original.

Witness ....

Medical examiner or agent if non-medical

Dated at .... this .... day of .... 19 ....

Signature of parent or guardian ....

CHILD - F.P.P. PART 2 - ENG.

REPORT OF MEDICAL EXAMINATION

Use space under "remarks" for details of any condition noted.

8. On examination is there any evidence of past or present disease of: Cervical glands? .... Lungs? .... Abdomen? .... Heart? State the pulse rate

9. Urinalysis: (Required if there is history of infectious disease or in every case over 5 years of age).

   Albumin　Sugar

10. Was birth premature or full term?

11. Does the life to be insured appear well nourished and in good health?

12. After careful examination are you satisfied that the life to be insured is well developed and free from disease, deformity or mental defect? Apparent age?

13. Give your opinion of the environment of the life to be insured.

14. (a) How long have you known the life to be insured? ....

    (b) Are you satisfied that the person being examined is the life to be insured named herein?

15. Do you unconditionally recommend the risk as first class?

Medical Examiner's Remarks ....

....

....

I hereby certify that, at .... o'clock $\frac{a.m.}{p.m.}$ this .... day of .... 19 .... I have made, in private, a personal examination of the life to be insured, herein named, and that the answers on this form are full, complete and true to the best of my knowledge and belief.

Signature of Medical Examiner .... P.O. Address ....

D58-6M-8-77-MPL

238

Main Types of Life Insurance

Life insurance is available in many different forms with a wide variety of options. Yet there are really only three basic types of insurance–term, whole life, and endowment. Each of these types is examined below.

Term Insurance

Term insurance provides temporary protection for a certain period of time–one year, five years, or until you reach a certain age, such as 65 or 70. Premiums for term insurance cost less than premiums for other types of life insurance. Group insurance is a common example of term insurance. Term insurance is much the same as home and car insurance. Your premium payments protect you against a certain risk for a specific time only. At the end of that term, you have to renew your policy if you want further coverage.

Term insurance is cheaper because it provides protection only for people in an age group where the probability of death is low. Even at age sixty, only about twenty out of every 1000 policyholders die. Because of this low mortality rate, premiums are low. Past age seventy, the risk rises rapidly and premiums are expensive. For this reason, most insurance companies will not usually issue term insurance to people over seventy years of age. Near the end of the term for which you were insured, you are often able to convert or change your term insurance into permanent insurance without a medical examination through most insurance companies.

Mark Wichrowski is a married man with a wife and two young children. He purchases $100 000 worth of term insurance at an annual cost of $250 for ten years to provide protection for his young family. If he dies within the ten-year period, his family will collect the value of his policy. However, if he dies even one day after the end of the period, his family will receive nothing.

If Wichrowski wants to renew his policy for another term, he can probably do so. But he will have to pay a higher premium each time he renews– as he gets older, he becomes more of a risk.

Whole Life Insurance

Whole life insurance protects policyholders their entire lifetime. Benefits are payable whenever the insured dies. Insurance protection continues as long as premiums are paid. Whole life insurance is often called permanent life insurance.

There are two basic types of whole life insurance: straight (or ordinary life) and limited payment life. Straight life premiums remain the same each year and are spread out over the insured's lifetime. If you were to purchase a life policy at twenty years of age, your premiums would be less than they would be if you purchased the policy at thirty-five years of age. Straight life insurance guarantees that you will pay the same premium every year that you have the policy. You are paying more than is necessary to protect you against risk in the first years of your policy. But you pay less in the later years when the risk of death is greater.

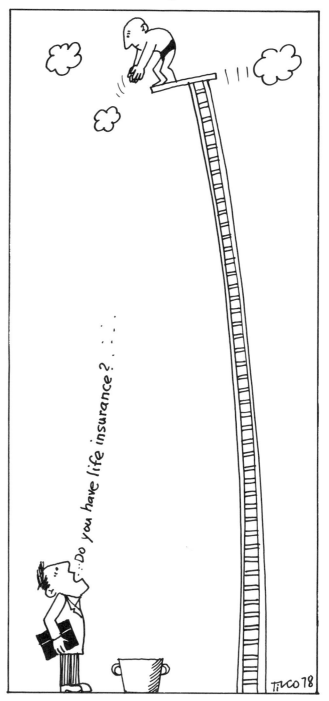

THE EMPIRE LIFE INSURANCE COMPANY Kingston Ontario № 8249

1. NAME of Life to be Insured:
(Circle given name most commonly used)

Mr. ☐
Mrs. ☐
Miss ☐

Surname | Given Names

2. ADDRESS ☐

Check box (√) to which mail is to be sent ☐

Present Residence

Former Residence Address (es)

Business Address

Social Insurance Number | Years Here

3. OCCUPATION: Give exact duties and badge #, if any -

Name of Employer -

4. DATE OF BIRTH of life to be Insured | Day | Month | Year | Age - (Nearest Birthday) | Place of Birth | Sex | Marital Status - Single ☐ Married ☐ | Widow (er) ☐ Divorced ☐ Separated ☐

5. Complete this section **ONLY** if Applicant is other than Life to be Insured:

Name of Applicant —

Occupation —

Address if other than in 2. above —

Employer's name and business address —

If Business, is it incorporated? Yes ☐ No ☐ If "Yes" under what law-

Social Insurance Number

If Child's Third Party, complete the following re Applicant:

Date of Birth -

Place of Birth -

Relationship to Life to be Insured -

6. BENEFICIARY (State relationship and give date of birth if a minor)

☐ Revocable   ☐ Irrevocable

Endowment policies, unless otherwise directed, will at maturity be payable to the Insured (i.e., Applicant/Owner).

10. Is beneficiary to have the right to commute the income under any CI Benefits? Yes ☐ No ☐

11. If third party application, state name in full of party who is to have applicant's rights and interests in the event of his prior death:

12. Who will pay the premiums? Applicant ☐ or

7. PLAN:

B.A. ☐   Cash ☐   Non-Par ☐
Div'd on Dep. ☐ Equity Divid. Opt. ☐

Premium for Plan selected
incl. WP ☐   not incl. WP ☐

MI 10 ☐
MI 20 ☐   AD ☐   DAD ☐

Guaranteed Insurability
with WP ☐   without WP ☐

Family Plan (FPP) ☐

CI Full Pay ☐   Limited Pay ☐
to Age   or   Years

S.I.R. ☐
Elected Payment Date:
(Pol. Anniversary Nearest Age   )

Ann ☐ Semi ☐ ACP ☐

Premium

Number of Units | Per Unit | For Policy

FOR H.O. USE

Annual Premium
Basic
WP

13. Has or does any of the proposed lives to be insured: Yes No

(a) made within the past 3 years or contemplate making any flights as a pilot, student pilot or crew member? Yes No Complete questionnaire if answer is "Yes". ☐ ☐

(b) participated or intend to participate in skin or scuba diving, auto or cycle racing or any hazardous sport? Complete questionnaire if answer is "Yes". ☐ ☐

(c) any other occupation or part-time employment? ☐ ☐

(d) contemplate any change in occupation, travel or residence outside of Canada or the U.S.A.? ☐ ☐

(e) had a request for life or health insurance or reinstatement of same postponed, rated, declined or restricted in any way? ☐ ☐

(f) presently have a pending application in this or any other Company? ☐ ☐

(g) have any insurance in this or any other Company which will be replaced by this application? ☐ ☐

For 13 (c) through 13 (g) give details where answer is "Yes".

8. Amount of Premium if Mode of Payment is Quart ☐ Monthly ☐

$

Policy Factor

Total Premium $

ADDITIONS AND AMENDMENTS

9. I/We the Applicant(s), have paid $.............. to cover

.... of the first .... premium.
(all or part)

I/We declare all statements and answers in all parts of my/our application for insurance to be full, complete and true to the best of my/our knowledge and belief and I/we agree: (1) In the event of any material misrepresentation or non-disclosure of any material fact the policy shall be void and all moneys paid forfeited; (2) Except as provided by the Conditional Interim Insurance Certificate, if any, issued in respect hereof, the Company shall not be under any risk or obligation unless (a) the first premium is paid, (b) the policy is delivered to me/us or to the beneficiary, (c) there is no change in insurability subsequent to the completion of the Part (s) 2 of this application; (3) If there are apparent errors or omissions in this Part 1 of the application or if the Company is only prepared to issue a modified policy it shall correct and complete this application or alter it accordingly, showing such changes in the space "Additions and Amendments" in the copy hereof in the policy submitted to me/us for acceptance and such changes will be deemed ratified and the policy accepted by me/us failing return within 30 days, of issue; (4) I/We reserve the right to change the beneficiary as permitted by law; (5) If the policy, as applied for contains variable insurance benefits, then (a) this application may be rescinded within 10 days of my/our signing and I/we acknowledge receipt of an information folder, (b) I/We may claim refund of any allowable additional premium payment within 10 days of its receipt at the Company's Head Office, if the charges applicable to such payment differ from charges applicable to similar payments as described in the policy or the latest premium notice issued by the Company; (6) If Payor insurance on disability or death of the applicant is requested, the statement and answers contained in Part 2 of the application respecting evidence of insurability of the applicant are declared full, complete and true and form part hereof and the agreement as hereinbefore contained shall be read and construed equally applicable to me as to the life to be insured; (7) In the event of the death of the life insured prior to exact age one year, the policy may provide for a death benefit less than the sum insured.

The undersigned acknowledge that they have been notified that a consumer report may be requested or a personal investigation conducted in connection with this application and hereby authorize The Empire Life Insurance Company to obtain such consumer report or to conduct or cause to be conducted a personal investigation.
If this application is accepted by the Company and a policy is issued I/we hereby request that it be issued in the English language.

Dated at ...., ..., this .... day of ...., 19 ....
I hereby declare that the declarations made by the applicant(s) are true and correct in all particulars and I consent to the issue of the policy as specified above.
It is hereby acknowledged that a Pre-Notice concerning the Medical Information Bureau was received.

Signature of ....
Applicant (s) *

....

....
Signature of life to be insured if other than applicant

Witness ...., Agent
* If applicant is a Company or Corporation its exact name must be given and an Officer (showing title) must sign.

PART I — ENG.

Limited payment life insurance offers lifetime protection too, but the insured person has to pay premiums for a specified number of years. This type of coverage remains in force for the rest of your life, although you pay premiums for a limited period of time such as ten or twenty years or most commonly, until age 65. Limited payment premiums are higher than straight life premiums since the insurance is paid up in a shorter time. These higher premiums are paid when the insured's income is probably at his or her highest level. And protection continues for the rest of that person's life when income may be more limited. This is an advantage of limited payment life insurance for many people.

Cash Surrender Value

Whole life insurance policies build up a **cash surrender value** or a cash value because, as explained previously, in such contracts not all the premium is needed to meet claims and expenses in the early years of the policy. The cash value of your insurance increases the longer you have the policy. During the first two or three years, costs of handling your policy and commission fees to the agent who sold you your policy come out of the premiums. It takes a few years before your policy begins to build up a cash value.

The cash value of a whole life insurance policy can be used in different ways. If you need to borrow money, you can borrow against the cash value of your policy. The interest rate that you pay for borrowing this money is lower than rates charged by many other lending agencies. The value of your policy is reduced by the amount of the loan, but the policy remains in effect. Once you have repaid the loan, your policy will be worth its full value once again.

If you want to cancel your policy, you will receive the cash value at that time in one lump sum or in instalments to provide you with a regular income. For example, you might want to cancel a policy worth $100 000 at death for $48 000 in cash now.

Endowment Insurance

Endowment insurance combines life insurance benefit features with features of a savings plan. It allows people to build up a fund of money to be paid to them on a particular date marked in the policy. If you don't survive to that date, the value of the policy will be paid to your beneficiary. Endowment policies can be obtained for various periods of time. Some people purchase these policies for the date

Analysis of Purchases of Individual Life Insurance Policies During 1976

	Per Cent of Policies	Per Cent of Amount
SEX OF INSURED		
Male	66	83
Female	34	17
Total	100	100
INCOME OF INSURED		
Under $5,000	2	1
$ 5 000 - $ 7 499	13	6
$ 7 500 - $ 9 999	18	11
$10 000 - $14 999	34	28
$15 000 - $24 999	24	30
$25 000 and over	9	24
Total	100	100
TYPE OF POLICY		
Whole Life	37	25
Limited payment life	17	7
Endowment	5	3
Retirement income	5	3
Level or decreasing term	18	39
Family policies	4	4
Other combination policies	14	19
Total	100	100
AGE OF INSURED		
Under 15	17	6
15 - 24	31	23
25 - 34	32	42
35 - 44	13	22
45 or over	7	7
Total	100	100
SIZE OF POLICY		
Under $5 000	11	1
$ 5 000 - $ 9 999	19	5
$10 000 - $14 999	25	12
$15 000 - $24 999	14	11
$25 000 - $49 999	19	26
$50 000 - $99 999	8	21
$100 000 and over	4	24
Total	100	100
MODE OF PREMIUM PAYMENT		
Annual	32	36
Semi-annual	6	5
Quarterly	2	2
Monthly debit	4	2
Salary savings	1	1
Monthly pre-authorized cheque plan	51	50
Other monthly	4	4
Total	100	100

Source: The Canadian Life Insurance Association
Reprinted by permission

when they expect to retire. Others purchase endowment insurance when their children are young; so that money will be available for further education after high school.

Assume that Phil Lightstone purchases a $10 000 fifteen-year endowment policy for his daughter, Marilyn, when she is three years old. The policy is to mature, or come due, when she is eighteen years old. Her father's plan is to have money available for her university education. This means that the full $10 000 value of the policy must be paid by the end of the fifteen years. If Marilyn should die as a result of an accident or an illness before the end of the fifteen-year period, her father and mother would receive the $10 000 as the beneficiaries of the policy. If Marilyn is alive at the end of the fifteen years, she will receive the full amount of money. Because of the high cash value to be paid, premiums for endowment policies are the most expensive to purchase.

Life Insurance Features

The three main types of insurance–term, whole life, and endowment–can be purchased with different options. Two of the more common options are waiver of premium and double indemnity.

Waiver of Premium

A waiver of premium is an option that keeps your insurance policy in force when premiums cannot be paid. If you become disabled and cannot work for a period of time, your premiums need not be paid. This option guarantees that your policy will not lapse while you are unable to work. You will be required to pay your premiums again once you are able to work.

Double Indemnity

A double indemnity clause in an insurance policy provides that the beneficiary will receive double the face value of the policy if the insured's death is an accident. This feature can be purchased as an option on a normal whole life policy. The premiums for a double indemnity option are not much higher than for a basic policy. Such causes of death as suicide and dangerous flying activities are not accepted in double indemnity claims.

Period of Grace

A few weeks before a premium is to be paid on an insurance policy, the company will send a renewal notice to the insured. All life insurance policies include a period of grace. This is a period of time, usually lasting thirty or thirty-one days after the premium due date, in which the insured is still protected by the policy. This applies even if the policyholder fails to pay the required premium on time. The policy remains in force and cannot be cancelled by the insurance company until after the end of the period of grace.

Annuities

Another form of financial planning available from insurance companies is an annuity. Life insurance is intended to provide your dependants with financial support after you die. An annuity is intended to provide you with a retirement income for as long as you live. The principle behind life insurance and an annuity is the same. Since you don't know when you will die or how long you will live, you contribute to a pool of funds with other people to share the risk of dying too soon for life insurance, and of living too long for annuities. Each of you gets some financial protection for yourself and your dependants.

The purpose of an annuity is to protect the income of insured people. Assume that Mr. and Mrs. Applegate have both retired from their jobs and have about $30 000 in savings. They will receive their Old Age Security Pensions and their Canada Pension Plan benefits. Are they able to live on their savings? Their pension plan payments will pay for most of their expenses for necessities such as food, clothing, and shelter. However, it is possible that some of their savings will have to be used to cover other expenses.

To guarantee that their savings will last as long as they live, the Applegates decide to put some or all of the $30 000 into the purchase of an annuity. They can start receiving monthly income from the annuity as soon as they want it. The insurance company can guarantee the Applegates monthly income payments as long as they live for the same reasons that the company can promise to pay insurance benefits for death of a person. This is because there are large numbers of people pooling their funds for annuity protection.

There are many annuity plans available, just as there are many life insurance plans. Before you purchase an annuity, obtain information from different insurance companies. Shop around and compare before making a decision. Annuity rates differ considerably from company to company.

APPLICATION TO
THE EMPIRE LIFE INSURANCE COMPANY

1. Full name of Annuitant ☐ Male ☐ Female

(Surname) (Given Names)

Social Insurance No.

5. Full name of Applicant, if other than Annuitant ☐ Male ☐ Female

(Surname) (Given Names)

Social Insurance No.

2. Date of birth of Annuitant

Day	Month	Year

Age nearest birthday

Place of birth
Name at birth if other than above

6. Address of Applicant ....

Street

City .... Prov. ....

7. Residence of Annuitant

3. Full name of Joint Annuitant (if applicable) ☐ Male ☐ Female

(Surname) (Given Names)

Social Insurance No.

Street

City .... Prov. ....

4. Date of birth of Joint Annuitant

Day	Month	Year

Age nearest birthday

Place of birth
Name at birth if other than above

8. Mailing address if different from 7.

Street

City .... Prov. ....

9. Plan (a) Systematic Investment Policy (SIP) ☐   (b) Variable Investment Policy (VIP) ☐
   (c) Pension Investment Policy (PIC) ☐
   (d) Immediate Single Life Annuity with a guaranteed period of 5 ☐ 10 ☐ 15 ☐ years
   (e) Deferred Single Life Annuity with a guaranteed period of 5 ☐ 10 ☐ 15 ☐ years
   (f) Other ☐ (describe fully)

10. Income applied for $..............

Commencing

Payable ☐ Monthly ☐ other ....
specify

11. I request that Premiums be payable

☐ In one sum ☐ Auto Monthly

☐ Annually ☐ Other

in the Amount of .... $............

12. Beneficiary (state full name and relationship to the Annuitant)

a. On death prior to the commencement of income ☐ Revocable ☐ Irrevocable

b. On death after the commencement of income ☐ Revocable ☐ Irrevocable

Consent of Irrevocable beneficiary is required for future dealings with policy.
IN QUEBEC appointment of spouse is irrevocable unless otherwise stipulated.

13. a. Is this contract intended to replace any contract in this or any other Company? .... *Yes ☐ No ☐

b. Is this contract to be registered under section 146 of the Income Tax Act? ☐ ☐

c. Is the premium to be paid out of an Approved Pension Trust fund or Registered Retirement Savings Plan? ☐ ☐

d. Does the Annuitant hold previously issued Insurance or Annuity contracts with this Company? ☐ ☐

*Give details here of "Yes" answers to question 13.

....

....

14. Additions and Amendments (For Head Office use only)

15. Special Instructions (For use of Applicant)

I/we declare all statements and answers in all parts of the application to be full, complete and true to the best of my/our knowledge and belief and agree that:

(i) The Company shall not be under any risk or obligation unless (a) the first premium is paid, and (b) the policy is delivered to me/us.

(ii) If any modified policy is submitted for acceptance and is not returned within 30 days of issue, then such policy shall be deemed to be accepted and any changes shown at (14) above will be deemed to be ratified.

(iii) I/we reserve the right to change the beneficiary as permitted by law.

(iv) If this application is for a Systematic Investment Policy, a Variable Investment Policy or a Pension Investment Policy then (a) this application may be rescinded within 10 days of my/our signing and I/we acknowledge receipt of the information folder, if any such folder is required, (b) I/we may claim refund of any additional premium payment within 10 days of its receipt at the Company's Head Office, if the charges applicable to such payment differ from charges applicable to similar payments as described in the policy or the latest premium notice issued by the Company.

If this application is accepted by the Company and a policy is issued I/we hereby request that it be issued in the English language.

I/We, the Applicant(s), have paid to .... $............ to cover .... of the first .... premium.
(all or part)

Dated at .... , ... , this .... day of .... 19......

I hereby declare that the declarations made by the applicant(s) are true and correct in all particulars and I consent to the issue of the policy as specified above.

Signature of Applicant(s)*

....

No 8239

Signature of Annuitant if other than applicant

Witness .... , Agent

Signature of Joint Annuitant

*If applicant is a Company or Corporation its exact name must be given and an Officer (showing title) must sign.

NON-EVIDENCE - ENG.

243

Shopping for Insurance

The amount and type of insurance that you purchase depends on the purpose for which you want the insurance. Be sure that you know what you want to protect before you buy insurance. This is the most important aspect of buying insurance. Do you want a large amount of term insurance at a low cost to protect a young family? Do you want to provide money for retirement income? Do you hope to buy insurance and establish a reasonable cash value in a specific period of time? These are some of the basic questions that need to be carefully considered.

Shop around for insurance and compare prices. Prices for the same kind of insurance differ considerably. A price variation of twenty per cent is not uncommon. Each insurance company has its own name for the different kinds of coverage. The Consumers' Association of Canada published *A Shopper's Guide to Life Insurance* in 1978. The guide compares prices and a variety of insurance policies, and is a useful source of information if you are about to purchase life insurance. The Canadian Life Insurance Association publishes a booklet, *How to Compare,* which outlines a method of comparison of life insurance policies.

In the latter part of the 1970s, more and more low-priced term insurance has been purchased by consumers for the basic insurance it provides. This term insurance has been supplemented with annuities for the savings they provide. These purchasing trends have resulted in a relative decrease in the number of whole life policies being purchased.

Health and Disability Insurance

Health insurance is necessary for everyone these days with the high and still increasing cost of hospital and medical expenses. Sickness and accidents can occur unexpectedly at any time. Some insurance is needed to provide protection if you become disabled or unable to work.

Hospital and Medical Insurance

All provinces have insurance plans to pay hospital and medical bills for their residents. Although the plans differ slightly from province to province, there are many common features.

Hospital insurance covers the cost of basic-ward accommodation, use of operating and delivery rooms, necessary nursing services, drugs ordered by the doctor, and other services needed for the diagnosis and treatment of an illness or injury.

Medical insurance covers the cost of the doctor's services. This includes services in your home or at the doctor's office or at the hospital. Surgery, treatment of fractures and dislocations, diagnosis and treatment of illness and injury are among other items included.

Much of the cost of these plans is covered by premiums paid by those persons enrolled in the insurance plans. The balance is paid from money raised by taxation.

Private insurance companies and other non-government organizations offer insurance plans to cover additional costs not included in provincial plans. One of the main additional costs is the difference between standard-ward and semi-private or private hospital room accommodation. Hospital and medical insurance do not cover your loss of income while you are sick or disabled. Insurance companies sell income and disability insurance to replace part of your income because of disability.

The Canada and Quebec Pension Plans, unemployment insurance, and workmen's compensation all provide disability insurance protection. Group insurance plans and annuities also provide protection against loss of income.

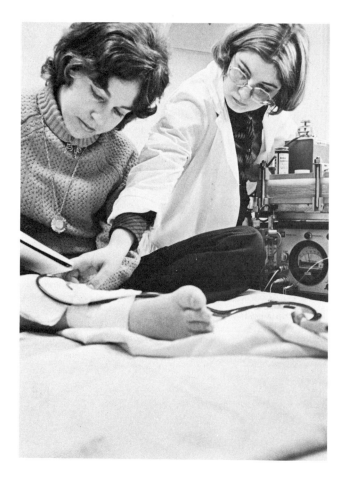

UNIT C

PROPERTY INSURANCE: CAR AND HOME

A home is probably the most expensive purchase you will make in your lifetime. After your home, a car is the next most expensive series of purchases. Nearly all homes and cars in Canada are insured against losses by fire and theft. Besides the obvious losses to property from fire and theft, you need protection against other people's losses or liabilities that occur on your property. As a homeowner, you are responsible for the safety of people in your home. This includes guests, service people who make repairs to appliances, baby-sitters, or anyone who enters your home. Car owners have a similar responsibility to passengers in their cars, other motorists, pedestrians, and to property. Thus, protection through insurance is a wise purchase for both home and car owners.

Car Insurance

It is likely that you will own a car some day. When you purchase your car, you should also consider the purchase of car insurance. It is an important form of insurance as the cost of cars increases every year. The damage that can result from a car accident is usually many times greater than the value of the car. Every year in Canada one car in ten is involved in an accident. The damage resulting from car accidents in Canada amounts to millions of dollars each year. Most people spend more money on car insurance than on home insurance. Why? Probably because more risks and losses are involved with cars. Cars can be stolen or damaged in accidents. Cars damage property and injure and kill people. Since most people cannot afford to pay the high costs involved in a car accident themselves, they need the financial protection provided by car insurance.

The Need for Car Insurance

Car insurance is a service that provides protection from financial losses that arise out of a car accident. Connie, a senior student in a Canadian high school, was involved with her friend Josie in a car accident with another car that had three people in it. Both cars were seriously damaged–the accident was Connie's fault. The driver of the other car and his passengers sued Connie for damages to his car and for their personal injuries. The case went to court, and as a result of the court action, Connie was required to pay the other driver $50 000 for personal injuries, $25 000 for injuries to his passengers, and $3 000 for damages to the car. In addition, repairs to Connie's car cost $2 000. The total cost of the accident was $80 000. Because of car insurance, Connie did not have to make these large payments herself. Her insurance company provided her with protection through her policy.

Financial Protection Through Car Insurance

From the example of Connie's car accident, you can see that her car insurance provided her with different kinds of protection. The basic types of car insurance available are:

Liability insurance-provided Connie with protection against the injuries to the driver of the other car, his car, and to his passengers.

Accident benefits-pay for death or rehabilitation of any passengers riding in the car, or loss of income of the injured passengers. These benefits are paid, regardless of Connie's fault.

Collision insurance-provided Connie with protection against the damage to her car.

Comprehensive insurance-protects against losses from such things as fire, theft, and glass breakage.

You can see that the driver of a car needs protection against several kinds of risks, but it is not necessary to purchase a separate policy for each risk. One policy can be bought to cover as many risks as you want protection for.

Liability Insurance

This type of insurance is necessary to protect drivers against claims of loss or injury by others as a result of an accident caused by the driver. The two types of liability insurance are bodily injury liability and property damage liability. These two forms of liability insurance are combined in a car insurance policy, which is a legal contract. They are commonly known as BI/PD (bodily injury and property damage) insurance. These combined benefits are described as third party liability insurance. You and your insurance company are the first and second parties to the contract. The injured person claiming against you is the third party.

Bodily Injury Liability Insurance

This insurance protects insured drivers against claims resulting from injury or death of passengers in their car, the driver or passengers in the other cars, or pedestrians. It is often called public liability insurance.

If someone is injured in a car accident that was your fault, your insurance company will pay the injured person up to the amount of insurance that you purchased. This payment covers such costs as medical treatment, hospitalization, time off work, permanent injury, and the cost of a lawyer defending you, if you are taken to court. If the court awards or gives the injured person more than the limits of your policy, you will be responsible for this extra payment yourself. In recent years, courts have awarded hundreds of thousands of dollars in individual damage claims to injured persons. One court settlement involved $875 000, and a settlement of one million dollars or more is now a real possibility.

Third party insurance is compulsory now in all provinces, except Ontario. Proof of such insurance is necessary in these provinces before licence plates are purchased. In Ontario third party liability insurance is not presently compulsory, although the Ontario government has announced that car insurance will be compulsory by December, 1979. However, most car owners have purchased it. All provinces have established a legal minimum amount to be purchased by persons buying car insurance. Higher limits may be purchased at a small and reasonable cost.

Property Damage Liability

This insurance protects insured people against claims resulting from damage caused by their cars to other cars or to property. If your car hit a hydro pole or bus owned by the city or the township, or your car ran over a person's front lawn, flower gardens, and into the side of the house, your property insurance would protect you. Property damage liability insurance does not cover the cost of damage to your car. Collision insurance is needed for this protection.

Collision Insurance

Collision insurance covers the cost of repairs to your car when it is involved in an accident. With this type of coverage, the insurance company is responsible for the damage to the car no matter who is at fault. The amount of money the company will pay for damages will not exceed the value of the car. If the damage to your car is estimated at $2 000 but your car is only worth $1 500, the company will only pay you $1 500.

Because of the high cost of car repairs, most collision insurance sections of a policy have a deductible feature. The most common deductibles selected are $50, $100, and $250. This means that the insured person pays the amount of the deductible, and the insurance company pays the balance of the cost. If there is a loss of $2 000 as there was in our example of Connie's accident, she would have to pay the amount of the deductible on her policy, for example, $250. Her insurance company would then pay the balance of $1 750. The higher the amount of the deductible, the lower the cost of the premium. This is because the risk of loss to the insurance company is less. Following are some sample rates for comparison:

Amount of Coverage	Annual Cost
$ 50 deductible	$53.00
100 deductible	44.00
250 deductible	33.00

Comprehensive Insurance

This type of insurance pays for loss or damage from any risk other than collision. Common risks include fire, theft, accidental glass breakage, vandalism, and weather conditions like floods and windstorms. These risks are items that are not covered by collision insurance. Comprehensive insurance does not cover wear and tear or mechanical difficulties to your car. A deductible clause is often a part of comprehensive coverage.

Canadian Auto Insurance Plans

In Effect March 1, 1978
Bodily Injury and Property Damage (BI/PD)

Region or Province	Legal Minimum Amount	Administration
Prince Edward Island	$ 35 000	Private insurers
Nova Scotia	35 000	Private insurers
New Brunswick	50 000	Private insurers
Newfoundland	75 000	Private insurers
Quebec*	50 000 (car damage)	Private insurers
Ontario	100 000	Private insurers
Manitoba	50 000	Government monopoly for basic insurance; for excess— government and private insurers compete
Saskatchewan	35 000	
British Columbia	50 000	
Alberta	50 000	Private insurers
Northwest Territories	50 000	Private insurers
Yukon	50 000	Private insurers

*From March 1, 1978 liability for bodily injury has been eliminated in Quebec.

Source: Insurance Bureau of Canada
Reprinted by permission

Auto Medical Benefits for you and your passengers

Accidental Glass Breakage

Vandalism

Falling Objects Missiles

Strike—Riot

Rental Reimbursement

Earthquake

Uninsured Motorist Protection

Fire

Theft and Theft Damage

Flood Rising Water

Windstorm Tornado

Explosion

Hail—Rain Snow—Sleet

Protection Against Uninsured Motorists

Special funds are available to compensate those people who are the victims of hit-and-run drivers and uninsured drivers. In those provinces in which car insurance is not compulsory, drivers who do not purchase insurance must pay a sum of money into a Motor Vehicle Accident Claims Fund. It is operated by the government in some provinces and by the insurance industry in other provinces. Thus, innocent victims are given some protection by law against uninsured motorists.

The payment of a sum of money into the Fund is *not* insurance. It does not protect uninsured motorists in any way. It simply allows these motorists to drive their cars. If such a motorist causes an accident and the claim is paid to the injured party out of the Motor Vehicle Accident Claims Fund, the uninsured motorist's licence will be suspended. All driving privileges are lost. The suspension remains in effect until the full amount of the court judgement has been paid or instalment payments have been arranged and started.

Uninsured motorists are responsible for the full amount of any judgements awarded by the courts to victims of an accident caused by these motorists. Such court judgements can financially ruin people who have not purchased insurance. Court awards are often based on the future earning power of the victim, and awards of several hundreds of thousands of dollars are becoming common.

The Cost of Car Insurance

Like all other kinds of insurance, the cost of car insurance depends on how serious the risks are. The premium rates that you pay are set so that the highest rates are paid by the people who have the biggest losses. The premiums each person pays are based on a number of factors.

Not All Drivers Are the Same

Generally, the single male driver under twenty-five years of age pays the highest premiums for insurance. This same male driver will often pay more than a single female driver under twenty-five. Insurance companies know from their records that drivers under the age of twenty-five have a greater chance of being involved in, and responsible for, accidents. Several insurers now give lower insurance rates to those young people who have successfully completed driver education classes in high school. These courses include both classroom and in-car instruction. Most insurance companies also believe that married people under the age of twenty-five are better insurance risks. Rates for insurance decrease as young people become older, get married, and as they develop safe driving records.

Crashes by Age of Drivers (1975)

	Fatal	Non-fatal	Property Damage Only	Total	%
Under 16	45	1 094	1 540	2 679	.2
16 - 19 years	1 177	33 182	101 260	135 619	12.2
20 - 24 years	1 632	44 134	144 871	190 637	17.1
25 - 34 years	1 828	54 865	190 529	247 222	22.2
35 - 44 years	1 022	32 104	113 482	146 608	13.2
45 - 54 years	797	24 789	87 049	112 635	10.1
55 - 64 years	525	14 339	51 014	65 878	5.9
65 and over	357	7 299	24 323	31 979	2.9
Not stated	313	31 675	147 419	179 407	16.1
Totals	7 696	243 481	861 487	1 112 664	100.0

Source: *Insurance Bureau of Canada*
From: *"Facts of the General Insurance Industry of Canada, 5th Ed."*
Reprinted by permission

Driver's Residence

Drivers who live in large cities are much more likely to be involved in accidents than drivers who live in small towns or rural areas. With heavier traffic, people in the cities face greater hazards while driving. Rates for insurance vary from city to city and are based on the frequency of accidents. This is one of the reasons why premium rates cannot be easily compared between different provinces.

The Driver's Record

Drivers with a good driving record who have not been involved in accidents for from one to five years usually pay less for their insurance. These drivers receive a preferred premium or discount that reduces the cost of their insurance by an appreciable amount each year. Drivers who are most likely to be involved in accidents are the people who pay the highest premiums. Nearly all insurance companies give lower rates to claim-free drivers. The method of granting the lower rate differs from company to company; so that it is wise to shop around when purchasing car insurance.

The Car and Its Use

Another factor that affects the cost of car insurance is the make, model, and year of the car, and also the number of kilometres driven each year. The more expensive your car, the more you drive it, the more expensive your insurance will be. This is because you are more likely to be involved in an accident and it will be costly to repair or replace your car. Some companies charge more for insuring high-powered cars for the same reason. People who own more than one car usually receive a discount on the additional car as it is not likely to be driven as much.

Increasing Premium Costs

Complaints come from drivers when the cost of their insurance increases. They have been driving their same car in the same way for years and have not been involved in any accidents. Why then has their insurance cost increased or just remained the same? As cars become more expensive to buy, the cost of repairs for accidents increases. According to the Insurance Bureau of Canada, the average BI/PD claim has been increasing every year as these figures show:

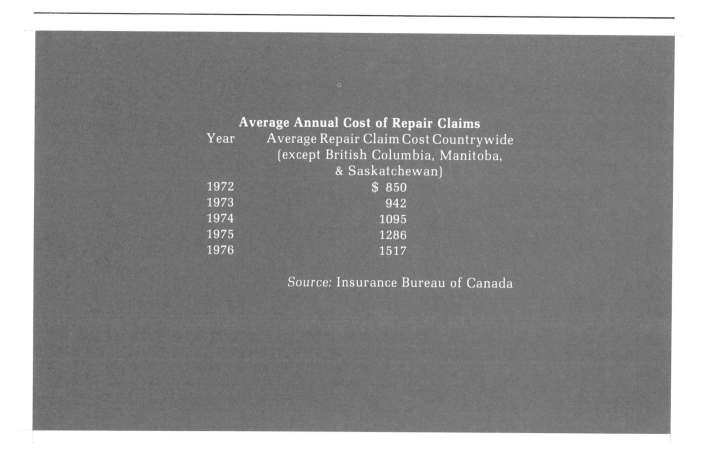

Average Annual Cost of Repair Claims

Year	Average Repair Claim Cost Countrywide (except British Columbia, Manitoba, & Saskatchewan)
1972	$ 850
1973	942
1974	1095
1975	1286
1976	1517

Source: Insurance Bureau of Canada

No-fault Insurance

To decrease the number of cases that go to court because of car accidents, several provinces have introduced a form of no-fault insurance. In the past, careless drivers had to pay through their insurance companies for the accidents they caused. This encouraged drivers to be more careful. But good drivers cause accidents too. Bad weather, poor road conditions, unsafe cars also cause accidents. It is becoming more difficult for the courts to determine who is to blame for accidents and to what extent they are at fault.

No-fault insurance describes the insurance plan that exists when fault does not apply to car accidents. There is no simple definition of no-fault insurance, and it is a complex legal matter. However, it suggests that each insurance company pays its own policyholder, no matter who is at fault. Some provinces have introduced no-fault insurance as part of their basic coverage. Most no-fault plans permit drivers to sue the party at fault for damages greater than the amount of money covered by the insurance plan.

Home Insurance

People purchase insurance as protection against a possible financial loss. As a homeowner, you may purchase a separate policy for protection against such losses caused by fire, theft, water, vandalism, personal liability, or other risks.

All property can be divided into two types: personal property and real property. Personal property is usually moveable and includes such things as clothing, furniture, jewellery, and books. Real property includes land, a home, garage, barn, and other buildings attached to the land.

Home insurance protects you against loss or damage to both real and personal property. It also covers damage you may cause to the property of others, and injuries to other persons on your property or caused by members of your family. Exceptions are damages caused by cars, aircraft, or other self-propelled vehicles.

The Major Risk of Fire

According to Statistics Canada, nearly 70 000 fires occurred in homes in 1976, killing 586 people and causing property damage of over $500 million. In 1973 the total damage was a little over $320 million from 74 000 fires. Although the number of fires has definitely declined, the total damage has considerably increased.

For all of Canada, careless smoking tops the list of causes of fire. It was responsible for about 10 000 of the nearly 70 000 fires in 1976. Property damage caused by cigarette-related fires amounted to about $40 million. Other major causes of fire are caused from electrical and heating equipment—stoves, furnaces, boilers, and smoke pipes. Fires from heating appliances numbered about 6 000 and caused about 38 million dollars' damage.

Liability Insurance

Many kinds of accidents occur in a person's home or apartment. Personal liability insurance protects home owners or tenants and their families against claims for injuries suffered by guests or workers while on the property. This type of insurance also pays legal fees if you are sued in court in a lawsuit.

Howard and Jeanette Echenberg own their own home. One weekend they had a party for several of their friends. During the evening, one of the guests tripped over a baby's toy and fell down a long flight of stairs. The guest suffered a broken leg and a sprained back. Personal liability insurance would protect the Echenbergs against any lawsuit started by the injured guest.

The Homeowner's Policy

Separate policies can be purchased for protection against fire, theft, personal liability, and other risks, but this can be a very expensive way to buy protection. Because of this cost, most people purchase a homeowner's policy. This type of insurance has become very popular because all of the property and liability needs of homeowners are included in this one policy. This policy covers a home and the contents of the home up to a fixed percentage of the value. It also provides protection against lawsuits or being taken to court—all in the one package deal. The advantages of this policy are that the cost of such insurance is usually less than that of several separate policies, and it is easier to keep track of premium payments.

A homeowner's policy is not just for those people who own their own home. Tenants or people renting apartments or homes might suffer a financial loss from damage, vandalism, or liability if their rental property were damaged or destroyed by fire or flood. It is a financial strain to replace furniture, clothing, and other personal items without adequate insurance. However, the rental home or apartment is not insured under the policy because tenants do not own it.

The Cost of Home Insurance

Home insurance costs, like car insurance costs, are based on a number of factors. One factor to determine is an estimate of the value of the home. A home built of brick and stone, for example, would be much less an insurance risk than a house of wood construction.

During the 1970s, the value of homes greatly increased. This higher value is, in part, a reflection of the increase in the costs of labour and construction materials. A home that cost $30 000 to build in 1971 might cost well over $60 000 to replace today. Because insurance coverage is directly related to construction costs, the average home insurance premium has also increased.

With the increase in value of real property, it is wise to make sure every few years that the value of your home insurance policy reflects this increased value. Some insurance companies automatically increase the value of policies each year to make sure that the actual replacement value of the property is insured.

The value of the contents in homes and apartments has also increased. According to the Insurance Bureau of Canada, fire claims and burglary claims have increased well over one hundred per cent in the last five years. Canadians own more things worth stealing now than five years ago. The things they own cost more than they did five years ago. All this means higher costs for home insurance.

Protection Against Fire

Another important factor to consider is how good a local or area fire department is, and how far your home is from a fire hydrant. If you live near a fire hydrant and have an efficient fire department, your insurance will be less than if you lived far away from a water supply and good fire protection.

Some insurance companies now consider the presence of a smoke detector in your home as a highly important factor. Most deaths from fire occur at night during sleeping hours, and deaths could be prevented if burning homes had fire-alarm systems to waken sleepers. Smoke reveals the presence of fire much sooner than heat does, and many people consider smoke detectors as potential life-saving devices. A matter of seconds or minutes can make the difference between life and death, once the warning sound is triggered on the detector. Alberta and Ontario now have legislation making smoke detectors mandatory equipment in all homes built after January, 1977.

THE STAGES OF FIRE

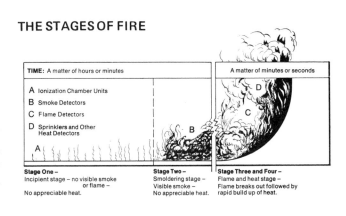

Stage One –
Incipient stage – no visible smoke or flame –
No appreciable heat.

Stage Two –
Smoldering stage –
Visible smoke –
No appreciable heat.

Stage Three and Four –
Flame and heat stage –
Flame breaks out followed by rapid build up of heat.

HERMAN

"If the smoke detector fails and your house burns down, we replace the unit plus batteries free of charge."

253

Other Factors to Consider

If crime rates are high in your neighbourhood or area, the cost of insurance protection will probably be high too. If losses resulting from a particular risk or hazard are low, insurance rates for that risk should be low. These, and the other factors already examined, are then considered with past experiences with various types of losses. This past experience is based on millions of cases over the years. Your specific premium rate comes from this analysis.

Recovering Losses through Home Insurance

When property is damaged, stolen, or destroyed, the property owners are always concerned about the amount of money they will receive for their losses from the insurance companies. Policyholders must make a claim in order to receive any money for losses.

Insurance companies require some proof of loss of the destroyed items before they will pay any claims. This places a responsibility on the insured to show how many items there were and how much these items cost when they were purchased. It is also useful to know what the items are worth today as this is more likely the replacement value that the insurance company will pay. Since the items have been used and are no longer new, the insurance company will not give policyholders the full value of the goods that they originally paid.

To have evidence for this proof of loss, people should keep an inventory list of the items in their homes. This inventory contains a list of the main items in the home, the date they were purchased, and how much they cost. Such a list can be prepared easily on your own, or printed inventory forms are available from your insurance agent. Some people take photographs of the rooms in their homes to provide additional proof to support their claims. It is important to add any new purchases made to your lists so that they are up-to-date at all times.

Shop Around for Property Insurance

Since costs and coverage may differ from company to company, it is wise to shop around. No matter where you live in Canada, the basic car insurance policy and homeowner's policy that you receive from any insurance company are much the same. The options that you choose and the amount of coverage you buy are the items that result in different costs. By shopping around you could save as much as twenty per cent on your purchases.

REVIEWING YOUR BUSINESS VOCABULARY

Write the number of each definition.
Write the word that matches each definition number.

UNIT A

actuary, agent, claim, insured, insurer, policy, premium, risk, term

1. Company that makes insurance protection available to others.
2. Person who buys insurance.
3. Sales representative of a life insurance company.
4. Chance or possibility of a loss.
5. Written agreement between an insurance company and the purchaser.
6. Payment for life insurance protection.
7. Period from the beginning to the end of an insurance policy.
8. Request for payment of losses.
9. Person who measures insurance risks and calculates premium rates.

UNIT B

annuity, beneficiary, breadwinner, cash surrender value, endowment, group life, mortality table, term, whole life

1. Person named in an insurance policy to receive the proceeds.
2. Set of statistics that estimates life expectancy.
3. Main earner of income in a family.
4. Insurance issued to an employer for the benefit of his employees.
5. Permanent life insurance that pays money when the insured dies.
6. Amount of money policyholders receive when they cash in their policies.
7. Contract between the insured and the insurer that guarantees the insured an income for a specific period of time.

8. Insurance in which the death benefit is payable only if death occurs within a set period of time.
9. Insurance payable to the beneficiary if the insured dies or payable directly to the insured if he or she lives beyond the time in which premiums are paid.

UNIT C

collision, comprehensive, deductible, homeowner's policy, liability, Motor Vehicle Accident Claims Fund, no-fault, personal property, property insurance, real property

1. Pays an injured party for damages caused by uninsured motorists.
2. Insurance that pays accident benefits to an injured party, no matter who is to blame.
3. Protects the insured against possible losses resulting from damage to the insured's property.
4. Insurance that provides complete insurance protection for a homeowner in one policy.
5. Insurance agreement that requires insured persons to pay a portion of the loss themselves.
6. Furniture and clothing.
7. A home.
8. Protection against financial losses resulting from injuries to other persons or their property for which the insured is responsible.
9. Pays for damages to the insured's car that is not covered by collision insurance.
10. Protects against losses resulting from damages to the insured's car, no matter who is at fault.

REVIEW QUESTIONS

UNIT A

1. What kinds of economic losses might a family encounter?
2. How can you reduce the possibility of risk of losses occurring in your lifetime?
3. What is meant by sharing economic risks? Does this sharing eliminate the risks?
4. How are risks shared with the purchase of insurance?
5. Who are the parties to an insurance policy?
6. What are the main types of losses for which people buy protection through insurance?
7. What are the two main factors a family must consider before buying insurance?
8. What are the four basic types of insurance commonly bought by Canadians?
9. What is an insurance policy? What are the essential parts of such a policy?
10. What is an insurance claim?
11. What three factors need to be considered in determining the cost of insurance premiums?
12. Why should a person shop around before buying insurance?
13. What is the function of a claims officer in an insurance company?
14. What is an actuary? Why is this career a key position in an insurance company?
15. List five basic careers that are available in the insurance industry.

UNIT B

1. Why do people purchase life insurance and health insurance?
2. Why is it so important for an insurance company to know a person's age?
3. Explain the difference between individual and group life insurance.
4. What are the three main types of life insurance?
5. What is the main advantage of term insurance? Why is the cost of term insurance higher each time the policy is renewed?
6. What are the two main forms of whole life insurance? What is the difference between each of them?

7. What is the cash surrender value of an insurance policy?
8. Which type of life insurance does not build up a cash surrender value? Why is this so?
9. What happens to the value of your insurance policy when you borrow against the cash surrender value of the policy?
10. What is endowment insurance? When can the insured collect the proceeds of an endowment policy?
11. What is a waiver of premium? Why is it a useful option to have on an insurance policy?
12. What is a period of grace, and how long is it?
13. What is the main difference between life insurance and an annuity?
14. In what two ways are hospital and medical insurance paid for?
15. List three forms of disability insurance protection.

UNIT C

1. What are the three basic types of car insurance that are available? What does each cover?
2. What is BI/PD insurance, and why is it often called third party liability insurance?
3. Why is property damage liability coverage important to car drivers?
4. What is the main difference between collision insurance and property damage liability insurance?
5. Explain what is meant by *deductible* as it applies to collision insurance?
6. What kinds of protection are included in comprehensive physical damage coverage?
7. What is the purpose of the Motor Vehicle Accident Claims Fund?
8. List four factors that must be considered by insurance companies in setting car insurance premium rates. Why is each important?
9. Who pays the highest premiums for car insurance? Why?
10. What is the difference between real and personal property? Give two examples of each.
11. What are some of the common risks for which people purchase home insurance as protection?
12. Outline the factors that an insurance company must consider in determining the cost of a homeowner's policy?
13. Why is it necessary to increase the value of your home insurance policy every few years?
14. What is meant by "proof of loss" as it relates to home insurance?

APPLYING YOUR BUSINESS KNOWLEDGE

UNIT A

1. Make a list of as many economic losses as possible that a business might encounter.
2. Why might you want to purchase an insurance policy while in high school?
3. Can risks ever be completely eliminated from a person's life? Why or why not?
4. Why do many people purchase insurance even if they do not expect to suffer any losses or be exposed to any risks?
5. Why might a football quarterback insure his passing arm? Is this a common risk? How would this effect the cost of his insurance policy?
6. Many people think that buying insurance is a form of gambling. Do you agree with this? Why or why not?
7. Would you be able to purchase a life insurance policy on your best friend's life? Why or why not?
8. Does a business person have an insurable interest in his or her partner's life? Explain.
9. Flight insurance is available for purchase at airports for people who are travelling between cities or between countries. Why is such insurance available?
10. Why are insurance companies major users of computer equipment?

UNIT B

1. Why do you think Canadians own more insurance per capita than people in any other country in the world?
2. What is the advantage of purchasing life insurance when you are young?
3. Why do insurance companies have different mortality tables for men and women?
4. Why are insurance premiums more expensive for people whose daily work is considered dangerous? List three types of occupations that you consider dangerous work.
5. What major benefit does group insurance have over individual insurance?
6. Why is group insurance a reasonably inexpensive form of insurance to buy?
7. Why won't insurance companies usually issue term insurance to people over seventy years of age? Do you agree with this?
8. What is a "convertible term insurance policy"?
9. Life insurance is often sold on a level premium basis. Explain the meaning of this statement as it applies to straight life insurance.
10. What is the main advantage for many people of buying limited payment life insurance?
11. What is the main advantage and main disadvantage of term insurance compared with whole life insurance?
12. Why do you think there are a large number of group health insurance plans available today?
13. Is it a good idea to get insurance protection for illness? Why or why not?
14. Why do provincial governments assume most of the responsibility for hospital and medical insurance?
15. Why do private companies sell insurance plans in the area of medical insurance?

UNIT C

1. Each province requires a driver to purchase a minimum insurance requirement of BI/PD coverage. Why might it be advisable to purchase more than the legal minimum?
2. If every driver on Canadian highways was considered a good, safe driver by their insurance companies, would there still be a need for car insurance? Discuss and support your answer with sound reasons.
3. Why do people who use a car for business purposes pay more for car insurance than people who use their car only for pleasure driving?
4. Has your province passed legislation requiring the compulsory wearing of seat belts by occupants in a car? What effect will such a law have on car insurance premiums?
5. What effect, if any, will these items have on car insurance premiums: reduced speed limits on highways; increasing costs of gasoline?
6. Why do insurance companies want to know the occupations of each policyholder? Do you think this is an important piece of information?
7. Why do you think insurance companies are prepared to give lower car insurance rates to young people who have successfully completed driver-education classes?
8. Do you believe that no-fault insurance is a good idea? Give reasons for your answer.
9. Although the number of house fires has decreased in recent years, why have total damage payments increased?
10. Why aren't automobiles included with other personal property in a homeowner's policy?
11. Where would the cost of fire insurance likely be higher—in rural areas or cities? Why?
12. According to insurance advisors, the amount of personal liability insurance you carry should reflect your financial worth, activity, and your property. Explain the meaning of this statement. Do you agree with it? Why or why not?
13. Why is it advisable to have a friend or neighbour check your home daily if you are absent from your home for any length of time?

PROJECTS AND PROBLEMS

UNIT A

1. Prepare a bulletin board display around the theme of **Insurance: The Sharing of Risk.** Divide your bulletin board into four subsections: Life Insurance, Car Insurance, Home Insurance, and Health and Income Insurance. Collect pictures and newspaper clippings that illustrate the kinds of risks and perils for which people need insurance protection. These risks include fires, floods, death, accidents, disability, and so on. Materials should be placed under the appropriate sections of the display. Sample insurance policies, forms involved in processing insurance claim, pictures of losses, and insurance company advertising might also be included as you become more involved in the study of insurance.

2. The Canadian Life Insurance Association publishes the booklets *Career Opportunities For You in Life Insurance,* and *What Will Your Career Be in Business?* Obtain a copy of these publications from your teacher or interview people working in the insurance industry. Prepare an oral report for the class on a career opportunity that interests you. Include the following items in the report:
   a job profile and description of what the job involves
   educational qualifications for the job
   availability of jobs
   salary range
   possibility of promotion and advancement.

UNIT B

1. Survey five of your family's friends or relatives and obtain answers to the following questions:
   a. How many have life insurance policies?
   b. What kinds of policies do they have?
   c. Why did they purchase these particular policies?
   d. When did they first buy their policies?
   e. From what companies did they purchase the insurance?
   f. Do they recommend that you purchase life insurance?

   Summarize your findings and report to the class.

2. Interview your parents or somebody familiar with your province's hospital and medical insurance plan. Obtain answers to the following questions:
   a. What is the name of the plan?
   b. Is the plan compulsory for all citizens?
   c. How often are premiums paid? What is the cost of the premiums for a single person, a family?
   d. Does the cost of the premium differ with the size of the family?
   e. What expenses does the plan cover?
   f. What other plans exist if you wish to purchase additional coverage?

   Summarize your findings and report to the class.

UNIT C

1. Check with a law student in your school or in some of the law texts in your school or community library. Read the details on five cases that involve injury to persons from car or home accidents. (A tort law chapter is a useful one to check.) Prepare an oral report to the class that summarizes:
   a. the facts of the case-who was involved and what happened.
   b. the result or judgement of the case.
   c. the adequacy of insurance coverage-would car or home insurance have been enough to cover this cost.

2. Choose one room in your home (bedroom, living room, family room, kitchen) and make an inventory list of everything that you can remember in that room. Prepare this list from memory. When you get home, compare this list with the actual inventory in that room. Did you miss any items? Were they big or small? Expensive or inexpensive? Is there a need for you to prepare inventory lists for every room in your home?

11 Law

UNIT A

BUSINESS LAW

There are many exciting and challenging aspects to the world of business such as marketing, accounting, and computers, but possibly no aspect is quite so intriguing as the part that involves business law. Much of business law is concerned with business transactions and the contracts that accompany them. A **contract** is a binding agreement between two or more parties. The parties refers to the people or organization involved in the contract.

Most consumers make hundreds of contracts in their lifetime. You will probably get involved in one before you get home tonight. For example, did you ride on the bus to school this morning? Or did you purchase something in the cafeteria today? If you did, then you were involved in a contract.

You may have noticed from the examples that not all contracts are written on paper. Actually, there are three different types of legal agreements.

Types of Contracts

One type of agreement is referred to as an **implied contract**. People become involved in an implied contract when their actions indicate that a business transaction is about to take place. When you board a bus, for example, this action would imply that you intend to be transported somewhere. The bus driver, in turn, assumes that you will pay for this service. Similarly, people who attend formal auctions to bid for merchandise are aware that a simple movement of the hand indicates an implied contract to a watchful auctioneer.

A second type of agreement is called an **oral contract**. As the name suggests, both parties agree to something verbally. You have probably been in a clothing store in which a sales clerk has offered some assistance. Perhaps you have even asked permission to try something on in order to see if it is the right size. The sales clerk does not assume a contract until you say that you wish to purchase the article.

The last type of agreement is a **written contract**. Agreements that involve large sums of money and last longer than one year are usually written contracts. Business transactions, such as buying real estate, life insurance, or something on the instalment plan are typical written agreements. The details of a bank loan, such as the rate of interest

and the length of time for the loan, are also written in the form of a **promissory note**

The Law of Contracts

Generally speaking, the people in a contract are entitled to the promises made by the other party. Under the law, however, some agreements are not considered **valid**. For a contract to be valid or enforceable, certain conditions must be met.

Mutual Agreement

The first necessary element of a contract is that both parties agree to all the contract details. This is sometimes referred to as a "meeting of the minds". A contract does not exist unless an offer has been made by one party and accepted by the other. "I'll have some french fries", constitutes an offer. When the waitress brings the food, the offer has been accepted.

> Herb Gough offered to sell his motorcycle to Barry Britton for $500. Barry said that he could only afford $450, and Herb refused to sell. A few moments later Herb said that he would take $475 instead. Barry went home to think about it. The next day, Herb said that Barry owed him $475.
>
> Does Herb have an enforceable contract?

An offer, however, must be definite and serious. Even though a frustrated student may proclaim that he would "sell this piece of junk for a dollar" when his motorcylce refuses to start after school, he probably does not intend it to be a serious offer. If a nearby student says "I'll buy it!", the surprised owner can refuse to sell it.

Remaining silent does not mean that one accepts the offer. A salesperson's statement to you that "If you do not notify me by tomorrow, I'll assume you've accepted", has no legal value. The other party must definitely state that they are willing to purchase in order for the contract to be enforceable.

261

Consideration

Consideration refers to what each party promises to do or give in exchange for what they are going to do. Usually one party provides a product or service in return for money. But if a person promises without being asked to do something for nothing, the item cannot be charged for later. The consideration must have some commercial or monetary value in order for the courts to recognize it as part of the contract. Suppose that Dave promises to pay his neighbour Joan $50 if she can sell Dave's car for $800. Dave's consideration is the promise to pay her $50. Joan's consideration is the service provided by selling the car. If Joan does manage to sell the car for the specified amount, she would be entitled to the $50. But if Joan had suggested to Dave without being asked that she would sell his car for him, legally, she would not be entitled to a fee.

Both Parties Must Be Competent

Contract laws have been designed to protect people from being taken advantage of when they enter into an agreement. Certain parties are not considered legally competent to understand the implications of a contract. These include minors or infants, the mentally incompetent, and the intoxicated. This means that if any of these people enter into a contract, they are able to withdraw, in most cases, with full protection of the law. Depending on the province, a minor is considered to be anyone under the age of eighteen or nineteen. Minors, however, are usually obligated to fulfil contracts that include basic necessities, such as food, shelter, clothing, education, and medical services.

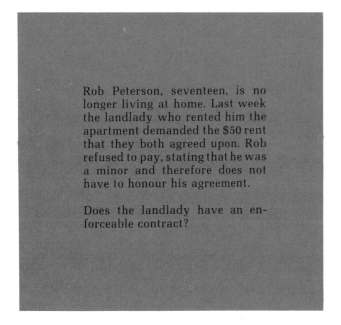

Rob Peterson, seventeen, is no longer living at home. Last week the landlady who rented him the apartment demanded the $50 rent that they both agreed upon. Rob refused to pay, stating that he was a minor and therefore does not have to honour his agreement.

Does the landlady have an enforceable contract?

Since parents are not liable for performing any part of a contract unless they sign it too, a business-person may ask that the parents co-sign an agreement with the minor. Without the parents' signatures, the store owner may only be able to recover the original article whatever its condition. If the contract has been co-signed by the parents, they are legally obligated to pay for the items.

Lawful Contracts

A contract involving dishonesty, illegality, or one that is against the public interest would not be considered valid in court. Suppose that Fred Johnson promised to pay Jack Sims $25.00 if he would steal a set of hub caps for him. Fred stole the hub caps and gave them to Jack, who then refused to pay. Fred could not collect because this is an unlawful agreement. Illegal contracts include anything that involves a criminal activity, operating an illegal gambling house, or doing business without a licence where one is required.

Written Contracts

Written contracts are probably the best type of agreement because they remove all doubts as to exactly what promises were made. For this reason, all important contracts should be in writing.

Any contract not to be carried out within one year must be in writing. This law was established because people tend to forget small details over a long period of time. The sale of buildings, land, or anything connected with land must also be in writing.

The court assumes that each party has read and understood all the terms of the agreement before signing. A signature on a contract is interpreted to mean that the signer agrees to everything stated in the agreement. The old adage "Always read the fine print before signing" is sound advice because once the paper is signed, all parties are committed to fulfil the requirements of that contract. Any oral agreements made after the signing do not alter the original contract and will not be enforced.

In summary, there are five elements that must be present in a contract in order to make it valid:

1. There must be mutual agreement
2. There must be consideration
3. Both parties must be competent
4. The contract must be legal
5. Certain contracts must be written.

Shirley Reiner signed an instalment contract to purchase a new car for $4500. After the agreement was signed, Shirley asked the car dealer if an optional AM/FM radio could be included for the same price. The car dealer said yes. When Shirley came to pick up the car the next day, the dealer refused to include the radio.

Is Shirley legally entitled to the radio?

LAWYER
LAWYERS HAVE LEGAL QUALIFICATIONS TO AD-
VISE CLIENTS ON THEIR LEGAL RIGHTS AND
OBLIGATIONS AND WHEN NECESSARY, REPRESENT
THEM IN COURTS OF LAW. THEY CONDUCT
CRIMINAL AND CIVIL LAWSUITS, AND DRAW UP
LEGAL DOCUMENTS. THEY ACT AS TRUSTEES,
GUARDIANS OR EXECUTORS. THEY MAY
TEACH COURSES IN LAW OR SPECIALIZE
IN ONE PHASE OF LAW. ADMISSION
TO PRACTICE LAW IN EACH PROVINCE
IS DIFFERENT.
NO MATTER IN WHAT AREA LAWYERS WORK, THEY
MUST ASSIST CLIENTS TO KNOW THEIR RIGHTS
UNDER THE LAW AND THEN HELP THEM ACHIEVE
THOSE RIGHTS BEFORE A JUDGE, JURY OR
GOVERNMENT AGENCY. THEY REPRESENT BUSI-
NESS OR INDIVIDUALS. FOR BUSINESS THEY
HANDLE TAX MATTERS AND ARRANGE FOR ISSU-
ANCE OF STOCK, HANDLE CLAIMS CASES, REPRE-
SENT THE FIRM IN REAL ESTATE DEALINGS
AND ADVISE THEM ON ALL LEGAL MATTERS.
FOR INDIVIDUALS THEY MAY DRAW UP WILLS,
ADVISE ON INCOME TAXES OR BUYING A HOME.
SOME WORK ENTIRELY IN THE COURTS WHILE
OTHERS CARRY ON BUSINESS SUCH AS DRAWING
UP MORTGAGES OR DEEDS AND DOING RESEARCH
IN A LAW LIBRARY OR COURTHOUSE. A NUMBER
OF LAWYERS WORK TO ESTABLISH AND ENFORCE
LAWS FOR THE GOVERNMENT, DRAFTING LEGIS-
LATION. THE MAJORITY OF LAWYERS ARE EN-
GAGED IN GENERAL PRACTICE HANDLING LEGAL
WORK OF ALL KINDS; OTHERS SPECIALIZE.
THROUGHOUT HISTORY, LAWYERS HAVE ALWAYS
BEEN PROMINENT AND RESPECTED INDIVIDUALS
ACTIVE IN PUBLIC AFFAIRS. THEIR WORK IS
STIMULATING FOR THEY ARE INVOLVED WITH
EVERY FACET OF HUMAN LIFE. TH__ MUST _

Breach of Contract

A breach of contract results when one party fails to fulfil any part of the contract. When this occurs, the other party is freed from all or part of his obligations under the contract. Suppose you have agreed to purchase a used car from a friend for $1200. When the car was delivered, however, it was not the original model described in the agreement. Since the seller has made a breach of contract, you are no longer obligated to buy the automobile.

Legal Advice

Major business transactions, such as the buying of a home or property, should not be undertaken without the help of a lawyer. A lawyer's research may prevent you from being involved in complex legal battles or paying hidden costs from the sale. For example, a person may sell you a home or cottage that has past taxes or a mortgage against it, or even unpaid repair work. The new owner is responsible for paying them.

UNIT B

RESPECTING THE RIGHTS OF THE INDIVIDUAL

Canadians are very fortunate. Unlike countries under dictatorships or countries under Communist rule, Canada has a democratic, modified free enterprise system that allows its people a large number of cherished freedoms. It also has laws ensuring that the legal rights of each individual are protected. Canadians are allowed to live a normal life without undue interference from neighbours or strangers. But, what are the rights of individuals? People have the right, in our society, to carry on everyday living without having the actions of other people interfere with their private property, personal safety, reputation, and standard of living. They also have the right to seek payment for personal losses or damages caused by the harmful actions of someone else.

The Law of Torts

The set of laws that deal with protecting the rights of individuals is called the Law of Torts. A **tort** refers to a civil wrong that someone has committed (other than a breach of contract). Courts use this set of laws to compensate the victim for any loss or damage suffered as a result of that wrong. **Compensation** refers to the payment of money, or something else that will make up for the personal injury or property damages caused by someone else.

In order for an individual to get compensation, that person must hire a lawyer and begin a
This means that the victim, called the **plaintiff**
court, must bring the other person to court and allow the judge to settle the dispute. This is commonly called suing someone. The person being sued is referred to as the **defendant.** Fortunately, only a few disputes ever reach this stage. Because of high legal expenses and the time lost when people are involved in court proceedings, most people prefer to settle their arguments out of court.

Types of Torts

A variety of "civil wrongs", for which people are liable, are underwritten by law. Being **liable** means that a person can be held legally responsible to compensate a victim.

Trespassing

Have you ever taken a short-cut across someone's property while walking home from school? If you did, you have committed a tort–a civil wrong. One of the rights individuals have in our society is the right to enjoy the privacy of their own property. Anyone who crosses private land without the owner's permission is guilty of trespassing. There are several reasons why property owners take offence against trespassers. Quite often, thoughtless people may cause damage to the person's property by doing such things as breaking bottles, littering, trampling flower beds, ruining the grass, breaking a fence or defacing buildings or structures on the property. The owner has the option, with the Law of Torts, of suing the trespasser for damages. The owner can even sue for invasion of privacy while on his or her property. For example, cottage owners do not like people using their private beach area. In the latter case, though, compensation is usually small because the courts find it difficult to assign a money value to loss of privacy.

Mr. Thompson owns a farm just outside Milk River, Alberta. On the weekend two people on snowmobiles came on his property. During their ride, the snowmobilers damaged a fence. Mr. Thompson stopped the people and demanded that they get off his property. The riders said that they did not mean to do any damage and left. Mr. Thompson is suing the riders.

Will Mr. Thompson succeed in his suit? Explain. Will the court compensate Mr. Thompson?

Defamation of Character

The law also provides a way to compensate a person whose reputation has been injured as the result of defamatory statements. A **defamatory statement** is one that lowers a person in the estimation of others. If the statement is spoken, it is referred to as **slander**. If the statement is written, or in a cartoon, it is called **libel**. Usually, the victim views the defamation as expressing hatred, contempt, or ridicule.

In a lawsuit of this nature, the wrongdoer must prove that the statements are true. It is not adequate to say that one mistakenly believed them to be true. Financial compensation varies in such cases. If the victim lost his job as a result of the statements, the court may award the amount of lost wages. The award may also take into account the social status of the injured party as well as the seriousness of the defamation. An important businessperson who depends upon the community's support to stay in business, for example, may receive a larger compensation than would a store clerk.

Dangerous Animals

Have you ever passed a neighbour's house and noticed a dog running loose in the yard? If a letter carrier or delivery person entered the yard and the dog attacked that person, has a tort been committed? The Law of Torts states that anyone who owns an animal is responsible for any harm that the animal may do. The owner must defend himself by showing that there was no reason to suspect that the animal was dangerous. However, if the animal has had a reputation for being vicious, then the owner may be forced to compensate the victim.

A person who kept a watchdog of a vicious nature allowed it to run loose in a closed yard. A gate was carelessly left open, and a student passing by was severely bitten and taken to hospital.

Explain the trouble the dog owner faces.

Wendy Fisher, a high school student, was riding up the escalator of a large department store when she tripped on a loose carpet at the top of the escalator. As she was falling, her coat caught on a clothing rack and ripped. A friend who had been at the store a day before said that she noticed the loose carpet as well. Wendy's mother decided to sue the store.

Does Mrs. Fisher have adequate grounds to bring an action against the store and if so how much compensation do you think the court will award Wendy?

A construction firm building a high rise apartment received a lawsuit from a boy's father. The boy had wandered on to the property through an open driveway used by the trucks and had fallen into a hole and broken his leg. It was dark at the time and neither the hole nor the driveway was fenced off.

Will the boy's father succeed? Explain. What compensation, if any, will the court award the father?

Dangerous Premises

Most retail stores take extra precautions to ensure that customers will not be harmed when they shop on their premises. Similarly, construction sites usually have high fences surrounding the property to protect people from the danger of the incompleted building. Under the Law of Torts, each property owner has a duty to ensure that the premises are as safe as possible. Even private homeowners can receive a lawsuit as a result of having a dangerous home. Suppose that a delivery person slips on a loose scatter rug and is injured. Because the homeowner had invited that person in, it was the owner's responsibility to make sure the premises were safe from hazards such as the loose rug.

Trespassers, of course, cannot obtain compensation because they are uninvited, but this is not true of small children who trespass. The law recognizes that, on occasion, dangerous premises present an attraction to children. The occupiers of the premises must be able to show that they had taken all reasonable precautions to prevent possible accidents. Examples of precautions include fences around private swimming pools or around repair work when it is left unattended for long periods of time.

Assault and Battery

Everyone is entitled to protection from aggressive people in our society. **Battery** refers to the physical striking of a person by another. The courts will compensate the victim for medical fees, loss of wages, scars, and inconveniences caused by the battery.

Assault is attempted battery. No actual physical hitting has to occur in order for a person to be sued for assault. A group of students blocking your way, threatening you, or pushing you, are examples of assault. Another example would be someone swinging a fist at you and missing. Even using words that shock the other person is considered to be a verbal assault. If, as a result of these incidents, mental anguish or suffering is evident, then the court will compensate the victim.

Negligence

Many torts committed in our society are unintentional. These torts are generally considered to be examples of negligence. This means that the person has no intention of committing a "wrong" but is just careless. The courts apply the principle of the "reasonable person" in order to make decisions in such cases. The idea is to consider how a reasonable person would have acted under similar circumstances.

There are many situations that require a person to take reasonable precautions. If people are careless while handling a car, poisons, chemicals, firearms, or sharp instruments, for example, they can be found liable for losses suffered by the victims of this carelessness.

Susan Brown has just bought her first car. One evening she parked the car on a hilly street overnight. Around 10 o'clock, the car began to roll down the hill and smashed into a *stop* sign. The City of Sudbury is suing Susan for damages.

If the city wins, how much compensation do you think the courts will award the city?

A boy playing with an air-rifle injured another boy. Legal action was taken against the boy responsible. During the trial, evidence was given showing that prior to the accident neighbours had complained to the father about his son's careless use of the rifle.

Is the father liable? Explain. Will the court compensate the victim?

Insurance Against Lawsuits

Awards for damages resulting from lawsuits may vary from small amounts to hundreds of thousands of dollars. Unfortunately, many defendants in tort cases have had to use all their savings and sell their property in order to pay a settlement decided upon in court. Indeed, some defendants may be poor the rest of their lives as a result of a heavy lawsuit. For this reason, many people make sure that they have **liability insurance**. This type of insurance protects the owner from the damages awarded by the courts.

People who live in apartments, for example, can obtain liability insurance that protects the owner from damages resulting from their own negligence. They may accidentally leave the water in the sink running or cause a fire, which damages surrounding structures.

Similarly, homeowners, can add liability insurance to their present home insurance. This additional insurance usually does not increase the premium by much. Under this type of insurance, situations such as someone being hurt on the property are covered.

It is not uncommon to find public liability insurance coverage for car owners ranging from $200 000 to $500 000. The laws regarding negligence in the operation of a motor vehicle are severe. A negligent driver can be charged by the police as well as suffer a large lawsuit from the injured party. Settlements in automobile accidents are growing increasingly higher. In some cases where the settlement is greater than the limits of the insurance, the defendant must make up the difference from personal savings. Liability insurance is well worth the investment.

UNIT C
CRIMINAL LAW

The Law of Torts, as you have read, deals with the compensation to a victim for losses and damages suffered as a result of a "civil wrong". Criminal Law has a different purpose. Its job is to punish criminals by such means as fines, jail sentences, and in some countries, death, referred to in law as **capital punishment.**

One drawback of Criminal Law is that although the criminals are punished, the victims are left to pay for the damages and personal injuries themselves. Suppose that a teenager in a stolen car leads a high speed chase down a main thoroughfare pursued by a police car. During the chase, the teenager strikes a pedestrian, killing her, then the car goes out of control, sideswiping three parked cars, before finally smashing into a town-owned cement lamp post.

Under the **Criminal Code,** the police will charge the teenager with reckless driving, manslaughter, and damaging public and private property. The court sentences the teenager to several years in jail. But who pays for the damaged cars, the city's lamp post, and the burial costs and wage losses to the family involved in the death of the pedestrian? The answer is that society bears the cost. Taxes are used to repair the lamp post and pay to keep the teenager in jail (about $20 000 per inmate a year). The car owners use their car insurance to cover their losses. And the relatives of the dead pedestrian may have to use their personal savings and life insurance to cover the burial costs and the adjustments to their lifestyle. The Law of Torts is insufficient in this case because the teenager may have no money or property to pay for the damages.

Every criminal act in our society provides a direct loss to the well-being of the people in it.

Why Criminal Laws Are Necessary

Any society with crowded conditions, mixed cultures, wide ranges in income, unemployment, and broken homes produces prejudiced, aggressive, and mentally disturbed people. These people pose a real threat to the stability of the rest of society, but fortunately, they represent only a small proportion of it. With police protection, the other 95% of society can continue living a normal life with reasonable expectations of remaining safe and enjoying the use of private property.

Criminal activities are actions (or emission of actions) that are harmful to the country as a whole. There are several types of serious crimes that cause a direct loss to the well-being of our society.

Arson

The crime of arson refers to a fire that is deliberately set and causes destruction to property. Usually, property insurance does not cover the total cost required to rebuild a structure. As a result, many buildings are not rebuilt unless additional money can be put into the project. There is also the danger that someone may be injured during the fire including the firemen who risk their lives in order to put it out. Because of the urgent need for fire-fighting equipment when a real fire occurs, false fire alarms are also considered to be a criminal offence.

Paul Kramer worked at a local restaurant during the summer months. One day after being late for work several times, the manager fired Paul. About ten minutes later a customer called one of the employees to come to the window. The employee saw Paul throwing lighted matches into a row of plastic garbage cans outside in the parking lot. The police were called.

What charge will the police bring against Paul? Explain what damage could have been caused.

Stealing

The Criminal Code describes various types of stealing. The seriousness of the crime is determined by such things as whether or not violence was used and the value of what was stolen.

Theft, which refers to stealing without the use of violence or a weapon, is divided into two categories. **Petty theft** includes the stealing of anything that has a value up to and including $200.00. **Grand theft** refers to situations in which the value of the stolen object exceeds $200.00.

Breaking and entering, commonly referred to as burglary, is considered to be a serious offence because of the dangers to the occupants of the building. Usually, the court interprets the unauthorized entering of a building as an intent to commit theft. If, for example, a stranger was found in the warehouse of a large department store that person would be charged with breaking and entering.

Identifying Types of Stealing

Type of Stealing	Description
Petty Theft	$200 or less
Grand Theft	Greater than $200
Embezzlement	Theft from one's own employer
Burglary	Also known as Breaking and Entering. Unauthorized entry into a building with intent to commit theft
Robbery	Theft that includes assault or battery
Armed Robbery	Theft that includes the use of a weapon

John Slater entered a department store one Saturday afternoon. After being dared by a companion, he slipped a bike part worth $1.98 into his coat pocket to see if he could sneak it out of the store. Just as he made it to the door, a store detective stopped him and took back the bike part.

The detective then took John to the administrative office and spoke with the manager. John explained the situation and offered to pay the $1.98. The manager refused to accept it, and called the police.

What charge could the police bring against John? Since only $1.98 is involved, would the police take it seriously? Why or why not?

Robbery is distinguished from theft in that robbery is stealing by using violence or a weapon such as a knife or gun. A robber with a weapon, or even a toy gun that resembles a real one, can be charged with armed robbery.

Embezzlement is the name applied to stealing items that were originally entrusted to that person's care. Often, such stealing is covered up by the employee by improper accounting methods or false reports.

Joanne Fraser, nineteen, works at a local credit union as an accounting clerk. She is in charge of the Petty Cash Fund, which is used to pay for small bills. When a senior accountant checked (audited) her books where she recorded all payments, he discovered that a total of $300 had been unaccounted for over a period of three months. After a long discussion between the manager, the auditor, and Joanne, the police were called in.

What possible charge could the police bring against Joanne Fraser? Explain what Joanne might have been doing illegally.

Mischief

The deliberate act of damaging or destroying another person's property is referred to as **mischief**. Such costly acts might include the damage of items such as car aerials, windows, and fences, or using spray paint to deface private property. If there is also a danger to life involved in the act, the court considers it to be a more severe offence.

Common Assault

The Criminal Code defines assault as a situation in which a person intentionally applies force to another person, or threatens to do so. If no bodily harm results, it is referred to as common assault. If a gun or weapon is used to cause bodily injury, a penalty of fourteen years can be imposed by the courts.

> On the way home from school Sandy Duncan and a girlfriend were stopped by three tough-looking high school seniors who proceeded to threaten and frighten the girls. When Sandy got home and told her parents of the incident, her parents called the police and the three boys were brought into custody. The boys stated that they did not touch nor harm the girls.
>
> Can the police lay a charge? If so, what would be the offence?

Homicide

Homicide is causing the death of another human being. If the death of the other person is intentional, then it is referred to as murder. A murder that is planned and deliberate is classified as "first degree murder".

Manslaughter, or "second degree murder", is not planned or deliberate. In this case, the accused may commit murder as the result of a heated argument. Although the accused may not have intended to cause the death, nevertheless, he or she must be punished for the loss of life caused by the action.

Summary Offences

Summary offences, also called misdemeanours, are less serious criminal offences for which the accused can be arrested or summoned to court without delay. The court in which summary offences are heard is called Provincial Court. No jury is used in these offences. Examples of summary convictions include traffic violations, unlawful assembly, common assault, or causing a disturbance. Once in court, people accused of a summary offence can

receive maximum penalties of $500.00 or six months' imprisonment.

Indictable Offences

Indictable offences, also known as felonies, are the more serious criminal offences. People accused of felonies first appear in the Provincial Court for a preliminary hearing. At the hearing, the judge listens to both the Crown Attorney and the accused's lawyer. If the judge thinks that there is adequate grounds for a trial, a date is set for the accused to appear in the County Court. The accused may elect to be tried by the judge in the Provincial Court or by judge and jury in the County Court. If the accused is found guilty, the penalty imposed is at the discretion of the judge and can be up to the maximum alloted by the Criminal code.

Rights of the Suspect

Before Being Arrested

If you are stopped by the police and the police have not said that you are guilty of any offence, it is not necessary to go to the police station, or answer any questions. The police are allowed, however, to search your van, car, or person if there is "reasonable grounds" to suspect that you are carrying drugs, liquor, or illegal weapons. This can be done without a search warrant. It is usually advisable to co-operate. If a citizen feels that the officer has not stated "reasonable grounds" for a search or arrest, he or she should secure the officer's badge number and the names of any witnesses. This will prove helpful at the court hearing or in a lawsuit.

After Being Arrested

In Canada, it is not necessary for an arresting officer to "advise you of your rights" or allow you a phone call. The officer should, however, tell you why you are being arrested. The Criminal Code allows the officer to use as much force as necessary in order to make the arrest, including the use of a weapon. In the case of indictable offences, usually the accused is taken directly to the police station where he or she is fingerprinted and a formal report is written out by the arresting officers. In serious felony cases, the accused will remain in custody until a judge or justice of the peace can set bail. In summary offences, the arresting officer can release the accused after informing that person the date to appear in court.

REVIEWING YOUR BUSINESS VOCABULARY

Write the number of each definition.
Write the word that matches the definition number.

UNIT A

breach of contract, competent, consideration, contract, mutual agreement, valid

1. A binding agreement between two or more parties.
2. A situation in which both parties agree to all the details.
3. A situation in which one of the parties fails to fulfil any part of the contract.
4. Something of value that each party agrees to exchange as part of the agreement.
5. For a contract to be legally enforceable, the parties must be sane, sober, and older than a minor.
6. A contract containing all the essential elements.

UNIT B

assault, battery, compensation, defamation of character, lawsuit, liability insurance, liable, negligence, tort, trespass

1. A legal action that involves taking another person to court in order to settle a dispute.
2. The term used when a person is physically struck.
3. The term used when someone has been physically threatened, but not actually beaten.
4. To commit a civil wrong.
5. To take a short-cut across someone else's property without permission.
6. The term used when a person's reputation has been injured by means of written or spoken statements.
7. When a person's careless actions cause loss or damage to someone else, that person can be held legally responsible.
9. A type of protection against lawsuits.
10. An unintentional tort in which a person's carelessness caused someone else an injury or loss.

UNIT C

arson, common assault, criminal code, felony, homicide, mischief, misdemeanour, robbery, theft

1. The set of laws that deal with crimes against society.
2. Stealing something without the use of violence.
3. Stealing that involves the use of violence.
4. Setting a fire deliberately with the intent of destroying property.
5. The deliberate pushing or shoving of someone or threatening bodily harm.
6. An act that causes the death of another human being.
7. Minor criminal offences, such as traffic violations or unlawful assembly.
8. A serious crime committed against society.
9. The deliberate act of damaging or destroying another person's property.

REVIEW QUESTIONS

UNIT A

1. Give one example of a business transaction.
2. What does the word "parties" in a contract refer to?
3. Name and explain the three types of contracts.
4. Explain how someone can get involved in an implied contract in the school cafeteria.
5. Why must a person be careful at an auction?
6. How does an oral contract differ from an implied contract?
7. List three business transactions that must have written agreements.
8. If the people in an agreement are entitled to the promises made by the other party, why does the law not enforce some agreements?
9. What does a "meeting of the minds" refer to?
10. Why have laws been designed to exclude minors, the mentally incompetent, and the intoxicated from contract obligations?
11. Who is considered to be a minor?
12. What type of contracts are minors obligated to fulfil? Give examples.
13. What is a co-signer?
14. Why do businesses prefer to have a co-signer along with a minor's signature?
15. Explain two general situations that require a contract to be in writing.
16. Why should a person read the fine print on a contract?
17. Name the five elements that must be present in a contract in order for it to be valid.
18. What does "consideration" mean?
19. Give two examples of contracts that would not be considered valid in a court of law.
20. Why consult a lawyer when buying a house?

UNIT B

1. What legal rights do individuals have in our society?
2. How do the courts use the Law of Torts to protect the rights of the individual?
3. Explain how someone can sue another person.
4. Why do only a small number of disputes ever reach the courts?

5. Explain why property owners take offence against trespassers.
6. Explain the difference between *libel* and *slander*.
7. When would the owner of a pet be forced to pay compensation to a victim?
8. Under the Law of Torts, what duty does a property owner or occupier have?
9. Give two examples of reasonable precautions homeowners should take around their property in order to prevent accidents.
10. What is the difference between *assault* and *battery*?
11. Name four examples of items on which a victim of assault and battery could claim compensation.
12. Explain the principle of the "reasonable person".
13. Give three examples of situations that require a person to take reasonable precautions.
14. What does it mean when the court finds a person "negligent"?
15. Why do people buy liability insurance?

UNIT C

1. What is the purpose of Criminal Law?
2. Explain one drawback of the Criminal Code.
3. Who pays for the actions of criminals? Explain.
4. Why are criminal laws necessary?
5. Why are false fire alarms considered to be a criminal offence?
6. What is the difference between petty theft and grand theft?
7. If you were caught in a locked building without permission, what may you be charged with? Explain why.
8. What does *embezzlement* refer to?
9. Give four examples of *mischief*.
10. Explain the difference between *murder* and *manslaughter*.
11. Name three misdemeanours that would be brought before a Provincial Court.
12. Describe how summary offences are handled by the legal system.
13. Describe how indictable offences are handled by the legal system.
14. Suppose the police stopped a van with two teenagers in it. On what "reasonable grounds" could they suspect the riders that would allow them the right to search the van without a search warrant?

APPLYING
YOUR KNOWLEDGE

UNIT A

1. Most people get involved in contracts on a daily basis. Explain two types of unwritten contracts that are common and give an example of each type.
2. If a passerby overhears a frustrated or angry owner proclaim that she will sell her property at a ridiculously low price, why will the court not uphold the contract if the passerby accepts the offer?
3. Suppose that a salesperson says to a customer that if the customer does not call back, the salesperson will assume the deal is accepted. Is that a legal contract? Explain.
4. Why do many businesses refuse to sell anything to a minor except on a cash basis? Explain how businesses can overcome this problem.

UNIT B

1. The Law of Torts provides guidelines that allow people to live a normal life without undue interference from neighbours or strangers. Explain what this means and why these laws are necessary.
2. Explain the difference between the *plaintiff* and the *defendant* in a lawsuit.
3. Suppose a local newspaper falsely accused you of stealing from the company for whom you worked. What tort has been committed? What situations might arise because of the false accusation? How would the newspaper defend itself in court?
4. How would a judge handle a tort case in which the defendant stated that there was no intention of committing a "wrong" but that it was just carelessness? What type of tort is this?
5. Why do car owners include liability insurance in their automobile insurance policy?

UNIT C

1. Several television programs are based on situations that involve policemen, detectives and criminals. In an effort to entertain the public, television writers include scenes of property destruction, violence, high-speed car chases, and physical injury. Is this form of "happy-ending entertainment" misleading?
2. Describe what you think would happen if everyone were allowed to do anything they liked without police interference.
3. One person, while being searched for drugs, was caught in the possession of tools that were designed to pick locks and windows. The police arrested the person and charged him with possession with intent to commit Breaking and Entering. Why would the judge consider this "reasonable grounds" for a trial?
4. Suppose that you are stopped by the police who proceeded to search you for drugs. If you reacted angrily or violently, what are the police allowed to do? Explain.

PROJECTS AND PROBLEMS

UNIT A

1. List each of the following transactions and beside each state whether it represents an implied, or a written contract.
   a. Taking a bus
   b. Purchasing clothing that needs alterations
   c. Buying a house
   d. Bidding at an auction
   e. Buying a magazine at a variety store
   f. Purchasing life insurance
   g. Getting a bank loan
   h. Purchasing a bike from a neighbour
2. Read the following case. Then list the five elements of any contract. Beside each one explain how each element applies in this situation.

   Joan Walker, nineteen, offers to sell her portable calculator to Maria DiGiandomenico, also nineteen, for $10. Maria says that she will purchase the calculator for that price if it includes the battery. Joan agrees.
3. The following statements are points concerning the Law of Contracts. Tell in your own words what each statement means.
   a. A "meeting of the minds" must occur before a contract can exist.
   b. Silence does not indicate acceptance of an offer.
   c. An offer must be definite and serious in order to be taken as part of a contract.
   d. Usually, there is monetary value attached to the consideration.
   e. Parties must be sane, sober, and of majority age.
4. Suppose that you wish to sell a two-year-old stereo set originally worth $250 to one of your classmates. Spend a minute negotiating with him or her, then draw up a written contract together describing the terms of the agreement. The contract should include:
   a. Title–Terms of Agreement
   b. The names of each party clearly printed
   c. The fact that both parties agree
   d. The agreed-upon price
   e. An accurate description of the article
   f. Date of transaction
   g. Signature of both parties.

UNIT B

1. List each of the following situations, then name the type of tort caused by each one.
   a. Making a statement that ridicules someone.
   b. Several boys harassing a particular passerby on several occasions.
   c. A tough senior physically striking a smaller grade nine student several times.
   d. A bank customer slipping on melted snow that has been tracked into the bank.
   e. A car driver tailgating a bicycle rider who suddenly falls from her bike.
2. Compensation refers to the money or anything else that the court awards to the victim of a tort. Read the following situations. Then suggest in each case what compensation would be fair. Explain why.

   a. The Montgomery family lost one of their two daughters in a drowning accident. Their neighbour had built a backyard pool last year, but had neglected to put up a protective barrier. The four-year-old child was playing unnoticed alongside the pool when she fell in.

   b. Two trespassers on some farm property caused a fire in a wheat field. Mr. Tornbee, the owner, claimed that a $1200 harvest was destroyed. On top of that, Mr. Tornbee had to pay the fire fighters and a lawyer for their services.

   c. Fran Simpson, a high school co-ed, suffered several cuts to her face when a bottle struck her during a football game. The cuts left several scars that needed expensive plastic surgery. As a result of her hospitalization, Fran did not complete her year at high school. The boy who threw the bottle was identified.

   d. Tony Woods got a job last week working at a local furniture store. Phil Burnhammer, who also wanted the job, told the owner that Tony associated with a local motorcycle gang. The owner, who had been harassed by such a gang last month, fired Tony even though Tony said he was not a member. Phil got the job instead. Angrily, Tony sued Phil for defamation of character.

UNIT C

1. List each of the following situations, then name the specific type of crime it represents.
   a. Deliberately setting a fire in order to destroy property.
   b. Stealing a 25 cent article from a variety store.
   c. Causing the accidental death of someone.
   d. Holding up a store with a gun.
   e. Breaking car aerials.
   f. Stealing from one's own company and hiding the theft with some illegal accounting.
   g. Stealing a car.
   h. Deliberately causing the death of someone.
   i. Entering a locked home uninvited.
2. List each of the following situations, then name each one as a *misdemeanour*, or *felony*, or *tort*. Stealing a bike; trespassing; breaking and entering; arson; traffic violations; causing a disturbance.
3. Most felonies involve some destruction or bodily injury. Read the following situation, then list five types of costs that society will have to bear because of that person's felonious actions.

   During a high speed car chase through a residential section, the pursued vehicle caused a two-car collision at one intersection as the other cars stopped suddenly. A small child chasing a ball into the street was killed just before the car went out of control and smashed into someone's front yard fence.

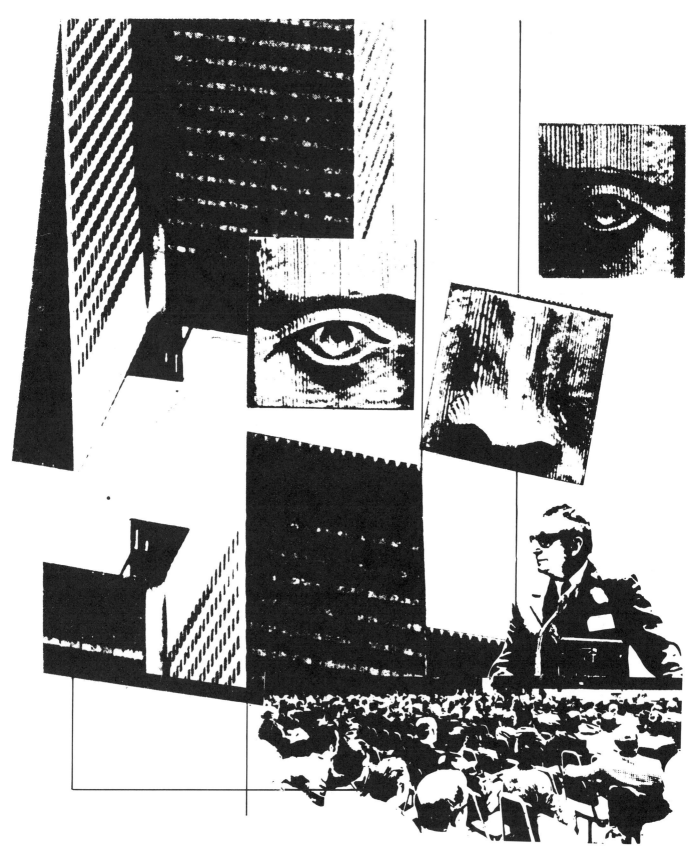

12 Government

UNIT A
THE ROLE OF GOVERNMENT

You will recall that Canada's economy was earlier described as a "modified free enterprise system". A "pure" free enterprise system is not influenced by governments. It is the presence of governments—federal, provincial, and municipal, that "modifies" our economic system. Governments are essential to the smooth operation of our economy. Although there is much criticism of governments, our economy could not operate without them. Governments, business, and the general public are interdependent.

In many ways, governments are like a big business. They are, collectively, Canada's largest employer—employing approximately ten per cent of the work force. They are also Canada's largest single producer of goods and services. Nearly one quarter of all of the goods and services produced in Canada in one year are produced by our governments. Like businesses, governments are also large consumers of goods and services.

Our various levels of government serve two basic functions in the Canadian economic system. The first is to produce certain goods and services. The second is to ensure that our basic democratic principles and freedoms are upheld. To accomplish the latter function, governments make laws and enforce them. Governments obtain their power from the people—you and me. We elect representatives to act on our behalf. Our representatives' decisions permit these two basic functions to be carried out.

Public Goods

Take a walk around your neighbourhood. Observe the numerous activities and services available that are not provided by private businesses. On the street corner you see a letter box. A mail carrier delivers the mail to your house. Cars and buses travel on the paved roads and obey street signs and traffic signals controlling the flow of traffic. On a neighbour's lawn is a fire hydrant. Two blocks away is the elementary school situated next to the park, playground, and arena. Electric power lines border the sidewalks. Most of these items and services are called **public goods.**

Businesses in Canada produce approximately seventy-five per cent of the goods and services consumed. These are called **private goods.** We purchase these goods from businesses. However, we tend to take public goods for granted. We use them without thinking about them, and it is difficult to determine how much individuals should pay for them. Most of them are considered to be essential, and there are good reasons why government, and not businesses provide them.

When people live together in groups, there is a need for certain goods and services that are shared by the community. Imagine the confusion if everyone had to build and maintain their own roads. Having five or six electric power companies competing for business in one area would be inefficient, to say nothing of the mess created by having numerous poles cluttering the neighbourhood.

As with all things of value, a price must be paid for having these goods and services. They are not free; someone must pay the bill. The next unit examines the costs of government.

Three Levels of Government

Because Canada's geography is very large, our predecessors established a federal system of government. This system was first described in our constitution, the *British North America Act,* which was enacted in 1867 by the British government.

The *B.N.A. Act* created the political country of Canada, with a central or **federal government,** and several **provincial governments.** The constitution divided the responsibility for making and enforcing laws between these two levels of government.

Provincial governments have granted certain powers to local governments in their provinces. These are also called municipal or regional governments.

Elected members of the federal government meet in Ottawa, and deal with matters affecting all of Canada. The federal government is responsible for national defence (the military), the post office, money and banking controls, social welfare plans, external affairs, natural resources, energy, and several other matters. This level of government also owns several federal crown corporations, the best known being Air Canada and the Canadian National Railways. Crown corporations have been established to provide some goods and services that are desirable but which private businesses will not produce because they are not profitable. Crown corporations operate as private businesses do, but report to a branch of government instead of shareholders.

Members elected to provincial governments meet in the provincial capitals and deal with matters such as public education, highways, and hospitalization.

Municipal governments are responsible for local matters within towns, cities, and regions. In most provinces, they share with the provincial government a responsibility for education. In addition, they build and maintain recreational facilities, local streets, sanitation systems, and administer **public utilities,** such as electrical power commissions and water commissions.

Government and Business

Government is Canada's largest single consumer of goods and services. The three levels of government are good customers for many Canadian businesses.

Governments provide assistance to businesses. The Federal Business Development Bank not only provides low cost loans to eligible Canadian businesses but also expert financial advice, particularly to new and small businesses. Governments run research laboratories whose objective is to find new and better methods to produce certain goods, particularly in the agricultural industry. In some instances, governments **subsidize,** which means they give financial aid to selected businesses to help them get established or stay in business in difficult times. Some local governments offer reduced taxes to businesses to attract them to do business in their areas.

Although most businesses operate fairly and honestly, there are a few that try to take advantage of consumers or other businesses. To help prevent this, governments control certain aspects of business. Some controls are designed to ensure that businesses compete fairly with one another. Except in special circumstances (public utilities are good examples), a monopoly–where one company gains sole control of the production of a particular good or service–is not permitted. Other businesses such as restaurants are controlled by licensing. And certain government agencies enforce high safety standards for manufacture of potentially dangerous products. The section on *Consumer Protection* in this book gives further details.

SMALL BUSINESS NEWS

FBB MANAGEMENT SERVICES

FEDERAL BUSINESS DEVELOPMENT BANK

The **Federal Business Development Bank** (FBDB) is a crown corporation providing financial and management services to assist new and existing business enterprises in Canada, particularly smaller businesses. FBDB's Management Services provide Management Counselling through CASE (Counselling Assistance to Small Enterprises), Management Training and Information Services.

Published by the **Federal Business Development Bank** to help smaller Canadian firms keep in touch with business developments.

278

GALLUP POLL

Government services are good, most agree

When Canadians were asked to rate six government services as "good value" or "not good value," a majority for each service felt they were getting their money's worth. But there were wide differences. For medicare, garbage collection, and fire protection, over eight-in-ten Canadians felt satisfied with the value. Only slightly fewer (79 per cent) felt this way about the police. Considerably lower were postal service (61 per cent) and education (52 per cent).

For the highly rated services, there has been little or no change from levels obtained in a 1976 study. Educational service, with 52 per cent currently satisfied has risen from a 47-per-cent level a year ago; while postal service has dropped from 68 per cent last year to 61 per cent today.

There are wide regional differences in the rating of both the postal service and education. In Quebec, while 80 per cent say they are getting good value for their postal dollars, only 46 per cent in Ontario and 50 per cent in British Columbia do so; while in the Atlantic provinces, 72 per cent think the educational dollars are being wisely spent, only 41 per cent in British Columbia and 43 per cent in Quebec think this way.

Personal, in-home interviews were conducted with 1 026 adults, 18 years and over, during mid-September. A sample of this size is accurate within a four percentage point margin of error, 19 in 20 times.

The question was:

"Let us think about some of the services provided by our governments, and paid for by you in a number of ways. Do you think you do, or do not get good value for the police, protection, medicare, etc.?"

	Good Value	Not Good Value	Can't Say
National Results:			
Medicare	88%	7%	4%
Garbage Collection	84	8	7
Fire Protection	83	7	10
Police Protection	79	15	7
Postal Service	61	36	4
Education	52	37	11

London Free Press
October 22, 1977

©The Canadian Gallup Poll Ltd.
Reprinted by permission

UNIT B

PAYING FOR GOVERNMENT

Total government expenditures in Canada in 1977 were over sixty-seven billion dollars. Out of a national income of approximately two hundred and seven billion dollars government expenditures account for approximately thirty per cent of the national income. National income in Canada is measured by calculating the total value of goods and services produced in the country in one year. This is called the   .
Where do governments get their money? How do governments spend money? What are the trends in government expenditures? These and other questions are answered in this unit.

Housewife cost hard to figure in Canada's GNP

By Don McGillivray
Southam News Services

OTTAWA-What are the economics of an unmade bed? How does a home-baked cake affect the gross national product? Is there a clear gain for Canada when a housewife finds a job as a super-market cashier?

These are questions about Canada's biggest but most invisible industry-housework. About two million Canadians work in factories. Government-including all its branches and crown corporations-also employs about two million. But there are at least two and a half million full-time housewives, and probably as many part-time housewives, not to mention househusbands.

An industry with a work force that large must have an economic impact. But because the workers are almost all unpaid and their product is impossible to measure and hard to estimate, the whole industry is outside most of the calculations of economists.

But perhaps they ignore the housework industry to their own confusion. It is possible that failure to take account of changes in the housework industry is creating large distortions in the "big numbers" by which Canada's economic performance is judged.

Statistics Canada estimates that there are about 4.9 million married women in Canada in the 20-to-64 age group. Of these, 2.3 million are either working or looking for work. The other 2.6 million are "not in the labor force". In other words, apart from a few unable to work, they are housewives.

Housework is skilled, specialized work. If the industry had to recruit workers in competition with other jobs, housewives would probably have to be paid at bonus rates because of the long, unpredictable hours.

But suppose the job is worth as much as that of the average worker in paid employment-about $12 000 a year. Then the efforts of Canada's full-time housewives are worth about $30 billion a year. If this were counted in the GNP, it would jump by about 16 per cent to $213 billion from the present estimate of $183 billion.

This is probably a very low estimate because it counts nothing for part-time housewives and nothing as a return on the large amount of productive capital invested in the household industry-washing machines, dishwashers, stoves, refrigerators, and the house itself.

But the failure to include more than $30 billion of production in the GNP is not the only distortion. It might be so if housework were a static, unchanging part of the economy. But the industry has been-and still is-in the grip of a massive revolution.

If the calculation above had been done 20 years ago-counting full-time housewives as being worth as much as industrial workers and adding this valuation of their output to the GNP-it would have increased the output estimate by 30 per cent instead of 16 per cent. The difference reflects the rush of women into the paid labor force and out of full-time housework.

For the past 20 years we have counted the economic output of women joining the paid labor force as a clear gain to the economy. It has been implicitly

Suppose the average housewife working outside the home can still be credited with half the housework output of a full-time housewife. This is a creditable performance, since she is doing a job and a half. But it means that when a housewife joins the paid labour force, $6 000 at average industrial rates must be deducted from her output at her new job in order to find the net benefit to the economy.

If she takes a job worth $7 000 to the economy, for example, the net gain to the GNP should be counted as $1 000 after the deduction for housework no longer being done not as $7 000. Of course, her total production has increased to $13 000 worth.

The Spectator, Hamilton
October 25, 1976
Reprinted by permission

280

The Budget

In an earlier chapter we saw that to prepare a personal budget, we simply estimate our various sources of **revenue** (income), and estimate our **expenditures** for various types of goods and services. If we plan to earn more money than we spend, then we have a **surplus** of funds at the end of the year. If we predict that our expenditures will exceed our revenues, we will have a budget **deficit**. In this case we either cut back on our expenditures to balance our budget or we must earn more revenue–perhaps we can borrow. A government budget, whether it be for federal, provincial, or municipal level works in exactly the same way. Each year, the treasurer of a government prepares a budget estimating its revenues and expenditures.

Sources of Revenue

Many individuals have only one source of revenue–their salary or wages: governments have developed several sources of revenue. Public utilities charge consumers directly for their services, as do crown corporations. There are direct charges made for some other types of government services, such as tolls for the use of highways and bridges, entrance fees to national, provincial, and local parks and recreation areas, and charges made for some government publications. The post office charges directly for the use of its services.

Various social welfare schemes such as unemployment insurance, government pension plans, and medical insurance are paid for by fees charged to individuals and families. Still other government departments charge licence fees for personal activities such as building houses, driving cars, and getting married. It is, however, difficult to charge individuals directly for many of government's services. How much money should you and your family be charged for your use of roads, sidewalks, a clean environment, and the upkeep of the military? Even if a reasonable charge could be calculated, the costs for collecting such fees would be very high.

Sources of Tax Revenue

Governments in Canada collect most of their revenues through various taxes. You have no doubt heard your parents complaining about the high personal **income taxes** that they pay–around tax-collection time in April of each year. Both federal and provincial governments levy personal income taxes. Personal income taxes are examples of **direct taxes,** because they are paid by the individual, and cannot be transferred to anyone else. These and other direct taxes produce most of governments' tax revenue. Corporation income taxes, however, are called **indirect taxes** because although the company pays the tax to the government, it collects it from the consumer of its goods and services by charging higher prices.

Most manufactured goods are subject to a federal **sales tax,** and several provinces have retail sales taxes charged on many items purchased by consumers in retail stores. Again, the federal sales tax is an indirect tax and the provincial retail sales tax is a direct tax. There are other types of taxes such as customs duties, gift taxes, and other business taxes. They produce relatively small revenues for governments. A new method for obtaining revenue has been popular recently–the lottery.

Revenue Canada Taxation   Revenu Canada Impôt

T1-1977

14

1977 Federal and Ontario Individual Income Tax Return
(and Canada Pension Plan Return, if applicable)

Identification

Family or Last Name (Please print)

Mr.
Mrs.
Miss

Usual First Name and Initials (Please print)

Present Address (Please print)

Number, Street and Apt. No., or P.O. Box No. or R.R. No.

City, Province or Territory   Postal Code

● Is this your first Income Tax return? Yes ☐ No ☐

If 'No', please state year for which last return filed. 19

Name on last return: same as above ☐ or

Address on last return: same as above ☐ or

Type of work or occupation in 1977

◆ Social Insurance Number   ● Date of Birth

As on your Social Insurance Number card   Day   Month   Year

◆ Province or Territory of Residence on 31st December 1977, was:

◆ If self-employed in 1977, please state province where business located

On 31st December, | Married Widow(er) Divorced Separated Single
1977, I was: | 1 ☐   2 ☐   3 ☐   4 ☐   5 ☐

● Usual First Name of Spouse

Address of Spouse: same as mine ☐ or

◆ Spouse's Social Insurance Number

◆ If you became or ceased to be a resident of Canada in 1977, please give:

Date of Entry   or Departure
         Day   Month   Day   Month

Name of present employer

Calculation of Total Income

$ c

Income from Employment

Total Earnings Before Deductions from Box C on all T4 slips (attach copy 2 of T4 slips)	**01**			⊙
Commissions from Box L on all T4 slips, included in above total **02**				
Other employment income including adult training allowances, tips and gratuities, etc. (Guide item 3; please specify)	**03**			⊙
Total employment earnings (add lines 01 and 03)	**04**			

Subtract: Employment expense deduction (Guide item 4)
If line 04 above is $8,333 or more claim $250.00
If line 04 above is less than $8,333 see Step 3 in Guide **05**   ⊙

Other allowable expenses (Guide item 5; please specify)
06   ⊙

Total employment expenses (add lines 05 and 06) 07   ◇

Net employment earnings (subtract line 07 from line 04) 08

Pension Income

Old Age Security Pension ($1,746.84 for year; for less than year, see Guide item 6)	**09**		⊙
Canada or Quebec Pension Plan benefits (attach copy 2 of T4A(P) slip)	**10**		⊙
Other pensions or superannuation (attach copy 3 of T4A slips)	**11**		⊙

Income from Other Sources

Taxable Family Allowance payments (Guide item 7; attach copy of TFA1 slip)	**12**		⊙
Unemployment Insurance benefits (attach copy 1 of T4U slip)	**13**		⊙
Taxable amount of dividends from taxable Canadian corporations (attach completed Schedule 4)	**14**		⊙
Interest and other investment income (attach completed Schedule 4)	**15**		⊙
Rental income (Schedule 7) Gross **83** Net	**16**		⊙
Taxable capital gains (Allowable capital losses)—complete and attach Schedule 2	17		
Other income (Guide item 17; please specify)	**18**		⊙

Income from Self-Employment

Report both 'Gross' and 'Net'. (Guide item 18). Provide other information concerning self-employment on page 3.

Business income	Gross **84**	Net **19**		⊙
Professional income	Gross **85**	Net **20**		⊙
Commission income	Gross **86**	Net **21**		⊙
Farming income	Gross **87**	Net **22**		⊙
Fishing income	Gross **88**	Net **23**		⊙

Total Income (add lines 08 to 23 inclusive — please enter this amount on line 24 on page 2) 24   ◇

14

Please do not use this area **82**

Please do not use this area **90**

283

The Weekend Poll-Taxes

This is income tax time, and Canadians don't seem to mind very much at all. The Weekend Poll of 31 urban centres finds that the sales tax, not income tax, is considered to be the most unfair form of taxation. Property taxes rank next in disfavour, followed by inheritance taxes and income tax. Excise taxes on cigarettes, alcohol and gasoline, followed by customs and import duties, are considered the most fair. Here are the proportions of Canadians who rate each tax as the least fair form of taxation.

Provincial sales tax	25%
Municipal property tax	18%
Inheritance taxes	17%
Income tax	17%
Excise taxes	9%
Custom duties	4%
Did not state	9%

These figures don't mean that income tax is popular. When asked if it is all right to take advantage of every exemption and loophole that the law allows, only 16 per cent say it is absolutely wrong; another 9 per cent say it is somewhat unacceptable. Forty-five per cent say it is absolutely right to pay as little tax as is legally possible, and another 28 per cent say it is generally acceptable.

One fact clearly emerges: the progressive income tax, in which the rate goes up as earnings go up, is over-whelmingly supported by Canadians. Eighty-three per cent believe that people earning less money than themselves should pay less income tax than they now pay. And 69 per cent believe that those earning more money than themselves should be paying more tax than they now pay.

Old people, many of whom are on pensions and pay no income tax, find municipal property taxes to be the most unfair form of taxation: 32 per cent of those over 55 take this view compared to 18 per cent of the national sample. Interestingly, few old people find inheritance taxes to be the least fair form of taxation–it's their heirs, the younger people, who complain; only 8 per cent of those over 55 think inheritance taxes are most unfair while 20 per cent of those from 18 to 45 think so.

The sales tax is the least progressive form of taxation, and predictably it is least popular in the lowest income group, those earning less than $5000. In this group 39 per cent find the sales tax the most unfair form of taxation compared to the national figure of 25 per cent.

The unpopularity of the sales tax does not have much to do with its rate. Residents of the Atlantic region pay the highest rate in the country but they complain less frequently about the sales tax than residents of other regions. Newfoundlanders pay 10 per cent and residents of the three Maritime provinces pay 8 per cent; only 11 per cent of them say the sales tax is the most unfair. In Quebec, where the rate is also 8 per cent, 29 per cent single out the sales tax as the most unfair. In Ontario and B.C. similarly large proportions reject the sales tax although the rate in these provinces is 7 per cent. Only on the Prairies is income tax rated as more unfair than the sales tax, and no wonder; Saskatchewan and Manitoba have sales taxes of only 5 per cent, and Alberta has no sales tax at all.

Source: Data Laboratories
Research Consultants
Weekend Magazine
April 22, 1978
Reprinted by permission

How the Tax Dollar Is Spent

Many people are surprised when they discover the variety of goods and services provided by the three levels of government. The amounts spent in 1977 by the ten largest ministries in the federal government are summarized in the chart. Notice that over half of the total expenditures of the federal government are made by only three ministries. For many years governments at the federal level have left budget deficits. There is now a large **public debt**: interest charges alone on this massive loan are approximately five billion dollars a year. To offset our debt, the federal government borrows money to finance deficits. One way of offsetting the debt is by selling Canada Savings Bonds to the public. The government is, in effect, borrowing money from its taxpayers.

The pie charts summarize the major sources of revenue and major expenditures of the provincial government of Ontario. Note that health and education costs account for well over half of this province's expenditures.

The two largest sources of revenue for municipal governments are property taxes on residences, businesses, land, and grants from the provincial government. Sanitation systems, water, police, fire protection, local road construction, and maintenance are provided to residents as well as many other services.

The Ontario Budget Dollar, 1978

Where it will come from . . .

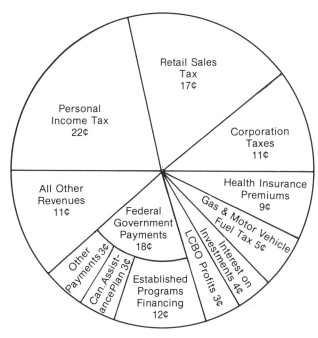

How it will be spent . . .

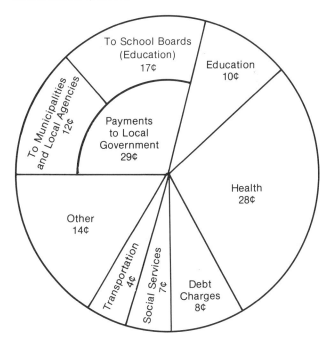

Source: 1978 Ontario Budget Release
Reprinted by permission

How the Federal Government Spends Its Revenue

	$ (billion)	%
National Health and Welfare	10.9	28.5
Finance	7.8	20.2
National Defence	3.4	8.8
Employment and Immigration	2.6	6.7
Energy, Mines, and Resources	1.7	4.3
Secretary of State	1.4	3.7
Transport	1.4	3.5
Post Office	1.1	2.9
Indian Affairs and Northern Development	0.95	2.5
Veteran Affairs	0.77	2.0
All other	6.5	16.9
Total	38.5	100

Source: Statistics Canada
Reprinted by permission

285

Someone must pay for the large number of goods and services provided by the three levels of government. Before the first World War, all three levels of government spent less than ten per cent of the total national income: today this expenditure is close to thirty per cent. Several reasons account for the increase.

Canada's population has grown dramatically since the first World War, meaning that government goods and services must be provided to more and more people. If all Canadians consume approximately the same amount of government goods and services, then a doubling of population will lead to a doubling in government expenditures.

Inflation has also accounted for a considerable part of the large increase in taxes. Today's dollar would purchase less than twenty-five cents worth of goods and services produced in 1925. Some economists believe that by deficit budgeting our governments (present and past ones), have been living beyond our means and have actually caused inflation.

A third reason for the increase in taxes is that the public has placed ever-increasing demands on all levels of government to provide more and better goods and services. In the past fifteen years, expensive new social welfare plans have been started, such as the Canada Pension Plan, the Unemployment Insurance Plan, Medical Care Plans, and Universal Baby Bonuses.

Obviously, taxes are necessary. Our economy would be in chaos without many of the essential services provided by our three levels of government. But how much government is essential? You and I–the voting public–must decide.

Dollar hits the table

Canadians will pay much more for imported fruits and vegetables this winter than they did last. The full impact of our devalued dollar will be felt at the family table, a more significant effect than price increases for such items as imported cards, electronic equipments, and textiles.

The Canadian dollar, hovering between 90 and 91 cents U.S., means an automatic increase of 10 per cent on foods coming into this country from south of the border. Many families, and people who live on fixed incomes, are hardest hit. Food prices are not controlled by the Anti-Inflation Board and they have been one of the chief causes of increases in the cost of living in recent years.

If it is any consolation, our devalued dollar makes Canadian exports easier to sell, though even this more cheerful aspect should not be overemphasized because our labor costs on the whole exceed those of our principal competitor, the U.S., and our unit production rate has been falling in recent years. These factors largely offset the advantages provided by our devalued dollar.

What all these things mean in simple terms is that our standard of living is declining. We cannot buy as much with our dollar as we could in former years. Orange juice, grapes, lettuce, and tomatoes will appear even more "expensive" in the months ahead than they have recently seemed. As a result they may not appear so often on Canadian tables, and mundane though it is, this is a sign of a declining living standard.

Canada is a rich country with abundant natural resources. Our devalued dollar is simply telling us that in the past we were spending more than we earned. The way ahead to renewed prosperity is open to Canadians. We have to learn to work harder, produce more and get less for it. If we do this, we shall avoid even harsher disciplines.

Canadians have no reason to look at conditions in the country today through rose-coloured glasses.

But, as Prime Minister Trudeau told an audience of high school students this week, this does not mean that we have to be despondent. There are indeed many people in other parts of the world who would give their right arm and leg to come to Canada and enjoy all the things this country still has to offer.

It's something too often overlooked by Canadians who in the past few years have seen their dream of endless prosperity rudely collide with cold reality.

The Spectator, Hamilton
November 19, 1977
Reprinted by permission

UNIT C

GOVERNMENT AND YOU

What Government Does For You

Our relationship with government is much like our relationship with business—we need each other. Governments serve us by providing many goods and services. These are called public goods, and include social welfare services, education, health and recreation services. Governments also help us by making laws that protect us as consumers.

Governments Have Jobs

Governments in Canada employ approximately one out of ten people working in Canada. This makes government the largest single employer. When you are making career plans, it is worthwhile to examine the number of job opportunities available in the various departments and agencies financed by government.

Governments employ people in almost any vocation or occupation you can think of. There is a constant need for people in office occupations, and many other skilled jobs. Professionals, such as accountants, lawyers, doctors, engineers, and teachers are also employed in many government jobs. Service people of all kinds are required, just as they are in any large business.

In the past salaries and wages paid by governments lagged behind those paid by business. This is not so today; people working in government jobs earn similar incomes to those working in related occupations in the business world.

A government employee is called a civil servant. They are part of the public or civil service. People who work in government jobs should have a desire to serve the public. The government exists to serve the public, not vice versa.

What You Do for Government

Businesses and the public share the responsibility for paying for the services of government. Every time you pay taxes, you are spending money that you could otherwise have spent on personal goods and services. But you also benefit from the goods and services that government provides, which you would have to buy from businesses or do without, if there were no government. Many Canadians work in the civil service, and thus provide the skills and knowledge necessary to produce government goods and services.

The public holds the key to government. Government has power because the people give it power. All governments in Canada are elected by the people—you and me. We are the electorate and have the choice to vote for the people or parties of our choice in federal or provincial elections held every four or five years, and in municipal elections held every two years.

Almost all Canadian citizens eighteen years of age or older have the right to vote in federal, provincial, and municipal elections. People eligible to vote are said to have the franchise. Some election officials, all judges of federal courts, mentally incapacitated persons, inmates of jails and prisons, and persons previously found guilty of dishonest election practices do not have the franchise. It is our responsibility to exercise this franchise. If we do not vote, we have only ourselves to blame when the government does something we criticize.

Because governments, like many businesses and people, have more needs and wants to satisfy than their revenue will permit, we should vote for the person or political party that we think will provide the types of goods and services that we consider are important.

How Much Government Is Enough?

Many people object to the increasing size of government although most Canadians agree that there are some essential services that governments must provide, such as protection, public education, and highways. But many Canadians, particularly business people, are upset about the continuing growth of government. They believe that governments should stay out of manufacturing activities, which compete directly with private business. Most Canadians would also agree that there is some need for government control over certain business activities, such as monopolies. However, business people argue that the government has gone too far, and that too much time is being wasted in making and enforcing regulations.

Governments have made mistakes. You can probably think of many. Most of us tend to look at government activities rather selfishly, and support those that we see directly benefiting us, while criticizing those that do not have any immediate personal benefit.

When you have the franchise, you will have an opportunity to help elect governments at all three levels. The more information and knowledge you have about our modified free enterprise system, the better prepared you will be to participate in the process.

REVIEWING YOUR BUSINESS VOCABULARY

Write the number of each definition.
Write the word that matches the definition number.

UNIT A

constitution, monopoly, crown corporation, municipal government, Federal Business Development Bank, provincial government, federal government, public utility

1. The branch of government responsible for the armed forces.
2. The *British North America Act*.
3. The government responsible for highways, schools, and police protection.
4. The government responsible for local matters such as parks and recreation.
5. A government agency providing expert advice to small businesses.
6. A business owned by the government.
7. A business that faces no competition.
8. A government agency providing water or electricity.

UNIT B

deficit, property tax, direct tax, public debt, gross national product, income tax, sales tax, indirect tax, surplus

1. The term that covers personal income taxes and retail sales taxes.
2. When expenditures exceed revenues.
3. The term for the total value of goods and services produced each year.
4. Taxes levied on goods and services.
5. The total money owed by government.
6. Taxes, such as corporation income taxes, that can be passed on to the consumer.
7. When revenues exceed expenditures.
8. Taxes on land and buildings.
9. Taxes on salaries and wages.

UNIT C

civil servant, franchise, electorate, public service

1. The right to vote.
2. The group of persons employed by the government.
3. An individual employed by the government.
4. All of the persons eligible to vote.

REVIEW QUESTIONS

UNIT A

1. Explain how business and government are interdependent.
2. What are the two basic functions of government in Canada?
3. What is a crown corporation?
4. List several ways in which business is helped by government.
5. Who gives governments the power to make and enforce laws?
6. Name three important goods or services provided by each of the three levels of government.

UNIT B

1. What is the difference between a budget deficit and a budget surplus?
2. Excluding taxation, state four other sources of government revenue.
3. Explain the difference between a direct tax and an indirect tax.
4. State three reasons why taxes have increased in recent years.
5. What is meant by the Gross National Product?
6. Explain why taxes are necessary.

UNIT C

1. Name five examples of goods and services consumed by government.
2. Name five different occupations available in the civil service.
3. Explain how you give government its power.
4. What groups of people in Canada do not have the franchise?
5. How is our relationship with government similar to our relationship with business?

APPLYING YOUR KNOWLEDGE

UNIT A

1. Draw up a three-column table, one column for each of the three levels of government. Provide the appropriate column headings. Use the table to classify the following services according to which level of government is responsible for them.

   highway repairs
   street repairs
   fire protection
   education
   old age assistance
   pollution control
   parks and
     recreation

   family allowance
     payments
   hospitalization
   defence (military)
   garbage collection
   customs and
     immigration
   agriculture

2. Name four privately owned businesses that have monopoly control of certain goods and services. Why do governments permit these monopolies to exist?
3. What advantages are there for the consumer in having public utilities owned and operated by governments?

UNIT B

1. Explain why there are direct charges for some government goods and services but not for others.

2. Assume that the interest charges on the public debt last year in Canada was five billion dollars. If the money borrowed by the government is earning interest at an average rate of 7.5 per cent, what is the total value of the public debt?
3. Does your province levy a retail sales tax? If it does, find out what types of goods and services are taxed, and what the rate(s) of tax is.
4. Explain how lotteries are a source of revenue for governments.
5. Explain how inflation has caused taxes to increase.
6. The payment of taxes in Canada is compulsory. Why?

UNIT C

1. Examine the *Help Wanted* section of your local newspaper. How many different types of government jobs are advertised? Which of these do you think you might be interested in?
2. What are the federal and provincial minimum wages in your province? Why do you think that Canada has minimum wage laws?
3. Find out when the last municipal election was held in your community. When is the next one to be held? How long must you reside in the community to be eligible to vote in a municipal election?

PROBLEMS AND PROJECTS

UNIT A

1. Draw up a one-page chart containing the following information:
   Names of all Canadian provinces
   Names of all provincial capitals
   Political party in power in each province
   Name of premier of each province.
2. Find the telephone listings for each of the three levels of government in your area in the telephone directory. Name at least five departments listed for each level of government. Beside each department describe briefly the service or services each provides to the public.
3. Al and Alice, a married couple, have no children, and don't intend having any. They are disturbed by the high costs of education. They state that they do not use the facilities of the school now, and do not expect to in the future, and therefore should not have to pay for these services. Discuss this problem in groups, and report to the class your group's feelings about the problem.

UNIT B

1. Prepare a list of ten goods and services provided by government. Beside each, indicate whether you benefit directly or indirectly from them. Compare your answers with those of your classmates. For review, indicate which level of government provides each of the services you listed.
2. Obtain a copy of the latest Canada Year Book. Prepare a bar chart showing the total revenues and total expenditures of the federal government for each of the last five years, using actual dollar values.
3. Obtain a copy of *How Your Tax Dollar is Spent* from Information Canada. Examine this booklet and answer the following question: If you were asked to eliminate thirty per cent of the federal government's expenditures, which activities would you stop? Explain your reasons for selecting these items and not others.

4. Visit a local business in your community. Find out what government regulations and taxes affect the operation of this business. Report the results to your class.
5. What is the cost of a marriage licence in your province? Where do you apply for the licence? What are the requirements you must meet before being issued the licence?

UNIT C

1. A few days before an election, you find that your name is not on the voters' list. What steps can you take to rectify this omission?
2. You learn that your local municipal government elected representative is in favour of installing street lights in your neighbourhood. You strongly disagree with his/her position. What steps can you take to make your views known?
3. What is meant by the consumer price index? What has been the trend in this index in the past ten years? What does this trend tell us about the government's ability to control inflation?
4. Select a job title of personal interest to you and which is represented by a civil servant in your area. As a class, generate a list of questions to be asked of people in these positions. Arrange an interview with a person in the job in which you are interested. Report the results to the class.
5. The aims of the Economic Council of Canada for the Canadian economy are summarized as follows:

   To promote and maintain a high rate of economic growth while maintaining stable prices and a strong international economic position.

   To ensure that incomes are fairly distributed to Canadians.

   To maintain full employment.

   What indicators are there that the federal government has been successful in achieving these goals in the last ten years? What indicators are there to the contrary?

13
The Working World

UNIT A
YOUR CAREER IN BUSINESS

You have now explored much of the business world. You have seen that businesses are organized to produce goods and services for consumers. You are both a producer and a consumer. You are now familiar with many of the thousands of possible jobs and careers available in business. Have you found your place in the business world? Some beginning high school students may have a clear idea of the job or career that they would like to follow. Most students, however, do not know what they want from the future. It is hoped that all of you have at least some idea now of the types of jobs that appeal to you, or which do not appeal.

Planning Your Career

It has been said: "If you are failing to plan, you are planning to fail!" Those activities and tasks that are planned are almost always more successful than those that are not planned. One of the most important tasks you face is to decide on a career. Effective planning involves gathering information about yourself and about possible careers. A careful study of this information will help you to develop one or more **career objectives** for yourself. Once you understand your career objectives, you can then plan what you must do to achieve your goals.

Know Yourself

Before you can plan a career, you must understand yourself. What do you like to do best? What do you least like to do? Do you enjoy being with others as part of a team or do you prefer to go it alone? Do you enjoy leadership roles? Do you enjoy travel and meeting new people? Do you enjoy the world outdoors? Which gives you the most pleasure—working with your head or working with your hands? The projects and problems at the end of this chapter should help you to understand yourself better. You will also find it helpful to assess your abilities and talents. To do this, look at your school record, your hobbies and spare time activities, your physical condition, and your personality. Knowing yourself will help you to choose a career that interests you.

Gathering Job Information

It is possible that you will work in some job for forty years or more. People who enjoy their work are fortunate. If you select a career that matches your own talents and personality, you will be happier then many people. Throughout this book, you have been encouraged to explore many different occupations. You may change your mind several times before you decide definitely on your career. It is wise to develop the habit of learning about occupations that interest you.

Working at McDonald's a religion

George A. Cohon says McDonald's, the hamburger chain, is a religion.

As president and chief executive officer of McDonald's Restaurants of Canada Ltd., he officiates over the Canadian branch of the United States-based fast-food chain.

Anyone who has observed the growth and operation of McDonald's will readily agree with Cohon that the owners and workers believe in their company religiously.

Cohon, 40, relaxed and chummy as if he were taking orders for a Big Mac dinner, gave a conference of businessmen at the University of Western Ontario school of business Friday some insight into his company's rites and practices.

Cohon's assignment was to discuss entrepreneurship, but his one-hour portion, including a promotion film, sounded like 30 continuous radio and television commercials calling the faithful to attend McDonald's hamburger temples.

To say that Cohon and his fellow toilers beneath the golden arches are enthusiastic and fired up about their product would be an understatement.

Everyone from Ray Kroc of Chicago, chairman of the parent McDonald's Corp., down to the teen-agers grilling hamburgers and sweeping the floor are dedicated to the McDonald philosophy.

"When you're No. 1 it makes you work harder," Cohon said. "We're not cocky or arrogant or flippant. You don't get a second chance to make a proper first impression. We have to deliver exactly what we promise."

Cohon said he visits McDonald's outlets frequently, talking with staff and customers, and suggested other executives should do the same within their organizations.

"Executives shouldn't be hiding behind wide, plush board rooms or hiding behind stilted news releases."

Cohon defended his company's donations to charity: "We're not do-gooders. It's good for the community."

He said McDonald's spends $125 million in the U.S. and $7 million in Canada on television advertising.

For its efforts, McDonald's 250 outlets in Canada will have gross sales of $300 million this year he said. The parent corporation earned $110 million after taxes last year.

The chain has 4 400 outlets in 23 countries, with most of them in the U.S., followed by Canada. World-wide, 500 outlets a year are being built.

Cohon said McDonald's outlets in Canada have higher sales volumes than their U.S. counterparts because "there are not as many first-class competitors here." Each outlet in Canada has sales "well in excess of $1 million, with several over $2 million," compared with $790 000 average sales per McDonald's outlet in the U.S.

What's the secret of McDonald's success?

"We stick to basics," Cohon said. "We serve 10 million hamburgers a day, one at a time. We take this business a lot more serious than anybody else."

Of the 20 000 McDonald's employees in Canada, about 16 000 are teenagers, paid less than the minimum wage of $2.50 for restaurant workers.

The teen-age employees are kept fired up and enthusiastic with interstore competitions and awards and an all-star competition for outlets across Canada.

Of the 250 outlets, 55 per cent are operated by the company and 45 per cent by franchise manager-owners, who earn 10 to 15 per cent of sales. Cohon said company store managers, whose average age is 25, earn $25 000 to $30 000 a year plus stock options after reaching certain standards.

A McDonald's franchise-and there's a long waiting list-now costs the adventuresome entrepreneur $210 000, of which $110 000 in cash is required. The rest can be financed.

"It's a myth that young people can't make a success of business if they have the ability to take risks and work hard."

London Free Press,
May 14, 1977
Reprinted by permission

Careers in the 1980s

What types of jobs are likely to be available when you are ready to enter the full-time work force? Consider the following predictions.

- The need for farmers, farm labourers and unskilled workers will decrease. Less than 8% of the work force will be employed in these occupations.

- Occupations increasing most rapidly are those requiring some education and training after high school.

- 20% of the work force will be employed in professional or technical occupations.

- At least 25% of all workers will be in office or sales occupations.

- Skilled craftspersons will continue to be in great demand.

- Demand for workers in service occupations such as nursing, medical technology, food, lodging, and social work are increasing.

Make use of as many different sources of job information as you can. Your teacher and school guidance counsellor can help you to find sources of information. Your public library has considerable information available, as does the Canada Employment Centre.

Your Career Objective

Objectives tell us what we would like to achieve. A **career objective** clearly describes what you want to achieve in your working career. John, who is not sure of his exact job choice, may choose as his career objective to "gain satisfying employment after high school graduation in a job working mostly outdoors, with other people." Mary, who is more definite, may choose as her career goal "to obtain a job as a nursery school teacher after completing the required training." What is your career objective?

ECONOMISTS THEREFORE
WORK IN BUSINESS AND INDUSTRY AND THE
UNIVERSITIES.   IN UNIVERSITIES ECONO-
MISTS TEACH AND USUALLY COMBINE THIS
WITH RESEARCH IN A PARTICULAR FIELD SUCH
AS LABOUR ECONOMICS OR BUSINESS FLUCTUA-
TIONS. THEY USUALLY WRITE ARTICLES
AND BOOKS TO ALLOW OTHERS TO USE THE RE-
SULTS OF THEIR RESEARCH. IN GOVERNMENT,
ECONOMISTS WORK FOR SUCH DEPARTMENTS AS
TRADE AND COMMERCE, INDUSTRY, HEALTH AND
WELFARE, MANPOWER, AGRICULTURE AND MIN-
ING. HERE THEY WILL BE REQUIRED TO KEEP
CLOSE WATCH ON CURRENT DEVELOPMENTS IN
TARIFFS, TRADE POLICIES, TRENDS IN EM-
PLOYMENT, WAGE RATES AND PRODUCTION IN
THE RESOURCE INDUSTRIES. THE DEPARTMENT
OF FINANCE AND THE BANK OF CANADA EMPLOY
ECONOMISTS TO STUDY MATTERS OF FINANCIAL
CONCERN TO THE COUNTRY. ECONOMISTS ARE
FOUND ON THE STAFFS OF CANADIAN TRADE
COMMISSIONS IN OTHER COUNTRIES.   IN BU-
SINESS, ECONOMISTS ARE EXPECTED TO KEEP
MANAGEMENT UP TO DATE ON THE BROAD ECO-
NOMIC AND POLITICAL TRENDS AFFECTING
THEIR COMPANY SO THAT PLANNING MAY BE
DONE ON A SOUND BASIS. SOME BUSINESSES
HAVE ECONOMISTS PREPARE REGULAR
PUBLICATIONS ON BUSINESS TRENDS AS A
SERVICE TO THEIR CUSTOMERS. PROJECTS
OFTEN TAKE SEVERAL MONTHS OF WORK AND
ALL REQUIRE CONSIDERABLE SPECIFIC DATA.
ECONOMISTS WHO TEACH WILL BE INVOLVED
WITH PEOPLE BUT THOSE IN RESEARCH WILL
BE LESS INVOLVED. SENIOR ECONOMISTS
OFTEN HAVE TO ADDRESS MEETINGS AND
ATTEND CONFERENCES AND PARLIAMENTARY
COMMITTEES. THE WORK REQUIRES MUCH
CONCENTRATION AND ATTENTION TO DETAIL
OFTEN UNDER PRESSURE. HOWEVER, AT
OTHER TIMES THE ECONOMIST HAS TIME TO
READ AND STUDY IN PREPARATION FOR
OTHER PROJECTS. ECONOMISTS SHOULD BE
INTERESTED IN ALL HUMAN ACTIVITIES
AND HAVE THE ABILITY TO WEIGH MANY
FACTORS IN MAKING JUDGMENTS. THEY
SHOULD BE ABLE TO COMMUNICATE IN SPEECH
AND WRITING EFFECTIVELY.   DURING THE
LAST TWENTY YEARS OPPORTUNITY FOR
ECONOMISTS INCREASED GREATLY AND THE

POLICE TRAINING

THERE ARE 3 LEVELS OF TRAINING:

1. AT THE LOCAL LEVEL: EACH FORCE MAY VARY IN ITS TRAINING & REQUIREMENTS BUT GENERALLY ADMISSION IS GRADE 12. A POLICE CADET (AGE 17-21) WOULD PROBABLY HAVE 3 WEEKS TRAINING BEFORE BEGINNING WORK. A POLICE CONSTABLE (AGE 21-35) RECEIVES A 6 MONTHS TRAINING. TRAINING IS SIMILAR FOR BOTH MEN AND WOMEN.

2. AT THE PROVINCIAL LEVEL (O.P.P.), GRADE 12 IS REQUIRED FOR ADMISSION. TRAINING TAKES PLACE AT THE POLICE COLLEGE IN TORONTO FOR 3 WEEKS. THEN THE RECRUIT IS PLACED ON A YEAR'S PROBATION ON A FORCE IN THE PROVINCE UNDER A SENIOR OFFICER. DURING THIS TIME HE/SHE WILL RECEIVE 2 SIX-WK. ADVANCED TRAINING COURSES AT THE ONTARIO POLICE COLLEGE, AYLMER, ONTARIO. IF THE RECRUIT IS SUCCESSFUL HE/SHE IS APPOINTED TO A FOR-CE. BOTH MEN & WOMEN ARE TRAINED IN OPP.

3. AT THE FEDERAL LEVEL (RCMP), APPLICANTS MUST BE AGE 18-29 TO BEGIN TRAINING WITH GRADE 11 EDUCATION. THEY MUST BE SINGLE AND IN GOOD HEALTH, WITH NO CRIMINAL RECORD. MINIMUM HEIGHT ACCEPTED IS 5 FEET 8 INCHES, AND MAXIMUM 6 FEET 5 INCHES. ONE YEAR OF BASIC TRAINING IS GIVEN AT REGINA FOR 6 MONTHS AND ON THE FIELD FOR 6 MONTHS. WOMEN ARE CURRENTLY BEING TRAINED IN THE R.C.M.P. ALL PREREQUISITES FOR ENTRY INTO THE R.C.M.P ARE THE SAME FOR WOMEN AS FOR MEN WITH THE EXCEPTION OF HEIGHT. THE MINIMUM HEIGHT FOR WOMEN IS 5 FEET 4 INCHES. FOR FURTHER INF. INTERESTED WOMEN MIGHT CALL OR VISIT R.C.M.P. DIVI-SION HDQTRS., 225 JARVIS ST., TORONTO, (416) 369-4578.

*COURSES FOR POLICE OFFICERS ARE BEING GIVEN AT UNIV. AND COLLEGES OF APP. ARTS & TECHNOLOGY. THEY ARE USUALLY TAKEN AS

RETAIL MERCHANDISING TRAINING

PROGRAMS ARE AVAILABLE IN FASHION MERCHANDISING, HOWEVER A BROAD EDUCATIONAL BACKGROUND - EITHER UNIVERSITY OR TECHNICAL SCHOOL IS ALSO ACCEPTABLE. MANY LARGE STORES HAVE MANAGERIAL TRAINING PROGRAMS FOR GRADUATES OF THESE SCHOOLS AND FOR VERY PROMISING EMPLOYEES.

```
     PROGRAMS IN RETAIL MERCHANDISING ARE
 AVAILABLE AT THE COMMUNITY COLLEGE
 LEVEL. STUDENTS COMBINE PRACTICAL
 ON-THE-JOB TRAINING WITH ACADEMIC STUDY.
 ADMISSION REQUIREMENTS ARE USUALLY AN
 O.S.S.G.D. (ACCUMULATION OF 27 CREDITS)
 OR EQUIVALENT.

     IF YOU INTEND TO ENTER A CAREER
 THROUGH IN-PLANT OR ON-THE-JOB TRAINING
 YOU SHOULD GIVE CAREFUL ATTENTION TO THE
 SELECTION OF COURSES THROUGHOUT YOUR
 SECONDARY AND POST-SECONDARY PROGRAMS SO
 THAT YOU WILL ACQUIRE THE ACADEMIC BACK-
 GROUND PREFERRED BY YOUR FUTURE EMPLOYER
 AS WELL AS THE BEST PREPARATION IN
 SKILLS REQUIRED FOR YOUR CAREER.
     WHILE A BACKGROUND OF COMMERCIAL AND
 TECHNICAL SUBJECTS MAY ASSIST YOU IN
 FINDING YOUR FIRST JOB, IT IS USUALLY
 THE STANDARD OF ACADEMIC COMPETENCE,
 PERSONALITY CHARACTERISTICS AND WORK
 HABITS WHICH PLAY A MAJOR ROLE IN
 ADVANCEMENT.
     IT MAY BE HELPFUL FOR YOU TO SEE
 YOUR GUIDANCE COUNSELLOR FOR MORE
 DETAILS RELATIVE TO YOUR INTENTIONS.

     **TYPIST TRAINING**
 NEATNESS, ORGANIZATION, DEPENDABILITY,
 GOOD GRAMMAR AND SPELLING SKILLS ARE ALL
 BASIC REQUIREMENTS OF A GOOD TYPIST.
     THIS TRAINING CAN BE OBTAINED IN
 SEVERAL DIFFERENT WAYS. MOST SECONDARY
 SCHOOLS OFFER EXCELLENT TYPING COURSES
 IN THEIR COMMERCIAL DEPARTMENTS. ONE-
 YEAR COURSES IN TYPING & BASIC SECRETAR-
 IAL SKILLS ARE OFFERED AT THE COMMUNITY
 COLLEGE LEVEL FOR WHICH THE ENTRANCE
 REQUIREMENT IS THE OSSGD. FEES ST
```

Education and Your Business Career

A large number of Canada's unemployed are non-skilled individuals in the 18-25 year age range. Most of these people have not completed their high school education. While having a good education is not a guarantee to a job, it can be a big help.

Most high schools offer several business education courses. Investigate those that interest you.

More and more high schools are offering **co-operative work experience programs** in which the student takes part-time classroom instruction, and gains practical experience in job situations in business and industry. These types of programs can help students to gain maturity, and to help them make a decision on their career objectives.

Your Career Choice Is Yours

When you have analysed your talents and personal qualities, and the requirements of occupations that interest you, you are well on the way to planning your future. No one can tell you exactly what occupation is best for you. The choice is yours. You may not be ready to select a specific job now, but you can identify fields in which you are interested. Take the time now to gather more information and experience, to narrow down your job choices.

Working but still in poverty

"They are poor because they want to be poor," went the old refrain. "If they didn't want to be poor, they'd get a job."

It is a myth that is repeated often enough to become an article of faith to some people. The belief that the poor don't work is often expressed in schemes for "workfare"–to get those idlers to work in return for social assistance.

But the plain fact is that 60 per cent of Canada's poor do work. According to an excellent study just published by the National Council of Welfare, not only do these people work, but they work hard, for low wages, and yet never stand a chance of living in anything but poverty.

The report says that the working poor are poorly educated. Thirty per cent are under 25, most of them single people. Of the remaining 70 per cent, two out of every three are heads of families with dependent children.

They work at jobs without the luxury of debating about the quality of their work–they worry more about simply keeping their jobs. Often they find that, no matter how hard they work, they can't get even the minimum amount of money necessary to adequately support their families.

Simply setting minimum wages doesn't help. The report notes that if the highest current minimum wage–$3 an hour–were in effect nationwide, single-earner families with three children would still fall $3 085 short of the poverty line.

Even if the minimum were $4 an hour those families would still be about $1 000 below the poverty line.

More than asking why some poor people don't work, it might be fair to ask why those who find themselves consistently working for an inadequate wage wouldn't simply stop working and throw themselves onto the welfare rolls.

The NCW suggests a two-point program to assist the working poor. Minimum wages should of course be maintained and upgraded as much as possible–but steep increases of the kind proposed by the NDP in Ontario are apt to have a negative economic impact.

But, the long-term answer is an income supplementation program administered through the income tax system–a guaranteed annual income, if you will–to bring working poor families up above the poverty line.

And, in order not to eliminate present poverty only to have the working poor retire into poverty, the public pension system should be strengthened.

There would have to be a higher contribution to the Canada Pension Plan for everyone and there would have to be a sliding scale of contributions, decreasing with income. The tax-based system is by far the most equitable and efficient way to redistribute wealth.

It would mean that the rest of the work force would supplement the pensions and the earnings of the working poor. But surely that is the minimum guarantee we would all want for our society–to work and live decently.

London Free Press,
June 18, 1977
Reprinted by permission

UNIT B

PREPARING FOR A BUSINESS CAREER

You will likely have five or more jobs in your working life. Each new job will help you reach more of your career goals. But each career plan must have a starting point. Your first job will be that starting point. It is important in many ways. It will help you identify your own interests and talents. It will also give you a chance to prove your abilities. Jobs that satisfy your interests and talents and allow you to use your abilities will allow you to be successful. Conditions of work vary with different jobs: some jobs involve inside work, others outside, some have night work, and some involve travelling. You will also find that some jobs offer many chances for promotions, and different jobs have different levels of salary and benefits.

As you will discover, your first job will help you find out a great deal about yourself, your career goals, and about jobs in general. Therefore, choose your first job wisely and gain as much experience as you can. This unit provides information to help you get your first job and also to improve or change your career as you continue to develop.

Sources of Job Information

There are many sources of job information to help you in your job search. These are available to you and require only some effort on your part to make use of them.

Student Services Department

Your counsellors and teachers can provide you with help in a job search. They can help you identify your interests and evaluate your special talents and abilities. They also receive notice of job vacancies from employers.

Newspapers

Most newspapers have classified advertisements that include a "help wanted" section. The jobs listed usually are of great variety and are available locally. The employers usually require the applicants to answer by letter or in person.

Canada Employment Centre

The Canada Employment Centre is a federal government agency that keeps files both on individuals available for work and on job vacancies. Its job is to help match the applicants with the employers. It also has special offices to help students find summer employment. These offices are often set up on college and university campuses.

Private Employment Agencies

These agencies offer many of the same services as Canada Employment Centres. They are owned by private businesses and charge a fee for their services.

Friends and Relatives

Friends and relatives are often a good source of job information. They will have inside information concerning the abilities needed for the job, the conditions of work, and the possibility of promotions. Employers usually prefer to hire someone who is supported by one of their own employees.

The "Beat"

Walking "the beat" means going to the personnel offices of all the businesses in a particular area and completing an application form. The personnel officer will usually accept and keep your application on file and will review it when a job vacancy occurs. It may be necessary to repeat this procedure later if you are not successful on the first attempt. Although you are working without leads, "the beat" can be effective because the employer will respect your determination.

Trade Journals

Magazines that specialize in particular businesses or industries, such as computers, real estate, or agriculture are called trade journals. These often contain job opportunities in these specialized fields. This information can be very useful after you have determined a career goal. Many employers looking for employees use trade journals to advertise vacancies in their companies.

The ability to get a job often depends on the general level of unemployment. If there are many unemployed workers in your area, it will be difficult to find a job because the competition for jobs will be strong. Do be realistic when looking for a job. Any job will help you to find out more about yourself and about the working conditions of jobs.

An Application Letter

An **application letter** is written by you to the employer asking for an interview. The letter introduces yourself and indicates your reasons for wanting the job. It also tells the employer when you are available and gives your name, address, and telephone number. Since the employer will get his or her first impression of you from your letter, make sure it is neat and contains no grammatical or spelling errors.

The Application

After you have found a job vacancy that appeals to you, your next step is making an application for that position. This procedure involves four parts.

```
                          Letter of Application

                                            21-16th Street, East
                                            Moncton, New Brunswick
                                            1978 09 16


        Ms. Toni Barris
        Personnel Manager
        Allan Products Limited
        197-41st Street, West
        Moncton, New Brunswick
        E5L 9T3

        Dear Ms. Barris:

        I wish to apply for the General Secretarial position advertised
        in the Tuesday edition of the Moncton Times by Allan Products
        Limited.

        I recently graduated from T.M. Bill Secondary School with a major
        in Business Subjects.  My typing speed is 65-70 words per minute,
        and I also have excellent standards in shorthand and accounting.
        A copy of my Data Sheet is enclosed.

        For the past two years I have been employed on a regular part-time
        basis at a local variety store.  My duties included receiving,
        pricing, stocking shelves, serving customers, handling cash, and
        keeping records of all kinds.  I enjoyed this work and found it
        very interesting.

        I would like to discuss the advertised position with you.  I am
        available for an interview at your convenience.  My telephone
        number is 964-2121.

        Sincerely yours,


        Judy Knot

        Judy Knot
        /jk

        encl.
```

Data Sheet

Judy Elizabeth Knot
21-16th Street, East
Moncton, New Brunswick
E5L 1P6

Personal

Age: 18
Height: 162 cm
Mass: 54 kg
Health: Excellent
Marital Status: Single

Education

1978 - graduated from T.M. Bill Secondary School with four-year
       diploma, major in Business Courses
     - won proficiency award in typing
     - excellent marks in Shorthand and Accounting
     - average marks in other subjects

Hobbies and Interests

- member of school drama club - 3 years
- member of community band - 2 years
- helped organize school trip to Vancouver
- play a variety of sports: tennis, curling, basketball, swimming

Experience

1974-1976 - babysitting
1976-1978 - worked in Sam's Variety on weekends for two summers

References

Mr. Sam Goldring - owner of Sam's Variety
29-12th Street, East
Moncton, New Brunswick
E5L 5J7

Ms. Ellen Woodbridge - Business Education Teacher
T.M. Bill Secondary School
147-14th Street, West
Moncton, New Brunswick
E5L 7M4

Ms. Mary Martin - Magistrate: Personal friend of family
196-13th Street, West
Moncton, New Brunswick
E5L 9V6

Data Sheet

A data sheet includes information about you that is important to the employer. It should list your name, age, state of health, and marital status. Your educational achievements should also be listed. This will include the year or grade attained in school, special awards, skill levels, such as typing speed, and specific courses that will be useful for that job. It is also useful to list your participation or responsibilities in any extra-curricular activities, such as sports, student council, social clubs, school band, etc. Your employer is also interested in other work experiences that you may have had. This involves other full time or part-time work and volunteer work. The data sheet should also list the names, addresses, and telephone numbers of your references. References are people who will recommend you to the employer. Be sure to ask the people you name for their permission.

Reference Letters

Reference letters are very helpful for any applicant. They should contain information about you that is important for a particular job. For example, if you are applying for a secretarial job, a letter from your secretarial teacher would be appropriate. It is also useful to have a letter from someone who is respected in the community and who can testify to your good character.

Application Form

The application form can be picked up from the employer's personnel office. It will ask for information that concerns the particular job. Fill in the information neatly and accurately. It is very useful to take the information from your data sheet. Generally, the following information is needed for the application form:

- Name
- Social Insurance Number
- Position Applied For
- Personal Data
- Educational Data
- School Clubs and Activities
- Hobbies and Special Interests
- Work Experience
- Personal References.

Be sure to have information on all the above with you to help you complete the application.

After you have completed the application form, you should submit all four parts of the application to the employer's personnel department or to the person named in the source. These four parts include your application letter, the data sheet, your reference letters, and your completed application form. The employer will review your application as well as those from the other applicants. If the employer is impressed with your application, you will be required to go to the business for a personal interview.

The Interview

The interview is a discussion between the employer and the applicant. Its main purpose is to determine if the applicant is the right person for job and if the job is the right one for the applicant. The employer will usually phone the applicant to arrange the time and place for the interview. You should be very polite and, if necessary, change your own schedule to meet the prospective employer's.

It is very important to be on time for the interview. Promptness indicates reliability. Since the interview is your first meeting with the employer, your appearance will create that very important "first impression". You should be courteous, neat, well groomed, and exhibit good posture. Above all, appear very interested. This gives the impression that "I want that job".

In some cases, it is important to take certain information with you. Take an extra copy of your data sheet, though you should also memorize the information on it. You can be sure the interviewer will refer to it and ask for more detail. It might also be useful to take some examples of your work or projects if they apply to the particular job and take along any reference letters that you did not include in your original application.

Most interviews last for twenty to thirty minutes. During that time you will be asked many questions. The questions usually start with the information on your data sheet, then they shift to information about you and why you want the job. Try to be positive and try to create the impression that you can help the employer and the employer can help you. The employer will probably ask questions or statements similar to the following: "What can I do for you? Tell me about yourself. Why are you interested in this job and this business?" To help you answer these questions, you should find out some information about the business. You can get this by talking to another employee or reading some pamphlets published by the business. These will let you know its products, services, and markets. Knowing something about the business will also give you confidence during the interview.

You should also know the name and title of the interviewer. Use his or her name during the interview, and treat him or her with respect, but not fear. The best rule to follow for a successful interview is "Be positive — Be prepared".

The interviewer will usually give an indication to bring the interview to a close. This can be a quick look at the clock, setting aside your application, or a question such as "Is there anything more you want to know about the job?" At that time, be prepared to ask any questions that you still have, but don't ask too many, and don't make them too long. Then make a polite departure and be sure to take all of your belongings with you.

Follow-up

A follow-up letter or telephone call may be in order after the interview. A short polite thank-you letter should follow a job offer from the employer. If you are not accepted, you can still write a letter thanking the employer for the interview and ask that your application be kept on file for any future job vacancy.

```
                                                      78-06-12


     Dear Kid:

     Today you came to me for a job.  From the look of your shoulders as you walked
     out, I suspect you've been turned down before, and maybe you believe by now that
     kids your age can't find jobs.

     But I hired a teenager today.  You saw him.  What was so special about him?
     Not experience; neither of you had any.  Attitude, son.  A-T-T-I-T-U-D-E.  He
     did his best to impress me.  That is where he edged you out.

     He wasn't dressed like Easter Sunday, but then that wasn't necessary.  His clothes
     were clean, and he had gotten a haircut.  He filled out the application form
     neatly and completely.  He did not ask to borrow a pen.  He carried his Social
     Insurance card, had basic identification, and did not ask, "What's a reference?"

     He didn't have two friends waiting for him by the pop machine.  He didn't start
     to chew gum or smoke while interviewing.  He didn't keep looking at his watch,
     giving me the impression that he had something more important to do.

     He took the time to find out how we "operate" here, and what his day-to-day tasks
     would be.  I think he'll keep his eyes open and work for me like he'd work for
     himself.

     He was willing to start at that point where I could afford to pay.  Someday,
     perhaps, he'll get to the point where he'll have more authority over others and
     a better paycheque.

     Maybe jobs aren't as plentiful right now, but there are jobs.  You may not believe
     it, but all around you employers are looking for young men and women smart enough
     to go after a job in the old-fashioned way.

     If you have even the vaguest of what I'm trying to say, let it show the next time
     you ask for a job.

     For both our sakes, get eager, will you?


            The Boss
     The Boss

     TB:eg
```

UNIT C

ORGANIZED LABOUR

Do you have a part-time job? Many students work after school or on weekends to earn some extra spending money. Such jobs might include delivering papers, babysitting, stock clerking, or helping in the family business.

Eventually, everyone seeks a full time job. The kind of job that a person obtains will depend upon the amount of formal education achieved, skills that have been learned, such as business or technical trades, and the availability of jobs in the job market. Anyone who is able to and is actively seeking work is considered to be part of the labour force. The present labour force in Canada is approximately nine million people, but not all nine million people have jobs. Those who cannot find work are referred to as the unemployed.

People are unemployed for several reasons. One reason is that they lack the skills or education necessary to perform a job. Most roles, such as those performed by an electrician, mechanic, computer operator, or keydisc clerk require at least a grade 12 education with emphasis in that particular skill. Indeed, because of the oversupply of workers, many businesses will choose the applicant who has additional college level training before hiring the high school graduate.

Another reason for unemployment is that some cities may have factories that have reduced their production because the demand for their product is down. With less products being manufactured, less people are needed to work in the factories. Some areas of Canada lack manufacturing industries entirely. As a result, as the population increases in these areas, more people are unemployed.

Labour Unions

Approximately 30 per cent of the people actively employed in Canada belong to organizations called labour unions. These organizations contain people who work in similar trades. Since not all unions are comprised of "trade" workers, the name "organized labour" is becoming more widely used. Some of the larger unions in Canada are the Canadian Union of Public Employees, which includes people who work for the government; the Automotive Union, which includes employees from the four major automobile manufacturers; and the Steelworkers' Union, which is made up of workers employed by steel-producing companies such as Stelco and Algoma.

Collective Bargaining

In earlier days, before mass production became popular, most shops and factories were small and employed few workers. If the workers wanted improvements in salaries, they would have to bargain with their employer on a one-to-one basis. During the depression years of the 1930s when millions of people were looking for work, employers could easily fire an employee who asked for a raise. There were many people to take his or her place. As a result, people worked long hours at harsh jobs for as little as two dollars a day.

These conditions gave rise to organized labour groups who would present their demands to the company through two or three spokesmen. If the company refused to accept their demands, the union would call for a strike, and plant production would come to a halt. This weapon gave the unions considerable power at the bargaining table. Most firms eventually realized that a shut down caused great losses in profits and considered negotiating with the labour unions on a regular basis. Today, instead of bargaining individually, most workers bargain together through their labour unions. This is referred to as collective bargaining.

How Collective Bargaining Works

When employees become dissatisfied with the salaries or conditions of work, their labour union elects a committee to represent them at meetings with the company management. The committee presents a list of demands to the employer. The employer studies the demands, then either accepts the items on the list or offers another proposal.

Usually several meetings of offers and counter-offers are held before an agreement is reached.

The agreement between the two parties is then written up in a formal document called a labour contract. Typical agreements last for one or two years before expiring. Since it is a legal binding contract, both parties are committed to uphold the terms of the agreement. The terms include all the promises made by both sides.

Typical Items in a Labour Contract

A labour contract usually states the wage rates for different kinds of jobs. Usually it specifies a higher rate of pay for overtime, such as time and a half; this means one and a half times as much pay per hour as during a regular working shift.

There are many other special considerations that concern bargaining committees. One is that inflation of prices tends to reduce the buying power of wages while the contract is in force. Rather than renegotiate a new contract each time the price of food and clothing increase, labour unions attempt to include an escalator clause in the original contract. The clause requires the company to alter the wage rates, up or down, as the prices for articles rise and fall. Another name for an escalator clause is cost-of-living allowance or "COLA".

In addition to regular wages, the negotiating committee will often bargain for fringe benefits. Fringe benefits include such items as dental and medical plans, paid vacations and holidays, sick leave, coffee breaks, and retirement funds. The cost of these benefits sometimes represents a large proportion of the total labour contract.

BANK CLERKS ORGANIZE

For over fifty years Canadian banks have operated without interference from labour unions, but this may soon change. Large unions associated with other industries are seeking ways to organize bank tellers and other clerks into a collective bargaining unit.

Several conditions have led bank workers to favour collective bargaining over the present fixed-rate system set by each individual bank. Wages paid by the banks do not compare favourably with similar "white collar" clerical jobs in industrial sectors. A bank teller, for example, may make $9 000 a year, while an office secretary may make $12 000.

Another issue that worries bank workers is the effect that computerization has had on job promotions. "Teller terminals" and "24 hour cash dispensers" both reduce the need for additional bank tellers. Even though more banking transactions are processed each day with the use of computers, the number of new job positions has not increased. Typically, chances of promotion are reduced in a labour force that stays the same size, compared to an expanding labour force.

Union organizers admit that it may take some years before the large number of individual bank branches will become part of one large union. So far, only a few individual branches have begun to bargain collectively.

Digest of Business News
Autumn 1978

Job security has become an important issue during times of economic recession. Workers want to ensure that they cannot be fired without "just cause". One way to achieve job security is to set up a grievance committee that can formally present arguments to management if a situation is being handled in an unfair manner. Another way to ensure job security is to include seniority rights in the labour contract. The term seniority refers to the length of time that an employee has worked for that company. The worker who has been with the company the longest has the most seniority. When the company is laying off workers because of reduced production, the last ones to go would be those employees with the most seniority. Similarly, when the need for additional workers arises again, the first ones to be re-hired would be those people with the most number of years of experience at that firm.

Conditions of work has become a common item to be included in labour contracts. This refers to such things as the degree to which the working area is comfortable and provides reasonable safety for the employees. It may also include a precise definition of what the job entails. Uranium miners have discovered that uranium-bearing rock emits a harmful radiation. Long exposure to the ore causes changes in the human body. Ways to minimize the harmful effects would be considered in the contract under the title "conditions of work". Asbestos workers

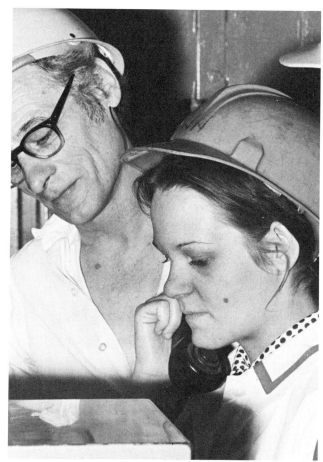

have been known to suffer lung ailments as a result of breathing in the tiny asbestos fibres. Acceptable working conditions in asbestos plants would include huge suction fans with air filters and the availability of filter masks for the employees.

Labour Unions Influence Legislation

Historically, organized labour groups have always searched for ways to improve the living standards and working conditions of their members. The use of strikes at a local factory may improve the situation in that area but leave a similar factory at another location unchanged.

National strikes involving work stoppages all across Canada can actually be harmful. A national transportation strike causes severe shortages of food, clothing, medical supplies, and increased prices for the products as a result. Consumers usually have to bear the loss for finding other more expensive shipping routes through price increase in the goods they buy.

Because local strikes are limited in their effect and national strikes are too unpopular, organized labour groups often create a political lobby group. This committee concentrates its efforts on writing and talking to politicians in the hopes of influencing the passing of new legislation in the House of Commons. Over the years, much new legislation has been passed that directly benefits workers. These laws include a minimum wage that must be paid by employees, an age limit that prevents small children from working in factories, a compensation fund for disabled workers and improved safety standards for factories, processing plants, lumber companies, and mining firms. One of the most active political parties in Canada that has supported such legislation is the New Democratic Party.

Wage Demands and Inflation

Inflation refers to a general rise in prices in goods and services across Canada. Inflation can happen for several reasons. One reason is that the demand for products is higher than the rate at which factories can make them. Since people are willing to pay higher prices, stores increase their prices until the demand levels off. Another reason is that workers demand higher wages, which causes the factories to increase their prices to consumers. As prices in stores increase, labour unions bargain for increasingly higher wages. This in turn causes the factories to increase their prices once again. This is referred to as the wage-price spiral, which means that demands for higher and higher wages causes inflation.

In the mid-1970s, the federal government introduced a wage-price legislation that limited wage demands for several years. Prices rose more slowly. Labour unions are becoming increasingly aware that they too can harm their employees by asking for too much all at once.

CONCLUSION

THE CHALLENGE OF BUSINESS

From a study of this text, you have been introduced to many areas of the world of business. The Canadian economy and the forms of business organization, the role of marketing and advertising, buying goods and services as consumers, consumer credit and financial institutions, the importance of computers and effective communication, the need for different types of insurance, and the roles of governments and unions in our society, were all discussed. You are now able to see that business and its many facets are all around us and that business is an essential and important force in Canadian society.

However, it is necessary for you to look into the future and be prepared to face some of the challenges that lie ahead. If we Canadians are to continue to enjoy a reasonable and comfortable standard of living, we must make some sacrifices and plan *now* for changes that will occur in our lifestyles. Among the major concerns to be faced are the pollution and energy problems, the related need to move from a consumer society to a conserver or "efficient" society, the consumer movement's demands for greater consumer protection, and the responsibility of corporations to attempt to meet society's needs before society demands that they do something about social, economic, and environmental problems. The corporation that is remote from society's concerns and needs will have little contribution to make in helping determine Canada's future.

You are now equipped with many new ideas, skills, and values in business that will help prepare you to face the future. These "life-coping skills and values" are a useful and a necessary preparation that will help make you more effective citizens. Obviously, you cannot be totally familiar with the details in each area, but you do now have a general knowledge so that you should be better off to enjoy a more comfortable standard of living. Together, you and business can work to make Canada a better country in which to live.

REVIEWING
YOUR BUSINESS VOCABULARY

There is no Unit A business vocabulary review as no new terms are introduced in this unit.

Write the number of each definition.
Write the word that matches the definition number.

UNIT B

application form, application letter, Canada Employment Centre, data sheet, interview, trade journal

1. A form required by an employer that includes important information about you.
2. A magazine that specializes in a particular business or industry.
3. A form supplied by a prospective employer to a prospective employee.
4. A federal government agency that keeps files on individuals available for work and on job vacancies.
5. A discussion between a prospective employer and an applicant.
6. A letter written by someone requesting a job interview.

UNIT C

collective bargaining, conditions of work, escalator clause, fringe benefits, job security, labour contract, labour force, labour union, political lobby, wage-price spiral, unemployed

1. People who cannot find work.
2. Organization of workers attempting to improve their job conditions.
3. Legal, binding agreement between employer and employees.
4. Item in a labour agreement that causes wages to rise and fall according to the cost-of-living index.
5. All the people in Canada capable of working.
6. Workers who bargain together through a labour union.
7. Items in a labour agreement that includes paid holidays, vacations, medical coverage, etc.
8. The protection of one's job or position in the company.
9. A term that defines what the job entails.
10. A group of workers who concentrate on writing and talking to politicians in hopes of influencing legislation.
11. A situation in which increased wages causes a similar rise in the prices of products.

REVIEW
QUESTIONS

UNIT A

1. Name four things that you can do to get to know yourself better.
2. Name five sources of job and career information available to you.
3. What is the relationship between education and unemployment in Canada?
4. What types of occupations are growing rapidly?
5. Why is a good education important when trying to find a job?
6. Why should you try to select an occupation that interests you?

UNIT B

1. Why is your first job important?
2. List at least seven sources of job information.
3. How can your teachers help you with a career search?
4. How does a private employment agency differ from the Canada Employment Centre?
5. Why are friends and relations a good source of job information for both the applicant and the employee?
6. How does the general level of unemployment affect your ability in finding a job?
7. What information should the applicant take to a job interview?
8. What information will be discussed during the interview?
9. Where can you get information about the business or employer? How can this information help you?

UNIT C

1. Describe three things that will affect the kind of job a person can get.
2. Explain two reasons why people are unemployed.
3. Why is "organized labour" a more accurate term than labour union?
4. What caused people to form labour unions?
5. Explain why an escalator clause is included in some wage contracts.
6. Name six fringe benefits that are typically included in a labour contract.
7. How do seniority rights provide job security?
8. What do you consider is the most important item among conditions of work? Why?
9. Why are national strikes an unpopular method of obtaining new labour demands?
10. Explain three laws that have been legislated because of the efforts of organized labour groups.

APPLYING
YOUR KNOWLEDGE

UNIT A

1. Some occupations require mostly physical work. Others require mostly mental work. Some require a combination of physical and mental work. List two jobs in each category.
2. List four reasons why different people choose different occupations.
3. List two jobs in which you have an interest. For each job, describe what you think would be satisfying about it. List any things that you would not find satisfying.
4. Select an occupation that interests you as a career. List several part-time or summer jobs that would give you some of the skills and experiences necessary in your chosen career.
5. List reasons why so many of Canada's youth are unemployed.
6. More and more women are entering Canada's work force. Why do you think this is so?

UNIT B

1. Find a friend or relative who has a job similar to one you want. Discuss the job with that person and write a short report on your findings.
2. Using your school course or program booklet make a list of all the courses in your school that would be helpful in your training for a particular job of your choice.
3. Select two different jobs that interest you. Write an application letter for each job. Use addresses of businesses in your community.
4. Prepare a data sheet for yourself. Include information about yourself that is accurate and up-to-date. Type the information in proper format.
5. Make a list of five reasonable questions that could be asked either by an employer or prospective employee for one of the following jobs: truck driver; accountant; teacher; department store manager; restaurant waiter or waitress; part-time service station attendant.

UNIT C

1. When the committee representing the labour union and the people representing the company get together at the "bargaining table", why does it take them so long to reach an agreement?
2. How could it be a disadvantage to the employer if only those with the most seniority were working during a production slowdown?
3. How does a company pay for items such as fringe benefits, higher wages, and improved working conditions for its employees?
4. How do wages cause prices to "spiral"?
5. Explain why wage-price legislation was introduced in the mid-1970s.

PROJECTS AND PROBLEMS

UNIT A

1. Name your favourite hobbies and spare time activities. What types of occupations might be suited to these natural interests?
2. Imagine a day in your life ten years from now. Describe at least three things about that day that would be proof to you that you are "successful".
3. Prepare a clear career objective for yourself. Discuss it with a group of students and your teacher. List five or six things you can do in the next two years to help you to achieve your career objective.
4. Some people think that earning a large income is the only source of satisfaction from a job. Do you agree with these people? Why or why not?

UNIT B

1. Obtain a blank job application form from a local business or government agency. Fill it out neatly and accurately. Get your teacher or a relative to explain any sections which you do not understand.
2. Investigate a business education course offered in the next grade in your school that you think might interest you. Examine the course description in your school program booklet, have the teacher explain to you "what the course is all about", examine the textbook used, and discuss the pro's and con's of the course with a student who is currently taking it. Prepare a one-page report summarizing your investigations.
3. Select a job that interests you. Bring to class three or more pieces of information you have found relating to the job. Search the *Help Wanted* section of your newspaper and cut out any advertisements for the job you selected.

UNIT C

1. List four labour unions or organized labour groups that operate in your community.
2. List each of the following items. Beside each item, state whether it would be classified as a *wage demand, fringe benefit, condition of work,* or *job security.*
a. An increase in the wage rate
b. Longer paid holidays
c. Two weeks' notice before firing
d. Filter masks provided for plant workers
e. Overtime rate to be set at time and a half
f. The last employees to be fired are those with the most seniority
g. Coffee breaks are to be twenty minutes
h. Handrails are to be installed on dangerous stairwells
3. Employers have certain responsibilities to their workers even though it may not be written in the labour contract. List four responsibilities that employers have to their workers. List four responsibilities workers have towards their employer.
4. Imagine yourself as a personnel officer for a large office building. List five characteristics that you would look for in a prospective employee that would help you decide whether or not to hire that person.

ACKNOWLEDGEMENTS

For permission to reprint copyrighted and trademarked material grateful acknowledgement is made to the following:

Photographs and Cartoons

Air Canada, p. 88; Agriculture Canada, Minister of Supply and Services Canada, p. 192; Bank of Canada, pp. 128-9; Canadian Imperial Bank of Commerce, pp. 91, 140; Canadian Standards Association, p. 204; © 1977 by *Creative Computing,* Morristown, NJ09760, p. 98; Dictaphone Canada Limited, p. 116; Duca Community Credit Union Limited, p. 218; T. Eaton Company Limited, p. 14; Employment and Immigration Canada, pp. 15, 287, 304, 306; Ford Motor Company of Canada, Limited, p. 50; Gulf Canada, pp. 15, 32; IBM Canada Limited, pp. 178, 179; Insurance Bureau of Canada, p. 254; Libby, McNeill and Libby of Canada Limited, p. 52; Loblaws Limited, pp. 174-5; Metric Commission Canada, p. 182; *Metric Monitor,* p. 181; Metropolitan Toronto Police, p. 264; Miller Services Limited, pp. 132, 193, 268; National Harbours Board, Vancouver, p. 48; Birgitte Nielsen, pp. 17, 33, 148, 149, 221; Olivetti Canada Limited, p. 118; Ontario Ministry of Industry and Tourism, pp. 23, 247, 288, 306; Ontario Ministry of Transport and Communication, p. 281; Procter and Gamble Company of Canada Limited, p. 51; Royal Bank, pp. 19, 130-1, 137, 152, 157, 160, 163, 164, 165, 215, 217; *The Spectator,* Hamilton, pp. 45, 86, 94; Toronto Fire Department, p. 231; Toronto General Hospital, pp. 232, 234; Cartoons © by Universal Press Syndicate, pp. 138, 253; *The Whig-Standard,* Kingston, pp. 182, 215, 252, 307; Xerox of Canada Ltd., p. 92.

Illustrative and other support matter

Bank of British Columbia, pp. 141, 143, 161; Bank of Montreal, pp. 143, 161; Better Business Bureau, p. 204; Campbell Soup Company Ltd., pp. 176, 189; Canadian Imperial Bank of Commerce, pp. 69-71; Canadian Life Insurance Association, p. 67; Consumers' Association of Canada, p. 204; Consumer and Corporate Affairs, Canada, pp. 186, 187, 188; Canadian Standards Association, p. 204; Consumers' Distributing Limited, p. 12; The Empire Life Insurance Company, pp. 234, 238, 240, 243; Canadian floral emblems, p. 197; © Grolier Limited; Kraft Limited, pp. 176, 189; Libby, McNeill and Libby of Canada Limited, pp. 176, 177, 191; Ontario Hydro, pp. 146-7; Procter and Gamble Company of Canada Limited, pp. 182, 191; Student Guidance Information Printouts, Ontario Ministry of Education, pp. 20-1, 58, 73-4, 89, 120, 153, 225, 263, 295-7; Revenue Canada, p. 283; Royal Bank of Canada, pp. 143, 161; Saskatchewan Consumer Affairs Department, p. 194; © April 1978, Washington Post Company, p. 303.